15
12/20/2007

1998

HANDBOOK
TO LIFE IN
ANCIENT EGYPT

SELECTED BOOKS BY THE SAME AUTHOR

Manchester Mummy Project: Multidisciplinary Research on Ancient Egyptian Mummified Remains (Manchester: Manchester Museum, 1979)

A Guide to Religious Ritual at Abydos (Warminster: Aris and Phillips, 1981)

The Ancient Egyptians: Their Religious Beliefs and Practices (London: Routledge, 1982)

Ancient Egypt (Oxford: Elsevier, 1989)

Discovering Ancient Egypt (New York: Facts On File, 1994)

The Pyramid Builders: A Modern Investigation of Pharaoh's Workforce (London: Routledge, 1997)

With A. E. David, *A Bibliographical Dictionary of Ancient Egypt* (Oklahoma: University of Oklahoma Press, 1997)

HANDBOOK TO LIFE IN ANCIENT EGYPT

ROSALIE DAVID

Facts On File, Inc.

Handbook to Life in Ancient Egypt

Facts On File, Inc.
11 Penn Plaza
New York NY 10001

Library of Congress Cataloging-in-Publication Data
David, A. Rosalie (Ann Rosalie)
    Handbook to life in ancient Egypt / Rosalie David.
        p.   cm.
    Includes bibliographical references and index.
    ISBN 0-8160-3312-9
    1. Egypt—History—To 640 A.D. I. Title.
DT83.D23 1998
932—dc21   97-35824

Facts On File books are available at special discounts when purchased in bulk quantities for businesses, associations, institutions, or sales promotions. Please call our Special Sales Department in New York at (212) 967-8800 or (800) 322-8755.

You can find Facts On File on the World Wide Web at http://www.factsonfile.com

Text design by Cathy Rincon
Cover design by Sholto Ainslie
Layout by Robert Yaffe

Printed in the United States of America

MP FOF 10 9 8 7 6 5 4 3 2

This book is printed on acid-free paper.

CONTENTS

ACKNOWLEDGMENTS

I am very grateful to Facts On File for advice and support given throughout the production of this book. I would also like to thank the following people who have contributed so much to its completion: Mr. G. Thompson of the Manchester Museum, University of Manchester for producing the photographs; Mr. A. Allen for the maps and line drawings; and Mrs. Audrey Johnston for all her help in typing the manuscript.

As always I am particularly grateful to my husband for his encouragement and practical help and advice.

Rosalie David
Manchester

INTRODUCTION

The civilization of ancient Egypt lasted for over 5,000 years, covering a period from c.5000 BC to the early centuries AD. Before the unification of the country in c.3100 BC, there were some 2,000 years (the Predynastic Period) during which the civilization gradually developed and the earliest advances were made in technology, arts and crafts, politics, and religion, laying the foundations for later developments. However, written records of this earliest period have never been discovered. After Alexander the Great (a Macedonian king) conquered Egypt in 332 BC, the country was ruled by a line of Macedonian Greeks who descended from Alexander's general Ptolemy (King Ptolemy I). Cleopatra VII (the last ruler of this dynasty) was forced to surrender Egypt to Roman rule, and the country became part of the Roman Empire in 30 BC. When the Roman Empire was divided into two sections in the fourth century AD, Egypt came to be controlled from Constantinople (Byzantium). Christianity was eventually adopted as the official state religion throughout the Roman Empire—thus affecting many aspects of Egypt's civilization—but some influences survived from the Pharaonic Period. However, when the Arabs conquered Egypt in the seventh century AD, Islam replaced Christianity as the major religion, and all outward expressions of the ancient civilization finally disappeared.

The basis of any modern chronology of ancient Egypt rests on the work of Manetho (c.282 BC), an Egyptian priest who wrote a chronicle of Egyptian rulers covering the period from c.3100 BC to 343 BC. He divided his king list into thirty dynasties, which are retained by modern historians (who have added an extra one). Egyptian historical accounts, the records left by Classical writers, and information provided by other contemporary sources (including Hebrew and Near Eastern historical and literary texts) all enable modern historians to compile a reasonably accurate sequence of rulers and their dates. Sometimes, however, the evidence is scanty or contradictory. The chronology followed in this book is based on the system given in the *Cambridge Ancient History*. The dynasties are arranged under the subdivisions "kingdoms" or "periods," which are generally accepted today in Egyptology.

There is no clear definition of *dynasty* or an explanation of why Manetho divided the king list in this way. If precise dates for a reign or an event are recorded, they are given in this book. When only approximate dates are known, they are written as c.240 BC (*circa*, or around the time of, 240 BC). If a date is written as c.240–c.160 BC, it means approximately 240 BC to approximately 160 BC. If it is written as c.240–160 BC, then it means approximately 240 BC to precisely 160 BC, while 240–160 BC means precisely 240 BC to precisely 160 BC.

Historical evidence about Egypt's civilization comes from various sources, including monuments, artifacts, inscriptions, and preserved human remains. The main aim of this book is to present information relating to Egyptian civilization from the Predynastic Period through to the end of Roman rule in Egypt. Although an outline of the historical background and context is provided in the back of the book, the chapters are organized thematically rather than chronologically so that readers can readily gain access to particular topics. There has been an attempt to separate archaeological, literary, paleopathological, or historical elements in the text and, whenever appropriate, the chapter combines current information from different areas of knowledge and research.

Although repetition of information is kept to a minimum, some topics can be viewed in more than one way and may therefore be covered in more than one section. Full use should be made of the index to find all references to a particular subject and also the meanings of particular words. The chapters provide summaries of current knowledge about the various topics, but further references are also included to guide the reader's own pursuit of the subject matter.

When special terminology or technical terms are used, such as *nome*, *ostracon*, or *cartouche*, a brief definition is provided. The most widely accepted versions of personal names are given, and sites are listed under the place-names by which they are best known; however, alternative ancient Egyptian, Greek, or modern Arabic versions are included where relevant. Regarding the spelling of kings' names, it is known that there were five main names in the pharaoh's royal titulary and the two most important were inscribed inside cartouches (a stylized loop of rope). In this book, the practice of using the one name by which the ruler is best known has been adopted. In some cases, this means that the Grecized rather than the Egyptian version of the name is retained (e.g., Cheops rather than Khufu); in others, the Egyptian name is used (e.g., Amenemhet rather than Ammenemes, and Senusret rather than Sesostris).

LIST OF MAPS

LIST OF ILLUSTRATIONS

HANDBOOK
TO LIFE IN
ANCIENT EGYPT

1

HISTORICAL BACKGROUND

The civilization of ancient Egypt lasted for more than 5,000 years. Climatic and environmental conditions have preserved a wealth of material evidence. The three main study sources for Egyptology are the monuments, objects, and artifacts from archaeological sites, and the literature. Before hieroglyphs were correctly deciphered in the nineteenth century AD, travelers and historians of the classical, Arab, and medieval periods were unable to fully understand the significance of the monuments and archaeological data. They reached ludicrous conclusions about the meaning and use of monuments such as the pyramids, and the interpretation of religious and funerary beliefs. However, following the decipherment of hieroglyphs, it became evident that some knowledge had been passed on through Hebrew and Greek literature and that Egypt was the source of many beliefs and customs that came to form the basis of "Western civilization."

Ancient Egyptian civilization covers a period from c.3100 BC to the conquest of Egypt by Alexander the Great in 332 BC. The Dynastic Period started in 3100 BC; in the Predynastic Period (c.5000–c.3100 BC), early communities made the first advances in technology, arts and crafts, politics, and religion and laid the basis for later developments. After Alexander the Great (a Macedonian king) conquered Egypt in 332 BC and subsequently died in Babylon, Egypt was ruled by a line of Macedonian Greeks who descended from Alexander's general Ptolemy (King Ptolemy I). Cleopatra VII, the last ruler of this dynasty, could not prevent Rome from absorbing Egypt as part of its empire in 30 BC. Egypt passed under the control of Constantinople (Byzantium) in the fourth century AD when the Roman Empire was divided into two sections. One significant development in Roman Egypt was the arrival and spread of Christianity, which became the official state religion.

This was replaced by Islam when the Arabs conquered Egypt in the seventh century AD.

The basis of any modern chronology of Egypt remains the work of Manetho (c.282 BC), an Egyptian priest who wrote a chronicle of Egyptian kings covering c.3100 to 343 BC. He divided this king list into thirty dynasties; historians still retain these and have added an extra one. They group these thirty-one dynasties into major periods: Archaic Period (Dynasties 1 and 2); Old Kingdom (Dynasties 3–6); First Intermediate Period (Dynasties 7–11); Middle Kingdom (Dynasty 12); Second Intermediate Period (Dynasties 13–17); New Kingdom (Dynasties 18–20); Third Intermediate Period (Dynasties 21–26); Late Period (Dynasties 27–31).

There is no clear definition of a "dynasty" nor any explanation of why the king list was thus divided into these dynasties. Some dynasties include rulers who were related by family ties and, if there were no direct descendants or another group seized power, then the dynasty changed. In other cases one family spanned more than one dynasty, and there was an apparently smooth and amicable transfer of power from one line to the next.

SOURCE MATERIAL

Monuments

Many monuments have survived. Some have always been visible above ground, but over the past 200 years, excavation has revealed and cleared many other tombs and temples. Main sites include domestic or "settlement" sites (cities, towns, villages, and fortresses) and cemeter-

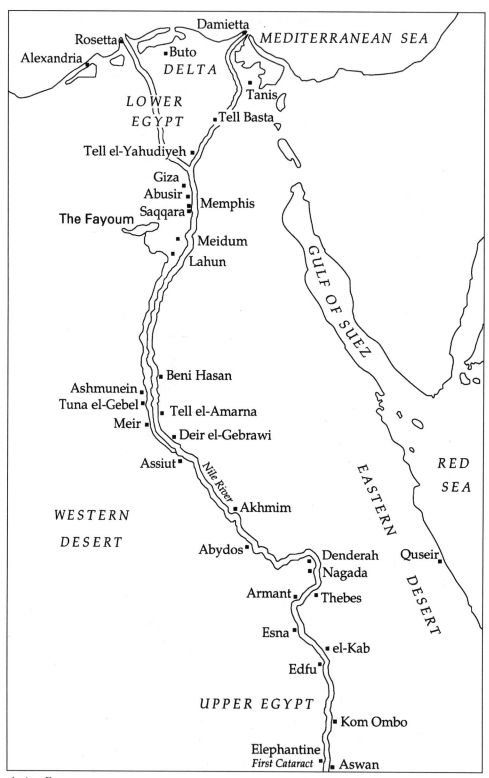

Ancient Egypt

ies (necropolises) with pyramids and other tombs for royalty and "private" tombs or graves for nobles, officials, craftsmen, and peasants. There are also some animal cemeteries. Intended to last for eternity, tombs and temples were generally built of stone, whereas domestic and military architecture mainly used mud brick and wood. The tombs and their contents have survived much better than objects found at domestic sites, partly because of the difference in building materials but also due to the fact that tombs were located on the desert's edge while dwellings were placed in the cultivated areas. Thus, more evidence has survived about funerary beliefs and customs than about daily life.

Objects and Artifacts

Archaeologists have recovered many objects placed in tombs or left behind at domestic sites. A belief in life after death led the Egyptians to equip tombs with a range of items. Some of these items (coffins, canopic jars, ushabtis, etc.) were for funerary use, but others (pottery, makeup, clothing, jewelry, weapons, tools, and food) were intended for use by the deceased in the next world. Thus, tomb goods provide evidence of religion and funerary customs as well as everyday life and technology.

Language and Literature

Decipherment of hieroglyphic and other scripts has provided direct access to an extensive religious and secular literature. Archaeological evidence (monuments and artifacts) can supply only limited information about a society, whereas knowledge of its literature reveals many other facets. Because of the preservation and understanding of both the archaeological and

A mummy of a child (second century AD*) from Hawara. The gilded cartonnage head-and-chest cover features inlaid eyes and molded imitations of jewelry, set with glass to represent semiprecious stones. In one hand, there is a molded wreath of red flowers.*

literary evidence, Egyptian civilization is more clearly understood today than are many other early societies.

Written sources exist from the historical period (c.3100 BC). Although no texts survive from the earlier (predynastic) cultures, excavations have revealed some facts about the structure and customs of those societies, and later writings also provide information. From antiquity there are writings about Egypt that include both Egyptian texts (on papyri, stelae, ostraca, and tomb and temple walls) and accounts by Classical travelers and authors.

EGYPTIAN SOURCES

These following sources supply the basis of the modern chronology of ancient Egypt.

Manetho His work, the *Aegyptiaca* (History of Egypt), is the most important source, although no complete firsthand record of this book survives and the facts it contained are not regarded as completely reliable. The work is preserved in edited extracts in the writings of Flavius Josephus (c.AD 70), a Jewish historian extensively used by Renaissance scholars as a source for ancient Egypt, and in an abridged form in the accounts of Christian chronographers Sextus Julius Africanus (c.AD 220), Eusebius (c.AD 320), and George the Monk (c.AD 800), known as Syncellus, author of the *History of the World from the Creation to Diocletian.*

Manetho, an Egyptian priest at the temple of Sebennytos in the Delta, lived during the reigns of Ptolemy I and II (c.305–246 BC). Knowledge of Egyptian hieroglyphs and Greek, firsthand experience of religious beliefs and customs, and access to king lists and registers held in the temples enabled him to complete his history. Written in Greek, his chronicle of Egyptian rulers extended from c.3100 BC down to 343 BC and was divided into thirty dynasties. A later chronographer added a thirty-first dynasty, preserved in the account of Sextus Africanus. According to Manetho, Menes became the first king of a united Egypt at the start of Dynasty 1 in c.3100 BC, but before this "dynastic period," the land had been ruled by gods and demigods (c.5000–3100 BC, known today as the Predynastic Period). Estimates of lengths of reigns and popular anecdotes about rulers' lives were also included.

Different accounts of lengths of reigns are often given in Eusebius and Africanus, and the chronology of the reigns and total years of each reign are unreliable. Some royal names are written in distorted forms, and only the overall number of kings is given for some dynasties. Anecdotal details cannot usually be confirmed by other sources. Nevertheless, Manetho remains the most comprehensive ancient source for the sequence of rulers and dynasties, and today many of his statements can be checked against archaeological evidence and other historical texts.

The King Lists Several lists survive that provide partial or damaged evidence about Egyptian chronology. Used for religious purposes and never intended to be historical records, these were incomplete and included only the names of previous rulers from Menes down to the king who had commissioned the list. Other kings were excluded if they were not regarded as "legitimate" rulers. No lists later than the reign of Ramesses II have yet been discovered.

Some king lists, inscribed on temple walls, were a key feature in the Ritual of the Royal Ancestors, performed daily in the royal mortuary temples to honor previous rulers and gain their acceptance of the current king. Priests brought food and other offerings from the god's altar, and these were then presented to the former kings, who were represented in the temple by the king list. The dead kings thus received sustenance and, in return, were expected to support the reigning king who had built the temple and provided their offerings. The known king lists include the following:

The Turin Canon Written in hieratic on papyrus and kept in the Egyptian Museum of Turin, Italy, this dates to the reign of Ramesses II (1304–1237 BC) and survives only in fragments. It preserves only between eighty and ninety royal names but provides some details that are also found in Manetho.

The Palermo Stone The largest fragment of a diorite stone is kept at Palermo, but other pieces probably from the same stone are in the Cairo Museum. When complete, this was perhaps an upright, freestanding oblong stone (stela), inscribed on both sides with horizontal registers and set up in a temple. Each register, divided vertically into compartments, contained hieroglyphic texts that would have supplied a continuous, year-by-year record of each reign. There were special references to outstanding annual events—victory over foreign tribes, building of a temple, festivals, and mining expeditions. Not all the fragments are present, but even when complete the stone recorded events in the reigns of the first five dynasties only.

The Table of Abydos Inscribed on a wall in the Gallery of Lists, Temple of King Sethos I (1318–1304 BC), this table includes seventy-six kings (starting with Menes) who preceded Sethos I. The accompanying wall scene shows Sethos I and his son, Ramesses II, offering food to the kings' names.

The Table of Karnak Inscribed on a wall in the Temple of Amun at Karnak, Thebes, this table dates to the reign of Tuthmosis III (1504–1450 BC). The list originally included sixty-one royal names, but only forty-eight were still visible when it was discovered in AD 1825. The sequence of names is incorrect, although some kings are mentioned who are not present in the other lists.

The Table of Saqqara Inscribed on the wall of the tomb of Tjuneroy, overseer of works at Saqqara, this table originally displayed fifty-seven names selected for inclusion by Ramesses II. Because of damage to the wall, only fifty are now visible.

CLASSICAL SOURCES

Attracted by the antiquity of the civilization, Greeks and Romans were enthusiastic travelers to Egypt. Several Classical authors left written accounts (see Chapter 7, Written Evidence) that, despite inaccuracies and embellishments, provide unique and often firsthand descriptions. They remained the most reliable source for ancient Egypt until Jean-François Champollion deciphered hieroglyphs and enabled Egyptian records to be translated and read. The most famous Classical sources are the writings of Herodotus (*The Histories*, Book II), Diodorus Siculus (*Universal History*, Book I), Strabo (*Geographia*, Book XVII), Pliny the Elder (*Historia Naturalis*), and Plutarch (*Moralia*).

TABLE OF EVENTS

Following is a selective list of important rulers and the main events that occurred in their reigns. All dates are BC, unless otherwise stated.

Predynastic Period (c.5000–3100 BC)

c.3400	The kingdom of Red Land is established in the north, White Land in the south; they are ruled concurrently under two kings.
c.3200	Scorpion, a southern king, makes preliminary attempts to conquer the northern kingdom.
c.3100	Menes (Narmer) subdues the north and unifies the two lands.

Archaic Period (c.3100–2686 BC)

Dynasty 1 (c.3100–2890)

c.3100–? Menes founds the unified kingdom of Egypt with capital at White Walls (Memphis). Beginning of the historical period.

c.2985–2930 Den pursues an active foreign policy, sending an expedition to Nubia. Innovations are introduced in design of royal burial monument at Abydos. Double Crown appears, symbolizing unity of the two predynastic kingdoms.

Dynasty 2 (c.2890–2686)

c.2700 King Peribsen and supporters of the god Seth lose struggle with supporters of the cult of Horus; Horus becomes royal patron deity.

Old Kingdom (c.2686–c.2181 BC)

Dynasty 3 (c.2686–2613)

c.2667–2648 King Djoser requests royal architect Imhotep to design world's first major stone building—the Step Pyramid at Saqqara.

c.2637–2613 Under Huni, construction is possibly started on the transitional Meidum pyramid.

Dynasty 4 (c.2613–2494)

c.2613–2589 Sneferu. Two pyramids are built at Dahshur, including the Bent, or Blunted, Pyramid; the Meidum pyramid is possibly also built.

c.2589–2566 Cheops. Great Pyramid at Giza is built; it is the largest pyramid ever constructed.

c.2558–2533 Chephren. Second pyramid as well as the Great Sphinx are built at Giza.

c.2528–2500 Mycerinus. Third pyramid at Giza is constructed.

c.2500–2496 Shepseskaf. In break with pyramid-building tradition, the mastaba tomb is revived with the building of the Mastabat Fara'un.

Dynasty 5 (c.2494–2345)

c.2494–2487 Userkaf. The sun cult is promoted. A sun temple is built at Abu Ghurob as well as a small pyramid at Saqqara.

A wooden, cat-shaped coffin containing a mummified cat (c.900 BC).

c.2487–2473 Sahure. The royal cemetery at Abusir inaugurated; Sahure and his successors build pyramids here, including one with particularly fine wall reliefs.

c.2473–2463 Neferirkare (Kakai). A pyramid is built at Abusir.

c.2463–2422 Niuserre. Builds sun temple at Abu Ghurob as well as pyramid at Abusir.

c.2375–2345 Unas. Pyramids are once again built at Saqqara; Unas's pyramid complex has the best-preserved causeway and contains the earliest examples of Pyramid Texts.

Dynasty 6 (c.2345–2181)

c.2345–2333 Teti. Builds his pyramid at Saqqara.

c.2322–2283 Pepy I. Also builds his pyramid at Saqqara.

2269–c.2175 Pepy II. The longest reign, but royal power declines and the kingdom disintegrates. Builds his pyramid at Saqqara.

First Intermediate Period (c.2181–1991 BC)

Dynasty 7 (c.2181–2173)

The Old Kingdom collapses, and a period of social upheaval and political chaos follows. Rapid succession of Memphis-based rulers.

Dynasty 8 (c.2173–2160)

Succession of Memphis-based rulers continues.

Dynasty 9 (c.2160–2130)

c.2160 At Heracleopolis, the local ruler Achthoes I seizes power and rules over parts of Egypt. He is suc-

ceeded by a line of seventeen kings ruling from Heracleopolis in Dynasties 9 and 10.

Dynasty 10 (c.2130–2040)

Dynasty 11 (c.2133–1991)

2060–2010 Mentuhotep (Nebhepetre), a local Theban prince, reunites Egypt and builds a unique and spectacular funerary monument at Deir el-Bahri, Thebes.

2009–1998 Mentuhotep (S'ankhkare).

1997–1991 Mentuhotep (Nebtowyre). The last ruler of Dynasty 11, he is assassinated. His vizier, Amenemhet, usurps the throne and founds the Middle Kingdom, ruling as Amenemhet I.

Middle Kingdom (1991–1786 BC)

Dynasty 12 (1991–1786)

1991–1962 Amenemhet I. Reorganizes Egypt and moves capital north to It-towy. He is buried nearby in a pyramid in the new cemetery at el-Lisht.

1971–1928 Senusret I. Coregent with Amenemhet I, he extends Egyptian power and furthers Egypt's interests abroad.

1929–1895 Amenemhet II. Continues pursuing contacts with Syria/Palestine. Builds his pyramid at Dahshur.

1897–1878 Senusret II. Undertakes a major land reclamation and builds works in the Fayoum, an oasis area. Constructs his pyramid at Lahun.

1878–1843	Senusret III. During a successful reign he completes the process of colonizing Nubia, where he builds or extends a series of fortresses. Abolishes powers and privileges of nobles (by unknown means), thus removing a great threat to royal power.
1842–1797	Amenemhet III. The Middle Kingdom reaches the pinnacle of its prosperity. Projects are built in the Fayoum, and quarrying expeditions are sent to Sinai.
1798–1790	Amenemhet IV. The kingdom begins to decline. He is ousted by his sister, Sobekneferu.
1789–1786	Sobekneferu. The queen regnant. Dynasty 12 comes to an end.

Second Intermediate Period (1786–1567 BC)

Dynasty 13 (1786–1633)

Line of sixty kings continues to rule from Thebes.

Dynasty 14 (1786–c.1603)

Simultaneous line of seventy-six kings rules from Xois in the Delta; this line had seceded and established its own dynasty of kings at the end of Dynasty 12.

Dynasty 15 (1674–1567)

The Hyksos invade Egypt and form two dynasties (15 and 16) of foreign kings.

| c.1570 | Hyksos ruler Auserre Apophis I encounters opposition from native Theban princes of Dynasty 17. |

Dynasty 16 (c.1684–1567)

Dynasty 17 (c.1650–1567)

| c.1575 | Theban ruler Seqenenre Ta'o II fights bravely against the Hyksos (Auserre Apophis I); possibly dies in battle. |
| c.1570–1567 | Kamose continues the war against the Hyksos. The Theban princes finally succeed in driving them from Egypt. |

New Kingdom (1567–1085 BC)

Dynasty 18 (1567–1320)

1570–1546	Amosis I. The founder of the dynasty expels the Hyksos from Egypt and pursues them to Palestine.
1546–1526	Amenhotep I. Lays the foundations for the Egyptian Empire with his conquests in Syria/Palestine. He builds a rock-cut tomb, rather than a pyramid, at Dra'abu el-Naga, Thebes, and founds a community of royal necropolis workmen.
1525–1512	Tuthmosis I. A great warrior, he leads campaigns in Nubia and Syria. His tomb is the first in the Valley of the Kings at Thebes.
c.1512–1504	Tuthmosis II. Marries Hatshepsut.
1503–1482	Hatshepsut. After seizing the throne from her stepson, Tuthmosis III, she becomes queen regnant. She builds a fine temple at Deir el-Bahri, Thebes.
1504–1450	Tuthmosis III. Upon reaching adulthood, he regains power from Hatshepsut to become

Egypt's greatest military leader. He extends the empire in Syria, crossing the Euphrates River and defeating Egypt's greatest enemy, the Mitannians.

Embarks on major building program at Temple of Amun at Karnak and elsewhere.

1450–1425   Amenhotep II. The son of Tuthmosis III is a great warrior and sportsman. His tomb in Valley of the Kings is used during Dynasty 21 to rebury a cache of royal mummies.

1425–1417   Tuthmosis IV. Creates peace alliance with Mitanni and marries a Mitannian princess. Aten starts to become a separate and important deity.

1417–1379   Amenhotep III. A great builder, he also promotes the cult of Aten. Tiye, his wife, is a powerful queen despite her nonroyal origins. Egypt's power and wealth are at their zenith; diplomacy replaces warfare.

1379–1362   Amenhotep IV (Akhenaten). A religious revolutionary, he disbands the traditional priesthoods and introduces an exclusive, near-monotheistic worship of the Aten. The court and capital are moved to Akhetaten (Tell el-Amarna), where he and his queen, Nefertiti, pursue the cult. Akhenaten produces no male heirs.

c.1364–1361   Smenkhkare. Son-in-law of, possibly half-brother of, and perhaps coregent with Akhenaten.

1361–1352   Tutankhamun. Another son-in-law of Akhenaten, he begins the gradual restoration of the traditional religion and returns the religious capital to Thebes.

He dies young, leaving no heirs; his tomb and treasure are discovered in the Valley of the Kings in AD 1922.

1352–1348   Ay. An elderly courtier, he inherits the throne and continues the restoration of religious traditions.

1348–1320   Horemheb. Of obscure, non-royal parentage, he was previously the army commander under Akhenaten.

In his Edict, Horemheb takes firm measures to restore the traditional religion as well as law and order. He obliterates traces of Atenism, and Akhetaten is finally deserted.

Dynasty 19 (1320–1200)

1318–1304   Sethos I. A warrior king, he reestablishes the empire in Syria/Palestine, which had been allowed to slip away during Akhenaten's reign. Along with Ramesses II, he undertakes major building programs, including temples at Thebes and Abydos. His tomb is the largest in the Valley of the Kings.

1304–1237   Ramesses II. A noted warrior and prolific builder, he is possibly the pharaoh of the Old Testament's Exodus.

Egypt wars against the Hittites before eventually making a peace treaty with them.

1236–1223   Merenptah. Son of Ramesses II, he defeats the threat posed by a coalition of Libyans and Sea Peoples.

Dynasty 20 (1200–1085)

1198–1166   Ramesses III. The last great warrior king defeats the Libyans (years 5 and 11) and Sea Peoples (year 8). He builds a magnificent temple at Medinet Habu, Thebes, and his tomb in the Valley of the Kings. The royal necropolis workforce conducts strikes.
The so-called Harem Conspiracy fails to assassinate the king.

1160–1156   Ramesses V. The Turin Papyrus and the Wilbour Papyrus are written.

1140–1121   Ramesses IX. Tomb robberies occur, while royal workmen's strikes continue.

1113–1085   Ramesses XI. The kingdom is virtually divided in half: the king rules the north, but the high priests of Amun seize power and attain near-equal status, effectively ruling the south from Thebes. Ramesses XI's royal burial is the last in the Valley of the Kings.

Third Intermediate Period (1089–525 BC)

Dynasty 21 (c.1089–945)

Seven kings rule nominally over the whole country but exercise their power only in the north from the delta city of Tanis. A line of high priests of Amun rule the south from Thebes.

Kings (Tanis)

1089–1063   Smendes. Founds Dynasty 21 upon succeeding Ramesses XI, under whom, as Nesbenebded, he virtually ruled the north.

1063–1037   Psusennes I. His daughter marries a Theban high priest, thus uniting the two ruling lines. His royal tomb is discovered intact at Tanis in AD 1940.

959–945   Psusennes II. As the son of a high priest of Thebes and a royal princess of Tanis, he unites the north and south once again. He rules all of Egypt from Tanis.

High Priests (Thebes)

1100–1094   Herihor. Inaugurates line of high priests who rule the south during Dynasty 21.

1064–1045   Pinudjem I. Effectively rules the south, first as high priest, then perhaps as "king" (1044–1026). He and Herihor order the reburial of the royal mummies of the New Kingdom in two caches.

985–969   Pinudjem II. Carries out rescue and reburial of the royal mummies.

Dynasty 22 (945–730)

945–924   Shoshenk I. The son-in-law of Psusennes II, he is from a family descended from Libyans who fought against Merenptah and Ramesses III and subsequently settled in the Delta. He inaugurates the dynasty and rules from Tanis, although he originates from Bubastis. He involves himself in foreign politics. References in the Bible name him as *Shishak*.

874–850   Osorkon II. Builds extensively at Tanis and Bubastis. His and other royal burials are discovered at Tanis in AD 1940.

Dynasty 23 (c.818–793)

Centered at Tanis, it is possibly contemporary with Dynasty 22.

Dynasty 24 (c.727–715)

Rules a limited area from the city of Sais.

Dynasty 25 (c.780–656)

716–702   Shabako. Egypt's first Nubian pharaoh. He establishes the dynasty at Thebes, building on the earlier efforts of Piankhy, ruler of the kingdom of Kush to the south (with capital at Napata) and who had begun the conquest of Egypt. Builds pyramid at Kurru (Kush) for his burial.

690–664   Taharka. Interferes in the politics of Judah, which leads to conflict with the Assyrians, who invade Egypt in 671 and again in 667 until 666. Flees to Napata and is buried in pyramid at Nuri (Kush).

664–656   Tanuatamun. The last Kushite ruler, he is defeated by the Assyrians.

Dynasty 26 (664–525)

The Assyrians install the princes of Sais as the native rulers of Egypt. Necho I (672–664), prince of Sais and vassal of Assyria, is killed by Kushite ruler Tanuatamun, who was attempting to regain power. However, Necho's son, Psam-

metichus I, becomes king and founds the dynasty.

664–610   Psammetichus I. Establishes the dynasty.

610–595   Necho II. Becomes involved in the politics of Judah and is defeated by the Babylonians at the Battle of Carchemish (605). He also initiates construction of the canal between the Nile and the Red Sea.

595–589   Psammetichus II.

589–570   Apries. The biblical Hophra, he becomes involved in the Judaean revolt against Babylon (588). Civil war in Egypt forces him from power.

570–526   Amasis. Army general. Checks the growing power of Greek residents, who have been causing concern among native Egyptians, and limits their activities to their city, Naucratis.

526–525   Psammetichus III. Defeated by Cambyses, king of Persia, at the Battle of Pelusium (525); Egypt becomes part of the Persian Empire.

Late Period (525–332 BC)

525–404   Dynasty 27. First Persian Period. Eight Persian kings rule Egypt as a satrapy of the Persian Empire.

525–522   Cambyses. Dedicates a sarcophagus of a mummified Apis bull at Saqqara as part of his religious duties as pharaoh.

521–486   Darius I. Actively promotes Egypt's religious customs and law reforms and completes the canal linking the Nile and the Red Sea.

404–399   Dynasty 28. Local rulers establish a limited, native kingship at Sais.

399–380   Dynasty 29. Another native line, based at Mendes, probably exercises control over a limited geographical area.

380–343   Dynasty 30. Native rulers, including Nectanebo I (380–363), are based at Sebennytos.

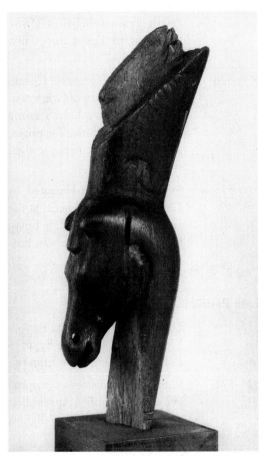

A wooden head representing a horse (c.1450 BC) that was perhaps originally part of a piece of furniture.

Persian Empire is revived and reorganized under Artaxerxes III, who reestablishes Persian control of Egypt in 343.

343–332   Dynasty 31. Second Persian Period. Includes the reigns of Persian kings Artaxerxes III, Arses, and Darius III.
The Persians are defeated by Alexander the Great, ruler of Macedon, who arrives in Egypt in 332.

332   Conquest of Egypt by Alexander the Great. Founds city of Alexandria; apparently undergoes some form of deification at the oracle of Siwa. Alexander rules Egypt as part of his empire until his death in 323.

Ptolemaic Egypt (305–30 BC)

305–283   Ptolemy I Soter. The Macedonian general of Alexander the Great who later became satrap of Egypt upon Alexander's death, he assumes the kingship in 305. Establishes the dynasty and ensures its continuation by means of coregencies and consanguineous marriages. Reorganizes the country.

283–246   Ptolemy II Philadelphus. He inaugurates financial administration in Egypt, introduces Greek farming communities in the Fayoum, and begins the abolition of the native aristocracy and the extensive Hellenization of Egypt. A great patron of the arts, he also undertakes major building projects.

246–221	Ptolemy III Euergetes I. Continues major building programs.
221–204	Ptolemy IV Philopator. Defeats Antiochus III of Syria at the Battle of Raphia in 217. There are nationalistic riots in Egypt.
204–180	Ptolemy V Epiphanes. Loses most of Egypt's foreign possessions as native uprisings continue. The Rosetta Stone, crucial to the decipherment of hieroglyphs, dates to his reign (196).
145–116	Ptolemy VIII Euergetes II (Physcon is a degenerate ruler). Numerous dynastic conflicts occur.
51–30	Cleopatra VII. The last Macedonian ruler, she reigns as queen with Ptolemy XII (51), Ptolemy XIII (51–47), and with Ptolemy XIV (47–30), and has liaisons with Julius Caesar and Mark Antony. Reputedly commits suicide at Alexandria after Augustus (Octavian) defeats her troops. Augustus conquers Egypt (30), which now becomes a province of the Roman Empire.

Roman Egypt (30 BC–c.AD 600)

AD 193–211	Septimius Severus. Persecutions of Christians occur and continue under emperors Decius (249–251) and Diocletian (284–305).
306–337	Constantine I. First Christian emperor issues various edicts ending the persecution of Christians; the Council of Nicaea attempts to resolve doctrinal conflicts within the church.
379–395	Emperor Theodosius I. Christianity is declared the official religion of the Roman Empire, and pagan temples and monuments are destroyed throughout Egypt and Syria.
395	The Roman Empire is divided into eastern and western portions; Egypt, now part of the eastern half, is placed under Constantinople (Byzantium).
600s	The Arabs conquer Egypt and introduce Islam.

PREDYNASTIC EGYPT

The Predynastic Period (c.5000–c.3100 BC) ended when King Menes (Narmer) founded Dynasty 1 and dynastic Egypt. Following climatic changes, the Neolithic communities of the Predynastic Period became established in the Delta and Nile Valley. They initiated many political, social, religious, and artistic developments that came to form the basis of civilization in later times. As communities, they were distinguished by certain common features: social aims; replacement of hunting with agriculture and farming; production of pottery, tools, weapons, and domestic utensils; and religious beliefs and customs that emphasized reverence for the dead and perhaps a belief in life after death. Knowledge about many aspects of their societies remains speculative because of a lack of written evidence and the absence of artifacts from domestic sites.

Later Literary Sources

According to Manetho, before Menes's reign Egypt was ruled by a line of gods, followed by demigods. The Turin Canon identified those rulers who preceded Menes as the "Followers of Horus" (perhaps the kings of the predynastic northern and southern kingdoms centered at Buto [Pe] and Hieraconpolis [Nekhen]). In dynastic times the Egyptians were evidently ignorant of their historical origins, and the period was obscured in mythology. No firm evidence exists to provide a chronology for lengths of individual reigns or cultural subperiods.

Archaeological Discoveries

Little was known of Egypt's history before the Old Kingdom—apart from references to Menes as the first king of a unified country—until excavations undertaken at several sites about 100 years ago revealed the existence of predynastic cultures. In AD 1894–95 Sir W. M. Flinders Petrie and J. E. Quibell excavated near the modern village of Nagada (southern Egypt), where they discovered cemeteries that represented the last two cultures of predynastic times. Because the remains did not appear to be Egyptian in origin, the excavators at first wrongly identified them as evidence of a "new race" that had arrived in the First Intermediate Period (c.2200 BC). Similar burials discovered at other sites, however, persuaded Petrie to recognize all of them as evidence of predynastic cultures, and he subsequently pioneered studies in this field.

Sequence Dating and the Predynastic Cultures

Sequence dating, one of Petrie's greatest contributions to Egyptology, is a method of dating a site's excavated material relative to its pottery, whose approximate age has been established by comparing it to other types of pottery from several sites and putting them in sequential order. This system has some problems, but it is still widely used today since there is no absolute dating method for this period.

Petrie divided these predynastic cultures into three groups—Amratian, Gerzean, and Semainian (names derived from local modern villages near his excavations). The term used today for the earliest identified predynastic culture is *Badarian* (named after the modern village el-Badari, where Winifred Brunton and Gertrude Caton-Thompson undertook important excavations). The terms *Nagada I* and *Nagada II* have replaced Petrie's Amratian and Gerzean periods, respectively (objects from both periods have been found at Nagada). *Semainian* is now a term used only for the earliest dynasties.

Many problems exist with regard to the Predynastic Period, and the pattern of cultural progress at the various sites remains unclear. At some sites, Badarian, Nagada I, and Nagada II cultures have been found in stratified layers, but elsewhere not all these stages are present. The various settlements were perhaps part of an overall culture, or they may represent distinct local variations. It is unclear if northerners and southerners had different racial origins, which group developed first in Egypt, and if there was a marked difference between their cultures. The communities obviously coexisted sufficiently well to enable them to develop without a constant threat of warfare, and they shared many important features. Cultural evolution occurred from one period to the next, with no well-defined break between Badarian and Nagada I. There were major innovations, however, at the start of Nagada II (c.3400 BC), which Petrie explained by the arrival of new people (his "Dynastic Race").

The Badarian and Nagada I Periods

Archaeological evidence from settlement sites is scanty, but it is assumed that most people lived in villages in dwellings built of perishable materials. Graves were generally situated away from the habitations. Grave goods, including implements, personal adornments, and food, were presumably intended for use in the afterlife. Most graves were shallow, oval depressions in the sand, situated on the desert's edge, and each contained a single burial. The body, contracted and placed on its left side with the head to the south so that it faced west, was often encased in coarse matting, a basket woven of twigs, or an animal skin. The heat and dryness of the burial environment desiccated and preserved the bodies, creating "natural mummies." A small pile of sand or stones probably marked each grave.

Grave goods included several distinctive types of pottery, stone vases, ivory figurines, amulets, and slate palettes. These continued to be present into Nagada I, when styles and materials show an increased foreign influence, perhaps due to increased trade. Animal cemeteries were located near human graves and included burials of dogs or jackals, sheep, and cows wrapped in linen or matting covers. These, together with animal statuettes placed in human graves, suggest that animal worship was already well established.

A copper mirror with a hard wood handle carved with the head of Hathor, goddess of beauty. Found in a workman's house at Kahun, c.1890 BC.

Nagada II Period and the Dynastic Race

Little is known of the political and social organization of this period, but communities gradually drew together in larger units, each with its own area capital, chieftain, and major deity. Larger geographical groups (probably approximate to the administrative districts termed *nomes* in later times) were formed from these units. Eventually two independent kingdoms, the Red Land (in the north) and the White Land (in the south), evolved. Communities came together to provide greater protection against attack and to fulfill a common need to irrigate the land and improve agriculture. Ultimately, at the close of Nagada II, King Menes united the two kingdoms (c.3100 BC) and established dynastic Egypt.

Important innovations occurred in Nagada II. In the burial customs the rulers and the ruled now had distinctive burials, whereas previously there had been little difference. The masses continued to be buried in shallow graves, but now the leaders had monumental brick tombs. In these the superstructure above ground was bench shaped (this is why Egyptologists call these "mastaba tombs," from the Arabic word for bench or bench shaped) and contained a complex of chambers that housed the tomb goods. The body was buried below ground in the substructure.

One theory claims that bodies in these and later royal and noble burials show physical differences from the masses interred in the pit graves. The apparently rapid change in burial customs c.3400 BC lends some support to Petrie's theory of a new people (the Dynastic Race) entering Egypt and bringing new ideas and customs with them. It is claimed that, once they had subdued the indigenous population, they imposed their innovations, which included a two-tiered burial system. This continued into later periods, by which time it no longer reflected differences in racial origin but simply in

A pottery dish from Kahun (c.1890 BC), probably used to serve food. Such dishes are usually oval in shape, made of fairly coarse red pottery, and incised on the inside with designs based on basketwork, animals, and (seen here) fish and lotus flowers.

status and wealth. Arguably, the descendants of this Dynastic Race would have formed the royalty and nobility of the early dynastic period.

Opponents of this theory argue that the innovations of Nagada II could have been initiated by the indigenous population without direct outside intervention. These advances, however, do not appear to have any direct precedents within Egypt. In addition to monumental brick tombs, the earliest known stages in the development of hieroglyphic writing now occur. There were also significant advances in arts and crafts, notably stone maceheads and inscribed cylinder seals, for which parallels have been found in other regions, and slate palettes decorated with motifs that represent strange composite animals not found elsewhere in Egyptian art.

The Dynastic Race, it is argued, entered Egypt from an area where these innovations had already been developed. Mesopotamia is one possibility, since cylinder seals and maceheads are found there and the composite animals on the Egyptian slate palettes could have been influenced by Mesopotamian artistic motifs. Monumental brick architecture, decorated with recessed paneling on the façade, occurs earlier in Mesopotamia than in Egypt, but in Mesopotamia it was used for temples rather than tombs, so possibly only the concept was adopted. Also, in Mesopotamia cuneiform writing (inscribed on clay tablets) predates any known examples of hieroglyphic writing found in Egypt, but the increased chance of discovery or preservation of clay tablets may explain this. Papyrus and wood used as writing materials in Egypt would have survived less well than clay tablets. Both writing systems, derived from pictographs (picture writing), differ greatly in appearance and language structure. If they ever had any direct connection, they must have diverged at an early date.

Mesopotamia was perhaps only a stage en route from another original homeland, such as Syria, Iran, or even an as yet undiscovered center which influenced both Egypt and Mesopotamia. Trade, rather than mass invasion or armed conflict, may have introduced these innovations into Egypt. This seems to be a one-way process, however, since no parallel Egyptian influence has yet been discovered in Mesopotamia or elsewhere that would indicate mutual trade.

Armed conflict is apparently depicted in the carvings on the ivory handle of the Gebel el-Arak knife. It has been suggested that one scene, showing a sea battle between ships tentatively identified as Egyptian and Mesopotamian in origin, represents an attempted invasion, but so far there is no physical evidence of any mass invasion. If newcomers did arrive, some may have used force whereas others were traders. They may have entered Egypt by different routes. Such incursions do not seem to have continued into the Dynastic Period, by which time any newcomers and their innovations would have been absorbed by the indigenous culture. By then the composite animal motifs had disappeared, the forms of the hieroglyphs and the language structure had become distinctively and uniquely Egyptian, and the brick architecture had developed into the more sophisticated tombs of the Archaic Period and the Old Kingdom.

The Two Kingdoms

Between c.3400 BC and c.3100 BC two independent kingdoms were established in Egypt. The Red Land was based in the Delta and extended south along the Nile Valley perhaps as far as Atfih. Its Delta capital was at Pe (near ancient Dep, later known as Buto). Today the site of Pe and Dep is known as Tell el-Fara'in (The Mound of the Pharaohs). Edjo (sometimes written as Wadjet) was the chief deity of the kingdom; a cobra goddess, she protected the king and was worshiped at Buto. Each kingdom had its own ruler; the king of the Red Land lived in a palace at Pe and wore the Red Crown.

The southern kingdom, the White Land, stretched along the Nile Valley from Atfih to Gebel es-Silsila. Its capital at Nekhen (later known as Hieraconpolis) lay near the modern city of Edfu. Situated on the west bank of the Nile, it was excavated by J. E. Quibell, F. W. Green, and S. Clarke in AD 1897–99. A great cache of votive offerings (the "Main Deposit") was discovered in the Nekhen temple; these mostly dated to the earliest dynasties. On the east bank opposite Nekhen, the town of Nekheb (el-Kab) was the cult center of the kingdom's patron goddess, the vulture Nekhbet. When Quibell excavated Nekhen and Nekheb, he proved that the southern capital and the predynastic kingdoms were historical realities. The evidence also indicated that it was a real historical person, Menes (Narmer) who had ultimately united these kingdoms. Even after the unification the existence of the two kingdoms was never forgotten: Egypt continued to be called the "Two Lands," the king now wore both the White and Red Crowns either separately or combined as the "Double Crown," and the symbols of the south (the sedge) and the north (the bee and papyrus plant) continued in art and architectural forms. Edjo and Nekhbet (known as the "Two Ladies") united in their roles as patrons and protectors of the king.

THE ARCHAIC PERIOD

"Archaic Egypt" is the term used to describe the first two dynasties, when Menes (Narmer) and his descendants established the main elements of a united kingdom—political, social, and religious systems; developments in administration, the judiciary, and writing; and technological advances in art, architecture, metalworking, and carpentry.

The Unification

Menes (Narmer), a southern king, united the predynastic Red and White Lands in c.3100 BC following preliminary moves by Scorpion, another southern ruler whose limestone ceremonial macehead was discovered at Hieraconpolis in AD 1898. Carved with scenes showing Scorpion engaged in an irrigation project and in military action, this may have commemorated his organization of Egypt following a great military success.

Menes (Narmer) is credited with the final conquest of the north and the unification of the Two Lands and with the subsequent establishment of dynastic Egypt after he became the first king of Dynasty 1. Tradition claimed that Menes was the founder of historic Egypt, and his identification with the person named Narmer is now generally accepted.

THE SLATE PALETTE OF NARMER

The votive offerings in the Main Deposit excavated in the temple at Hieraconpolis (Nekhen) included a slate palette, possibly placed there by King Narmer as an offering of thanks to the god for his victory. This large, ceremonial palette (now in the Cairo Museum) is a fine example of the type that developed in later predynastic times from the small, plain slate slabs included in many graves as part of the cosmetic equipment used for grinding eye paint. The large ceremonial palettes were carved with scenes and became vehicles for recording important historical events.

The Narmer Palette commemorates the unification of Egypt. On the obverse the king is shown wearing the White Crown and smiting a captive northern chieftain; he is followed by a servant carrying a waterpot and the king's sandals, and below this group are two slain men. Hieroglyphs above the northern chieftain's head probably read "Horus brings [to the king] captives of Lower Egypt." On the reverse the sequel shows the conquest of Lower Egypt. The king wears the Red Crown (to mark his defeat of the north) and, with his standard-bearers, leads a ceremony to inspect ten slain northerners who are shown bound and beheaded. This may have taken place on the battlefield or at the temple at Nekhen where the victory was marked with the sacrifice of several captives. Other elements on the reverse include two entwined composite animals held by two men who grasp the ropes around the animals' necks. Thus, the palette commemorates Narmer as a southern conqueror (obverse) and as the victorious ruler of a united Egypt (reverse).

Memphis as Capital City

Scenes carved on a contemporary macehead show Narmer wearing the Red Crown and participating in a ceremony that possibly represents his marriage to the heiress of the Red Land. This union would have consolidated his claim to the northern kingdom and established the legitimate rulership of his descendants.

One of his first actions as king was to found a new capital city in the north, at the apex of the Delta. Probably originally called "White Walls," it was known later as Memphis and became one of the great cities of the ancient world. The royal family lived there, and it also probably accommodated the administration, judiciary, treasuries, and center for foreign trade, although already there were government offices at provincial centers. Memphis became a great metropolis for arts and crafts, and during the Old Kingdom it dominated all aspects of society.

Royal Burial Sites at Abydos and Saqqara

Although Memphis became very important, the early kings also emphasized the role of the old southern capital of This (near Abydos) as their foremost religious center. The exact location of the royal burials of the Archaic Period remains unresolved. The names of some kings and a queen of this era occurred on stelae and tomb goods found in brick pit tombs discovered at Abydos in 1895. At first Egyptologists identified these tombs as the royal burial places, and lack of any human remains there was explained as the result of plunder or marauding animals.

In 1938 however, a series of brick mastaba tombs was discovered at Saqqara (the cemetery of Memphis); these contained skeletal remains but had no stelae with names of individual owners. Inscriptions identified each tomb with a particular reign but not with a ruler; therefore, they may have belonged to courtiers or been royal tombs. The Abydos and Saqqara monuments were both probably royal funerary sites built to mark the kings' roles as rulers of north and south. It is most likely that the rulers were buried at Saqqara and had cenotaphs at Abydos. There is evidence at both sites that servants were taken to accompany their rulers in the afterlife. Subsidiary graves contained bodies of women servants, artisans, and pets to serve and entertain the owner and to repair his tomb throughout eternity. They were probably poisoned before burial. This custom had ceased by the end of the Archaic Period, and model figures of servants were placed in tombs as substitutes for human sacrifices.

Funerary Customs

Mastaba tombs continued in use for royalty and nobility, and the masses were buried in pit graves. The mastaba represented a house for the deceased. Important architectural changes were introduced to provide greater security for the burial and more space for tomb goods. By the end of Dynasty 2, tombs for royalty and nobility had become standardized, with size and number of chambers indicating the owner's wealth.

A range of goods and equipment was supplied for the owner's afterlife. An eternal and continuing food supply was very important. Some tombs included a complete meal, and additional offerings were left there by relatives. A stela inscribed with a "menu" was placed inside the tomb to provide a magical, alternative supply in case the real food was destroyed or the provisioning of the tomb was neglected. Early attempts were made to preserve the body by physical measures so that the owner's spirit could use it to receive sustenance from the food offerings. Gradually, use of some of these funerary preparations filtered down through society, but most people continued to be buried with basic grave goods in pit graves.

THE OLD KINGDOM

The foundations of society were established in the Archaic Period. By the Old Kingdom (Dy-

nasties 3–6), Egypt had become a highly organized, centralized theocracy. There were great advances in many fields including art, architecture, literature, medicine, and technological skills such as stone masonry and metalworking. The king held absolute power, which enabled him to devote a considerable proportion of the country's wealth and manpower to construct a great monument as his burial site. The Great Pyramid built for King Cheops at Giza (Dynasty 4) was the zenith of burial construction, but pyramids became a great economic drain on Egypt's resources and eventually contributed to the decline and disintegration of the Old Kingdom.

Structure of the Society

Society reflected the pyramid structure, with the king at the top and a broad base of peasantry at the bottom. Egypt revolved around the concept of a god-king and this held the country together as a political state. This idea was more evident in the Old Kingdom than at any other time. Each king was believed to be half divine, born of the union of the leading god and the Great Royal Wife (the previous king's chief queen). This unique status placed an impassable chasm between the king and his subjects and, in the Old Kingdom, supported the idea that only the king had an individual eternal life, which he spent sailing with the gods in the heavens. His status also gave him the power to mediate between gods and men. In theory he owned all the land, its resources, and its people, but in practice he was subject to *ma'at*, the principle of balance and order, and was constrained by precedent. Many of his duties in religion, law and justice, politics, warfare, and social affairs were delegated to royal officials, who advised him on state matters.

A glazed cosmetic dish in the shape of a fish, probably used to mix eye paint.

The king's role had developed out of its predynastic origin when he was recognized as the most powerful of many tribal leaders. By the Old Kingdom it had grown into a ruler surrounded by a large court and bureaucracy. Kings practiced polygamy and there were sometimes disputes among the royal children over the succession. Marriage to the royal heiress (Great Royal Daughter—eldest daughter of the previous king and chief queen) ensured accession to the kingship. To offset the rivalry of his siblings and relatives, the king gave them the most influential positions in government and provided them with wealth and lavish tombs. In the Old Kingdom these men and their families formed the nobility. At first their official appointments, given by the king, were held only throughout their lifetime. In later times, to offset a decline in royal power, the king appointed men outside the royal family in addition to his own relatives, and positions became hereditary in a vain attempt to ensure their loyalty. The king gave royal land and possessions to his nobles and tombs close to his own pyramid. These were provisioned with goods and supported and maintained by estates also provided by the king. The king's bounty and approval were required in order that the nobility could hope to achieve some kind of immortality after death.

An extensive hierarchy of minor officials supported these great administrators and governors. Their departments were accommodated, together with the royal domestic quarters, in a large complex known as the "Great House." This was at Memphis, Egypt's capital, where the chief royal residence, administrative headquarters, and great religious center were situated during the Old Kingdom.

The royal burial sites were near to Memphis at Saqqara, Giza, Meidum, and Dahshur, and

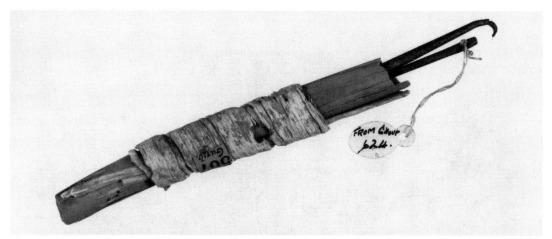

A reed and fiber needle case containing copper needles. From Gurob, c.1450 BC.

many artisans and craftsmen lived at Memphis, preparing the burial monuments and producing fine objects to be placed in the tombs. Wealthy residents were also supplied with furniture, jewelry, toilet equipment, and other articles for their daily use.

The majority of the population (perhaps 80 percent) were peasants. They were not slaves because they were not "owned," but their lives and opportunities were very limited. For most of the year they irrigated the land and grew crops to feed the population and provide the perpetual offerings presented at the tombs and pyramids.

When inundation made cultivation impossible for three months of each year, the peasants may have been paid by the state to labor on the pyramid. They could also be conscripted to undertake military duties and accompany royal expeditions to obtain hard stone or gold from the south.

Foreign Affairs

Egypt traded with and sometimes campaigned against her neighbors, seeking gold, hard stone, turquoise, good quality timber, and incense and spices. Through the port of Byblos (on the Syrian coast), Egypt obtained timber to construct tombs, coffins, ships, and doors. From Punt (probably situated on the east coast of Africa near the south end of the Red Sea) was acquired myrrh and frankincense for use in religious rituals. Expeditions were sent to Sinai to obtain turquoise, and there were extensive contacts with Nubia (to the south of Egypt). Here commercial expeditions, supported where necessary by military force, sought hard stone and exotic goods including ebony, ivory, incense, oil, and panther skins.

Religious Organization

There were now attempts to rationalize various aspects of religion. Village communities had worshiped local tribal gods in predynastic times, and in the early dynasties these gods had been brought together to form a confusing pantheon. During the Old Kingdom, as some cities emerged as major religious centers associated with particular gods or groups of gods, efforts were made to give some kind of structural order to the various elements of religious beliefs and practices. Each center had a powerful priesthood that developed a distinctive theology. This promoted the god's supremacy and claim to be the creator of the universe. The most important centers were Heliopolis, Memphis, and Hermopolis, where the gods Re, Ptah, and Thoth, respectively, were worshiped. The priesthoods each stated their god's supremacy in a "Creation Myth."

THE SUN GOD

The most important and successful deity during the Old Kingdom was the sun god Re, whose center was at Iwnw (later known as Heliopolis). From Dynasty 2 each king declared his allegiance to Re by adopting the title Son of Re as part of his royal name. The cult of Re played an important part in pyramid and solar temple development, in the Pyramid Texts and creation myths, and in political and religious events in Dynasty 5. There are a number of important myths associated with Re. He assimilated the cult center (Iwnw) and some of the characteristics of an earlier god, Atum, and as Re-Atum was worshiped as creator of the world. He had various physical forms. As Khepri, shown as a dung beetle pushing the sun in front of him (in the way dung beetles propel dung balls in front of them), he became a symbol of renewal and self-generation, representing the sun as he appeared in the early morning. Another form was Re-Harakhte (Re in his horizon).

The sun, regularly appearing at dawn and disappearing at sunset, was regarded as an eternal and self-renewing force. Re, it was believed, sailed a daily course around a circular ocean in the center of which lay the earth (believed to be flat and formed by the back of the earth god Geb). The circular ocean's upper half formed the sky above the earth, while the lower half

flowed through the underworld. The sun emerged at dawn on the earth's surface and spent the day in the sky, illuminating the earth, and at night it passed below the horizon into the underworld. This daily birth, death, and rebirth in the sun's cycle were regarded as the pattern for the king's own life, death, and resurrection.

The sun cult played an important role in two major monuments of the Old Kingdom: pyramids and solar temples.

PYRAMIDS

The classic form, with smooth sloping sides, was developed from the step pyramid. While the step pyramid may have been associated with star worship, the classic (or "true") pyramid was probably linked with the sun cult, which may have superseded star worship. The true pyramid possibly represented a sun ray, providing a ramp to heaven that would enable the king buried within the pyramid to ascend and join the gods, particularly Re, on the daily celestial journey in the sacred bark. The first stone pyramid—Djoser's Step Pyramid at Saqqara—was built in Dynasty 3. The pyramid complex as an architectural form reached its zenith at Giza in Dynasty 4, but from Dynasty 5 the pyramids declined. They ceased with the collapse of the Old Kingdom. Although reintroduced in the Middle Kingdom, they were finally replaced by rock-cut tombs.

SOLAR TEMPLES

In Dynasty 5 the kings gave unprecedented support to the sun cult and its priesthood and built six special solar temples to Re. Resources were allocated to these rather than to the kings' own pyramids, which were now built to inferior standards. These temples were modeled on the original sun temple at Heliopolis (which has never been located). This apparently contained as a central feature the benben stone, which represented both a sun ray and the god's cult symbol.

THE FIRST INTERMEDIATE PERIOD

Decline of the Old Kingdom

By Dynasty 5 there was a decline in standards of pyramid construction, and in Dynasty 6 the king's power and wealth were depleted. With the death of the aged King Pepy II at the end of Dynasty 6, the kingdom and centralized government collapsed. Egypt entered a period of disorder and disillusionment (Dynasties 7–10) that only ceased with the emergence of a strong ruler in Dynasty 11. This transitional phase (Dynasties 7–11) is known as the First Intermediate Period.

Various causes contributed to this collapse: political, economic, and religious. Throughout the Old Kingdom a number of economic factors ensured a gradual but inevitable equalization of wealth. Royal estates and wealth, through the king's presentation to the nobles, gradually passed into a widening circle of inheritance. Once given away these lands were also usually exempt from taxation, so eventually the king lost both the "capital" and the "interest." Kings also incurred great expense in building new pyramid complexes and maintaining the associated endowments and priesthoods, in addition to repairing and provisioning their ancestors' pyramids.

It was probably toward the end of Dynasty 4 that the king's power and wealth began to decline while the nobles and priests increased their position. In an attempt to win support from these "power groups," the king took action that ultimately exacerbated the problem. There were further tax exemptions, and the king now sometimes married outside the royal family into the increasingly wealthy nobility. This destroyed the fiction of the divinity of the royal line on which the king's right to rule and to enjoy an exclusive afterlife was based. Granting hereditary governorships to nobles and advancing the sun cult and temples at the expense of the king's own status further undermined royal power. Finally, the aged King Pepy II, who ruled for over ninety years, was incapable of rescuing the situation. Internal weakness and dissolution allowed an external danger to erupt when Bedouin nomads on the northeast frontier infiltrated Egypt.

Literary texts (Admonitions of a Prophet and Prophecy of Neferti) provide the main source for knowledge of the ensuing civil war and widespread chaos. The country suffered political upheaval and social disintegration. Royal authority collapsed, and the old order disappeared. This led to major religious changes: The masses questioned the king's absolute divinity and unique claim to individual immortality, and a democratization of religious and funerary beliefs and customs now emerged. The royal god Re was replaced as supreme deity by Osiris who offered eternity to rich and poor.

The Egyptians never forgot this period. It replaced the certainties of the Old Kingdom which came to be regarded as a "golden age." People now questioned their most fundamental beliefs, and at every level the country underwent profound religious and social change.

History of the First Intermediate Period

There are five distinct but overlapping stages in this period.

1. Disintegration of the country at the end of Dynasty 6 and ensuing chaos. Many ephemeral kings ruled from Memphis during Dynasties 7 and 8.

2. The collapse of centralized government at Memphis, which was followed by civil war between provincial governors. This was exacerbated by Bedouin infiltrators. The loss of centralized control resulted in widespread conflict, famine, and disease.

3. Emergence of a new line of rulers, governors of Heracleopolis, who gained control over the area of Middle Egypt between Memphis and Thebes. Led by a man named Akhtoy, this line ruled during Dynasties 9 and 10 and achieved a temporary cessation of warfare and anarchy.

4. A family of rulers, centered at Thebes, now rose to power and came into conflict with the Heracleopolitans. The first three of this line were named Inyotef (Antef).

5. The greatest ruler of this family was Mentuhotep Nebhepetre, who gained rulership over Egypt and made himself the first king of Dynasty 11. Little is known of his campaigns to overcome the Heracleopolitans and terminate the period of civil war and anarchy. He made Thebes the capital of Egypt and was buried there in a unique funerary monument. There was a general revival in monumental building and the arts, and a "Theban" art style brought a new vigor to wall reliefs and statuary and replaced the classic royal Memphite art of the Old Kingdom.

Literature

Texts that form part of the so-called Pessimistic Literature are believed to describe the events of the First Intermediate Period. Prophecy of Neferti and Admonitions of a Prophet both take the form of a prophetic speech, although they were actually composed after the events they describe.

Prophecy of Neferti (found in Papyrus Leningrad 1116 B, written during the reign of Tuthmosis III, c.1460 BC) describes how a wise man (Neferti) is summoned to appear before King Sneferu (who ruled at the beginning of Dynasty 4) and entertain the king. Asked to prophesy about future events, he describes the internal strife and foreign intervention that will afflict Egypt, but claims that the situation will be saved by a great king, Ameny (Amenemhet I, founder of Dynasty 12).

In Admonitions of a Prophet (Papyrus Leiden 344), the text probably describes events at the close of Dynasty 6. A wise man, Ipuwer, arrives at the court of an elderly, infirm king (probably Pepy II) who, protected from reality by his courtiers, is unaware of the dangers threatening his country. Ipuwer describes in vivid detail the horrors that already exist and foretells future events, and he begs those who hear him to act urgently to fight the king's enemies and restore the worship of the gods. He tells of conditions that prevail throughout the land: the overthrow of order, reversal of the positions of rich and poor, violence, robbery and murder, famine, disease, and foreign infiltration. The people themselves threaten the administration which soon disintegrates. Internal chaos results in neglect of irrigation and farming, bringing economic hardship and famine, and foreign trade collapses. People now long for death, but even this brings no peace because materials are often no longer available to provide appropriate burials, and tombs and bodies are plundered.

Ipuwer's pleas are ignored, conditions worsen, and the old order is swept away, possibly with the overthrow and removal of the king himself.

Religious Developments

Osiris began to supplant the Old Kingdom god Re throughout the First Intermediate Period as part of the general democratization of religious and funerary beliefs and customs. Kings of Dynasty 11 elevated their own local Theban war deity, Montu, to be their royal patron and supreme state god.

The troubled conditions of Dynasties 7–10 probably limited the ability of the rulers to build great burial monuments, but in Dynasty 11 Mentuhotep Nebhepetre resumed the tradition and constructed a great funerary complex at Thebes. It included a burial area and a mortuary temple where the funerary rituals could be performed and was built to a unique design. Set against the cliffs at Deir el-Bahri on the west bank opposite Thebes, little of the original monument survives today as the stone was used to construct the later adjacent temple of Queen Hatshepsut (Dynasty 18). The complex also included the burials of other members of the king's family. Democratization and decentralization affected the Old Kingdom custom of

Stone and faience jars for holding perfumed ointments and oils. The small vases with broad, flat neck pieces fixed on separately (left and center front) contained kohl for outlining the eyes. From Kahun, c.1890 BC.

locating nobles' tombs near the king's burial place. From the end of the Old Kingdom to Dynasty 12, provincial nobles increasingly chose not to be buried near the king but to prepare fine, rock-cut tombs in the cliffs near their own centers of influence along the Nile. Generally, the democratization of funerary beliefs encouraged a massive expansion in the production of various categories of goods for inclusion in the tombs.

THE MIDDLE KINGDOM

Domestic Policy

The last ruler of Dynasty 11 was probably assassinated by his vizier, Amenemhe, who seized the throne and became King Amenemhet I, the founder of Dynasty 12. He and his descendants ruled Egypt for the period that Egyptologists have named the Middle Kingdom, when the country flourished again as in the Old Kingdom.

Amenemhet I's father was not royal, and he and his descendants had no legitimate claim to rule, but they took several shrewd political measures to establish and promote their dynasty. They chose a new and more central site for their capital at It-towy, some distance south of Memphis. Thebes was retained as a great religious center. Amenemhet I introduced coregencies to counteract any attempt to place a rival claimant on the throne after his death. In year 20 of his reign he made his eldest son (later Senusret I) his coregent, and they ruled together for twenty years. This custom was continued throughout the dynasty and ensured a smooth succession even when violent events such as the probable assassination of Amenemhet I occurred.

These kings also dealt with the problem of the powerful provincial nobility, which had contributed to the downfall of the Old Kingdom. Under Amenemhet I the nobles retained many privileges and built magnificent rock-cut tombs in their own provinces. Their political and military strength still posed a threat to the king, and a later ruler of Dynasty 12, Senusret III, took decisive action and suppressed these men, removing their rights and privileges and closing their local courts so that they never again challenged royal authority. Their great provincial tombs ceased after his reign, and a new middle class, consisting mainly of craftsmen, tradesmen, and small farmers, replaced the nobles. They were grateful to the king for their advancement and were directly responsible in their government duties to the king or his deputy, the chief minister (vizier).

Foreign Policy

The political reorganization of the country was accompanied by an active building program with construction of religious and secular buildings throughout the country. There was also renewed royal interest in foreign policy, which was dictated both by trading and military needs. Trading contacts were renewed with Byblos and Phoenicia, and expeditions were sent to Punt (on the Red Sea coast). During the First Intermediate Period trading and military relations with Nubia had ceased, and a new and more aggressive people had entered Nubia. In Dynasty 12 the Egyptians initiated an active military policy there to reduce the Nubians to submission. An important feature of this was the construction of a series of large brick fortresses along the river between the cataracts. These were intended to present Egypt's might to the local population and provide a basis for the garrisons to control the waterway and ensure a safe passage for goods brought from Nubia to Egypt. Gold was the main commodity sought, but Nubia was also the source for ebony, ivory, giraffe tails, leopard skins, ostrich feathers, and monkeys.

During the Middle Kingdom there was also military engagements with other neighbors. The 'Aamu ("Asiatics" or Bedouin) had infiltrated through Egypt's northeastern border during the First Intermediate Period. Amenemhet I now constructed the Walls of the Ruler (perhaps a line of fortresses) in this area to repel them. There were probably other military actions taken by the Egyptians against their northern neighbors, but the Egyptians also developed diplomatic and trading relations with them during Dynasty 12. They had both peaceful and warlike relations with Syria/Palestine, and their connections with the Minoan civilization and the Aegean world probably included an interchange of ideas and products. One of the most significant discoveries at sites in Egypt has been Minoan pottery.

Pyramid Building

The kings of Dynasty 12, emphasizing their credentials to rule Egypt, returned to the Old Kingdom tradition of building pyramid complexes, although some new architectural features were introduced. The main cemetery of the capital city It-towy has been identified at the nearby site of el-Lisht, where the pyramids of two kings—Amenemhet I and Senusret I—have been discovered. These kings basically followed the Old Kingdom plan. Other rulers chose to return to Dahshur for burial in the southernmost area of the Memphis necropolis, first developed in the Old Kingdom. In the royal family burials associated with two of these pyramids (those of Amenemhet II and Senusret III), archaeologists discovered treasure and jewelry belonging to the queens and princesses.

One area, however, was particularly chosen by the kings of Dynasty 12 to accommodate their burials. The Fayoum, an oasis of great beauty and fertility to the west of the Nile Valley (southwest of Cairo), was extensively developed at this time. Senusret II built his pyramid here at Lahun, and in an associated family tomb archaeologists found the treasure of Princess Sit-Hathor-Iunut, which was similar to the Dahshur jewelry. In the 1890s the British archaeologist Petrie discovered and excavated the nearby and contemporary town of Kahun, which once housed the pyramid workforce and its families. Amenemhet III built his pyramid at nearby Hawara where a legendary building, the "Labyrinth," described by the Classical writers Herodotus, Diodorus Siculus, and Strabo, was also excavated by Petrie. The Labyrinth was built with interconnecting passages and chambers, and its unique plan incorporated the mortuary temple of Amenemhet III's pyramid, administrative quarters, and possibly a royal residence. This king undertook other major building works in the area, and he and Senusret II are accredited with the construction of the local Lake Moeris, although it was probably a natural feature around which the kings undertook an extensive program of land reclamation.

Nonroyal Tombs

The democratization and decentralization of power from the end of the Old Kingdom throughout the First Intermediate Period resulted in important changes in the construction and location of nonroyal tombs. Instead of grouping their tombs around the king's pyramid, the provincial nobles built rock-cut tombs at their own centers along the Nile. These were usually cut into the mountainside or cliffs bordering the river in parts of middle and southern Egypt, and each contained an offering chapel and a burial chamber. Major sites include el-Hawawish, Aswan, Assiut, el-Bersha, and Beni Hasan. These large tombs continued to be built in the earliest part of Dynasty 12, until the king curtailed the powers and privileges of the provincial nobility.

A particularly interesting group of tombs at Beni Hasan was built for the rulers of the sixteenth nome (district) of Upper Egypt who lived at the town of Monet-Khufu. The wall scenes in these tombs show various daily activities including food and textile production and military training. Once the provincial tombs ceased to be built, there was a return to the tradition of constructing tombs in the proximity of the king's pyramid.

Gods and Religion

The kings of Dynasty 12 promoted the Theban god Amun as their royal patron and protector. For the first time the Temple of Amun at Karnak, Thebes, became a national religious center, and Amenemhet I may also have constructed the nearby temple to Mut, Amun's consort. Later in the New Kingdom the Karnak complex would become Egypt's greatest religious center.

In the First Intermediate Period and the Middle Kingdom, however, the cult of Osiris became supreme. Osiris was one of Egypt's greatest gods whose story symbolized the triumph of good over evil and life over death. In the Middle Kingdom his supposed ability to offer immortality to all, regardless of wealth or position, mirrored the contemporary pattern of religious democratization. He gained widespread importance, and many features of the funerary cult are associated with his myth and worship. This emphasized the new belief that everyone, not only the king, could enjoy access to eternity. This concept inspired the mass production of funerary and tomb goods—coffins, canopic chests and jars, models of servants and boats, ushabtis (figurines of agricultural workers), soul houses, and other equipment—which characterized the Middle Kingdom.

THE SECOND INTERMEDIATE PERIOD

Historical Background

The long and successful reign of Amenemhet III (Dynasty 12) was followed by that of his coregent Amenemhet IV whose sister, Sobekneferu, succeeded him as the last of the dynasty. Under Amenemhet IV and Sobekneferu the country was beset with problems, and in the ensuing years (which Egyptologists call the Second Intermediate Period) Egypt suffered many difficulties. The Second Intermediate Period was at first a time of internal collapse when a rapid succession of kings failed to hold the kingdom together. Eventually native centralized government was restored by a line of Theban princes. In between these events, however, foreign rulers (whom we know as the Hyksos) entered Egypt and established their dynastic control over the country. They were not a minor harassment as the intrusion of foreign tribes had been in the First Intermediate Period but were regarded by later generations as foreign conquerors. Their advent profoundly changed the Egyptian attitude toward her neighbors and regarding warfare techniques.

The Second Intermediate Period includes Dynasties 13 to 17 and in many ways reflects the dissolution and decentralization of the First Intermediate Period. Dynasty 13 appears to have succeeded Dynasty 12 without major political upheaval, and the rulers of the two dynasties may have been related by ties of blood or marriage. The many rulers of Dynasty 13 had short reigns and were possibly puppet kings dominated by a line of powerful viziers. They ruled from Memphis and wielded power in Egypt and abroad, but toward the end of the dynasty lack of a strong ruler undermined the country. The dynasty no longer ruled all of Egypt. (Dynasty 14, centered on the city of Xois in the Delta, and other lines of rulers seem to have existed concurrently with Dynasty 13.)

The Hyksos Period

During Dynasties 15 and 16 the Hyksos took advantage of Egypt's internal weakness and seized control of Egypt. Their arrival (once viewed by scholars as an invasion) was probably achieved by infiltration rather than by significant military conquest. They probably represented a change of rulers rather than a massive influx of a new ethnic group.

Literary tradition provides some information about the Hyksos. Flavius Josephus (in *Against Apion*) claims to quote Manetho in stating that the invaders of an obscure race came without warning to conquer Egypt in the reign of King Tutimaios. They took the land without striking a blow and then ravaged the countryside, burning the cities, destroying temples, and massacring the people or taking women and children into slavery. They then appointed Salitis, one of

their own, as king. He ruled from Memphis, levied taxes on the whole country, and positioned garrisons to protect his gains. He rebuilt and massively fortified the city of Avaris on the east bank of the Bubastite branch of the Nile. Josephus also refers to Manetho's suggestion that *Hyksos* meant "Shepherd Kings" and was derived from *hyk* (meaning "king" in the sacred language) and *sos* (meaning "shepherd" in the vulgar tongue). Josephus adds his own interpretation that *Hyksos* meant "captive shepherds" from the Egyptian word *hyk* for a "captive." He believed this tied in with the idea (not supported by most modern scholars) that the Hyksos's arrival in Egypt, their occupation, and final expulsion were the basis for the Biblical account of the sojourn and Exodus.

The name *Hyksos* is in fact derived from two Egyptian words meaning "rulers of foreign lands." This term was used in the Middle Kingdom to refer to the leaders of the Bedouin tribes who infiltrated Egypt. It was now, however, applied to the new foreign rulers who were almost certainly not a new race. Manetho's account (preserved in Josephus) probably distorts the degree of severity of the rule that the Hyksos imposed. Probably based on an early account compiled under the Theban rulers who finally expelled the Hyksos, it doubtless reflects strongly propagandist influences, vilifying the Hyksos to justify Theban military action. In reality the Hyksos probably adopted and carried on existing Egyptian roles and powers, appointing Egyptian bureaucrats to administer the country and supporting native traditions. Even their policies of taxation and taking tribute from vassal rulers in the south merely perpetuated Egyptian practices. The Hyksos also encouraged native arts and crafts and patronized literary composition. Royal programs of temple building were initiated, and they elevated Seth as their patron god. He was probably more

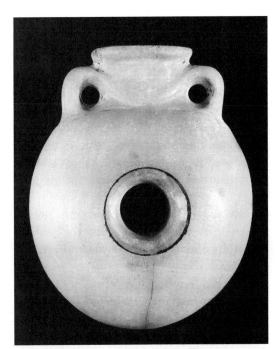

A doughnut-shaped alabaster vessel from Abydos (c.1450 BC) that may have contained perfumed oil. Alabaster was a favorite material for perfume jars, as it kept the oils and unguents cool.

closely associated with one of their own Asiatic deities than the "Evil One" in the Osiris myth, and his cult center was at Avaris. The Hyksos also promoted the worship of Re, Egypt's traditional royal god. The facts, therefore, do not bear out the literary claim that they set out to make extensive political, social, or religious changes in Egypt. Also their rule probably did not extend over the whole land, as Josephus claimed, but was limited to the north. The Theban princes of the south appear to have retained a considerable degree of autonomy, although they paid taxes to the Hyksos.

Josephus and some modern scholars have claimed that the Hyksos were a race of invaders who first conquered Syria and Palestine and then pushed onward into Egypt. Manetho claimed that they were Arabians and Phoenicians. Another theory stated that they had originated in Asia Minor and included Hurrians (people from the Caspian region) who, when they passed through Syria/Palestine, were joined by Semitic peoples who accompanied them in a mass invasion of Egypt. This is based on the idea that their conquest of Egypt was easy because they used the horse-drawn chariot which, it is claimed, was of Aryan origin (the Hurrians were Indo-Aryan). The technical terms associated with the horse-drawn chariot may be Indo-Aryan in origin, but horses and chariots were known in Mesopotamia long before the Hurrians appeared. Also, there is no real evidence that the Hyksos made use of the horse in Egypt until the end of their rule. The Hurrians and others exerted pressure downward into Syria for many years, but there is no conclusive evidence that they were a major element in the Hyksos invasion of Egypt. The Hyksos were most probably a small group of people of Semitic origin (the names of their chieftains indicate this) who moved from Palestine to Egypt, where internal dissension allowed them to impose their dynastic rule over part of the country.

CONFLICT BETWEEN THE HYKSOS AND THEBANS

Toward the end of this period some hostility appears to have developed between the Hyksos and the native population. Foreigners were used increasingly to administer Egypt, and this may have led to resentment. The conflict came to a head in a confrontation between the Hyksos and the native Theban rulers (Dynasty 17). Later generations regarded these princes as heroes who expelled the Hyksos, pursuing them into southern Palestine where they finally subdued them. The Theban princes established Dynasty

18 and the New Kingdom when the Egyptian Empire was founded.

Three Theban rulers were especially involved with the expulsion of the Hyksos—Seqenenre Ta'o II and Kamose of Dynasty 17 and Amosis I who founded Dynasty 18. Various sources (the Carnarvon Tablet, a stela, and fragments of a historical inscription discovered at Karnak) provide details of Kamose's campaigns against the Hyksos ruler Auserre Apophis I. They indicate that Kamose was assisted by Nubian soldiers from the south and reached Avaris where he attacked the Hyksos before returning to Thebes. His brother, Amosis, finally drove the Hyksos from Egypt and brought about the fall of Avaris. In the tomb of Ahmose, son of Ebana, at el-Kab, a wall inscription describes Ahmose's role as a fighter who accompanied Amosis on this expedition. It mentions Sharuhen in southern Palestine, which was probably the northernmost extent of the Egyptians' pursuit of the Hyksos. Another tomb inscription at el-Kab, belonging to a younger relative, Ahmose Pennekheb, provides other details of military action during this period.

LASTING INFLUENCE OF THE HYKSOS

The Hyksos rule marked a turning point in Egyptian history. National character and attitudes changed. The Egyptians no longer remained an isolated though brilliant society but became an empire-building people who sought not only resources but also power abroad. The Hyksos interlude forced the Egyptians to realize that unless they adopted an aggressive foreign policy, others would attempt to seize Egypt. Toward the end of their rule the Hyksos adopted new skills and war techniques from the north to help them subdue the Egyptians. When they won the The-

ban princes took over these innovations and used them to lay the foundations of an Egyptian empire. A professional army was also established, and the soldiers were paid by gifts of land from the king that remained in the family as long as they continued to fight for Egypt.

The Hyksos changed Egyptian attitudes toward political and military matters and also introduced important technical ideas and developments such as a special type of fort, weapons including the khepesh sword and composite bow, the horse-drawn chariot, advances in metalworking skills, the vertical loom for weaving, humped cattle, the lyre, and the lute.

The Hyksos period was not a time of anarchy, but it led to important changes. The Hyksos seem to have had no common language or culture to impose on Egypt, and whenever possible they adopted Egyptian customs. They were important as carriers of new ideas, however, and their rule prepared the Egyptians for the new challenges that faced them in the New Kingdom.

THE NEW KINGDOM

Amun, God of Thebes

The Theban princes who had driven out the Hyksos established their own dynasty (18) which ruled the whole of Egypt and founded an empire. In their early years, close dynastic marriages (in which the royal wives transmitted the kingship) helped them to consolidate their rule. The dynasty retained its local center, Thebes, as the new capital city, although major cities and military bases continued to flourish in the north at Memphis, Heliopolis, and other Delta sites.

The rulers of Dynasty 18 attributed their success over the Hyksos to the support of their local god, Amun, and later credited him with their military advances in Asia, which laid the foundations of their empire. Amun, originally a god of the air, now acquired roles as god of fertility and warfare. To ensure he had no rival, the kings associated him with the northern sun god Re, creating an all-powerful deity, Amen-Re. As Egypt's foreign conquests reached their peak (mid-Dynasty 18), the god's universality and role as creator of all peoples were emphasized. His temple at Karnak, Thebes, came to wield unequaled and unprecedented power. His priests promoted Thebes as the original place of creation and developed a new cosmogony (creation myth) to emphasize this role. He became the supreme state god, the "King of Gods," who assimilated the characteristics and powers of other major deities such as Re, Min, and Ptah. His consort Mut, a vulture goddess, was worshipped with him at Karnak but also had her own temple nearby (Temple of Luxor). Their son Khonsu, the moon god, also received worship at Karnak. Amen-Re protected the kings and supported their claim to rule Egypt. His cult center, Thebes, became the most important religious and political city in Egypt and the empire. Amen-Re's priesthood achieved great political power, not least because the priests came to control the royal succession: If succession was disputed or if there was a weak claimant, the priesthood granted or withheld the god's approval for a particular ruler. At the end of Dynasty 18 (Amarna Period) the priests' power was so great that the kings attempted to change this balance. They did not succeed, however, and the problem continued through later dynasties.

The priesthood of Amen-Re also possessed great economic strength. This was largely the result of direct royal policy, since the kings returned with booty and prisoners from their military campaigns in Asia and made large donations to Amen-Re's temple as an offering in gratitude for their success. The temple complex was expanded and enhanced by many rulers, and great estates were established to support the temple personnel.

Religious Developments

Opposite the city of Thebes, on the west bank, the kings selected a new burial site. Known today as the Valley of the Kings, this barren area in the western hills was selected for its relative isolation and proximity to the capital. Abandoning the custom of building pyramids (perhaps because of their vulnerability to tomb robbers), the kings now chose to be buried in deep, rock-cut tombs. These were also plundered, however, with the exception of Tutankhamun's burial which was discovered virtually intact in 1922. Later in the New Kingdom favorite royal wives and princes were buried in similar tombs in the nearby Valley of the Queens. Tombs for nobles and officials were arranged in several major groups scattered across the mountainside.

Another major architectural development of the New Kingdom was the royal mortuary temples, also situated on the west bank. Unlike the cultus temples (built to house the gods and to provide a place for worship), these were used for the performance of the royal burial rites and subsequently for the perpetual rituals to ensure the king's life in the next world. Originally attached to the pyramid, there was now no space in the Valley of the Kings to build the temple adjacent to the tomb, so they were situated on the plain between the Nile and the necropolis.

Egypt's Empire

The wealth and cosmopolitan outlook that the Egyptians enjoyed by mid-Dynasty 18 resulted from their foundation of the world's first empire. The kings first restored control over Nubia and then began to campaign in Palestine, where there were many small, independent states. This policy brought them into conflict with the other great powers of the area, first the Mitannians and then the Hittites. Under the powerful rulers of Dynasties 18 and 19, the Egyptians successfully established an empire that stretched from Nubia to the Euphrates River in Asia. There was extensive colonization and Egyptianization in Nubia so that it virtually became part of Egypt. In the north the control was less direct; the Egyptians gained the allegiance of the small, semi-independent states, where the native princelings were allowed to rule as long as they pledged allegiance to Egypt.

The military valor and prowess of the kings of Dynasty 18 were legendary. The achievements of Tuthmosis I were surpassed only by those of his grandson Tuthmosis III who undertook fourteen campaigns to Syria/Palestine in sixteen years in order to control the area. Eventually, under Amenhotep III, peaceful diplomacy, the exchange of royal gifts, and marriage between the royal families replaced active warfare. After Egypt's influence abroad had largely disappeared during the Amarna Period, however, the kings of Dynasty 19—Sethos I and Ramesses II—again took up arms in the north, this time against the Hittites. Both sides soon realized that neither could win outright and so, in year 21 of his reign, Ramesses II made a treaty with the king of the Hittites that brought peace to the area. It was followed by friendship between the two royal families and the marriage of Ramesses II to a Hittite princess.

The Amarna "Revolution"

Toward the end of Dynasty 18 there was a political and religious upheaval that had far-reaching repercussions. Amenhotep IV inherited the throne of Amenhotep III and began to make unprecedented changes. At first he lived at Thebes with his queen Nefertiti. Apparently he had already started to promote the cult of his favorite god, the Aten, by building temples to the deity in proximity to Amen-Re's temple at Karnak. Unlike other rulers Amenhotep IV did not simply wish to claim the superiority of his god. He attempted to impose a form of solar monotheism on Egypt based on the worship of the life force present in the sun and symbolized by the Aten (sun's disk). This cult, unlike others, did not tolerate the existence of other deities.

As his relationship with Amen-Re's priesthood deteriorated, Amenhotep IV took radical steps. He disbanded the priesthoods of all gods except the Aten, obliterated the gods' names from the monuments, and diverted the income from those cults to support the Aten. He expressed his allegiance to Aten by changing his name to Akhenaten ("servant of the Aten"). Finally, he moved his capital city from Thebes to a new, specially selected site in Middle Egypt. Here he built Akhetaten (known today as Amarna, or Tell el-Amarna) as his political and religious capital.

He moved his family, court, professionals, officials, and craftsmen to Amarna and built special temples there for the worship of the Aten, several royal palaces, and tombs for his family and courtiers. He pursued the exclusive worship of the god and appears to have neglected administration of the empire. With no direct male heir to continue his policies, however, a counterrevolution, probably initiated by senior courtiers, soon followed, and the royal family and court returned to Thebes. Amarna was eventually abandoned, but the religious ideas and distinctive art style that had flourished there seem to represent a unique experiment.

The Ramessides

There has been much discussion about Akhenaten's aims. Some regard him as a visionary and revolutionary religious and political leader, whereas others interpret his moves as politically expedient attempts to curtail the excessive power of the priests of Amen-Re. With the return to Thebes the traditional religious values were restored and the Egyptians again worshipped a multitude of gods. The kings of Dynasty 19 continued this policy.

When Ramesses II, a leading ruler of Dynasty 19, died after a long and impressive reign, he was succeeded by his thirteenth and eldest surviving son, Merenptah. It has been argued that the biblical Exodus probably occurred in the reign of Ramesses II or Merenptah. In year 5 of Merenptah's reign he faced an attack by a coalition of Libyan tribes and the Sea Peoples (migrants who approached Egypt from the eastern Mediterranean region and Aegean Islands). They wished to settle in the fertile lands of the Delta, and the Sea Peoples brought their wives, children, cattle, and possessions. Merenptah repulsed them, but Ramesses III (arguably Egypt's last great king) faced them again in years 5, 8, and 11 of his reign. He succeeded in defeating them, and most of the Sea Peoples traveled on to settle in other Mediterranean countries and islands. Ramesses III enjoyed a prosperous reign, which is evidenced by his mortuary temple at Medinet Habu. However, the kings who followed were less successful, and with the death of Ramesses XI the New Kingdom and Dynasty 20 drew to a close.

THE THIRD INTERMEDIATE PERIOD

Division of the Country

After the end of Dynasty 20, Egypt began a slow but inevitable decline. The Third Intermediate Period, like the First and Second Intermediate Periods, was characterized by internal dissolution. It includes Dynasties 21 to 25, covering a period when the country was sometimes subject to foreign rule.

When Ramesses XI died Nesbenebded took the name Smendes and founded Dynasty 21. His line chose the Delta site of Tanis as the capital and main residence. Pierre Montet discovered several royal tombs here in AD 1940. Although the environmental conditions in this area were less ideal for preserving artifacts than those at Thebes, Montet's excavations revealed a magnificent royal treasure that included gold and silver coffins and sets of jewelry. There was also a solid gold face mask, and the treasure rivaled the contents of Tutankhamun's earlier tomb.

The rulers of Dynasty 21 are recorded as the legitimate kings, but in fact they only exercised their power in the north. A line of high priests of Amun, established by a priest named Herihor in Dynasty 20, dominated the south from Thebes. The arrangement appears to have been amicable. One of the priests, Pinudjem I, had recognized Smendes as king and founder of Dynasty 21, and in return Smendes acknowledged him as the effective ruler in the south. These two lines had mutually recognized rights of succession in the north and south, and the families were joined by marriages arranged between Tanite princesses and Theban high priests. Through their mothers the Theban high priests thus became the legitimate descendants of the Tanite kings. Despite these arrangements, however, the country suffered from the lack of a strong, unified government.

The Royal Mummies

During Dynasty 21 the Theban high priests rescued and reburied some of the royal mummies of the New Kingdom. Their tombs and mummies had been desecrated by robbers. To give them another chance at eternity, Pinudjem I and Pinudjem II ordered the reburial of the bodies and the surviving tomb goods. Some were placed in a tomb belonging to Queen Inha'pi, south of Deir el-Bahri, and in later years mummies of other members of the royal family and priests were added. The inhabitants of the nearby village of Qurna discovered this cache, and in AD 1881 investigations carried out by the director of the Antiquities Service led to the removal of the mummies and tomb goods to the Cairo Museum. Another cache of royal mummies was buried in the tomb of Amenhotep II in the Valley of the Kings. This was discovered by the archaeologist Victor Loret in 1898, and the bodies were again transported to Cairo. The villagers of Qurna identified another important tomb in 1891 near Deir el-Bahri, where G. Daressy (excavating for the Antiquities Service) found many funerary objects belonging to the family of the high priest Menkheperre and to the priests of Amun. These caches provide invaluable information about New Kingdom religious and funerary practices.

Libyan Rulers (Dynasties 22 and 23)

On the death of Psusennes II, last ruler of the Tanite dynasty, there was no male heir, so his son-in-law, Shoshenk, a powerful chief and army commander, founded Dynasty 22 (sometimes called the Bubastite Dynasty because Shoshenk was from the Delta city of Bubastis). His family, who originally called themselves Chiefs of the Meshwesh, were of foreign origin. They were descended from the Libyans who had attacked Merenptah and Ramesses III and subsequently made their homes in the Delta, where they became successful and prosperous.

During this dynasty the capital was situated either at Tanis or Bubastis, and Thebes continued as the great religious center in the south. Despite Shoshenk I's action in appointing his second son as high priest of Amun and thus gaining control of Thebes, the country still suffered internal conflict. Inscriptions on the entrance (the Bubastite Portal) into the main temple at Karnak that Shoshenk I erected describe the troubled events of this period; however, the rulers were still powerful enough to build their monuments at Bubastis and Tanis and to be buried with magnificent treasure which Montet uncovered in their tombs at Tanis. Shoshenk I was also sufficiently confident to take action abroad again, trading with Nubia and intervening in internal politics in Palestine. Identified in the Bible as King Shishak, he removed a large amount of tribute from the temple and palace in Jerusalem.

The succeeding dynasties are poorly documented. According to Manetho, Dynasty 23 consisted of four kings who ruled from Tanis. This line may have ruled at the same time as some of the kings of Dynasty 22, reflecting a breakdown of centralized government. Manetho's Dynasty 24 is certainly limited to one area, and its one recorded king ruled from Sais in the Delta. This line was descended from a prince of Sais, Tefnakhte, who had attempted to extend his power southward. His plans were curtailed by Piankhy, the ruler of a kingdom that was situated far south of Egypt. Its capital, Napata, lay near the Fourth Cataract on the Nile, where the people worshipped Amen-Re and continued many traditions of Egypt's Dynasty 18. Piankhy campaigned in Egypt, subdued the south, and gained submission from the north before returning to Napata.

Nubian Rule

Egypt continued to be segmented and ruled by various princes, but Piankhy's brother and successor, Shabako, returned there to defeat Tefnakhte's successor at Sais. He then founded Dynasty 25 (the Ethiopian or Kushite Dynasty) and, as Egypt's first Nubian ruler, chose Thebes as his capital. He eventually returned to Napata and, like his predecessor Piankhy, was buried in a pyramid at Kurru. The custom of pyramid building was revived by these rulers although it had ceased in Egypt hundreds of years before.

Shabako's successors, Shebitku and Taharka, inherited the kingship and Taharka was crowned at Memphis. He was an effective ruler, but he soon came into conflict with the new power in the area, the Assyrians. When the king of Judah, Hezekiah, asked Egypt for help against the Assyrians, the Egyptian forces were defeated at el-Tekeh. Assyrian expansion to gain control of the small states in Syria/Palestine met with opposition from Egypt, to whom these states appealed for help. Resentful at Egypt's intervention the Assyrians attempted to invade Egypt (674 BC), but they were defeated. However, in 671 BC the Assyrian ruler Esarhaddon drove Taharka out of Memphis. He destroyed Memphis and removed booty and people from Egypt while Taharka fled to the south.

Esarhaddon now appointed rulers for Egypt who were selected from local governors and officials loyal to the Assyrians. One of these,

Necho of Sais, would become the founder of Dynasty 26.

Esarhaddon's death allowed Taharka to reinstall himself at Memphis, but the Assyrian king Ashurbanipal attacked Egypt and regained Memphis in 662 BC, driving Taharka first to Thebes and then to Napata. Further intrigues followed, and eventually Taharka's nephew and successor, Tanuatamun, reestablished the dynasty's power at Memphis. However, Ashurbanipal returned again, and Tanuatamun fled to Thebes and then to Napata, while the Assyrians ransacked Amun's temple at Thebes and transported booty back to Nineveh.

The Nubian kingdom soon ceased to exert any claim over Egypt, continuing to exist within its own boundaries. Its northern boundary was probably fixed south of the Third Cataract. The Nubians established a new capital at Meroë and continued to trade with Egypt. Aeizanes, ruler of Axum, finally destroyed Meroë in AD 350, but throughout this period a form of Egyptian culture continued to exist there. Egyptian-style temples flourished, and royalty were buried in pyramids; their language was written in hieroglyphs, and they produced two distinctive scripts known today as Meroitic.

THE LATE PERIOD

Assyrian Policy

The Assyrians discovered that the local Egyptian princes whom they had installed as governors in Dynasty 25 were poor allies. The princes had switched allegiances and now gave political and military support to the deposed Nubian ruler Taharka, causing the Assyrians to remove them to Nineveh. Ashurbanipal subsequently restored Necho of Sais (a Delta town) and his son Psammetichus as petty rulers in the Delta. The latter would become the first king of Dynasty 26.

This line of native rulers brought many changes to Egypt, and there was a brief resurgence of national power and pride. But the country's international significance was never regained, and the gradual but inevitable decline continued. Necho had established an important kingdom in the western Delta and probably began to rule as a local king at Sais in 672 BC. He was killed, however, by the Nubian Tanuatamun who briefly regained Egypt in Dynasty 25, only to lose it to Psammetichus who founded Dynasty 26 and claimed the kingship of Egypt. At first he probably ruled only in the north while Tanuatamun still controlled the south. When Tanuatamun finally left Egypt for Nubia, Psammetichus took charge of the whole country.

The Divine Wife of Amun

Psammetichus continued an important tradition established by earlier rulers by making his daughter Nitocris the Divine Wife of Amun at Thebes. In the New Kingdom the king's chief wife had carried this title and acted as the god's consort in state festivals. From Dynasty 21, however, the title came to have political significance. It was now accorded to the king's daughter who became a priestess with extensive political and religious powers as well as great wealth and possessions. As the wife of Amun at Thebes, she owned property and land, controlled officials, and performed rituals for the gods. She was not allowed to marry but had to adopt the daughter of the next king as her own daughter and successor.

This practice continued into Dynasty 25, when it was established as a vital method of ensuring the unity of the kingdom and preventing the division into northern and southern bases of power, which had happened in Dynasties 20 and 21. It also ensured that each king gained control over the south through his daughter's unrivaled position at Thebes. There she had equal status to the king, but her power was limited to that city. Since she could not marry, her husband and sons could not threaten the king's supremacy, and while she ruled at Thebes no male rival to the king could seize power there. The process of adopting the next divine heiress ensured a safe and smooth transition of her title and power.

Saites and Mercenaries

The Saites (rulers of Dynasty 26) had gained the throne with the help of Greek mercenaries, and the line continued to rely on foreign naval and military skills as well as foreign merchants. They pursued a policy of encouraging foreigners to settle in Egypt, since foreigners provided the Saites with strength against other local princes. These foreigners included Greeks, Carians, Jews, and Syrians, but because the native population came to resent them, it became necessary to establish separate districts where they could live. Psammetichus I built the city of Naucratis in the Delta specially to accommodate Greek residents.

Another reaction to this influx of foreigners was the native revival in religious and artistic traditions. This expressed itself in an increased interest in the particularly Egyptian custom of worshiping animals and in an archaistic tendency in literature and art, where styles found in the Old Kingdom were now revived. This dynasty produced the last fine quality goods of local manufacture, with special emphasis on funerary goods such as ushabti figures.

SAITE FOREIGN POLICY

Psammetichus I's son and successor, Necho II, was interested in exploration and trade; he began the construction of a canal between the Nile and Red Sea and established a fleet of triremes. The Phoenician sailors he employed voyaged around Africa for three years, taking a route from the Red Sea around the Cape and then returning via Gibraltar. His reign, however, was mainly dominated by foreign affairs. As the power of Assyria waned and the Babylonians became the new force in the area, Necho II became engaged in the politics of Syria/Palestine. The Babylonian ruler, Nabopolassar, came to regard Egypt as an enemy, and his son, Nebuchadnezzar, soundly defeated the Egyptians at Carchemish in 605 BC, pursuing them in the district of Hamath and making them flee. Later the Babylonians seized all of Egypt's foreign territorial possessions.

When Nebuchadnezzar became ruler of the Babylonian Empire, he was able to campaign against Egypt in 601 BC, but he was unsuccessful and was forced to return to Babylon. Although the brief reign of Psammetichus II, son and successor of Necho II, was concerned with domestic policies, his own heir, Apries, again became involved in foreign affairs when King Zedekiah of Judah rebelled against Babylon. The exact role Apries (the biblical pharaoh Hophra) played against the Babylonians is not clear, but Jerusalem was captured by the Babylonians, Zedekiah was taken prisoner, and a large proportion of the population was removed to Babylon while the prophet Jeremiah led the remainder to Egypt.

LATER SAITE RULERS

Internal politics in Egypt finally resulted in the removal of Apries and his replacement as ruler by an army general, Amasis. The events of his life and reign are provided by Herodotus, and it is clear that although Amasis continued to use Greek mercenaries in Egypt, he was mindful of native feeling since he owed his kingship to the Egyptian population. He checked the growth of Greek merchants in Egypt by limiting their trading ventures to the city of Naucratis.

Amasis's son, Psammetichus III, ruled for only a few months before Egypt was taken over by the Persians. Cyrus II, the Achaemenid ruler who founded the Persian Empire, defeated Nabonidus, the last king of Babylon, in 539 BC after he had overcome Media, Lydia, and the cities of the Ionian coast. Persia became the great new power of the area, and Cyrus II's son, Cambyses, was sent to subdue Egypt. He defeated the Phoenicians and took possession of their fleet before proceeding to rout the Egyptians at the Battle of Pelusium (525 BC). A final seige of Memphis resulted in the death of Psammetichus III and the annexation of Egypt. This first Persian period (Manetho's Dynasty 27) lasted until 404 BC.

Persian Rule

As a satrapy (province) of the Persian Empire, Egypt was governed by a satrap on behalf of the Persian king. The Persian kings, however, seem to have taken on the title and role of pharaoh and to have performed religious duties and upheld Egyptian traditions. Herodotus is again a main source for this period, characterizing Cambyses as a cruel tyrant who may have suffered from insanity. By contrast Darius I was regarded as a positive ruler who, according to Diodorus Siculus, was a lawgiver. Whereas Cambyses apparently neglected the Egyptian gods, Darius supported their cults and made additions to their temples. He also completed (518 BC) the canal to link the Nile and the Red

Sea, which had been started by Necho II. His son and successor, Xerxes, was a tyrant to the Egyptians and put down a series of uprisings. Disturbances continued under his successor Artaxerxes I. Eventually a local chieftain, Amyrtaeus of Sais, seized some power; he is recorded by Manetho as the only ruler of Dynasty 28. In the two succeeding dynasties native rulers continued to claim power, but Artaxerxes II began to prepare to reestablish Persian control over Egypt and sent forces there under the satrap Pharnabazus. However, local circumstances including the Nile inundation helped the Egyptians to repel them.

This was merely a temporary respite, however, and when Artaxerxes III became emperor (358 BC) he reorganized his forces and marched against Egypt in 343 BC. He was successful and destroyed the walls of the most important cities and removed treasure and inscribed records from the temples. Finally, before he left for Babylon he installed a new satrap, and a second Persian period ensued. This Dynasty 31 was added later to the thirty dynasties given by Manetho. Persia's control of Egypt came to an end in 332 BC when Alexander the Great, king of Macedon, took the country and laid the foundations for the Ptolemaic Period.

The periods of Persian domination, like the Assyrian, had no profound effect upon Egypt. Despite Herodotus's claims of tyranny, it is unlikely that their rule was excessively cruel. They had little impact on Egyptian civilization although communities of foreigners now resided in Egypt, Egyptian soldiers fought in Persian campaigns, and artists and officials were taken to work in cities in Persia. Nevertheless, the Egyptians welcomed the arrival of Alexander the Great as their savior from Persian domination and segmented native rulership.

THE PTOLEMAIC PERIOD

Alexander the Great

When Alexander the Great arrived in Egypt (332 BC), communities of Greeks had been resident there since the Saite rulers had brought in mercenaries to establish their dynasty and to fight against the Persians. The Greeks had modernized the Egyptian army and introduced new fighting techniques. There was also a substantial community of Greek merchants who were established in their own Delta city of Naucratis. A period under Persian domination, interspersed by ineffectual native rulers, made the Egyptian people very receptive to Alexander the Great's conquest.

Alexander the Great was the son of Phillip II, the ruler of Macedon. When Phillip was assassinated supporters helped Alexander gain his throne, and from this base, he set out to conquer the known world. Under his brilliant leadership his forces were able to annex the lands of the Persian Empire, and the tribute which the subject peoples had formerly paid to the Persian king was now handed over to Alexander. His rapid conquests were, however, accompanied by a relatively benign rulership which brought long-term benefits to his empire. Common social and economic interests were developed alongside the freedom to practice individual religions and customs, and this unified the diverse peoples whom Alexander ruled. He also founded new cities to disseminate the Greek culture.

CONQUEST OF EGYPT

After his conquest of Syria/Palestine and the siege of Tyre, Alexander attacked Gaza before he reached Egypt in 332 BC. He was welcomed by the population as a liberator, and the Persian satrap surrendered without opposition. He was invested by the Egyptian priests as a pharaoh and spent six months in the country, establishing important guidelines for the future government of the people. A viceroy was appointed, together with six governors (two Macedonians with military powers, and two Greeks and two Egyptians with civil powers). Garrisons were placed at Pelusium and Memphis, and Macedonian commanders were put in charge of the Nile fleet. Military matters and finance were put under a Greek system of control, and arrangements were made for the imposition and collection of taxes.

During his brief stay in Egypt Alexander founded the new city of Alexandria, lying on the west mouth of the Nile and the Mediterranean coast. Its position ensured that it would become the great commercial center of the area. Planned and built as a Greek city, Alexandria became Egypt's new capital and a great center of Hellenistic knowledge and learning. Alexander also paid special attention to the Egyptian gods, and he was probably crowned as king in a traditional ceremony at Memphis. He visited the famous oracle of Jupiter Amun at the oasis of Siwa where legend claimed that the god recognized him as his own son and promised him rulership of the whole world. This seems to have been interpreted as a form of personal deification for Alexander, which the Egyptians accepted as a special divine recognition, according Alexander and his successors, although foreign, the legitimate right to rule Egypt.

Alexander left Egypt to pursue further conquests but fell ill on returning from India and died in Babylon in 323 BC. His empire was now divided between his generals, and the Macedonian general in charge of troops in Egypt, Ptolemy, son of Lagos, became satrap of Egypt first under Philip Arrhidaeus, Alexander's half brother, and then under his son, Alexander IV. In 305 BC Ptolemy became independent king of Egypt, taking the title Ptolemy I Soter (Savior) and founding the Ptolemaic dynasty.

The Reign of Ptolemy I

Ptolemy I was determined to establish himself as a regenerator of Egypt and to ensure the succession within his own family. He appointed his son as coregent and reintroduced the custom of royal brother-sister marriages. He reorganized the country and adopted the title and role of pharaoh. This allowed him to claim the religious right to rule Egypt and the political justification to own the country's resources and impose heavy taxes. His role as pharaoh was further emphasized when he built temples to the Egyptian gods. Five examples survive at Edfu, Denderah, Esna, Philae, and Kom Ombo, where the Ptolemies are shown in the wall scenes as Egyptian kings performing the divine rituals. Ptolemy I also introduced the cult of a new hybrid deity, Serapis, who was worshiped as a combination of the Egyptian god Osiris and various Greek deities. At Alexandria he founded the cult of Alexander the Great, which laid the foundations for the later official state cult of the Ptolemaic dynasty.

There was also a dedicated attempt at Hellenization by Ptolemy I and his successors. Large communities of Greeks were now established at Alexandria, Naucratis, Ptolemais, and also in country districts like the Fayoum where farming was developed. The Ptolemies actively patronized the arts, particularly at Alexandria where the Great Library and Museum were established, and foreign scholars were encouraged to come to the city. Greek language and culture now predominated in these new centers, although settlers in the country districts were more exposed to the continuing Egyptian traditions, and a degree of hybridization occurred in aspects of art, religion, and architecture.

Changes under the Ptolemies

The Greeks now formed the new upper classes in Egypt, replacing the old native aristocracy. In general the Ptolemies undertook changes that went far beyond any other measures that earlier foreign rulers had imposed. They used the religion and traditions to increase their own power and wealth. Although they established a prosperous kingdom, enhanced with fine buildings, the native population enjoyed few benefits, and there were frequent uprisings. These expressions of nationalism reached a peak in the reign of Ptolemy IV Philopator (207–206 BC) when rebels gained control over one district and ruled as a line of native "pharaohs." This was only curtailed nineteen years later when Ptolemy V Epiphanes succeeded in subduing them, but the underlying grievances continued and there were riots again later in the dynasty.

Family conflicts affected the later years of the dynasty when Ptolemy VIII Euergetes II fought his brother Ptolemy VI Philometor and briefly seized the throne. The struggle was continued by his sister and niece (who both became his wives) until they finally issued an Amnesty Decree in 118 BC.

Cleopatra VII

The final stages of this dynasty centered around the life and death of Cleopatra VII. She became joint ruler with her father Ptolemy XII Auletes in 51 BC and then ruled successively with her brothers Ptolemy XIII and Ptolemy XIV to whom she was also married. Cleopatra, however, was ousted from the joint rulership in favor of her brother Ptolemy XIV. She seized her opportunity for power when Gaius Julius Caesar, Roman dictator from 49 to 44 BC, followed his enemy the Roman consort Pompey to Egypt. Pompey had been appointed by the Roman Senate as the guardian of Cleopatra and her brother when their father died, but Pompey was killed by some Egyptian courtiers. Caesar now spent time in Egypt (47 BC), and Cleopatra's plea to him to restore her throne was granted. Her royal powers were reinstated, her brother drowned in the Nile, and her son by Caesar, Ptolemy XV Caesarion, was adopted as her coregent. Cleopatra and Caesarion appear together in a wall scene at the Temple of Hathor at Denderah.

Cleopatra's involvement with Marcus Antonius (Mark Antony) ultimately led to the end of her dynasty. He was a Roman consul and triumvir whose early career at Rome had been supported by Julius Caesar. He had also married Octavia, the sister of Gaius Julius Octavianus, who was to become the first emperor of Rome and take the title of Augustus when he became sole ruler in 27 BC.

Mark Antony may have initially intended to turn Egypt into a client state of Rome, but Cleopatra used her political and personal skills to persuade him to abandon this scheme. The couple spent time together at Alexandria, and Mark Antony made many gifts to the queen, incurring the displeasure of the Roman Senate. Their relationship aroused the displeasure of Augustus, Mark Antony's brother-in-law, who also probably regarded Mark Antony's base in Egypt as a threat to Rome. His verbal hostilities persuaded the Senate that Mark Antony was a traitor of Rome, and Augustus's personal declaration of war against Mark Antony and Cleopatra resulted in their defeat at the Battle of

A plaster head of a woman that was originally placed over a mummy. From the cemetery at Mallawi (near Beni Suef), which was once the location of a Roman garrison. The head dates to the second century AD, *and such examples seem to have occurred only in this area for a period of about eighty years.*

HISTORICAL BACKGROUND

Actium in western Greece in 51 BC. The queen, followed by Mark Antony, fled to Alexandria where for ten months they awaited the arrival of Augustus. Unable to bear the humiliation that Augustus would have imposed on them when he took Alexandria, they chose to commit suicide.

Augustus was declared pharaoh of Egypt on August 31, 30 BC when Egypt became a Roman province and lost all independence.

THE ROMAN PERIOD

Administration of Egypt

When Augustus (Gaius Julius Octavianus) was declared pharaoh of Egypt in 30 BC the country became a Roman province. Unlike other major provinces governed by the Roman Senate, however, Augustus gave Egypt a special status as his personal property. It was administered by a prefect (viceregal governor) who was directly responsible to Augustus. Now regarded as a district to be administered to benefit the empire, Egypt no longer had its own king or capital city. An administrative system was set up that retained the structure and officials that the Ptolemies had used but introduced some important new elements such as Roman law.

The political stability of the Roman Empire ensured that Egypt flourished, but the main aims were to collect taxes and ensure that the country supplied the commodities, such as corn, papyrus, and glass, that Rome required. There was no investment to improve the lives of the native population who enjoyed few of the benefits of their own prosperity. Roman control was extended as far south as possible, and an expedition was sent to the Theban district, while the emperor founded temples as far south as Nubia.

Roman Emperors as Pharaohs

Augustus and his successors followed the example of the Ptolemies in becoming pharaoh and taking on the role and titles of the divine son. This gave them the legitimate right to rule Egypt and, as they chose to interpret this power, to exploit the people and resources. Several of the emperors visited Egypt and traveled to see its ancient monuments. At Alexandria, which Augustus preserved and enhanced, a center for the divine cult of the Caesars was established, while throughout the Greek cities of Egypt the use of the Greek language persisted and the Hellenistic culture survived.

The emperors continued to build and add to Egyptian temples where their role as pharaoh was emphasized. Many are well preserved, and with only minor variations, they continued the traditions of pharaonic temples. They have the same architectural and ritual features, but some new details were added including a birth house (mammisi) where the god's birth was celebrated.

Christianity

The most profound change in Egypt during this period, in terms of religion, art, and language, was the arrival and spread of Christianity. As early as the first century AD, Christianity was introduced to Egypt through Alexandria where friends and relatives of the Jewish community brought it from Jerusalem. Its concepts of disinterest in worldly goods and mutual support made it immediately relevant to the Egyptian poor who eagerly adopted the new faith. Despite persecution by several emperors (Septimius Severus's edict of AD 204 forbade Roman subjects to embrace

Christianity; Decius ordered the persecution of Christians in Alexandria; and Diocletian instigated persecutions in 302 that lasted for ten years), the reign of Constantine I changed these attitudes.

Constantine, the first emperor to support the growth of Christianity, introduced a series of measures. He ended the persecutions started by Diocletian and issued the Edict of Toleration in 311 and then in 313 the Edict of Milan, which restored the property of the churches. Public funds were now allocated for building and restoring churches, and in 324–30 Constantine founded Constantinople, which became the first Christian city. The founding of Constantinople also had political significance for Egypt since it lessened the importance of Alexandria as the foremost city of the east; Constantinople joined Rome as a major recipient of Egypt's grain.

Christianity now spread throughout Egypt. The Caesareum at Alexandria that had accommodated a cult to the Roman emperors now became a church dedicated to St. Michael. Later it was established as the seat of the Patriarch of Alexandria. Christianity brought profound changes in art as well as religion. The pharaonic and Hellenistic traditions had previously inspired its development, but new art forms now emerged by the fourth and fifth centuries that had a great impact on the paintings, sculpture, and textiles used to decorate monasteries, churches, and houses. Egypt's climate has ensured the survival of Coptic or post-pharaonic textiles, which include religious and secular clothes, burial garments and wrappings, and domestic furnishings. The Coptic language was developed for religious scriptures and the liturgy. The Greek alphabet and some additional letters were used to convey this final stage of the ancient Egyptian language, which had previously been written down in hieroglyphs, hieratic, or demotic.

The territories of the Roman Empire, divided into eastern and western portions in 305, were now ruled from Constantinople and Rome. Egypt, controlled as part of the Eastern Empire, became a focus for various theological and doctrinal conflicts that were addressed at a series of councils (the most famous was held at Nicaea). These problems had a profound effect upon the development of Christianity and the Christian church.

Christianity had been officially adopted as the religion of the empire following the baptism of Theodosius I (379–95) soon after his accession. This was formally declared in his edict (384), which also ordered that the temples to the old gods should be closed. There was now widespread persecution of those people who clung to the old religions, and temples and monuments were destroyed throughout Egypt and Syria. However, ancient Egyptian religion continued to be practiced until, in the reign of Justinian (c.540), the temples to the cult of Isis on the island of Philae in southern Egypt were finally closed.

Christianity ceased to be the official majority religion after the Arab conquest of Egypt in 641 when Islam was introduced. Many Christians were converted, but strong Christian communities also survived, especially in the south. These Christian Egyptians came to be called "Copts," a term first used in sixteenth-century Europe to distinguish them from other Egyptians. (The words *Copt* is originally derived from the Greek *Aigyptios*, meaning Egyptian, which became *Qibt* after the Arab invasion.) With the arrival of Islam the Roman rule of Egypt came to an end and the country underwent radical changes.

PROMINENT KINGS AND QUEENS

The following selected biographies are in chronological order. The dates give the lengths of reigns.

ARCHAIC PERIOD

Menes (Narmer) King, Dynasty 1, c.3100–? BC. He was the founder of historic Egypt and unifier of the Two Lands, and he built the first capital, White Walls (later known as Memphis). As a southern ruler he conquered the north and subsequently unified the two regions. This is probably commemorated on the Narmer Palette. He possibly married a northern princess in order to consolidate the country's unification, and he is accredited as the first lawgiver and the ruler who brought civilization to Egypt.

OLD KINGDOM

Djoser King, Dynasty 3, c.2667–2648 BC. Djoser was probably the founder of the Old Kingdom, and his reputation as a great king survived for centuries. He introduced the custom of royal burial in a pyramid, and his architect, Imhotep, designed the Step Pyramid at Saqqara as his tomb. This was a new architectural form and marked a major development in stone building techniques.

Hetepheres Queen, Dynasty 4, Reign of Sneferu, c.2613–2589 BC. Hetepheres was the wife of Sneferu, the first king of Dynasty 4, and the mother of King Cheops. Her undisturbed tomb was discovered at Giza in AD 1925, and it contained jewelry, furniture, and mummified viscera, although the body was missing. The original burial had probably been robbed, and

Cheops thus provided his mother with a new tomb and tomb goods. The viscera (which presumably survive from the initial burial) provide the first known evidence of true mummification.

Cheops King, Dynasty 4, c.2589–2566 BC. Khufu (Greek: Cheops) was an absolute ruler with unchallenged access to Egypt's resources and manpower, which enabled him to build the Great Pyramid at Giza as his funerary monument. Herodotus represented him as a cruel tyrant, but he was also accredited with great sacred wisdom and knowledge and the authorship of a hermetic book.

Chephren King, Dynasty 4, c.2558–2533 BC. Khafre (Greek: Chephren), the son of Cheops, built a pyramid complex at Giza that is the best-preserved example still in existence. The Great Sphinx, a unique feature of this complex, is said to portray Chephren's own facial features. Herodotus described him as a cruel tyrant whom the Egyptians despised.

Mycerinus King, Dynasty 4, c.2528–2500 BC. Menkaure (Greek: Mycerinus) was the son of Chephren and built the third pyramid at Giza. It was completed by his successor, Shepseskaf, and sculpture from both Chephren's and Mycerinus's pyramid temples provide examples of the finest royal art of the Old Kingdom. Mycerinus, the last great ruler of the dynasty, was described by Herodotus as kind, pious, and just.

FIRST INTERMEDIATE PERIOD

Mentuhotep Nebhepetre King, Dynasty 11, 2060–2010 BC. Following the period of civil war and conflict, Mentuhotep Nebhepetre reunited the kingdom and founded Dynasty 11. To establish his rule he had to subdue the princes of Heracleopolis and their supporters and regain control of Nubia. He built extensively throughout Egypt but is most famed for the unique complex at Deir el-Bahri, Thebes, where he and his family were buried. He established his capital at Thebes and elevated Montu, god of war, to be patron deity of his dynasty.

MIDDLE KINGDOM

Amenemhet I King, Dynasty 12, 1991–1962 BC. Amenemhet I (Greek: Ammenemes) was the founder of Dynasty 12 and the Middle Kingdom. He was of humble origin but, as vizier of Mentuhotep Nebtowyre, the last king of Dynasty 11, he managed to usurp the throne. He reestablished the unity of the kingdom, moved the capital to It-towy, and introduced the system of coregencies to protect the dynastic succession. He campaigned in Nubia and traded with Syria/Palestine. Amun was promoted as the dynasty's patron god, and his cult was developed at Thebes. Amenemhet I was possibly assassinated by palace conspirators and was buried in a pyramid at el-Lisht.

Senusret III King, Dynasty 12, 1878–1834 BC. Senusret III (Greek: Sesostris), the son of Senusret II, was the greatest ruler of Dynasty 12. He abolished the power of the provincial nobility, thus obliterating their threat to royal supremacy, and consolidated the annexation and colonization of Nubia, where he built a string of fortresses. He was buried in a pyramid at Dahshur, and in AD 1894, in a nearby tomb, archaeologists discovered the treasure belonging to the queens and princesses of his family.

Amenemhet III King, Dynasty 12, 1842–1797 BC. Amenemhet III (Greek: Ammenemes), son of Senusret III, was a great ruler who consolidated Egypt's control of Nubia and expanded the domestic economy. His power and

influence extended from Nubia to Syria, and he sent quarrying expeditions to Sinai. At home he initiated major land reclamation and building schemes in the Fayoum (including his famous Labyrinth which probably combined a funerary monument, palace, and administrative headquarters) and built two pyramids at Dahshur and Hawara.

NEW KINGDOM

Amosis I King, Dynasty 18, 1570–1546 BC. The son of Seqenenre Ta'o II and Ahhotpe, Amosis was the brother of Kamose, whose daughter, Ahmose-Nefertari, became his chief queen. He expelled the Hyksos from Egypt and pursued them into southern Palestine and then founded Dynasty 18 and established the New Kingdom. He reestablished the internal administration of Egypt and was able to hand on a united realm to his son, Amenhotep I. His capital was at Thebes, where he fostered the cult of the dynasty's patron god, Amen-Re; he was buried there in a rock-cut tomb at Dra'abu el-Naga.

Amenhotep I King, Dynasty 18, 1546–1526 BC. Amenhotep I (Greek: Amenophis), son and successor of Amosis I, extended Egypt's boundaries and campaigned in Syria. At home he rebuilt temples and restored prosperity. He was particularly associated with his mother, Ahmose-Nefertari, with whom he founded the community of royal necropolis workers at Deir el-Medina and shared a tomb at Dra'abu el-Naga, Thebes.

Tuthmosis I King, Dynasty 18, 1525–1512 BC. As the son of Amenhotep I by a nonroyal wife, Senisonb, Tuthmosis I had to claim the throne through his marriage to Princess Ahmose, the sister of Amenhotep I. Tuthmosis I was a great military pharaoh who campaigned as far as the Fourth Cataract in Nubia where he established fortresses; he also extended Egypt's power in Syria as far as the river Euphrates. He was the first king to have a tomb in the Valley of the Kings at Thebes with a separate mortuary temple on the Theban plain.

Hatshepsut Queen regnant, Dynasty 18, 1503–1482 BC. The daughter of Tuthmosis I and his Great Royal Wife, Ahmose, Hatshepsut married her half brother Tuthmosis II (the son of Tuthmosis I by a secondary wife, Mutnefert). This strengthened Tuthmosis II's claim to the throne, but when he died, and his son Tuthmosis III (born to a concubine) inherited the kingship, Hatshepsut herself seized power. Supported by officials and the priesthood of Amen-Re she ruled as senior pharaoh, although she was eventually overthrown by Tuthmosis III, who destroyed her monuments. She pursued an active building program, and she is best known for her mortuary temple at Deir el-Bahri, Thebes. She also sent expeditions to Byblos, Sinai, and Punt for commodities including timber, turquoise, and incense. She was buried in the Valley of the Kings at Thebes.

Tuthmosis III King, Dynasty 18, 1504–1450 BC. The son of Tuthmosis I by a concubine, Isis, Tuthmosis III was prevented from ruling by his stepmother, Hatshepsut, when he ascended the throne as a minor. Later, he was able to seize the throne and to erase traces of Hatshepsut's reign. He was regarded as Egypt's greatest ruler and established his country as the area's foremost military power. He led many campaigns in Syria/Palestine, crossing the Euphrates River and conquering the Mitannians. In Egypt he undertook major building programs, especially in the Temple of Karnak at Thebes. He was buried in the Valley of the Kings.

Amenhotep II King, Dynasty 18, 1450–1425 BC. Amenhotep II was the son of Tuthmosis III and Hatshepsut-meryetre and married his full sister, Tio. He retained the empire established by Tuthmosis III and campaigned in Nubia and Syria. At home he had an extensive building program and excelled as Egypt's greatest royal sportsman. His tomb in the Valley of the Kings was used for the reburial of some of the royal mummies in Dynasty 21.

Amenhotep III King, Dynasty 18, 1417–1379 BC. The son of Tuthmosis IV and Queen Mutemweya, Amenhotep III enjoyed a reign when military activity was largely replaced by diplomacy and marriages with foreign royal families. Egypt's empire and wealth were at their zenith, and Amenhotep III was able to patronize the arts and build great monuments. His chief wife, Tiye, was the daughter of commoners, and his sons included Amenhotep IV (Akhenaten) and possibly Smenkhkare and Tutankhamun. Akhenaten may have been the coregent of Amenhotep III for a time. Amenhotep III continued to worship Amen-Re as the chief state god, but he also enhanced the cults of other gods, particularly the Aten, in an attempt to restrict the traditional priesthood's power.

Tiye Queen, Great Royal Wife of Amenhotep III, Dynasty 18, reign of Amenhotep III, 1417–1379 BC. Tiye was the daughter of commoners, Yuya and Thuya. She nevertheless married Amenhotep III and became his chief wife and mother of his heir, Amenhotep IV (Akhenaten), and possibly grandmother of kings Smenkhkare and Tutankhamun. She exerted great political influence on state affairs that continued even after her husband's death: Foreign rulers continued their correspondence with her, which was subsequently preserved in the archive known as the Amarna Letters. She lived with

Amenhotep III in the palace at Malkata, Thebes, and later spent time at Akhetaten (Tell el-Amarna). She was worshiped as a goddess in cults in Nubia and Thebes and was probably buried in her husband's tomb in the Valley of the Kings.

Akhenaten (Amenhotep IV) King, Dynasty 18, 1379–1362 BC. The son of Amenhotep III and Tiye, Amenhotep IV changed his name to Akhenaten in year 5 of his reign to mark his allegiance to the god Aten. He introduced and promoted a unique form of monotheism based on the worship of the sun's disk (the Aten) which had been in existence for many years. He built special temples to the Aten at Thebes and then closed the temples to other gods throughout Egypt and disbanded their priesthoods. Next, he moved his political and religious capitals from Thebes to Tell el-Amarna, which became a focus for the new religion and where artists were encouraged to experiment with distinctive art forms.

His wife, Nefertiti, is famed for her beauty, which is evident in the contemporary sculpture and paintings. They had six daughters but apparently no sons, and Akhenaten took Smenkhkare (who was possibly his half brother) as his coregent. When they both died without direct male heirs the throne passed to Tutankhamun (probably another young half brother of Akhenaten) who restored the traditional gods and moved the capital back to Thebes. Akhenaten was probably buried in the Royal Tomb at Amarna. He is a controversial figure, whom scholars variously regard as a fanatic, political opportunist, or a visionary.

Nefertiti Queen, Great Royal Wife of Amenhotep IV (Akhenaten), Dynasty 18, reign of Akhenaten, 1379–1362 BC. Nefertiti is renowned for her beauty, which is apparent in her famous sculptured head now in the Berlin Museum. Her parentage is unknown, but she became the Great Royal Wife of Akhenaten, the mother of six daughters, and the mother-in-law of Smenkhkare and Tutankhamun. She played an important political and religious role in the cult of the Aten and was depicted in scenes in the Aten temples at Thebes and Amarna, participating in the god's cult as an equal partner with Akhenaten. There are no known references to her after year 12 of his reign, however, and it has been suggested that she may have died or fallen from favor. She was perhaps also buried in the Royal Tomb at Amarna although her body has never been discovered.

Tutankhamun King, Dynasty 18, 1361–1352 BC. Tutankhamun was possibly the son of Amenhotep III. He married Ankhesenpaaten, the third daughter of Akhenaten and Nefertiti, and ascended the throne while he was a child. On the advice of his courtiers he restored the worship of the traditional gods, particularly Amen-Re, and reinstated Thebes as the religious capital. He died as a young man and was buried in the Valley of the Kings where his tomb and magnificent treasure were discovered by Howard Carter in AD 1922.

Horemheb King, Dynasty 18, 1348–1320 BC. Horemheb's parentage is unknown, but he married Mudnodjme who was possibly the sister of Queen Nefertiti. He was commander of the army under Akhenaten and succeeded another royal courtier, Ay, as king. Supported by the army and the traditional priesthood he restored the old divine cults and reinstated law and order after the Amarna Period. He was buried in the Valley of the Kings.

Sethos I King, Dynasty 19, 1318–1304 BC. The son of Ramesses I, Sethos I restored Egypt's glory by reclaiming the empire in Syria (his campaigns are depicted in wall scenes in the Temple of Karnak). He built and refurbished several major monuments at Thebes and Abydos and was buried in the finest tomb in the Valley of the Kings, which was excavated by G. B. Belzoni in AD 1817. His well-preserved mummy was discovered in the cache of bodies that were reburied at Deir el-Bahri by the priests during Dynasty 21.

Ramesses II King, Dynasty 19, 1304–1237 BC. The son of Sethos I, Ramesses II was a famous warrior who fought the Hittites but eventually concluded a peace treaty with them in year 21 of his reign. He subsequently marked the alliance by marrying Hittite princesses. He had many wives and fathered more than 100 children. He built impressive monuments at Pi-Ramesse, Memphis, Abydos, Thebes, and Abu Simbel and was buried in the Valley of the Kings, although his body was finally discovered in the Deir el-Bahri cache. He may have been the pharaoh associated with the biblical Exodus.

Nefertari Queen, Dynasty 19, reign of Ramesses II, 1304–1237 BC. Nefertari was one of Ramesses II's principal queens and mother of several of his children. She pursued a diplomatic friendship with the Hittite queen once the peace treaty was concluded with the Hittites, exchanging letters with the Hittite royal family. Ramesses II built a fine tomb for her in the Valley of the Queens at Thebes and also a temple for her worship adjacent to his own monument at Abu Simbel.

Merenptah King, Dynasty 19, 1236–1223 BC. Ramesses II was succeeded by his thirteenth son, Merenptah, whose mother, Istnofret, was a principal queen. He led expeditions to Canaan and Syria and in year 5 defeated a coalition of Libyans and Sea Peoples who threatened Egypt. The Israel Stela from his temple at Thebes has an inscription that provides the first known reference to Israel. He was buried in the Valley of the Kings, but his mummy was subsequently moved by the priests to the tomb of Amenhotep II.

Ramesses III King, Dynasty 20, 1198–1166 BC. Ramesses III was the son of Setnakhte and Queen Tiye-merenese. He was Egypt's last great warrior king, and he defeated the Libyans in years 5 and 11 and the Sea Peoples in year 8. Details of these encounters are preserved in the Great Papyrus Harris and in wall scenes in his temple at Medinet Habu. He survived an assassination attempt by the women of the royal harem, but his reign was also troubled by the strikes of the royal necropolis workmen. His principal queen was Ese, and he fathered many children. His mummy was found in the Deir el-Bahri cache.

LATE PERIOD

Alexander the Great King of Macedon, ruled Egypt 332–323 BC. Alexander was the son of Philip II of Macedon. He established a vast empire, conquering Egypt in 332 BC. He subsequently founded Alexandria as the new capital and visited the oasis of Siwa in the Western Desert, which resulted in his apparent belief in his personal deification. He left a small army in Egypt when he pursued further conquests elsewhere. On returning from India he died at Babylon in 323 BC, and his body was reputedly brought to Egypt for burial, although his tomb has never been found.

PTOLEMAIC EGYPT

Ptolemy I Soter King, Ptolemaic dynasty, 305–282 BC. Ptolemy, the satrap whom Alexander left in charge of Egypt, assumed the kingship after Alexander's death. He established the Ptolemaic dynasty, reorganized the country, and restored the native temples, as well as introducing the cult of a new god, Serapis, who was supposed to provide a focus for both Greek and Egyptian worshipers. Ptolemy I founded the city of Ptolemais and also inaugurated the museum and library at Alexandria. He introduced consanguineous marriages into the royal family as a means of continuing and supporting his family's dynastic claims.

Cleopatra VII Queen, Ptolemaic dynasty, 51–30 BC. Cleopatra VII was the last Macedonian ruler of Egypt. She ruled jointly with her father Ptolemy XII Auletes and then with her brothers/husbands Ptolemy XIII and Ptolemy XIV. Her romantic liaison with the Roman ruler Caesar helped her to regain her throne, and she ruled jointly with Ptolemy XV Caesarion, her son by Caesar. A love affair with another Roman leader, Mark Antony, was bitterly opposed by Mark Antony's brother-in-law, Augustus (Octavian), who campaigned against Cleopatra and Mark Antony. They chose to commit suicide in Alexandria before the victorious Augustus arrived there and took Egypt for Rome in 30 BC.

OTHER PROMINENT PEOPLE

The history of Egypt largely centers around the lives of kings and queens (see above). For selective references to other prominent figure see the following: for authors and wise men (Chapter 7), Classical writers (Chapter 7), architects (Chapter 6), army commanders (Chapter 8), and doctors (Chapter 11).

READING

Source Material

Cambridge Ancient History 1962: textbook on history of Egypt (and neighbors); Gardiner 1961: chronological history of pharaonic Egypt; Herodotus 1961: English translation of Book II, dedicated to history and social conditions in Egypt; Diodorus Siculus 1954: English translation of Book I, describing the customs of ancient Egypt; Baines and Málek 1980: topographical account of major ancient sites.

Historical Periods

PREDYNASTIC EGYPT

Baumgartel 1955: account of the evidence for predynastic Egypt; Quibell and Green 1900–1902: excavation report of Hieraconpolis; Adams 1974: study of remains from Hieraconpolis; Hayes 1964: account of predynastic times; Derry 1956: theory of the Dynastic Race; Kantor 1942, 1952: possible links between Mesopotamia, Egypt, and Dynastic Race.

ARCHAIC EGYPT

Emery 1961: history and archaeology of first two dynasties; Emery 1949, 1954: discovery of royal tombs at Saqqara; Petrie 1900 and 1900–1901: discovery of royal tombs at Abydos; Reisner 1936: history of architectural development of tombs in earliest dynasties; Kemp 1966: study of early tombs; Mercer 1962: study of history and characteristics of god Horus.

OLD KINGDOM

Edwards 1985: classic account of history and construction of pyramids; Reisner 1942, 1955: study of pyramids and tombs in Giza cemetery; Drioton and Lauer 1939: pyramid complex at Saqqara; Mendelssohn 1973: theories about the collapse of the Meidum pyramid; Faulkner 1969: translation of the Pyramid Texts.

FIRST INTERMEDIATE PERIOD

Winlock 1947: history of the period; Edwards 1985: development of pyramids.

MIDDLE KINGDOM

Winlock 1947: description of events at Thebes in Middle Kingdom; Edwards 1985: pyramid development; Baines and Malek 1980: description of tomb and pyramid sites; Budge 1911: account of cult and mythology of Osiris; Griffiths 1966: discussion of cult of Osiris; Griffith 1970: translation and commentary on Plutarch's *De Iside et Osiride*; Faulkner 1973–78: translation of Coffin Texts; Aldred 1971: includes description of Middle Kingdom royal jewelry.

SECOND INTERMEDIATE PERIOD

Van Seters 1966: origins and problems associated with Hyksos; Engelbach 1939: theories about the role of the Hyksos.

NEW KINGDOM

Edgerton 1933: account of family conflict between Hatshepsut and Tuthmosis III; Emery 1965: Egypt's relations with Nubia; Mercer 1939: translation of archive of correspondence between Amarna rulers and other kingdoms; Smith 1912: account of the discovery and investigation of royal mummies; Davies and Davies 1915–33: recorded scenes from Theban tombs, with commentary; Černý 1973: study of royal workmen's village and life; Aldred 1988: account of reign and religious beliefs of Akhenaten; Martin 1974, 1989: discovery and description of Royal Tomb at Amarna; Redford 1984: examination of Akhenaten's political and religious motives, and roles of his successors; Smith and Redford 1977: study of Aten temple blocks discovered at Thebes; Kitchen 1975–90: translation of texts from Ramesside Period: Martin 1976–79: excavation of Horemheb's tomb at Saqqara; Carter 1923–33: discovery and excavation of Tutankhamun's tomb; Reeves 1990: study of evidence relating to Tutankhamun; Kitchen 1981: account of reign and politics of Ramesses II; Breasted 1903: the classic battle between Egyptians and Hittites; Edgerton and Wilson 1936: translation of inscriptions in reign of Ramesses III.

THIRD INTERMEDIATE PERIOD

Kitchen 1973: history of the period; Montet 1951–60: tombs and treasures of Tanite rulers; Reeves 1990: account of tombs and burials in Valley of Kings; Smith 1912: description of discovery and study of royal mummies; Dunham 1950: account of excavation of royal cemeteries of Dynasty 25.

LATE PERIOD

Posener 1936: account of first Persian period of occupation of Egypt.

PTOLEMAIC PERIOD

Wilcken 1932: biography of Alexander the Great; Bell 1956: history of Egypt in Ptolemaic and Roman times; Fraser 1972: account of Alexandria; Bowman 1986: chronological and social history of Egypt in Greco-Roman Period; Austin 1981: history of Ptolemaic Egypt; Bevan 1927: account of the reigns of Ptolemies.

ROMAN PERIOD

Bell 1956: history of Egypt under Roman Empire; Bowman 1986: Egypt in Ptolemaic and Roman times; Jones 1964: account of the later Roman Empire.

Prominent Kings and Queens

Gardiner 1961: history with details of major rulers; David and David 1992: selective biography of kings, queens, and other persons with individual bibliographies.

2

GEOGRAPHY OF ANCIENT EGYPT

Land and Climate: Impact on Civilization

The nature of the land and the climate profoundly influenced the civilization of ancient Egypt. Today a map shows that most of the country is desert; however, the Delta (the inverted triangle of cultivation at the mouth of Egypt through which the Nile fans out to join the Mediterranean), the Nile Valley, and the far-flung oases in the Western Desert are fertile.

In the Paleolithic period (before c.5000 BC) the Delta and Nile Valley were virtually uninhabitable. The annual flood (inundation) of the river Nile would have placed all areas of the Nile Valley under water for three months of each year, and at other times it was covered with thick vegetation that provided habitation for a variety of wild animals. In the north much of the low-lying Delta was covered with papyrus swamps. At this time people lived on the desert spurs and hunted the prolific game. As the climate became drier and the vegetation in the Nile Valley gradually changed, they were able to move down into the valley once the inundation receded. Here during the Neolithic period (c.5000–4000 BC) they began to live together in communities and to cultivate the land, growing grain and learning to domesticate animals. This settled existence gradually replaced their hunting activities.

It was during this period that the people's earliest concepts and religious beliefs and experiences developed. They were always aware of their environment and of the impact of the natural forces upon their daily lives. The power of the sun was regarded as the great creative force and sustainer of all living things, and the sun god Re was one of their most important deities. Every day the people observed the cycle of the sun's birth, life, and death.

Similarly they witnessed the annual miracle of the river floodwaters' restoring life to the parched land. Osiris, the god of vegetation and king and judge of the underworld, symbolized this annual rebirth of the land, and through his own resurrection was thought to be able to offer eternal life to his worshipers and adherents. From the cyclical processes that they observed around them in the natural world, the Egyptians appear to have believed from the time of their earliest religious awareness that mankind's own existence had a similar pattern in which birth, life, and death were followed by individual resurrection as the reward for a virtuous life.

The landscape provided a sharp contrast between life and death in terms of cultivation and the desert. The Nile flood brought with it the rich black mud that, every year, was deposited on the river banks. The mud fertilized the soil, making the land very productive, and over the centuries the Egyptians labored successfully to produce an abundance of crops. They called their country "Kemet," meaning the "black land," in reference to the rich black soil. Here in this narrow strip and in the fertile Delta people grew their food, reared their animals, and established their towns and villages.

On either side of this cultivated area, stretching away to the horizon or rising into steep cliffs along the river's edge, there was the desert. The Egyptians regarded this as a place of fear, terror, and death, where wild animals roamed; they called it "Deshret," meaning the "red land," on account of the predominant coloring of the landscape. Our own word *desert* is derived from this. Because the extent of the cultivation was so limited, the land had to be used to maximum effect for growing crops and accommodating the population. There was no additional space here for the graves of the dead; therefore, from

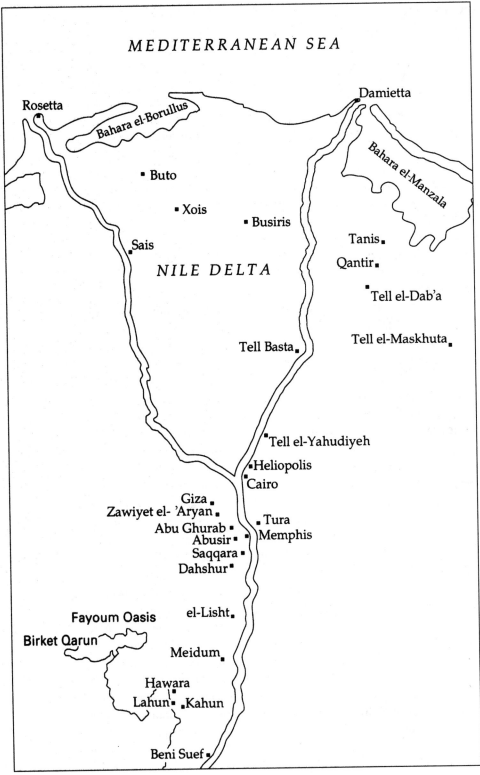

Lower Egypt

earliest times corpses were buried on the desert edges. This custom profoundly affected the Egyptians' religious beliefs and practices.

The country also divides naturally into distinct northern and southern regions, the Delta and the Nile Valley. Only the Nile, flowing from south to north, truly unites these two areas, and Egypt has always been a country that is politically difficult to control. There was a common need to cooperate over the irrigation schemes that had originally brought isolated village communities together; the river was both a means of transport and communication for them and also a life-giving force that had to be harnessed to provide the means of existence.

During the Predynastic Period (before c.3100 BC) when the communities were increasingly drawn together into larger units for mutual protection and support, the Egyptian peoples eventually organized themselves into two kingdoms, the northern Red Land and the southern White Land. Each had its own king, capital city, patron gods, and distinctive features. Even after these kingdoms were unified under one ruler in c.3100 BC, they retained something of their original independence and individuality throughout the next 3,000 years. The political duality of Egypt's origins was never forgotten, and these areas were often referred to as the Two Lands.

Again geographical factors dictated this duality. The Delta faced the Mediterranean and became an early crossroads for peoples, ideas, and influences from Africa, Asia, and Europe. It was here at the apex of the Delta that Memphis, the country's first capital, was established; thousands of years later the Arabs founded their own capital, which later became Cairo, just to the north of Memphis. This region had obvious advantages for a conqueror who wished to control both the north and the southern hinterland, and most of the major cities of Egypt developed in the Delta region. One important exception was Thebes (modern Luxor), the capital city of the New Kingdom, which was established some 400 miles to the south. Generally, however, the Nile Valley, which was hemmed in by the deserts, was more traditional and less influenced by events elsewhere than other regions were.

The Egyptian civilization is unique and distinctive. Over a period of 3,000 years there were few major developments that produced marked differences in the culture. The casual visitor to an Egyptian collection in a museum would observe a continuity of style in the various classes of objects. This, of course, was because the underlying beliefs and concepts remained constant and the distinctive art forms, architecture, decoration, and religious beliefs had developed and become established during the earliest periods without the disruption of foreign conquest and intervention. By the time Egypt directly encountered other civilizations the basic concepts were so firmly entrenched that any foreign impact was minimal. Indeed, foreign ideas, gods, and customs were quickly absorbed into Egypt's own culture.

Again it was geographical factors that gave Egypt natural barriers and initial protection against foreign invasion. The Mediterranean to the north ultimately became a trading route between Egypt and surrounding lands, but in earliest times it was a formidable barrier against invaders. To the west there was the Libyan Desert with its chain of oases. There had always been close contact between the Libyan tribes and the inhabitants of the Nile Valley, and trade flourished between them. It was only in the later periods that Egypt faced a political threat from this direction.

Nubia lay to the south; this was the land (occupying approximately the area that today covers southernmost Egypt and northernmost Sudan) that supplied the Egyptians with good building stone and much of their gold. To ensure that access to these commodities remained unhindered, the Egyptians pursued a policy of colonization in this area from earliest times.

On the eastern side the Red Sea provided further protection, but above it, to the northeast, there was one relatively easy route across the northern Sinai Peninsula, which provided overland access to the Delta and the Nile Valley. The earliest infiltrations (possibly of the so-called Dynastic Race) may have followed this route.

Compared with other ancient civilizations of the Near East, however, Egypt did not suffer continuous waves of invasion, and one civilization was not replaced by another. Natural protective barriers, a relatively regular and predictable climate, and a countryside in which patient and diligent husbandry could produce an extraordinarily abundant harvest were all predominant factors in the development of Egypt's remarkably stable and continuous civilization.

SOURCE MATERIAL

Both Classical and medieval writers provide literary accounts that refer to the geographical background of Egypt. The most important Classical writers were Herodotus, Diodorus Siculus, and Strabo (see Chapter 7, Written Evidence). The account by Herodotus contains both historical and geographical information, but it is particularly important because it provides a firsthand description of his own travels in Egypt. He refers to the geological formations and the geographical features and describes the Nile, together with its sources and inundation, and the different characteristics of the various parts of the country. He also discusses the animals and in particular the peculiarities of the hippopotamus, ibis, crocodile, and phoenix. He states that the phoenix only visited Egypt every 500 years on the occasion of the death of the parent bird (this had been reported to him at Heliopolis).

The geographer Strabo also visited Egypt. He wrote seventeen books (known as the *Geographia*) that compiled facts about the Roman world; the last was an account of Egypt's geography. It is mainly a topographical list of towns and resources with additional references to historical facts and monuments.

Medieval and later writers also added to geographical knowledge about Egypt. Some were derivative, largely based on the Classical accounts; others included the firsthand observations of the authors. The latter included works by Father Claude Sicard, an Arabic scholar, who traveled in Egypt between 1707 and 1726; George Sandys who made a journey in the Mediterranean and Egypt in 1610; Richard Pococke who traveled to Aswan in 1737; and Frederick Lewis Nordern who attempted to reach the Second Cataract. In 1768 the famous traveler James Bruce sailed up the Nile to seek its source and visited many sites and monuments on the way that he described later in his writings.

INUNDATION OF THE NILE

The Nile and the sun were the two great life-giving forces that shaped Egypt's civilization. Although the country has a negligible annual rainfall, centers of population were able to de-

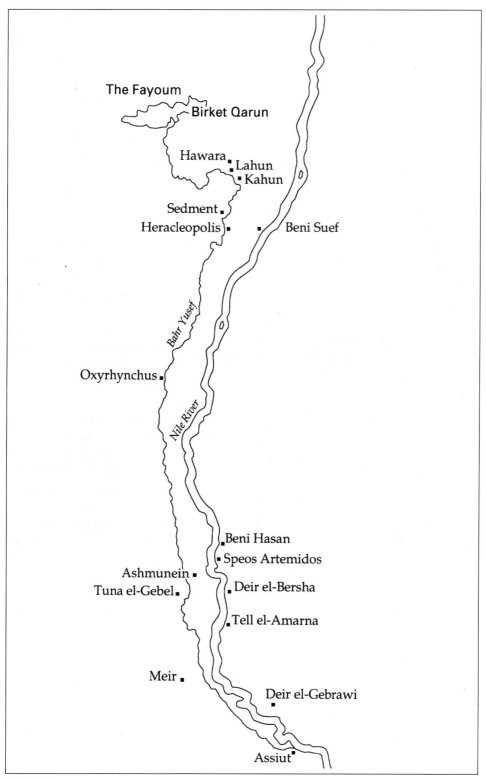

The Fayoum
Birket Qarun
Hawara
Lahun
Kahun
Sedment
Heracleopolis
Beni Suef
Bahr Yusef
Oxyrhynchus
Nile River
Beni Hasan
Speos Artemidos
Ashmunein
Tuna el-Gebel
Deir el-Bersha
Tell el-Amarna
Meir
Deir el-Gebrawi
Assiut

Middle Egypt

velop and flourish in the Delta and the Nile Valley because of the phenomenon of the river's inundation.

Hecataeus, a Classical writer, has provided the often repeated phrase that Egypt is the "gift of the Nile," and probably no other civilization was so absolutely dependent on the regular occurrence of one natural event. In antiquity the country and its people only survived because the Nile brought its floods with the result that the harvests could be reaped. To ensure a successful outcome Hapy, the Nile god, and Osiris, the god of vegetation and rebirth, were worshiped throughout Egypt.

Within Egypt the Nile cuts a course of some 600 miles from Aswan in the south to the Delta, where its two main branches flow into the Mediterranean through Rosetta in the west and Damietta in the east. Its long journey begins far to the south of Egypt, however, rising three degrees south of the Equator in the region of the Great Lakes. In its upper course it is called the Mountain Nile; then it joins with the Bahr el-Ghazel to become the White Nile. In the highlands of Ethiopia the Blue Nile rises in Lake Tana, and ultimately at Khartoum in the Sudan the two Niles join and become the river that continues down through Egypt to the Mediterranean. This river, the longest in Africa, today travels through several countries and a variety of landscapes and climates. Within Egypt itself there are marked variations in the weather, and Upper Egypt's high temperatures contrast with the more moderate climate found in the Delta.

Between Khartoum (the modern capital of Sudan) and Aswan (Egypt's southernmost city), a series of six cataracts interrupt the course of the Nile. These are not dramatic features and do not include waterfalls; they are merely scattered groups of rocks that cause an obstruction of the stream across the width of the river. At the Fourth, Second, and First Cataracts, this obstruction has always affected the river traffic.

The original boundary of ancient Egypt was located at the First Cataract, which lies just to the south of ancient Elephantine (modern Aswan). Later rulers pushed the boundary south and built fortresses to regulate the local population. From Aswan north to the Mediterranean coast, the Nile's course continued uninterrupted in antiquity, although dams have been built across the river in modern times.

There are dramatic changes in the scenery between Aswan and Cairo, Egypt's modern capital, which is positioned at the apex of the Delta. The Nile has forced its passage here through this valley. In some parts there are steep, rocky cliffs on either side that descend abruptly to the river's edge, while in other areas the flat cultivated plains stretch away to the desert. This rich, cultivated strip varies in width but can only be farmed to a maximum distance of some thirteen miles.

When the river reaches Cairo and passes into the Delta its appearance changes as it continues over a low plain and fans out toward the coast. Some of the Delta land can be cultivated, but much of it is waterlogged marshland.

The inundation was an annual event until recently. The rains fall every year on the highlands of Ethiopia in tropical Africa and increase the waters of the Nile so that until the dam system was built the river became swollen and flooded out over its banks, depositing the rich black silt that fertilized the land.

In Egypt the flood occurred first in the region of the First Cataract in late June. The effect reached Cairo in the north at the end of September, and then the waters gradually receded until they reached their lowest level in the following April. This annual miracle brought renewed life to the parched land and was eagerly awaited by all inhabitants of the country.

There was always the fear that, one year, the river would not rise, resulting in death and destruction, and this was always a focus for people's prayers. Even though this perceived disaster never became reality, a low Nile could bring famine while an excessive inundation could flood the land, ruin the crops, and bring devastation. The unpredictability of the inundation was a constant concern that threatened the country's safety and prosperity.

Modern technology has today enabled a series of dams to be built across the river at certain points; the most famous is the High Dam at Aswan. These dams ensure that the volume of water can be held back (it is now stored in Lake Nasser behind the High Dam) and then released for irrigation, as required, through a series of canals.

In antiquity the water levels were measured and recorded on nilometers positioned along the river. At two nilometer sites (one south of Cairo and the other near Aswan), which were believed to be the "caverns" or "sources" that controlled the Nile flood, as well as near other nilometers, a ritual was performed to bring about the force of the flood: Cakes, fruit, sacred jewelry, and sacrificial animals were thrown into the river, and to ensure the Nile's fertility female figurines or "dolls" were also included.

AGRICULTURE

From earliest times people were aware that in order to control and regulate the Nile waters and to organize an efficient irrigation system to benefit all the communities in the Delta and Nile Valley they would have to act communally.

This need undoubtedly gave the people a common goal and was an important incentive for the unification of Egypt as a state, despite the geographical problems of controlling such a long, narrow, inhabited area. King Menes (Narmer) unified Egypt in c.3100 BC, but it is evident that an earlier southern ruler, Scorpion, had started this process. Scenes carved on a ceremonial limestone macehead discovered at Hieraconpolis in AD 1898 show military activities but also depict Scorpion undertaking, and perhaps initiating, an irrigation program. This macehead may commemorate an early reorganization of the country.

The irrigation system was complex; it used the Nile flood and its attendant deposits of rich black mud to cultivate the land as far as possible on either side of the river. Earth dikes were built to divide the land into compartments of varying sizes, and when the river rose the water was diverted into these areas through a system of canals. It was kept there until the black silt was deposited, and once the river level fell any remaining water was drained off from these compartments. The remaining rich soil could be plowed and sown with crops.

Most of the population worked on the land. The peasant worked either with his family or in a gang and cultivated crops for the state and for his own needs. The state organized the irrigation system and also the storage of the country's food supply in granaries. Officials who controlled these aspects were responsible to the king who in theory owned all the land.

Egypt's main crop was cereals. Knowledge of their cultivation was introduced from the Near East in Neolithic times. The farmers grew two kinds of wheat (spelt and emmer) as well as barley, and these provided the Egyptians with the basic requirements for their staple diet of bread and beer. Stages in the production of these

A tomb scene, c.1400 BC, showing stages in plowing (right) and preparing the ground, followed by the scattering of the seed. A worker (top left) takes a drink from a waterskin suspended in a tree.

Agricultural tools include a wooden hoe (center) and rake (top right) used to clear the ground before plowing; a sickle (bottom right) for reaping the harvest; a wooden winnowing scoop (top left) for tossing grain; and a wooden scoop (bottom left) for collecting the grain off the threshing floor. From Kahun, c.1890 BC.

cereals are depicted in many tomb scenes to ensure an ample food supply for the deceased in the next life.

Once the Nile waters had receded in the autumn, seed was scattered on the earth and then plowed into the soil by a peasant who either used a wooden hoe or followed a plow dragged by two cows. Next, sheep and pigs were set loose on the plowed area to trample the ground. The harvest was gathered in the spring. The men worked together in a group and cut the stalks with wooden sickles fitted with flint blades. Once the short sheaves had been made into bundles, donkeys carried them to the threshing floor where animals trampled the stalks and separated the ripe grain from the husks. It was then further separated with a brush and winnowed by using a wooden scoop to throw it into a high wind before it was sieved. The by-product, straw, was set aside for making brick while the corn itself was measured and kept in sacks in large silos.

The other major product of Egypt was linen. This textile was widely used for clothing and other domestic purposes as well as for mummy badges. It was produced from flax, and tomb scenes often show this being gathered. Peasants worked together in the fields to pull the flax fibers before they bundled them; then they prepared the material for spinning and weaving.

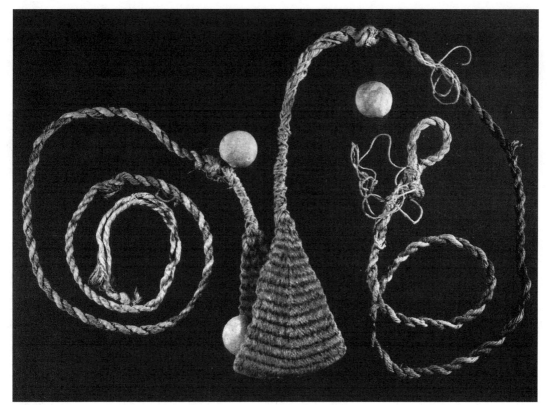

A woven sling with long cords, one of which ends in a loop to retain it on the finger. Found with the three sling-stones which were probably flung from the sling simultaneously, perhaps to frighten away birds in gardens and vineyards. From Kahun, c.1890 BC.

Scene from the tomb of Ipy, c.1500 BC. To cultivate plants in gardens, servants sometimes brought water from the river by hand, but a single workman could increase the volume of water he could raise by using a water-raising machine, the shaduf (shown here).

Cotton cultivation was introduced into Egypt from Nubia during the Coptic Period, and from the nineteenth century AD it became one of Egypt's major industries. Cereals and linen (which was produced to an extremely high quality) were Egypt's main exports in antiquity.

The Egyptians were also market gardeners. Whereas irrigation was carried out only once a year in antiquity (it is now continuous), allowing the fields to be watered and cultivated, the orchards and gardens near the cultivated basins or compartments could be used all the time because the river regularly fed them with water. The gardeners were assiduous in transporting water to these areas, either bringing it from the Nile in two large pots suspended from a yoke or using a SHADUF. The shaduf, introduced in the New Kingdom, had a bucket on one end of a rope that was lowered into the river; this was counterbalanced by a weight at the other end of the device.

In the gardens near their houses and on the mud dikes the peasants grew beans, lentils, chickpeas, fenugreek, radishes, onions, cucumbers, lettuces, and herbs. Plants also produced perfumes, dyes, and medicines; oil came from castor oil plants, Arabian moringa, and the olive tree. Flowers, including cornflowers, chrysan-

A tomb scene, c.1400 BC, showing wine production. The grapes are picked (right), then trampled in the winepress (left), and finally the extracted juice is collected in jars (center).

A tomb scene (c.1450 BC) in which the owner (right) is seated in a kiosk, overseeing work on his estate. Under an inspector's direction, his laborers winnow the grain (top left) and scoop it off the threshing floor (bottom left).

themums, and lotus, were also grown in gardens for the production of bouquets and garlands. Fruits that added variety to their diet included figs, grapes, sycamore figs and dates, and pomegranates.

Wine production was another major industry. The vine may have been introduced to Egypt from Asia before 3000 BC. Grapes could be picked throughout the year to provide table grapes and grape juice, but there were regular heavy vintages when the grapes were picked and processed before the wine was poured into amphorae (tall jars with pointed bases) where it was left to age.

The production of papyrus was also important. It was used for writing paper, ropes, sails, baskets, mats, and sandals. There had always

been huge thickets of papyrus in the marshlands, particularly in the Delta, and later it was grown in cultivated fields. Laborers cut down the papyrus stems and transported them to workshops where they were turned into the required products.

In earliest times there was abundance of animal life in Egypt. Once hunting had given way to farming, people began to domesticate animals. In predynastic times dogs were trained to hunt and guard the herds. By the time of the Old Kingdom donkeys, cows, oxen, and sheep were used for a variety of agricultural and other tasks, and pigs were later introduced for trampling the sown fields.

There were two breeds of oxen in ancient Egypt, and cows and bulls roamed the grasslands.

Other animals, kept for meat, milk, and leather or as sacrificial beasts, included goats, gazelles, and oryx. By selection of the animals in temple herds the Egyptians were able to improve breeds of sheep and cattle. Birds were also specially bred and fattened for the table. They included geese, ducks, cranes, and pigeons.

Although land cultivation was very important, the population was small enough to ensure that they were not forced to overwork the land. Large areas of marsh were left for hunting and fishing. Fishermen used traps and nets to take a wide variety of fish and nobles made their catches with harpoons. Birds were hunted with boomerangs and with civets, mongooses, and wild cats; large clap nets were used to trap quantities of geese and wild duck.

NATURAL RESOURCES

As well as benefiting from a rich agriculture, Egypt provided its inhabitants with fine quality stone for building monuments and carving statues and with supplies of gold from Nubia and the Eastern Desert. Stone came from a variety of sources. White limestone was carefully cut from special quarries such as Tura near Memphis. This limestone was specially used to cover the walls of temples and mastaba tombs as it was a good surface for bas-relief carvings. Yellow sandstone came from Gebel es-Silsila, and red and yellow quartzite (often used for statuary) from Gebel el-Ahmar. There was schist for statues from Wadi Hammamat; basalt was favored for paving stones and lower courses in temples, while statues and vases were produced in a variety of stone, including diorite, porphyry, marble, and serpentine. Alabaster, used in buildings and for small objects, was found in the Eastern Desert where the main quarry was at Hat-nub, about twelve miles from Tell el-Amarna (Akhetaten).

Granite from the Aswan area provided material for buildings, sarcophagi, and statuary. It occurred in a variety of colors—red, gray, black, and blue. Once it had been cut from the rock (by a process that is still not fully explained), it was transported by river downstream to the major building sites (the capitals of Memphis or Thebes and elsewhere).

The quarries (and mines) were a royal monopoly. Some were situated in remote parts of the desert. None was worked continuously; when the king decided that he wished to build or adorn a temple, an expedition was organized and dispatched to the quarry. Some of these were large operations on the same scale as an army; they were in fact administered by the army, although the government itself organized the workforce (which consisted of craftsmen and forced labor raised from the peasantry) and communications. Even by the New Kingdom their only tools were copper or bronze (iron was not introduced into Egypt until the period between 1000 and 600 BC). In earliest times only stone had provided tools and weapons, including arrowheads, hammers, teeth of sickles, and knives. Stone continued as the most important material for these purposes for many years, and even in the Middle Kingdom, it was retained, whenever appropriate, alongside metal. Flint was the traditional stone used for many of these items.

Some details of the expeditions have survived in the inscriptions left by the leaders in the quarries; they indicate that elaborate preparations were undertaken and that final reports were written by scribes and kept as temple archives in the "House of Life."

They also searched in the deserts for the semiprecious stones used by the jewelers.

Some (turquoise, malachite, and emerald) came from the eastern mines, while carnelian, amethyst, and jasper came from Nubia or the Eastern Desert. Other natural stones included garnets, green feldspar, and obsidian. The Egyptians also used calcite or rock crystal backed with colored cements to produce artificial substitutes. Lapis lazuli was imported from the region known today as Afghanistan via the Euphrates River region.

The Egyptians regarded gold as one of their most precious substances, a divine metal that ensured eternal life. Used for royal and noble burial goods as well as for jewelry, gold also became a form of currency by the New Kingdom. As wages were paid in kind, however, it never gained widespread use throughout the society.

Gold was found both in Egypt and Nubia in the quartz present in the eastern and southeastern mountains. Wadi Hammamat and the area to the east of Edfu were both important gold working areas. The Royal Treasury owned all the mines, and the mining expeditions were directed by officers and soldiers; only state workers were allowed to mine and handle the gold. Electrum, the natural alloy of gold and silver, was found in Nubia but not in Egypt. Pure silver, regarded as a type of gold, did not occur in Egypt and was imported from the north or east. Following their conquests in Asia the Egyptians had greater access to it, but silver never became as popular as gold.

The country was also not particularly rich in copper. In predynastic times little use was made of it except for small decorative objects, but by Dynasty 2 (c.2700 BC) copper was used for statues of kings and gods. Gradually it became an increasingly popular metal in the Old and Middle Kingdoms for objects such as weapons, tools for carpentry and stoneworking, statuary, jewelry, mirrors, razors, vases, and furniture fittings.

From Dynasty 3, the Egyptians exploited the copper mines in Sinai, where expeditions were sent for turquoise and copper. These were soon worked out, however, and copper was increasingly brought from Cyprus and Syria. Copper and bronze ingots were imported into Egypt, and in c.2000 BC advanced metalworking techniques were brought from Asia with the result that bronze gradually replaced copper for all industrial uses.

In addition to a scarcity of metal ores, Egypt also lacked wood. This affected the availability of fuel supplies and timber for doors, coffins, boats, furniture, and statuary. From c.2700 BC cedarwood was imported from Lebanon to be used for temple doors and flagpoles, the best ships, and the finest coffins. Ebony was brought via Nubia and used for inlay and fine furniture.

Native woods included palm trunks (beams were made of this), sycamore (used for making poorer quality coffins and statues), and acacia (used for building river barges). These, as well as willow and thorn trees, were also used in the production of weapons, stelae, domestic furniture, and other articles. Domestic fuel was scarce; either charcoal (allocated by the government) or dried dung supplied most of their needs.

NEIGHBORING LANDS

Nubia

In antiquity, Egypt's southern neighbor was known as Nubia. From earliest times the Egyptians had exploited Nubia to gain access to the region's products—stone, minerals, and later, gold—and used it as a route to obtain exotic goods from central Africa. As early as the Archaic Period the Egyptians had annexed the area around Elephantine and made it part of Egypt's southernmost nome (district), fixing the boundary at the First Cataract.

By the Old Kingdom the Egyptian rulers were sending an increasing number of trading expeditions to Nubia. Some of the men who led these enterprises were buried in the rock-cut tombs near Elephantine where the wall inscriptions are very informative. When necessary the expeditions were supported by military force. The Egyptians sought exotic products such as incense, ivory, ebony, and panther skins. One particularly interesting account in the tomb of the local governor Harkhuf (Dynasty 6) at Aswan provides details of four expeditions to Nubia; these were probably undertaken partly by river and partly overland by donkey. The inscription also includes the text of a letter, sent to Harkhuf by the boy-king Pepy II, anxiously inquiring about the dwarf that the expedition was bringing back for him.

Trading expeditions ceased during the troubled times of the First Intermediate Period, and this policy was replaced in the Middle Kingdom by colonization of Nubia and direct military control. The Egyptians conquered Nubia as far as Semna, south of the Second Cataract, and the area was now systematically organized and exploited. Kings Senusret I and Senusret III, who campaigned in Nubia and consolidated the area, subsequently built a string of brick fortresses between Semna South and Buhen at the Second Cataract.

During the Second Intermediate Period when the Hyksos ruled Egypt, the Nubians gained power and independence and even helped the Hyksos to hold onto Egypt. With the establishment of the New Kingdom, however,

the kings of Dynasty 18 reaffirmed Egyptian control over Nubia. Tuthmosis I extended his dominion beyond the Fourth Cataract, and his grandson Tuthmosis III fixed the last major outpost at Napata near the Fourth Cataract. The Middle Kingdom fortresses were now either augmented or largely superseded by additional fortresses built to protect the new boundary. These, also garrisoned by Egyptian soldiers, incorporated temples, cemeteries, and living quarters. Important fortresses were built at Sai, Sedeinga, Sulb, and Napata. Nubia was effectively Egyptianized during this period and became an integrated part of the Egyptian political system.

Nubia was divided into the subprovinces of Wawat (from Elephantine to the Second Cataract), or Lower Nubia, and Kush (from the Second to the Fourth Cataracts), or Upper Nubia. In the New Kingdom the whole area south of the First Cataract was administered autonomously for the pharaoh by a viceroy; in the reign of Tuthmosis IV he received the title "King's Son of Kush," although none of these deputies were actually royal relatives. By the middle of Dynasty 18 the viceroy's area also included the three southernmost nomes of Upper Egypt.

The main duty of the viceroy was to oversee Nubia's natural resources and ensure that the annual tribute was paid into Egypt's treasury. The name "Nubia" is derived from the Egyptian word *nub*, meaning "gold," and since the Middle Kingdom the Egyptians had extensively exploited the region for gold. This came mainly from mines in Wawat that were worked by slaves, prisoners of war, and convicted criminals. In wall scenes such as those in the Tomb of Huy, viceroy of Nubia, at Thebes the Nubians are depicted bringing gold deben (rings) to King Tutankhamun as part of their annual tribute; gold also arrived in Egypt as bars or ingots or stored as gold dust in bags.

Gold was a government monopoly by the New Kingdom, but since early times Nubia had also been an important source for hard stone (granite) for monumental buildings in Egypt. The great temples of the New Kingdom continued this tradition with their granite doorways and obelisks. Other tribute brought to Egypt included ostrich plumes, precious stones, exotic animals, leopard skins, and slaves. These items are depicted in some of the wall scenes in contemporary tombs; the Egyptian artists also depicted the black peoples of central Africa with whom, through Nubia, they now came into contact for the first time.

The local inhabitants of Nubia had gradually adopted Egyptian religion, customs, and writing. Egyptian influence now reached its zenith, and, under Amenhotep III and Ramesses II, personal cults were established for these kings in Nubia, where they were worshiped as gods in magnificent temples built at Soleb and Sedeinga by Amenhotep III and at Abu Simbel by Ramesses II. Nubia became so Egyptianized that major campaigns were no longer required to subdue the population, and expeditions were only sent to control the desert tribesmen. For many centuries Nubians had been recruited to serve as "Medjay" in the Egyptian police; they also joined the army.

When pharaonic power began to decline after the New Kingdom, however, the Nubians reasserted their independence. A great kingdom now emerged in which the Egyptianized rulers of Napata (Gebel Barkal), situated near the Fourth Cataract, achieved great power and reversed the process of colonization by taking control of the Nile Valley. They imposed their rule on Egypt for about 100 years until they were driven out by the Assyrians. Their intervention in Egypt stopped, and they broke off all political association with the north. In their kingdom to the south of the Fourth Cataract the Nubians continued their own form of Egyptian civilization. After the Napatan Kingdom was finally overthrown by the Abyssinians and the capital was moved south to Meroë (north of Khartoum) in AD c.300–350, rival rulers continued to reside at both Napata and Meroë where they continued to build temples and pyramids. The term "Meroitic culture" is sometimes applied to this period; hieroglyphs continued to be used for writing, and two distinctive scripts were developed which are known today as Meroitic. With their construction of Egyptian-style temples and burial of their royalty in pyramids, these people continued to develop Egyptian culture long after it had died out in Egypt. The end came when Aeizanes, ruler of Axum, destroyed Meroë in 350.

Nubia, therefore, was of great importance to Egypt for thousands of years. In recent times, many of its sites and monuments were placed in danger by the increased water levels that resulted from the decision to construct dams at Aswan. The first Aswan Dam was built and subsequently heightened in the early part of the twentieth century; the Egyptian Survey Department set up a rescue project, the Archaeological Survey of Nubia, with the task of describing the entire area and listing the sequence of cultures, excavating any sites of particular importance, and excavating and examining the large quantities of skeletal remains found in the ancient cemeteries.

In the late 1950s the governments of Egypt and the Sudan decided to build the High Dam at Aswan, and this necessitated further urgent action. The creation of Lake Nasser behind this dam was destined to flood some 300 miles of Nubia, with the consequent loss of many archaeological sites. A UNESCO appeal for international help to save a maximum number of monuments before the dam was completed in 1965 resulted in international cooperation on an unprecedented scale. In addition to two major missions to rescue the temples at Abu Simbel and on the island of Philae and relocate them in new, safe positions near their original sites, a selection of other temples and monuments were moved and rebuilt in an open-air museum at New Kalabsha near Aswan.

In return for their cooperation in sending specialist help for the project, several countries received a major share of the antiquities found in the course of the rescue excavations. Also, some endangered temples that would otherwise have been lost were presented by Egypt to other countries and rebuilt at new sites (usually within museums) in Europe and the United States.

Egypt's Empire

In the Middle Kingdom the rulers of Dynasty 12 pursued active domestic and foreign policies. Both military and trading considerations influenced their conduct with neighboring countries, but at the same time foundations were also laid for Egypt's future empire-building role.

The kings restored trading contacts with Asia Minor, particularly Byblos and Phoenicia, and possible connections between Egypt and the Aegean Islands are the subject of considerable scholarly interest and debate. Expeditions sent to Punt (an area of the Red Sea coast, possibly modern Somalia) in the Old Kingdom were reintroduced, and the Egyptians again brought back the highly valued incense and incense trees that grew there. The copper and turquoise mines in Sinai were also reopened.

When a new and more aggressive people settled in Nubia during the First Intermediate Period, the Egyptian rulers were forced to adopt a strong policy in this area in order to ensure safe passage of the valuable and essential commodities (gold, hard stone, and exotic goods) that

Egypt sought from the south. Military campaigns were sent to subdue the local population and impress them with the pharaoh's might and authority. The Egyptians built a string of large brick fortresses along the river between the cataracts in Nubia; they eventually became permanent stations staffed by Egyptian soldiers and officials. These actions established the concept of the colonization of Nubia and laid the foundations for Egypt's empire. During the Hyksos Period (Dynasties 15 and 16) when a line of foreign kings ruled Egypt, the Nubians became powerful and independent. The Hyksos Period marked a turning point in Egypt's history and profoundly changed the national character. The Egyptians became aware that if they did not adopt an aggressive policy, other people would attempt to seize their country as the Hyksos had done. Egypt could no longer remain an isolated society. It had to seek to impose control over neighboring lands not only to gain access to their resources but to found the first empire. The Egyptian princes of Thebes, who eventually drove out the Hyksos and became the first kings of the New Kingdom, adopted new skills and war techniques, introduced from the north by the last Hyksos rulers, in their attempt to subdue the Egyptians. Also, for the first time, New Kingdom rulers established a professional army, paid by gifts from the king of land, which remained in the family only as long as they continued in military service.

Egypt's first step to establish this empire was to repossess Nubia. Several kings of Dynasty 18 campaigned vigorously in this area, including Amenhotep I and Tuthmosis I who extended Egyptian control to its furthermost point beyond the Fourth Cataract. His grandson, Tuthmosis III, finally established the frontier at Napata near the Fourth Cataract, and a series of new fortresses were built. Nubia was integrated into the Egyptian administration and governed by a viceroy on behalf of the pharaoh. His main tasks were to ensure that the district remained peaceful and to supply the treasury with its annual quota of tribute.

Egypt's relations with Syria/Palestine during the New Kingdom were rather different. At the beginning of Dynasty 18, the situation was dominated by events surrounding the expulsion of the Hyksos and their subsequent overthrow by the Egyptian rulers who besieged them in southwestern Palestine.

By the beginning of Dynasty 18, ethnic movements in the Near East had created a power vacuum that was now filled by a people known as the Mitannians. Their homeland (Mitanni) occupied the land of Naharin, between the Tigris and Euphrates Rivers, where the Hurrian population (who had originated in the region to the south of the Caspian Sea) were ruled by an aristocracy of Indo-Aryan origin. The Mitannians were to be Egypt's first adversary in Syria/Palestine although they later became their allies.

Having first secured their southern flank in Nubia the Egyptian kings were now ready to launch aggressive campaigns in Syria/Palestine where the Mitannians had attempted to push southward. Egypt's aims were to break the Mitannian power and to establish Egypt's northern boundary at the Euphrates. The petty city-states that occupied Syria/Palestine were not a threat to either Egypt or Mitanni, but they did become involved in the conflict between the two great powers.

Tuthmosis I launched the first major offensive in Syria and crossed the Euphrates into Mitanni (Naharin). His son, Tuthmosis II, also campaigned in Palestine, but it was his grandson, Tuthmosis III, who really established Egypt's power. He fought seventeen campaigns and drove the Mitannians back beyond the Euphrates; details of his campaigns are preserved in the inscriptions and wall scenes in several temples and on stelae (inscribed stones). Tuthmosis III regarded his victory at Megiddo (a fortified town overlooking the Plain of Esdraelon) as his most significant achievement.

An important aspect of Tuthmosis III's campaigns was the detailed organization and preparation of his troops and supplies. For example, in his eighth campaign, he crossed the Euphrates and defeated the king of Mitanni. He achieved this by using boats to cross the river; these had been built at Byblos on the Syrian coast and then transported overland by wheeled wagons drawn by oxen. The subjugation of Byblos and other harbors along the Syria/Palestine coast was a key preliminary strategy, for Tuthmosis III could use them to provision his campaign in the hinterland.

Another fruitful policy was to bring the princelings of Syria/Palestine firmly into Egypt's sphere of influence. Egypt controlled these areas through methods that differed from those employed in Nubia. Here, the native governors were left in charge of their own cities, but the Egyptians, to obtain their loyalty, removed their children or brothers as hostages to Egypt where they were educated as Egyptians.

Egypt thus controlled the first empire in the region with boundaries fixed in southern Nubia and at the Euphrates. It was, however, small in comparison with the later empires established by the Assyrians and Persians. As the greatest military power, Egypt now received vast wealth not only in terms of gifts sent by other countries but also as booty brought back from military campaigns. Much of this booty was presented to the god Amen-Re and his priesthood in the Temple of Karnak at Thebes because the early rulers of Dynasty 18 credited their military success to Amen-Re as their patron deity. Consequently this temple and its priesthood became so wealthy and powerful that, by the end of Dynasty 18, the priests posed a considerable political threat to the royal line.

Tuthmosis III was Egypt's greatest military leader, and his son, Amenhotep II, tried to emulate his victories. However, his successors, Tuthmosis IV and Amenhotep II, pursued different policies. It became clear to both Egyptians and Mitannians that neither would succeed in permanently establishing supremacy in northern Syria; therefore, they concluded a peace, and Tuthmosis IV married a daughter of the Mitannian king. Friendship between the two royal families continued under Amenhotep III, who himself married two Mitannian princesses, and correspondence between the two families is preserved in the archive of clay tablets (the Amarna Letters) discovered at Tell el-Amarna. Toward the end of this period another power, the Hittites, emerged as the new threat to Egypt. The Hittite king Suppiluliumas attacked Mitanni and destroyed the kingdom. In Dynasty 19, the Egyptian kings Sethos I and Ramesses II faced this new enemy, but again total supremacy was unachievable, and Ramesses II eventually made a peace treaty with the Hittite ruler and received a Hittite princess as his wife.

It was the arrival of the Sea Peoples (a collection of itinerants who were seeking new homelands) that eventually marked the final decline of the Egyptian Empire. Although the later Ramesside kings successfully repulsed them, their effect upon Egypt and her Mediterranean neighbors was profound. The Sea Peoples dramatically changed the balance of power in the area, and after Dynasty 20 there was a rapid disintegration of Egypt's once-great possessions.

A GAZETTEER OF PLACE-NAMES

Abu Ghurab Site of six sun temples of Dynasty 5, although only those of Userkaf and Niuserre have been discovered and excavated. The wall reliefs are now in the Cairo and Berlin museums.

Abu Simbel Rock-cut temples built by Ramesses II (Dynasty 19) to impress the Nubians. The Great Temple dedicated to Amen-Re and Re-Harakhte and the smaller temple dedicated to Hathor and Nefertari were relocated by a UNESCO project.

Abusir Group of pyramids belonging to kings of Dynasty 5, excavated by the German Oriental Institute; also some important tombs. Czech archaeologists have recently discovered and opened the tomb of Ifuaa, a lector-priest and controller of the palace. This rare example of an intact tomb dates to Dynasty 26 (c.600 BC) and contains a magnificent sarcophagus.

Abydos A very ancient and important political and religious site; the capital during Dynasty 2; first devoted to the god Khentiamentiu, and then became the great center of Osiris. Famous early dynastic tombs, and the temples of Ramesses II and Sethos I (with the Osireion cenotaph).

Akhmim Center of the god Min. The temples are now much destroyed; nobles' rock-cut tombs (Dynasty 6) nearby.

Ashmunein Town of Hermopolis where Thoth was worshiped. Nothing remains of its Old Kingdom importance; its rulers were buried at Deir el-Bersha.

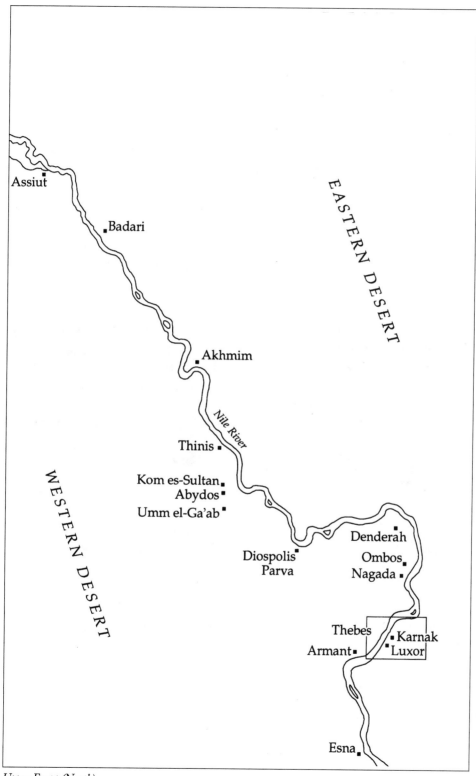

Upper Egypt (North)

Assiut Ancient center of god Wepwawet; particularly important in the First Intermediate Period and Middle Kingdom. Local rulers buried in rock-cut tombs nearby.

Aswan and Elephantine The island and town of Elephantine marked Egypt's boundary with Nubia in the Old Kingdom. Rock-cut tombs of the local governors dating to the Old and Middle Kingdoms are nearby. Granite quarries in the vicinity and the site's command of the First Cataract and of trading routes to Nubia made it significant.

Beit el-Wali Rock-cut temple built by Ramesses II and dedicated to Amen-Re now relocated in Kalabsha Open-Air Museum.

Beni Hasan Rock-cut tombs (First Intermediate Period and Middle Kingdom) of provincial governors with fine painted scenes of daily life.

Busiris Ancient Delta town that was one of Osiris's main cult centers.

Buto Pe, the capital of Lower Egypt, was situated here in the Predynastic Period; cult center of goddess Edjo (Wadjet).

Coptos Town dedicated to Min; commercial center for caravans going to Punt via the Red Sea.

Dahshur Site of five pyramids; two built for Sneferu (Dynasty 4) and one each for Amenemhet II, Amenemhet III, and Senusret III (Dynasty 12).

Deir el-Bersha (el-Bersha) Important Dynasty 12 rock-cut tombs of the governors of Khnumu (Ashmunein) similar to those at Beni Hasan.

Deir el-Gebrawi Rock-cut tombs of Dynasty 6 belonging to local governors; fine wall paintings of daily life scenes.

Denderah Well-preserved temple of Greco-Roman date built on earlier temples. Dedicated to Hathor, worshiped here from Old Kingdom. Interesting sanatorium for medical treatment.

Edfu Important center from Old Kingdom; site of best-preserved temple (Greco-Roman Period), dedicated to Horus the Behdetite, husband of Hathor.

Esna Partially excavated temple of Khnum (Roman Period), with some of the last extant hieroglyphic inscriptions.

Fayoum Fertile oasis attached to the Nile Valley; favored for hunting and fishing by kings and rulers of Dynasty 12 who were buried there (pyramids at Lahun and Hawara).

Gebel es-Silsila North of Aswan and considered the source of the Nile; festivals to the Nile god Hapy were held here. Important quarries with many rock-cut stelae and graffiti.

Giza One of the world's most famous sites, this was the necropolis of the kings of Dynasty 4. Its monuments include the Great Pyramid (Cheops) and its solar barks; pyramid, valley temple, and sphinx (of Chephren); pyramid of Mycerinus; smaller associated pyramids; and the nobles' cemeteries.

Hawara Pyramid of Amenemhet III (Dynasty 12), and his "Labyrinth," housing his mortuary temple and administration headquarters. Mummy portraits found in the nearby Greco-Roman cemetery.

Heliopolis Ancient center of sun cult, and claimed to be original site of creation. First sun temple with Benben (solar cult symbol) built here.

Heracleopolis Magna Cult center of god Herishef. Very little remains of the town and tombs.

Hieraconpolis With the neighboring site of el-Kab this formed the predynastic capital of Upper Egypt where the goddess Nekhbet was worshiped. Hieraconpolis became the center for the worship of Horus, the first royal patron deity.

Kahun Royal workmen's town (Dynasty 12) built to house the workforce engaged in building the nearby Lahun pyramid for Senusret II.

Kalabsha The largest freestanding temple in Egyptian Nubia, originally located near the town of Talmis; relocated in recent years to the Open-Air Museum at New Kalabsha, a promontory near Aswan.

Kom Ombo Unique double temple (Greco-Roman period) dedicated (southern side of building) to Sobek and (northern side) to Haroeris. Interesting carved panel of "medical instruments" on back wall.

Lahun Pyramid of Senusret II (Dynasty 12) and shaft tombs of his family where the spectacular royal jewelry and treasure were found.

Lisht (el-Lisht) Site of It-towy, capital city during Dynasty 12; site of pyramids and nobles' tombs of reigns of Amenemhet I and Senusret I.

Meidum Unfinished pyramid probably built for Sneferu (Dynasty 4), that apparently collapsed; associated mortuary temple and nobles' tombs.

Meir Rock-cut tombs of local governors (Dynasties 6 and 12), with some of the most interesting wall scenes of the Middle Kingdom.

Memphis White Walls, first capital founded by Menes; cult center of Ptah. Its strategic importance ensured that it remained a great political and economic center until Greco-Roman times.

Nagada With Badari, this was the site of some Egypt's earliest predynastic burials. Nearby are the ruins of Ombos, predynastic capital and cult center of the god Seth.

Oxyrhynchus Ancient site of Per-medjeh and a substantial Greco-Roman period town best known for its wealth of Greek, Coptic, and Arabic papyri.

Philae Island near Aswan, once occupied by temples including that of Isis, as well as those of Osiris, Harpocrates, Nephthys, Hathor, Khnum, and Satet. In recent years the buildings have been dismantled and reerected on a nearby island in a UNESCO rescue project.

Qantir Possibly the site of Pi-Ramesse, the Delta residence built by the Ramesside kings (town called Ramses in the biblical exodus).

Sais Delta city dedicated to goddess Neith; capital of Egypt in Dynasty 26.

Saqqara Famous necropolis of Memphis with monuments from most periods. Most famous are Djoser's Step Pyramid (Dynasty 3), Persian shaft tombs (Dynasty 27), pyramid of Unas (Dynasty 5), mastaba tombs of Ti and Ptah-hotep (Dynasty 5) and Mereruka, Kagemni, and Ankhmahor (Dynasty 6). Also, the Serapeum, subterranean galleries that housed the mummified remains of Apis bulls; these cult animals, each worshiped in its lifetime as the incarnation of the divine Apis bull, were finally interred here in great stone coffins.

Tanis Capital during Dynasties 21 and 22 with continued importance in Roman times. Royal tombs and treasure discovered here.

Tell el-Amarna City of Akhetaten built by heretic pharaoh Akhenaten (Dynasty 18). Cult center of the Aten; temples to the Aten, royal palaces, and important nobles' tombs.

Tell Basta City (Bubastis) was used by kings of Dynasty 22; cult center of Bastet, the cat goddess; a large necropolis and extensive cat cemetery.

Tell el-Dab'a Recent excavations have indicated that this is probably Avaris, the capital city founded by the Hyksos (Dynasty 15).

Tell el-Maskhuta Possibly the ancient city of Pithom mentioned in the biblical exodus.

Tell el-Yahudiyeh This town may have been founded in the Middle Kingdom or Second Intermediate Period, but most remains date to Ramesses II (Dynasty 19).

Thebes Great capital of the New Kingdom; many spectacular monuments survive today including the Temples of Luxor and Karnak on the east bank and the cemeteries and mortuary temples on the west bank, such as the Valleys of the Kings and Queens, many famous nonroyal tombs, and the mortuary temples of Sethos I (Qurna), Ramesses II (the Ramesseum), Ramesses III (Medinet Habu), and Hatshepsut (Deir el-Bahri).

This Southern capital city in the earliest dynasties with neighboring tombs.

READING

Source Material

Africa 1963: discussion of accounts of Herodotus and Diodorus Siculus; Fagan 1977: details of early accounts of Egypt; Bowersock 1965: discussion of Strabo.

Inundation of the Nile

Baines and Málek 1980: historical atlas of Egypt with detailed maps and commentary on sites; Kees 1961: discussion of the topography of Egypt; Butzer 1976: a study of the irrigation methods in Egypt.

Living off the Land

AGRICULTURE AND FARMING

Bender 1975: account of farming in early communities; Ucko and Dimbleby 1969: study of the use of plants and domesticated animals in early communities; Ucko, Tringham, and Dimbleby 1972: urban development in early communities.

NATURAL RESOURCES

Lucas 1962: detailed, scientific account of ancient Egyptian materials and industries; Aldred 1971: useful account of materials used in jewelry.

Neighboring Lands

NUBIA

Gardiner 1961: good general history of Egypt with details of Egypt's relations with Nubia; Emery 1965: account of Egypt's relations with Nubia; Kitchen 1973: scholarly discussion of Dynasty 25, the "Ethiopian Dynasty"; Adams 1977: general account of Nubia.

EGYPT'S EMPIRE

Emery 1965: op cit; Gardiner 1961: op cit; Trigger 1976: Egypt's domination of Nubia.

Gazetteer of Place-Names

Baines and Málek 1980: op cit.

3

SOCIETY AND GOVERNMENT

THE KEYS TO STABILITY

There were few changes in the social organization and system of government over a period of 3,000 years. This orderly arrangement was only punctuated by a possible revolution of some uncertain kind at the end of the Old Kingdom, followed by temporary collapse and disintegration, and by intermittent times of civil war (during the First, Second, and Third Intermediate Periods), when local princelings challenged central authority and established their own power bases. The system was supported and preserved, however, by patterns of marriage and inheritance: People tended to marry within their own social groups, and offices and trades were passed down from father to son. Such stable and centralized government set the framework in which it was possible to construct great monuments and establish an empire; it also ensured that the people were fed. During the periods of collapse and disintegration, there were, nevertheless, civil wars, famine, disorder, lawlessness, and even foreign infiltration and invasion.

The king was central to the government and to religion. He was regarded as half-divine. From the New Kingdom, the term *pharaoh* was adopted as the title for the king (derived from the Egyptian *per-wer*, meaning the "great house" [the royal palace]). The king acceded to the throne and received the divine right to rule at his coronation when he became the earthly incarnation of the god Horus. It was believed that each new ruler revitalized the universe and reestablished the original creation. The king ruled Egypt subject to Ma'at, the goddess who symbolized the equilibrium of the universe. Everything emanated from the king, and he theoretically owned all the land, people, and possessions. His individual resurrection after

death and continuation as a god in the next world was of paramount importance not just for himself but for the survival of Egypt. To this end all the funerary beliefs and customs were initially designed and developed for the king's use. However, even his seemingly unlimited powers were kept in check because he had to observe precedent and obey the principles of *ma'at*. Although regarded as part-divine, his subjects did not give each king their blind acceptance and approval but judged him according to his deeds.

From prehistoric times the country had been divided into administrative districts (for which modern historians use the Greek term *nomes*). The nomes had grown out of those areas originally controlled by the separate tribes, and they persisted into the historic period, each being placed under a district governor (nomarch) who was appointed by the king. Toward the end of the Old Kingdom these became hereditary posts, and subsequently the nomarchs became virtually independent rulers. They were only finally subdued by the king in the Middle Kingdom, and the nomes were redefined in the New Kingdom as a larger number of smaller areas, each strictly controlled by central government. Despite the changes they underwent, the nomes remained the basic administrative unit of Egypt.

Insufficient evidence exists to reconstruct a clear picture of how the economy was organized and how it functioned. In general the land owned by the king was administered by royal officials or presented as a perpetual gift to the temples. Some land was also managed for the king by officials according to a life tenure system: They looked after the estate and in return received revenues from it. Since the Old Kingdom, wealthy individuals had owned some land privately, but the total amount of this property and the number of persons whom they employed were small compared with the possessions of the state or the temples. Other tasks which were necessary to enable the state to run efficiently, such as working the land, brickmaking, and quarrying, were carried out by the peasants who were all liable to corvée duty.

There were sufficient foodstuffs to support the country's relatively small population and also a surplus that was used to trade with other countries. Egypt's exports included paper (papyrus), cereals, textiles, and dried fish; gold and luxury manufactured goods were also traded for the commodities the country lacked: sufficient wood for building, copper, silver, and spices. In addition to trade the Egyptians used diplomacy, conquest, and colonization to acquire these requisites.

Warfare and subsidies of gold were used in Egypt's relations with Asia, whereas colonization and direct control were employed in Nubia. When Egypt had established its empire in Asia, the subordinate city-states there were governed through a system of local rulers who gave allegiance to the Egyptian king. To ensure their continuing loyalty their children were removed to the Egyptian court for education; this also allowed the Egyptians to instill their own ideas and values in the next generation of vassal princes.

Within Egypt the economic system revolved around the payment of wages in kind (usually in food such as corn, barley, fish, and so forth) to various groups of employees, such as scribes, priests, farmworkers, and artisans. The three major employers—the state, temples, and nobles—paid their employees from the rents and dues they received themselves. Revenue and payments depended on a fairly rapid redistribution system of the food that was grown and collected annually.

Because an essential feature of the organization of the temples and tombs was their continuing commitment to offer food regularly to the gods and the dead, they were closely involved

with the general economic policy of the state. Indeed, much of the country's labor and production, which were centered around food, building materials, and other commodities, were directed toward meeting the needs of the gods and the dead.

DIVINE KINGSHIP

The king's role originally developed out of the de facto custom in predynastic Egypt that the most powerful of the tribal leaders became the leader of the country. By the Archaic Period when he took up residence at Memphis and the political structure began to be established, the

A pendant in the form of a bivalve shell, beaten out of gold. The name of King Senusret III has been worked in gold wire and soldered to the shell; it appears in a cartouche that is supported by two uraei. These gold shells were based on the real pearlized shells that were trimmed to shape and inscribed with a king's name. From Riqqeh, c.1850 BC.

king was already regarded as an absolute monarch, identified with the royal hawk god, Horus. Each ruler was believed to be the god's earthly embodiment and carried the title of Horus during his lifetime. When he died, he handed on this title to his successor.

The idea of rule by a god-king was central to Egypt's political and religious development. The order of succession, which passed through the king's principal queen (Great Royal Wife), was probably established as early as the Archaic Period. Subsequently the Egyptians fostered the fiction that every king was the child of the union between the chief state god and the ruling king's principal queen. This unique origin, which provided the heir with a divine father and a human mother, was believed to endow him with special qualities for kingship. It enabled him to mediate between gods and men and to perform the rituals for the gods in the temples. It also separated the king from his subjects not only in his lifetime but also after death when, at least in the Old Kingdom, he alone could expect to experience an individual eternity. Then, and even later when concepts of immortality had become more democratic, the king was expected to pass his afterlife in a different set of circumstances from his subjects, sailing in the divine bark in the company of the gods and encircling the heavens.

His divinity also gave the king theoretical ownership of Egypt, its resources, and its people and freedom to dispose of them as he wished. He was, however, subject to Ma'at (goddess of truth) in his decisions and actions and had to obey the principles of balance and order. In reality he was advised by his counselors and administrators.

Because of the need to ensure that the next king was born to a woman of the purest royal blood and because the role of the Great Royal Wife was of the greatest importance to the succession, the ruling king was usually married to the Great Royal Daughter (who was customarily his sister and the eldest daughter of the previous king and his Great Royal Wife). Inheritance thus passed through the female line; to substantiate his claim to the throne and gain acceptance of his own son as the next heir, each royal heir presumptive had to marry the Great Royal Daughter. Sometimes the system broke down because the king and principal queen did not have a son and daughter who could marry each other. If a royal heir did not have a full claim (perhaps he had been born to a secondary royal queen), however, he could ensure his succession by marrying the Great Royal Daughter. Even claimants who had only tenuous links with the main royal line could legitimatize their kingship if they married the royal heiress.

The concept of the god-king is most clearly defined in the Old Kingdom when it was emphasized in the burial customs—the king rested in his pyramid while his subjects were placed in tombs and graves. The relationship between the kings and the gods was never entirely comfortable, and the chief god and his priesthood always presented a threat to royal supremacy. When the kingship was strong this was less apparent, but even when the kings were powerful and successful, as in early Dynasty 18 when they presented the god Amen-Re with booty from the military campaigns, their actions were ultimately increasing the god's wealth and influence at their own cost.

The landmarks in the relationship between the king and the gods give some indication of the power struggles and the actions that both sides took in order to gain advantage. Although the king was omnipotent in the early Old Kingdom, he took the additional title of "Son of Re" in Dynasty 2, indicating that his relationship with the sun god was already becoming filial rather than one of equal partners. By Dynasty 5, when the priests of Re may have helped to place that line of kings on the throne, it is clear that the cult of Re became preeminent, and the kings ceased to prepare well-constructed pyramids for themselves but instead channeled their resources into building sun temples for the god's worship.

In the Middle Kingdom, when there was democratization of religious beliefs and customs and Osiris achieved widespread acclaim, the new rulers replaced Re (the royal patron deity of the Old Kingdom) with Osiris. This god was featured in the Pyramid Texts (Old Kingdom), supporting the king's personal resurrection.

These kings may have given Osiris royal patronage then in order to counterbalance the power of the priests of Re. In the Middle Kingdom, however, Osiris became the supreme royal god, closely associated with the divine rituals performed at the kings's accession and coronation, and whereas the living king was regarded as the incarnation of Horus at death he now became Osiris, god and judge of the underworld.

By the New Kingdom when Amen-Re (Amun) had been elevated as chief god of the state, the early Theban kings honored their god with campaign booty and a magnificent temple

A scene shows King Horemheb carried by his soldiers, while two fan-bearers walk in front and behind. His throne is decorated with the figure of a lion.

at Karnak. Because the high priest of Amun had the power to approve the royal heir on behalf of the god, he had direct control over the kingship. Toward the end of Dynasty 18, Akhenaten (Amenhotep IV) introduced a monotheistic cult centered around the Aten (sun's disk), perhaps in the hope of destroying the priests' power (the cults of all other deities were terminated and their priesthoods disbanded). He and his immediate predecessors had also abandoned the custom of marrying the Great Royal Daughter and took their principal wives from outside the royal family.

The experiment was a failure, and the traditional gods and their priesthoods were restored. In Dynasty 21 a line of high priests of Amun gained virtual autonomy in the south, although they acknowledged the nominal supremacy of the dynastic kings who now ruled from the north. In effect, however, the country was split and the two lines had their own mutually recognized rights of succession.

In Dynasty 21, a new role was introduced for the Divine Wife of Amun. Originally this title had been borne by the principal queen, but now it was the king's daughter who assumed this position with its extensive power and possessions. She was required to live at Thebes, the cult center of Amun, where she had great power and endowments; in many respects her status equaled that of her father. Her influence was limited to the Theban area, however, and as the god's wife, she was forbidden to take a human husband. Her court was also subject to the rule of chastity since these women were Amun's concubines.

By the start of Dynasty 25, this position had become an instrument of great political power. It allowed the king to keep control over Thebes through his daughter's status there. Each divine wife adopted as her successor the daughter of the next king. Their main function was to prevent seizure of political power at Thebes by a man who could threaten the king's supremacy, and they prevented any repetition of the division of the kingdom. The use of this role and title became another royal attempt to limit the political aspirations of the priesthood.

SOCIAL STRUCTURE

Egypt's social structure originated in the scattered communities of the Predynastic Period. Gradually, as these came together into larger units either through mutual cooperation or because one area conquered another, they established communities that enjoyed mutual protection and schemes such as irrigation which benefited everyone. Each unit retained its independence and had its own capital city and an area of land to support its inhabitants. Eventually these units combined to form larger districts and these became the main administrative divisions of later times (known as "nomes"). Around 3400 BC two kingdoms, the Red Land and the White Land, were established in the north and the south, respectively. With the unification of the country in c.3100 BC the whole area came under one ruler, but the symbolic parallelism of the "Two Lands" was always retained and the nomes continued to form the basis for administering the country.

By the Archaic Period some of the political and social systems that continued in later times were already in place. But it was in the Old Kingdom that the pattern of Egypt's social structure (which, with relatively minor adjustments, was to continue until the Ptolemies and Romans brought in their own systems) had already emerged.

The king (regarded as a partly divine being) had a unique status and role around which the society revolved. Kingship had developed out of the role of tribal chieftain, and theoretically the ruler's duties included political, religious, social, economic, military, and legal commitments. As the kingdom developed, however, these were increasingly delegated to royal officials. The kings were polygamous, and there were usually secondary branches of the royal family descended from minor queens and concubines. This family background not infrequently led to rivalry and dispute over the royal succession, although theoretically the eldest son of the king by his principal queen became the royal heir. Because of the importance of the queen in the royal succession, she exercised great power in the royal household.

In the Old Kingdom the king had attempted to secure the loyalty of his relatives by granting them the major positions in government. He also gave them gifts of royal land and possessions, and their children were educated at the royal court. He provided them with tombs, funerary goods, and estates to maintain their tombs, and they could only expect to attain immortality through his bounty. But by the end of the Old Kingdom the situation had changed: Many of the governorships and top posts had become hereditary so that the king no longer controlled them, and increasingly these positions were given to nonroyal persons who had no direct ties with the king's family.

After the king the most important position was held by the vizier (prime minister). He was head of the judiciary, chief royal architect, and keeper of the state archives. The country was divided into districts that were administered by local governors. In times of internal dissension these petty rulers became semi-independent, reverting almost to the pattern of tribal chieftains that had existed in predynastic times. The kings

needed their support, but the viziers posed a constant threat, and it was not until Dynasty 12 that the problem of the provincial nobility was resolved. King Senusret II took decisive action and deprived them of their rights and privileges; it is not evident how he achieved this result, but from then onward the political strength of these governors (nomarchs) was destroyed. Members of a new middle class consisting of craftsmen, tradesmen, and small farmers formed the new administration, organized so that they were directly responsible to the king or the vizier.

The other great threat to the king's power was the priests, and this relationship was never satisfactorily resolved. The highest levels of the priesthood wielded considerable political influence.

The top level of the government was supported by an extensive bureaucracy. This was run on a daily basis by a hierarchy of officials who organized the treasuries, which dealt with revenue and expenditure, the armory, granaries, and public works. Traditionally these departments were housed in a palace complex in the capital city where the living quarters of the royal family were also situated. The complex was known as *per-wer* (the "great house") and eventually this term was also applied to the person of the king as the title of pharaoh. There were also extensive administrations for the great temples and for the royal burial center and its associated temples and residence cities.

As the country developed some kings occupied several major residence cities, and the administration in response became increasingly complex. Some areas of the administration were organized on a local basis with officials placed in the various districts. In the New Kingdom the acquisition of an empire extended the bureaucracy still further.

Below the government officials there were the craftsmen and artisans who produced a wide range of goods for the living and the dead. These people worked in communities: Many lived in the capital city, and particular schools or styles of art developed in the great centers; others were employed in the temple workshops; and the elite were engaged in preparing and decorating the royal burial place. They were accommodated near the worksite in specially constructed towns. Advances in technology, originally developed for funerary architecture and goods, were soon employed in the service of the living to produce furniture, jewelry, toiletries, pottery, and clothing.

At the bottom of the society were the peasants (perhaps representing 80 percent) who worked on the land. They were responsible for providing the food, resources, and manpower for the whole country. Their work on the land was governed by the annual inundation and the seasons, but they attempted through their arduous labors to produce enough food to satisfy their own limited needs. Through their taxes they also fed the rest of the society and supplied the offerings for the tombs and temples (which were ultimately presented to the priests).

For three months each year, when the inundation covered much of the land with water and rendered it impossible to cultivate, the peasants probably undertook alternative employment. They may have worked at the royal burial sites receiving food for themselves and their families as payment. Such work would have prevented starvation and ensured that they did not have time and opportunity to cause problems.

The peasants were liable to corvée duty (the king could call upon them for any duty). Indeed, this applied to all his subjects, but the wealthier could pay someone else to take on their allocated tasks. These conscripted peasants could be used for stone quarrying, gold mining, building works, and before a professional army was established in the New Kingdom, they were sent on military service.

GOVERNMENT AND BUREAUCRACY

The pharaoh was supreme overlord of Egypt. In his name the administration controlled the lives of the populace and the court and ordered the economy. There was a strictly organized hierarchy directed from the offices of the royal residence; under this, local governors supervised the bureaucracy of each administrative district. At the central level there were departments of granaries, agriculture and farming, and building works, as well as the army, ships, frontiers, trading expeditions, foreign relations, justice, prisons, and health. Temples and wealthy landowners also had their own administrations, which were sometimes independent but at other times came under direct government control. The arrangements were generally complicated and involved the lives of many people since most holders of offices in the system were employed either by the state or the temples.

Even in the Archaic Period some centralized departments had already been established at Memphis, the new capital city. These included the administration, judiciary, and foreign trade and also the treasuries of the Two Lands (named the White House and Red House), which collected and redistributed the national revenue. These departments were probably already connected to the provincial administration, and the two levels addressed the problems of governing a country that included settled urbanized and closely organized communities as well as more loosely structured agricultural units.

In the Old Kingdom pyramid building had required the existence of a fully supportive, highly organized bureaucracy, and consequently a very centralized government emerged. This subsequently broke down, and in the Middle Kingdom a new system was introduced by the rulers of Dynasty 12 who usurped the throne. By the New Kingdom the establishment of a permanent army and an empire, as well as greatly expanded temple estates, resulted in many changes in the administration of the country.

It was this bureaucratic system that enabled civilization to flourish in Egypt. A complex society emerged with well-developed institutions and a king as the central figure who represented divine rulership and embodied the state. He was assisted by a group of deputies who headed the administration, the army, and the priesthood. They were paid large salaries, and they received rent from the land and royal gifts in addition to a share of the temple revenue at certain periods and the gift of a tomb from the king.

The administration was headed by the vizier (*tjaty*), who was usually appointed from the ranks of the scribes. His job was to advise the king from whom he directly received his orders. As head of the judiciary and with responsibility for the whole administration, his powers were extensive. At some periods there were two viziers to serve the northern and southern parts of Egypt, and the office of vizier was in place from Dynasty 4 until the fourth century BC.

There were many minor officials below the top ranks including scribes, priests, and artisans. These were the retainers of the upper classes; they were paid in kind and were fairly affluent. Below them were the peasants. They had worked on the land and had also probably been part of the labor gangs at building sites in the Old Kingdom. By the Middle Kingdom the peasantry included not only native Egyptians but also some prisoners of war. All the peasants were liable to corvée duty; they worked in the fields, on building sites, in the workshops, mines, and quarries; in early times they were also obliged to fight as soldiers for their overlords. Their lives were organized by the office to which

they were attached—the state administration, temple, or private individual—and their work was essential to the state.

The extent to which some of the peasants were slaves in the modern sense is unclear. The government, the temples, or wealthy individuals seem to have "owned" some workers in that they had the right to buy, sell, bequeath, or emancipate them. However, slaves could also own land and possessions and sell or bequeath them as they wished; they could also marry freeborn women and employ servants. Therefore, the concept of a slave as someone who is totally owned by another did not exist in ancient Egypt. Even the kind of slave labor that did exist was not a major factor in the economy, and early projects requiring large scale labor, such as the Old Kingdom pyramids, would have been built by native serfs rather than slaves.

The government was upheld by a police force basically employed to protect the weak against the strong. The police had local responsibilities to guard the farmers against theft and attack and to expel troublemakers from the community; they were also expected to use persuasion and even physical force to ensure that the peasants paid their taxes. Other groups patrolled the east and west frontiers of Egypt or sought out and returned escaped slaves and prisoners to their captors. The police were not part of the army. In Dynasty 18 a special group was established in the force when the Medjay (nomads from the Nubian desert) were enrolled and became a very effective law enforcement branch.

The government was supported by the treasury and by trade. The main export trade was a royal government monopoly, and the king protected the state's interests by imposing customs duties at Egypt's frontiers. Access for foreign merchants was probably strictly limited, and when they were permitted to enter the country they were controlled by the government and sometimes confined to their own cities within Egypt.

Taxation was heavy and could be administered universally because an elaborate bureaucracy was in place. The districts paid some taxes to the Crown in gold, and this was used for subsidies in foreign diplomacy and for paying the salaries of government ministers. However, the state's most important duty was to pay its many officials, and to build up a food stock for the times of famine. The economy was based on a barter system, and the taxation procedure rested on a regular census of the fields, herds, and gold that was undertaken from the Old Kingdom onward. Each year for the agricultural census officials were sent out to measure the arable area and to compile a list of the institutions and private owners who held the land. This enabled them to estimate the year's crop and the probable tax that it would yield; once the crops had begun to grow other inspectors would return to make a final tax assessment.

Laws and Punishment

Compared with other ancient civilizations Egyptian law has yielded little evidence of its institutions. It was, however, clearly governed by religious principles: Law was believed to have been handed down to mankind by the gods on the First Occasion (the moment of creation), and the gods were held responsible for establishing and perpetuating the law, which was personified by the goddess Ma'at. She represented truth, righteousness, and justice and maintained the correct balance and order of the universe. Theoretically the god-king was the sole legislator with power of life and death over his subjects, but in reality his freedom in legal matters, as in other areas, was determined by precedent. As chief official of the judiciary the king was a priest of Ma'at, and the vizier, as the king's delegate, was head of the courts of justice. Officials of the judiciary were also priests of Ma'at.

Inscriptions in tombs and on stelae and papyri, which provide the earliest extant legal transactions, can be dated to the Old Kingdom. They indicate that the legal system was well developed by this date and suggest that there must have been a long period of experimentation beforehand. Egyptian law ranks with Sumerian as the world's oldest surviving legal system, and its complexity and state of development are on a level with ancient Greek and medieval law.

In general there are many transactions that deal with funerary property. Although the king had absolute rights over his subjects and their property, in practice there was private as well as royal law, and property was often dealt with through private legal transactions. There was no formal law code (such as the Code of Hammurabi in Babylon), and cases were largely decided on precedent. The laws were generally humane (more than those of other ancient societies), and they controlled and regulated an essentially law-abiding society. Men and women of all classes were treated equally, and there was great emphasis on protection of the family within the society. The punishments were generally severe, and there was a complex system of procedure within the law courts.

Some evidence still exists of legal transactions during the Old and Middle Kingdoms, but most information derives from the New Kingdom. Major changes were introduced under the Ptolemies and Romans.

Ownership and transfer of property were the subject of either Crown or private transactions. In ownership cases, the original owner drew up a special document setting out the terms of the transfer, which was then passed to the new owner. This document was witnessed by three persons, and then the papyrus was rolled up and sealed by a high official. These were usually prepared for houses and other valuable possessions; wills in the modern sense were unknown, but a person could leave a transfer document to pass on, at his death, a valuable item to someone else.

Special arrangements were made to protect the provisioning of the tomb. Because family commitments to bring food offerings to the tomb were often neglected, a legal arrangement existed which provided an "insurance policy" against this omission. The tomb owner would set up an "eternal property" from a profit-bearing part of his estate. From this, a selected special priest (ka servant) would receive a perpetual income in exchange for a legal agreement to place offerings at the tomb. When the priest died his heirs would inherit his income and this obligation. Even this arrangement was not entirely satisfactory, however, and the offerings would lapse, so the tomb owner also resorted to magic and provided his tomb with wall scenes and models depicting food in addition to an inscribed menu.

The legal system operated through the law courts, although it was possible to reach private agreements. There were two types of court: the local courts (kenbet) included local dignitaries under a chairman and they dealt with most cases; the High Court sat at the capital under the vizier and tried serious cases, particularly those entailing capital punishment. The courts admitted and considered all kinds of evidence, which was studied by the judges, but a case did not end with the judgment: It had to be followed by a declaration of submission by the defeated party. Documentary evidence (particularly tax rolls in deciding ownership cases) was often used.

A change that was introduced in Dynasty 19 marked a deterioration in the system. A verdict was now sometimes obtained by means of an oracle. The statue of a god became the judge, and its decision was ascertained through ceremonies performed in front of the image. A list of named suspects would be read out, and the statue was supposed to give a sign at the name of the culprit. The system was clearly open to corruption and abuse.

Punishments were severe and were intended to deter future offenses. Officials could pursue ruthless interrogation of the suspect in court, beating him until he confessed, and independent witnesses could also receive severe treatment so that their "evidence" would be presented to support the desired outcome of the case. Minor misdemeanors could be punished with 100 strokes, and imprisonment and forced labor in the mines and quarries were also often imposed. If prisoners tried to escape their ears and noses were sometimes amputated before they were sent back to their captors.

The death penalty offered a number of options. Some criminals were left to be devoured alive by crocodiles. As a special favor or indication of high status, some individuals were allowed to commit suicide. Children who killed their parents underwent an ordeal in which pieces of their flesh were cut out with reeds before they were placed on a bed of thorns and burnt alive. However, parents who killed their children were not put to death but were instead forced to hold the dead child's body for three days and nights. Deserters were also spared death, but they suffered great disgrace (although they could be reinstated to favor if they later performed a courageous deed). The operating principle here was that disgrace could often be worse than death. Also, a rehabilitated person could be useful again to society whereas an executed criminal could never contribute. Sometimes a whole family might be punished for the actions of one member.

Other punishments included the emasculation of a man who committed rape against a freeborn woman; the amputation of the hands of dishonest officials; and the removal of tongues of those who released military secrets. If a man committed adultery with a woman's consent he would receive 1,000 blows, but she might suffer amputation of her nose, or she might be divorced or even burned to death.

Although the law makers were men, the system safeguarded the financial position of women and children and attempted to protect and promote the family. Property was invested in women in the same way that the kingship was invested in the Great Royal Wife. On marriage a woman retained her own property, and under the terms of the marriage contract the husband sometimes transferred the whole of his property to his wife to hold and pass on to their children. This transfer of property was probably more theoretical than actual, and in most cases the man would have retained the right to administer and use his own property, at least until divorce. Outside the royal family bigamy and polygamy were rare, although some men had serf concubines as well as a wife. Divorce was possible for both men and women; legally, it was easier for a man to divorce his wife, but if he did so he had to pay her compensation and she retained the property she had brought to the marriage.

Archival material that illuminates the Egyptian legal system is rich and varied. It includes papyri fragments from town archives; temple documents that provide details of the trial of men and women implicated in a harem conspiracy to assassinate the king; and well-preserved papyri that record the trials of the royal tomb robberies in the Ramesside Period.

Taxes and Finance

In theory the king owned all land and possessions. In reality, although he was the largest landowner and possessed areas within each nome (administrative district), the temples and even private individuals owned substantial real estate. The royal lands were officially registered and administered by an overlord appointed by the king. The Crown also constantly acquired new land; sometimes this would be bought from men who had lost their own wealth and needed to exchange their land for other commodities.

It was the main duty of provincial and town governors to collect taxes for the king. There is more information about taxation in the New Kingdom than there is for earlier periods; for example, in the reign of Tuthmosis III it is known that taxes were collected in the form of cereals, livestock, fruit, and provisions, as well as gold and silver rings and jewels. The governors annually assessed the cereal payable for that year, basing their calculations on the surface area of each nome and the height of the Nile rising. The levels of inundation were recorded on nilometers; built at the river's edge, nilometers were designed to measure the annual height of the inundation. If there was a low Nile when the water did not reach the usual level, the tax to be paid that year was reduced accordingly. There was also a tax on livestock based on a general census of the herds; this was carried out every second year by the government inspectors who visited the privately owned estates to assess their liability.

The temples had gained major concessions from the king as early as the Old Kingdom when he gave land to the priesthood and signed decrees that exempted them in perpetuity from taxation of goods or services. They also had other important privileges: Some temple personnel could not be used for the service of the king or the royal household, and the king could not remove funds allocated to the god's worship to use for his own benefit. Despite Akhenaten's closure of the temples, once they were restored under Horemheb the priesthood continued to amass great wealth as before, and the temples once again owned vast property.

Under the administrative system the country was divided into nomes: twenty-two in southern Egypt and eventually the same number in the north. There was a leading city in each nome where the district governor and his staff had their headquarters. These governors (who replaced the virtually independent local rulers of the Middle Kingdom) were appointed by the king. Their many duties covered the areas of public works, law and order, provision against famine, and raising taxes. An important task was to build up a reserve food supply after a good harvest that would offset the dire consequences of a future low inundation.

Individuals also owned land or sometimes administered the king's estates as a way of earning a living. This was a desirable position as the official could keep some of the profits from the royal estate for himself. Another way in which individuals acquired land and property was through inheritance, or sometimes the king provided high-ranking officials with tombs and with the land to supply their tomb offerings. From the New Kingdom onward land was also given to professional soldiers as a reward for military service; this remained in the soldier's family as long as they continued to fight for the king.

The Egyptians were among the first people to pay tax. The most important was the poll tax. The revenue officer regularly gathered the information to raise this tax from the head of each family. He had to declare all the members of his household including servants and slaves; the number of pregnant women in each household was also noted so that the officer could assess how many new taxpayers might be expected the following year. Taxes were paid in kind since Egypt had no official coinage until the Persian Period (c.525 BC). They were not only collected in the form of agricultural commodities; by the New Kingdom craftsmen had to hand over to the state a proportion of the articles they produced. The commodities paid to meet tax demands were stored in government treasuries and then redistributed to meet the state expenses.

It is not surprising that the Egyptians incurred debts. A debtor would swear an oath in which he invoked the king or a god, and confirmed that he would repay this obligation in the future. The rate of interest on loans was 100 percent per year, and at the end of each year the outstanding interest was added to the capital sum, and a further 100 percent was charged on this. Payment consisted of any objects the creditor would accept, and all commodities were valued against a general standard.

In the Late Period (c.700 BC) it was possible to enter into a "self-sale"; this involved a person selling himself into servitude in order to meet the demands of an overdue loan (working off his debt) or selling himself to become another person's "son." This carried certain obligations to the "father," such as ensuring that the correct burial procedures were carried out on his behalf. If a couple were childless they would sometimes enter into such an agreement and adopt an adult "son" to ensure that their burial was performed correctly. In return, under the law of succession, the person who carried out the burial rites would inherit the deceased's property.

Reading

Divine Kingship

Fairman 1958: description of kingship rituals; Gardiner 1950: coronation of the king.

Government

BUREAUCRACY AND ADMINISTRATION

Edgerton 1947: aspects of the government system.

LAWS AND PUNISHMENT

Blackman 1925, 1926; use of oracles; de Buck 1937: trial of the royal tomb robbers; Peet 1925: the royal tomb robberies; Edgerton 1951: industrial disputes of the royal workmen; Goedicke 1963: aspects of the trial related to the Harem Conspiracy; Černý 1973: legal aspects of the community at Deir el-Medina.

TAXES AND FINANCE

Montet 1965: general account that includes information about the taxation system.

4

RELIGION OF
THE LIVING

Religion was an integral part of the lives of the ancient Egyptians and permeated most aspects of everyday existence in addition to laying the foundation for their funerary beliefs and customs. Religion was practiced at the state level with the king acting as the unique link between the gods and men, and the temples played an important role in this respect too. There is also ample evidence of personal piety and worship by ordinary people who prayed to special deities in their own homes.

STATE RELIGION

We have very limited knowledge of the religious rites and customs practiced by the living during the Predynastic Period since no chapels or sacred centers have been identified (they would have been constructed of perishable materials). This is in contrast to evidence of early funerary beliefs and burial customs based on cemeteries and grave goods that have survived. However, scenes painted on pottery found in graves depict figures of deities and gods' shrines carried on boats in religious ceremonies, and depictions of early shrines occur on cylinder seals and ebony and ivory tablets of the Archaic Period.

Early Animal Cults

Before the unification (c.3100 BC) it seems that there were many localized and unconnected cults, and each community worshipped its own deity. Most were originally represented in animal or fetish form, and the importance of animal cults in later times is already emphasized in these early societies. There were animal burials in some villages in which dogs or jackals, sheep, and cows were wrapped in linen and matting and interred among human burials. Amulets in the form of animals were placed with human burials to provide protection and a food supply for the deceased, while animal gods were presented on the painted pottery of the Nagada II period. There were also animal statuettes and slate palettes in the form of animals in many of the early graves. The reasons behind the deification of animals in ancient Egypt are not clear: Possibly some were worshiped because they assisted mankind, while others, who were feared (such as the jackals who ransacked the cemeteries), were deified in an attempt to propitiate them.

It is evident, however, that animal and fetish forms were regarded as symbols through which the divine power could manifest itself and that animal worship continued to be extremely important throughout the historic period. A few of the gods, such as Ptah the creator god of Memphis, were always represented with a full human form, but most retained some animal characteristics.

In the early dynastic period there was a gradual anthropomorphization of the animal gods, who began to be represented with animal or bird heads on human bodies. By Dynasty 2, some animal gods appear with fully human forms. Throughout the historic period, however, animal deities continue to display a variety of forms; some have complete animal bodies, some have animal heads and human bodies, and a few take on a completely human appearance.

Cosmic Gods

During the Predynastic Period a group of deities emerged whom Egyptologists now term "cosmic gods." They differed in several respects from the local, tribal gods, and it has been suggested that they may have been introduced into Egypt from another area, possibly by the Dynastic Race. Although many of the older tribal gods survived virtually unchanged, some may have been fused with the cosmic deities so that the latter could adopt some of their characteristics and take over their cult centers. Another explanation is that the cosmic gods were not introduced by a new race entering Egypt but had always been worshiped by the indigenous population. Because of their remoteness and inaccessibility, however, they were possibly not at first attributed forms or centers by their worshipers. It was only later that the cosmic forces (the sun, moon, stars, and elements) were in some cases fused with local gods and thus acquired specific names, attributes, and centers. Cosmic and local gods continued to be worshiped throughout the historic period, with the cosmic deities usually assuming roles as state gods.

The Pantheon of Gods

As political development occurred in predynastic times and the villages joined together to become clans and eventually districts (nomes), the gods of each community were amalgamated and transformed from local deities into gods of the nomes. In this process called syncretism, deities of conquered or subordinated areas would be absorbed into the god of the victorious community. Any desirable features or characteristics of the conquered deities would be assimilated by the victorious god to enhance his own powers, or sometimes they would become assistants or followers of the god or would cease to exist. The chief god of a nome provided the regional chieftain with protection and had extensive powers; he would be represented by the ensign of the nome.

This amalgamation of local cults that had followed the political pattern resulted, by the Old Kingdom, in an expanded and confusing pantheon. It has also formed our probably erroneous impression that the Egyptians worshiped many gods; in practice each individual probably worshiped only one local god or group of gods. Nevertheless, there was such confusion by the Old Kingdom that the priesthood attempted to organize the gods in the pantheon either into family groups or into ogdoads (group of eight gods) or enneads (group of nine gods) according to their direct associations with particular cult centers. Creation myths (cosmogonies) and other mythologies were developed to emphasize the relationships between the deities of each group or family.

A pantheon of gods thus emerged and continued throughout the historic period. Some retained only local or limited significance, although they had cults and were worshiped in temples. Sometimes a particular line of rulers would elevate their own local god to become the dynasty's royal patron, with the deity acquiring, if only temporarily, the status of a state god. Nevertheless, most state gods continued to hold their place in the top league of deities throughout many centuries. Their powers extended throughout the whole of Egypt even if they had particular associations with certain cities and cult centers. They received cultic worship in the temples and were believed to influence the power and success of the nation in internal affairs and in foreign conquests. The divine patron and protector of each line of rulers was one of the state gods, and he became the supreme deity of that dynasty. Some, such as Re the sun god, Osiris the god of the dead, Isis the wife of Osiris, and Amun the king of the gods, achieved almost continuous and even international acclaim and worship as supreme deities.

THE GODS AND GODDESSES

There were hundreds of deities in the Egyptian pantheon. Here are some who represent the three main categories of state, local, and household gods.

State Gods

GODS OF THE ELEMENTS

According to the Heliopolitan cosmogony, Atum ("the Complete One") emerged from the primeval ocean (Nun) either as the son of Nun or by self-creation to bring forth the world from himself. His first act was to bring into existence the mound ("Island of Creation") on which he first stood; this was believed to be the location of the later temple of Heliopolis. As the earliest god to be worshiped at this center Atum was later associated with the sun god Re, to become Re-Atum, and was subsequently worshiped as a sun god. Since he was alone in the world, Atum had to create other gods from his own substance, and he proceeded to give birth to his son Shu (god of the air) by spitting him out and to his daughter Tefnut (goddess of moisture) by vomiting her forth.

Shu and Tefnut carried on the creative cycle, and from their union a son Geb (the earth god) and daughter Nut (the sky goddess) were born; their arrival completed all the cosmic elements necessary for creation (light, air, moisture, earth, and heaven). Geb and Nut in turn became the parents of two sons, Osiris and Seth, and two daughters, Isis and Nephthys, who were not cosmic deities. These gods made up the Heliopolitan Ennead (group of nine gods); this

Heliopolitan cosmogony was the most famous of the creation myths. Osiris married Isis, and Seth became the husband of Nephthys; the mythology surrounding Osiris's family is one of the greatest religious sources from ancient Egypt.

OSIRIS

Although Osiris was one of the greatest gods the Myth of Osiris is preserved completely only in Plutarch's writings, *De Iside et Osiride*. This relates how Osiris was an early human king who ruled Egypt and brought civilization and agriculture to the people. Murdered by his jealous brother Seth, Osiris's body was dismembered and scattered throughout Egypt. Isis (his sister-wife), however, gathered together and magically reunited his limbs and then posthumously conceived Osiris's son Horus. When grown, Horus sought to avenge his father's death by fighting Seth in a bloody conflict. Eventually their dispute was brought before the tribunal of gods whose judgement favored Osiris and Horus. Osiris was resurrected and continued his existence in the underworld where he became king and judge of the dead, while Horus became king of the living; Seth, now identified as the "Evil One," was banished.

In the Middle Kingdom the cult of Osiris became widespread and important; it offered resurrection and eternal life to followers who had lived according to the rules and emphasized that goodness rather then wealth ensured immortality. The two great cult centers of Osiris were Busiris and Abydos, which became a place of pilgrimage. The cult of Osiris had a profound effect on religious belief and practices, and the triad of Osiris, Isis, and Horus became a symbol of family virtues. Osiris and Horus were also directly associated with the concept of kingship, and Isis became the supreme mother goddess.

THE GODS OF MEMPHIS

Ptah was the creator of the universe and master of destiny according to the Memphite creation myth. He absorbed the functions of all the other gods and established ethics and morals, as well as creating food and drink, towns and buildings, and the forms and images of the gods. He achieved this through divine utterance. He is always shown in completely human form as a mummy. Later he acquired funerary characteristics and was associated with Osiris and with Sokar, the hawk-headed guardian of the Memphite necropolis. He was also worshiped in animal form as the Apis bull. This cult was practiced at Memphis where a bull selected because of its distinctive markings was kept in a sacred stall and, after death, mummified and buried in a special gallery (the Serapeum) at Saqqara. Ptah, however, never received widespread acclaim because his worship lacked a mythology that had popular appeal. Ptah's wife was the lioness goddess Sekhmet; their son was Nefertem, often shown as a youth seated upon or crowned with a lotus flower.

THE THEBAN TRIAD

Amun, chief god of Thebes, was originally one of the eight gods of Hermopolis. His cult increased in importance at Thebes from Dynasty 12, when a temple was built there for his worship. In Dynasty 18, when a family of Theban princes became kings of Egypt, Amun's cult reached unprecedented status. He became associated with and absorbed the characteristics of Re of Heliopolis to form the deity Amen-Re. Although briefly eclipsed as supreme state god by the Aten toward the end of Dynasty 18, Amun was soon reinstated as the great royal deity who was "Father of the Gods" and ruler of Egypt and the peoples of its empire. The conflict between the status and power of the king and of Amun was never resolved. Amun's consort Mut had an important center (the Temple of Luxor) near Amun's great complex at Karnak. Their son Khonsu was the moon god.

THE CULT OF THE ATEN

In the reign of Amenhotep IV (Akhenaten), the cult of the Aten ("sun's disk") became a form of monotheism; the temples of other gods were closed down and their priests were disbanded. The worship of the Aten was centered at a new capital city, Akhetaten (Tell el-Amarna). Although the doctrine of Atenism included some new concepts, many of the ideas, such as the god's international role and association with plant and animal life, were developments of earlier beliefs.

ASSISTANT GODS

Some deities played important roles as assistants in the major mythologies. Thoth, the ibis-headed scribal god of wisdom and writing, had an important cult and creation mythology associated with Hermopolis. He also featured in the mythologies of Ptah at Memphis, Re at Heliopolis, and Osiris. In the Osirian Judgment of the Dead he recorded the verdict of the Negative Confession. Anubis, the jackal-headed god of cemeteries and embalming, also assisted at this occasion, weighing the heart of the deceased in the balance.

Local Gods

Some gods retained only a local importance and were worshiped in temples at particular sites. Sobek, the crocodile god, was a form of Seth and had temples at various places, but particularly in the Fayoum and at Kom Ombo. Montu, the falcon-headed god of war, was worshiped at

Armant, but in Dynasty 11 he was elevated to become the protector of the royal line that originated there. These are just two examples of a wide range of local gods.

Household Gods

Some deities did not receive temple cults but nevertheless played an important part in protecting and comforting people of all classes. They were worshiped at shrines in the home. The best known are Bes and his consort Tauert. Bes, represented as an ugly dwarf wearing a feathered crown, protected children and women in childbirth; he was the god of marriage and jollification. Tauert, shown as a pregnant female hippopotamus, was a symbol of fecundity and assisted all females (divine, royal, or ordinary) in childbirth. (A discussion of household gods and domestic worship follows later in this chapter.)

TEMPLES AND TEMPLE ART

There are two temple traditions in ancient Egypt. The sun temples of Dynasty 5 and Aten temples of Dynasty 18 probably derive from the same concept that may have been introduced into Egypt from elsewhere. The cultus and mortuary temples of the New Kingdom, however, developed from the predynastic local shrine that contained the cult statue; the leader of each village or community would have erected a primitive shrine (probably constructed of a matting of woven reeds attached to a wooded framework) in which he enacted the rites to honor the local god. By contrast the later temples were massive stone monuments, but they retained the same basic plan and features of the earliest hut shrines. The most powerful chieftain eventually became the king. His local god was translated into the national deity, and so it was the king (or his delegate, the high priest) who continued to perform the rituals in the temples, offering food, drink, and clothing to the deity's statue.

Cultus and Mortuary Temples

The temples, like the tombs, were designed to last forever and consequently were built of stone. The uses of "cultus" and "mortuary" temples were distinct, but their architecture and rituals had much in common. The cultus temple was a place where the god's statue could be housed and protected; as a place of great sanctity, it provided a location of spiritual potency where the king or priest could approach the god and, through the rituals, present offerings from which the god would derive benefit and sustenance. In return it was believed that the god conferred bounty upon Egypt, the king, and the people. Without such a relationship and performance of the rituals, it was feared that disaster would befall the country.

The mortuary temple had an additional function. Originally attached to the pyramid as part of the king's burial complex in the Old and Middle Kingdoms, the mortuary temple was the place where the funerary rites were performed and where perpetual offerings were placed to ensure the continuing sustenance of the spirit of the deceased ruler. When the kings ceased to build pyramids, however, and began in the New Kingdom to construct rock-cut tombs in the Valley of the Kings, there was no longer

The hypostyle hall in the Temple of Hathor at Denderah (Ptolemaic Period) has columns with capitals that represent Hathor as a cow-eared deity with a human face. Scenes on the walls and columns depict rites once performed in the temple.

sufficient space to build adjacent mortuary temples or offering chapels. Instead the mortuary temples were now separate buildings, mostly erected on the west bank at Thebes. They still provided a place where the dead, deified ruler continued to be worshiped and to receive food offerings. These temples also had a cultus function since they were dedicated to the cult of the chief local deity, and thus they incorporated rituals for both the god and the king.

All cultus and mortuary temples had the same basic layout and architectural features, but there were some minor differences. Cultus temples had space and provision only for the rituals offered to the resident god, whereas mortuary temples included additional areas for the worship of the dead, deified king and for his predecessors, the royal ancestors.

Temple Architecture and Design

Mythology and ritual requirements dictated the basic form, layout, and architectural features of the temple so that there are only minor variations between temples of different dates and at various sites. There are three major mythological interpretations of the temple: It was the "Mansion of the God" where the deity resided; it was the "Island of Creation" where the god on the "First Occasion" had created all the elements of life and universe; and it was a microcosm of the universe or a reflection of the heavens.

As the House of God it fulfilled the same function as the domestic home for its owner or the tomb for the deceased: It provided shelter, protection, and, as at the tomb, a place of worship. The design of the temple thus followed the pattern of the house; enclosed within a mud brick wall, the temple was rectangular and provided accommodation for the god equivalent to a bedroom, reception area, and storerooms for possessions. However, the plan was modified to accommodate a central processional route and to provide space for the rituals, so the building was elongated in plan. Leading from one or two courts (open to the sky) at the front, a central doorway on the main axis of the building gave access to the area that was covered by a roof. Here a processional route passed through one or two hypostyle (columned) halls (the reception area) into the sanctuary (bedroom) situated centrally at the rear of the temple. Arranged around the sanctuary were several chambers where the god's possessions were stored.

That the temple was the Island of Creation was also reflected in the architecture. The enclosure wall was constructed in sections in which the bricks, arranged in alternative concave and convex sections, formed wavy lines which represented the primeval ocean from which the island had emerged. The heavy stone columns in the hypostyle halls had palmiform, lotiform, or papyriform capitals which represented the lush vegetation on the island, while the ceiling was decorated to symbolize the sky above the island, and a frieze of plants carved on the base of the walls recreated the island vegetation. Even the floor level, gradually ascending from the front of the temple to the sanctuary and then sloping down again at the rear, reproduced the shape of the island with the god's resting place at the highest point.

Wall Scenes

The wall scenes in every temple had specific functions: In some areas (hypostyle halls) they represent historical events such as the coronation ceremony or foundation of the temple,

An early twentieth-century photograph showing temples on the island of Philae, partly covered by the annual inundation. After the first dam was built at Aswan, the island was submerged for much of the year, but following the construction of the High Dam in the 1960s, the temples were dismantled and moved to a neighboring island, as part of the UNESCO Salvage Campaign.

whereas in others they depict the different rituals that were once performed in those parts of the building. Arranged in two or three horizontal registers on each wall, the scenes always show the king (as the god's divine son and rightful heir) performing the rites for the god. He alone, because of his uniquely divine nature, would be efficacious in presenting the offerings, although in actuality it would have been the high priest as his delegate who usually performed the rites.

The scenes show the figures in poses that are in strict accordance with the principles governing religious art. The accompanying inscriptions give the title of each rite and the speeches of the king and gods in the scene as they address each other. This selection of scenes would have been taken from a complete version of the ritual, which was preserved on papyrus.

PRIESTS

Role in Society

The Egyptian term that is now translated as "priest" actually meant "god's servant." This title was held by a man whose main duty was to act on behalf of the king (god's son) in the temple, performing the rituals to fulfill the deity's needs. State religion was believed to perpetuate and maintain the equilibrium of the universe; the rituals ensured the king's immortality and success over his enemies and also the fertility of the land and its people. If these duties were neglected or abandoned the result would be chaos and disaster. The priests, however, had no pastoral duties and were not expected to preach to the people or oversee their moral welfare; indeed, they played no direct role in developing the religious awareness or beliefs of the masses.

Although the priests' training, preserved in the Instructions in Wisdom, emphasized the need for moral and social standards of behavior including discretion in speech, honesty, and fairness toward others, those entering the priesthood were not considered to have a vocation or to belong to a special sect of people who had experienced divine revelation. They were expected to become dedicated officials and functionaries who performed their temple and liturgical duties efficiently. It was the wealth and privilege that a career as a priest offered that attracted ambitious, able, and even sometimes unscrupulous candidates.

The role of the priest can be traced back to the time of the predynastic communities when the leader would approach the local god on behalf of his people, presenting regular food offerings to the god's statue in the village shrine. Most of these functions continued, although on a grander scale, until well into the Greco-Roman Period when Christianity became widespread in Egypt and all the temples were finally closed.

Recruitment and Training

Priests were recruited in various ways. It was traditional for a son to follow his father, as in other professions and trades; however, the appointment of high priests and some promotions were made by the king, exercising his ultimate right of selection. He could move men from one temple to another or even from the royal court or the army into the priesthood. In other cases candidates were selected for vacancies by a committee of priests, and sometimes an office was purchased by the payment of a fee.

After his appointment the novice priest probably underwent training in religious knowledge and ritual practices before he was initiated into the secret wisdom of the god's cult. One important aspect was the fact that most of the temple employees were lay priests, particularly during the Old and Middle Kingdoms. Even in later times when the larger temples had a class of permanent priests, the lay or part-time priests continued to predominate in the smaller communities.

Duties and Restrictions

Their duties were organized around a system in which four groups of lay priests in each temple performed the duties for the god. Each group consisted of the same number of priests and served on a rotational basis for three months each year. A term of duty lasted for one month, followed by a three-month break before the next commitment. In the free period they could pursue ordinary lives and other careers (often as doctors, scribes, or lawyers); they could marry and live outside the temple except during their periods of duty when they were expected to reside within the temple enclosure.

At the bottom of the hierarchy was the *waab* priest, a term that indicated he was ritually pure and could therefore enter the presence of the divine statue and have direct contact with the god's possessions. To reach this level of physical purity the priest had to wash in cold water twice a day and twice at night (usually carried out in the Sacred Lake of the temple) and clean his mouth with natron (a mixture of sodium carbonate and bicarbonate of soda, which occurred in natural deposits in Egypt and was also used for mummification and laundry purposes). He was also required to shave his head and body every day. Priests were circumcised (probably after they had entered the priesthood) and were expected to practice sexual abstinence while they were performing their temple duties. They could only wear linen clothes and shoes made from plant products; materials such as wool and leather which came from living animals were forbidden. Some foods were also prohibited; fish and beans were probably generally unacceptable, and permission to eat many other items such as pork, lamb, beef, pigeon, and garlic may have varied from one area to another where particular plants or meats were associated with individual deities.

Temple Hierarchy

Some temples, such as that of Amun at Karnak, owned vast estates and had large numbers of employees. In the reign of Ramesses III it is recorded that there were over 80,000 employees at Karnak and that it owned more than 2,000 square kilometers (772 square miles) of land. The most important post was that of high priest of Amun (First Prophet of Amun); this carried great political power (generally, the temples became the largest employers in Egypt), extensive wealth, and the ownership of a great house and large estates. From the New Kingdom onward, the high priest of Amun had the right to confer or withhold the god's approval of the royal heir (thus giving him control over the kingship). At the great assemblies to which the temples sent priests to represent their views to the king on matters such as temple taxes, revenues, and building programs, the high priests also exercised considerable power.

Below the high priest were the ranks of the fathers of the god (the Second, Third, and Fourth Prophets of Amun) and then the ordinary priests (*waab*). The lay workers who serviced the temple, its estates, and workshops included stewards, overseers of granaries and estates, clerks, and police.

In smaller institutions there were generally three categories of employees. The senior priests performed the daily rituals for the gods and included among their ranks the specialists who worked in the "House of Life." This institution was attached to all the major temples; here, the sacred texts that perpetuated the divine cult were composed and copied, and the scribes (who included priests and lay scholars) discussed and developed the god's theology and mythology, composed religious, astronomical, and medical texts, and probably gave instructions to students.

There were also minor clergy who assisted with various religious duties and rituals and conducted the more mundane aspects of running the temple, such as supervising the renovation and decoration of the temple. Finally, there was the auxiliary staff: architects, painters, sculptors, doorkeepers, guards, estate workers who produced the food for the god, craftsmen who made the god's clothing and the utensils used in the rituals, and the butchers, bakers, confectioners, and florists who prepared the divine daily offerings. There were also temple cleaners. None of these workers were priests, but their services were vital.

RELIGIOUS RITUALS

The Egyptians believed that the living, the dead, and the gods all had the same basic needs—shelter, food and drink, washing, rest, and recreation. The living were accommodated in houses, the dead were provided with tombs, and the gods resided in temples. Food was supplied for the dead by means of the funerary cult, and the god's needs were met through the divine rituals. Once performed within certain areas of the temple, they are still depicted and preserved in the scenes carved and painted on many of the interior walls of the temple.

Usually arranged in two or three horizontal registers, some scenes have a formal content or depict a single, important event in the reign such as the king's coronation or the foundation or consecration of the temple. Others, however, represent rituals that were once performed regularly in certain areas of the temple. Arranged in a particular sequence and order, these show the content of each rite, while the accompanying inscriptions provide its title and the speeches of the god and king as the king performs the sacred actions for the god. The scenes not only supply evidence that indicates the ritual use of that area or chamber but also preserve important information about the rituals that were once enacted in the temple.

It was believed that the Ceremony of Opening the Mouth, performed at the consecration of the temple when it was formally handed over to the resident god, would recharge the vital energy of the building and all the wall reliefs and statues within it. The temple would thus assume all the spiritual potency of the original "Island of Creation," the location it sought to re-create, and the rituals depicted in the wall scenes would through magic continue to be performed on

A temple scene (c.1450 BC) in which the king drops pellets of incense into an incense burner. Used as a fumigant, incense was an important element of many temple rituals, and the Egyptians traveled to Punt to obtain it.

behalf of the god even if the rites should be discontinued at any time.

Daily Temple Rituals

One group of temple rituals was enacted on a daily basis, and these followed the same pattern for all temple gods throughout the country. The Daily Temple Ritual was carried out in all cultus and mortuary temples from at least as early as Dynasty 18. It provided a ritualized and dramatized version of the mundane processes of washing, clothing, and feeding the god's cult statue in the sanctuary. The priest (acting as the king's delegate) entered the sanctuary each morning and lifted the god's statue out of its box shrine and placed it on the altar immediately in front. He then removed its clothing and makeup of the previous day, before fumigating the image with different kinds of incense and presenting it with balls of natron (which the Egyptians chewed in order to cleanse the breath). The priest then dressed the statue in fresh clothes, decorated its face with makeup, and presented it with jewelry and insignia. Finally he gave the god the morning meal and withdrew backwards from the sanctuary. He presented two other meals at noon and in the evening before replacing the statue in the box shrine.

This ritual included elements from the mythologies of Re and Osiris and was intended to revitalize the god and reaffirm his daily rebirth. Neglect of these duties would, it was believed, ensure the return of chaos, the state that had prevailed before the universe was created. Correct observance of the rites would, however, be rewarded by divine favor: Temple religion, based on a compact between gods and men, ensured that the gods received temples, food, and other offerings, and booty from military campaigns in return for their gifts of power, fame, immortality, and success in battle for the king and fertility, peace, and prosperity for Egypt and its people.

From the New Kingdom onward another ritual was performed in the mortuary temples at the conclusion of the Daily Temple Ritual. Known as the "Ritual of the Royal Ancestors," this attempted to ensure that the former legitimate kings of Egypt gave their support to the reigning king. After his death this ruler would join them, and so the ritual also sought to gain benefits and eternal sustenance for him.

The food was removed from the god's altar at the conclusion of the Daily Temple Ritual and taken to another area of the temple. After some preliminary rites it was offered to the ancestors (usually represented in the temple in the form of a list of kings inscribed on a wall). The food was subsequently removed intact from this altar and taken outside the temple to be divided between the priests as their daily payment. In the cultus temples this division took place immediately after the Daily Temple Ritual.

Festival Rituals

The second group of rituals represented the festivals. These did not follow the same order in all the temples but varied from place to place, reflecting the unique mythology of each deity. They were held at regular, often annual, intervals and celebrated special events in the gods' lives. Festivals which marked the annual death and resurrection of Osiris, god of the dead, and the conjugal visits between other famous deities were most popular. Some stages of these events were performed inside the temples, but there were also celebrations outside the temple enclosure when the god's portable statue was paraded in a sacred boat and carried among the crowds. This public procession was the only occasion when the masses had the opportunity to see the god and participate in his worship. These were noisy and spectacular events accompanied by singing and dancing, and the most important festivals attracted large numbers of pilgrims who traveled from all over Egypt.

Role of the King

Although the priests acted as the god's servants and in reality performed all the rituals, it was the figure of the king who was shown performing this role in all the temple wall scenes. This preserved the fiction that he alone carried out every rite in all the temples. As the incarnation of the god Horus and the son of Re and divine heir only he could act as mankind's agent in the presence of the gods. The Egyptians considered the rituals to be effective only if they were enacted by the king to whom the gods had given the rulerships; only he could attend to their needs and execute their orders. Originally each tribal chieftain had performed all the rites on behalf of the local god, but in later times the kings could not personally attend to all the state and religious duties. These were largely delegated to senior officials and functionaries, although the king may have continued to perform the Daily Temple Ritual in the main temple of the chief god and to attend the consecration ceremony of each temple built during his reign.

RELIGIOUS ARTIFACTS

The Egyptian belief in magical powers and properties influenced many areas of their lives. Inanimate objects were believed to have the ability to affect events once they had been charged with magical force. Objects and wall reliefs in tombs and temples were "brought to life" with the performance of the "Ceremony of Opening the Mouth." Although it was originally used only in royal tombs and temples, this rite was eventually also employed in nonroyal situations to restore the life force and original qualities to mummies, statues, models, and wall reliefs within the tomb. The priest would cense, sprinkle with water, and touch the mouth,

A wall relief (Temple of Amun, Karnak) depicting a festival procession; priests are shown carrying the god's statue in a bark outside the temple precinct. The king (left) offers burning incense to the god, purifying the space around the bark. c.1450 BC.

hands, and feet of the mummy, statue, or wall relief with an adze to enable the owner's spirit to enter the image and partake of the food offerings placed at the tomb.

Amulets

Funerary equipment was considered to have magical properties that could bring special benefits to the deceased. Amulets formed an important group of jewelry since they acted as lucky charms and could be worn by rich and poor alike. They were carried by the person when alive and placed with the deceased to provide help in his future existence. The term *amulet* that is applied to this particular type of jewelry comes from the later Arabic word *hamulet* meaning "something that is borne or carried." The primary function of all Egyptian jewelry was to protect the wearer against a range of hostile forces and events, which included ferocious animals, disease, famine, accidents, and natural disasters. Amulets were believed to possess special beneficial properties and, by the principles of sympathetic magic, to be able to attract good forces to assist the wearer or, conversely, to repel a variety of evils and dangers.

Some amulets were regarded as universally beneficial while others had particular significance only for the owner. Essentially they were charms that had been magically charged in order to bring about the desired results. Some were designed to strengthen the owner's ability to overcome the dangers he encountered and took the form of images of power such as miniature crowns, scepters, and staffs of office while others represented gods or animals. Another group were believed to have an impact on any physical weakness or disability from which the owner might suffer; these were modeled to simulate the limbs in the hope that the amulet would attract magical strength to heal the afflicted part or that the disease would be transferred from the limb to the amulet "double."

Other amulets represented offerings (food, drink, or clothing) and possessions to ensure that the owner would continue to enjoy wealth and prosperity. A number of amulet forms were considered to be particularly potent. These included the Sacred Eye of Horus (Wedjat), which symbolized completeness or wholeness; the *ankh*, which represented life; the *djed* pillar, which was associated with resurrection and rebirth as well as strength and stability; and the *tit* symbol, which signified fertility. The scarab (dung beetle) symbolized eternal renewal of life. The Egyptians made this association because when they observed the habits of the beetle each new generation seemed to emerge, self-generated, from the sand. This assumption was, of course, inaccurate; the adult beetle lays its eggs in the sand from which the new beetles emerge sometime later.

The shape of an amulet conferred power and strength on its owner, but some materials and colors were also believed to possess special hidden qualities that could bring health and good luck. Stones such as carnelian, turquoise, and lapis lazuli were much favored because of the magical properties of their colors, and they were often used in the manufacture of jewelry and amulets. Sometimes stones were selected for amulets if they duplicated the color of the original limb or organ, and this authenticity was expected to bring additional benefits to the owner.

Divine Possessions

The clothes, crowns, jewelry, and insignia that belonged to the god were considered to be especially sacred because of their physical proxim-

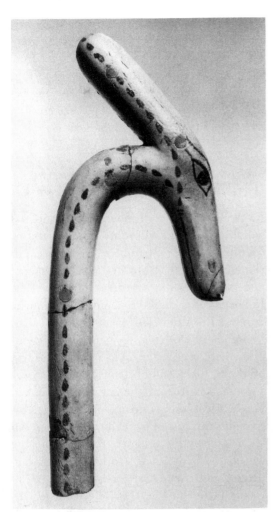

A faience was-scepter representing a gazelle head. Scepters were believed to give the owner spiritual dominion, and they are often shown in the hands of gods and kings. This example, from Nagada (c.1450 BC), may have been used in temple rituals.

It was also essential that the priests who came into direct contact with the divine statue and possessions should be ritually pure, and this was achieved by the observance of special procedures and prohibitions. The god's crowns were believed to give particular strengths and powers to the deity, and the colors of these and the cloths which were placed on the cult statue each gave him their own protection.

CREATION MYTHS

Creation myths (cosmogonies) attempted to explain the origin and creation of the universe. They were first formalized during the Old Kingdom, when the priesthoods of the most important gods tried to rationalize and coordinate the multitude of cults and multiplicity of deities that made up the predynastic pantheon. Some cities became great religious centers associated with particular gods or groups of gods who each had their own theology. Every center tried to claim the supremacy of its own god and to establish his principal role in the creation of the universe, all other gods, and mankind. The three main cosmogonies were established during the Old Kingdom, but others (such as the Theban cosmogony, centered around Amun) developed later.

All the major myths claimed that each center was the place where the primordial mound, the "Island of Creation," had emerged from the ocean. Life had begun here and each priesthood claimed that their own god's temple was the physical location of that mythical island and therefore a place of great spiritual and magical potency. At this "First Occasion" light and land came into existence and the first god, in the form

ity to the divine cult statue in the temple. Similarly the utensils used to prepare and carry the god's daily food offerings in the temple rituals had their own magical properties. These possessions were kept in special rooms in the temple and were regularly cleansed in the ritually "pure" waters of the temple's sacred lake.

of a bird, alighted on the island. After this there was a gradual but steady development in the process of civilization until a golden age emerged when the gods ruled on earth, establishing law, ethics, and all the elements for orderly human existence. At the end of this era the gods returned to the heavens, but they directed the king to rule Egypt as their heir and successor according to the principles of *ma'at* (divine order, equilibrium, and justice) in order that the conditions of the golden age could be continued forever.

The Heliopolitan Myth

The most famous and influential cosmogony emerged at Iwnw (Heliopolis); it centered around Re-Atum (Re, the sun god, had assimilated some of the characteristics of Atum, an earlier deity at the site). The main source for this Heliopolitan myth are the Pyramid Texts, and the myth clearly had a great influence on many aspects of religion.

Two groups of gods feature in this myth; these are the Great Ennead (group of nine gods), which included Re-Atum, Shu, Tefnut, Geb, Nut, Osiris, Isis, Seth, and Nephthys, and the Lesser Ennead, which was led by Horus, the son of Osiris and Isis. Re-Atum brought himself into existence by self-generation and produced children (Shu and Tefnut, representing air and moisture) who in turn became the parents of Geb (the earth) and Nut (the sky). These gods were all cosmic deities and personified the elements that were required for creation to take place. The children of Geb and Nut—Osiris, Isis, Seth, and Nephthys—were not cosmic.

The myth recounts that Re-Atum took the form of the mythical Bennu bird and alighted on the benben (a pillar associated with the sun god) when he arrived at the island. In Re's temple at Heliopolis the benben was the god's cult symbol. It had probably been there from the earliest years of the cult, and it was perhaps a conically shaped stone. The Egyptians believed that it marked the exact place of creation where the sun god had first alighted.

The Memphite Myth

Re-Atum's greatest rival was Ptah, who was worshiped as the supreme creator god at Memphis. The Memphite creation myth claimed that Ptah was in fact Nun (the state of nonexistence prior to the creation) and that he had begotten a daughter, Naunet, by whom he fathered Re-Atum. This placed Ptah ahead of Re-Atum in the creation geneology. Memphite theology (preserved in a much later text on the Shabaka Stone) claimed that Ptah was supreme creator of the universe who had brought everything into existence through his thoughts (expressed by the heart) and his will (expressed by his tongue). Ptah created the world, the gods, their centers, shrines, and images and the cities, food, drink, and all requirements for life. He also established abstract concepts and principles such as divine utterance and ethics. Ptah's mythology had no widespread popular appeal, however, and although he received royal support he was never adopted as supreme royal patron.

The Hermopolitan Myth

The third great cosmogony emerged at Hermopolis, the cult center of Thoth, god of wisdom. There were several versions of the Hermopolitan myth, but they all attempted to establish the center's supremacy and primal role in creation. In one account the Hermopolitan Ogdoad (group of eight gods) played the major role: the four males—Nun (primeval waters), Huh (eternity), Kuk (darkness), and Amun (air)—and their female consorts—Naunet, Hauhet, Kauket, and Amaunet—created the world immediately after the First Occasion. When these frog-headed males and serpent-headed females eventually died, they continued their existence in the underworld where they made the Nile flow and the sun rise so that life could continue on earth.

In another version a cosmic egg replaced the primordial ocean as the source of life. A bird (either a goose called the "great Cackler" or an ibis representing Thoth) laid this egg on the island and, when it opened, it contained air (essential for life) or, in a variant, the god Re was inside a bird when he proceeded to create the world. Yet another account describes how the ogdoad created a lotus flower that arose out of the "Sea of Knives" (perhaps the Sacred Lake of the temple at Hermopolis). When the flower opened its petals it revealed either the child Re who then created the world or a scarab that changed into a boy whose tears became mankind.

Later Myths

In the New Kingdom the Theban cosmogony, which was developed at the Temple at Amen-Re at Karnak, claimed that Thebes was the original site of creation where Amen-Re had made all gods and mankind. A later, less important myth described how Khnum, the ram-headed god of Elephantine, had modeled men and women on his potter's wheel.

HOUSEHOLD GODS AND DOMESTIC WORSHIP

Although ordinary people may have understood something of the god's role within the temple and had contact with the temple deities during the festival processions, their religious practices were generally directed toward another group for which we use the term "household gods," since they were generally worshiped at small shrines in houses. People approached these gods for guidance and assistance about various aspects of their lives and, although the gods did not possess temples, cults, or priesthoods, they were worshiped at all levels of society.

Evidence for this popular religion has to be sought in the settlement sites (cities, towns, and villages), which have survived less well than the tombs or temples. However, three of the towns that were populated by the workers (and their families) who constructed and decorated the royal tombs have been discovered and excavated. Objects and documents found at these sites have provided insight into the personal religion of these families.

Religious Worship at Deir el-Medina

It is evident that the tomb laborers and their families considered religion to be very important. At the site known as Deir el-Medina, where a town was built to accommodate the workmen who constructed the royal tombs in the Valley of the Kings during the New Kingdom, there were several important cults. Perhaps surprisingly the great state god Amen-Re was treated by these residents as their local god and

A terra-cotta figure of the god Bes, represented here as a Roman soldier. Shown as a bowlegged dwarf wearing a feathered headdress, Bes was popular as a magical protector, and his influence continued into later times. Roman Period.

been introduced into Egypt from Asia or Ethiopia at a very early date. As the god of love, marriage, dancing, and jollification he also assisted at childbirth and protected the young and weak. He attended the circumcision ceremony and defeated the forces of evil by making music, singing, and dancing. Represented as a bowlegged dwarf with a feathered crown, he always wore a hideous mask and was often shown playing a musical instrument.

Bes's consort, Tauert, was the goddess of fertility and childbirth who was present to assist women of all classes at the birth of their children. She was depicted as an upstanding pregnant hippopotamus. Other important goddesses at Deir el-Medina were Hathor the cow goddess, Mertetseger the serpent goddess of the Theban necropolis, and "Peak-of-the-West" the personification of the mountain situated above the Valley of the Kings. At Deir el-Medina there is also evidence of several Asiatic gods.

An important aspect of popular religion at Deir el-Medina was the use of an oracle. This was worked by the priests (who were chosen from within the workforce by the workmen themselves) who held the god's statue in front of the petitioner and made it move in a particular direction in response to his inquiry. The priests claimed that through them the deified Amenhotep I thus gave advice to the petitioners over personal quarrels and family concerns; he even ruled on law cases since it was acceptable to seek an oracular answer instead of the decision given by the local law court. The priests also organized local festivals when the divine statues would be carried in procession through the town. In general this community enjoyed great religious and legal autonomy.

Domestic gods were worshiped at a shrine filled with stelae, offering tables, water jars, braziers, and vases in a separate area of the

regarded as the arbiter of divine justice and protector of the weak and poor. These families worshiped Amun and addressed their personal prayers to him. There was also an important cult to the royal patron and founder of the community, King Amenhotep I and his mother Queen Ahmose-Nefertari. They received the unusual honor of deification and personal worship even after death.

Two gods were widely worshiped at Deir el-Medina and throughout Egypt. Bes was a jolly but grotesque dwarf whose cult may have home. Worship at home probably reflected the rituals performed in the great temples and would have included the presentation of food offerings and libations and the burning of incense in front of the god's statue.

At Deir el-Medina there is evidence of a particularly interesting and very unusual aspect of personal piety. Memorial stelae (stones) set up in some of the offering chapels by the workmen have inscriptions in which the workmen appeal to the gods for help. Some express humility (a rare admission in formal inscriptions in Egypt) and gratitude to the god for delivering the person from illness or affliction believed to have been the result of his own sins. These appeals for mercy and confession of sins have prompted scholarly interest; one suggestion is that these were new ideas perhaps introduced by Syrian immigrants, but others claim that such concepts had probably always been part of popular faith, but because of the high level of literacy at Deir el-Medina they were more frequently written down there and have therefore survived. The workmen's transgressions appear to have included impiety and swearing falsely by a god's name; blindness seems to have been regarded as a special punishment for sins against a god.

Religious Worship at Tell el-Amarna and Kahun

At the other royal workmen's towns at Tell el-Amarna and Kahun similar household cults have been discovered. Although Tell el-Amarna was the capital built at the end of Dynasty 18 specifically to promote King Akhenaten's monotheistic cult of the Aten, the workmen's village provides evidence that they retained their religious independence and continued to worship such popular deities as Bes and Tauert.

At Kahun some aspects of the community's religious practices that are somewhat unusual may be due to the presence of foreign immigrants among the workforce. Nonetheless, the gods worshiped in this town (built in Dynasty 12) include the usual domestic deities, and it is evident that offerings of food were presented in household shrines. Several roughly carved stone dish stands have been discovered in the houses, and these were probably used for offering bread or dough to the god's statue. Although these incorporate unusual features, it is difficult to determine if they really represent foreign religion or if they were a purely local development of Egyptian popular cults. Another strange religious custom found at Kahun was the practice of burying babies in boxes underneath the floors of some of the houses. In Egypt it was usual to inter the dead on the edge of the desert, but similar intramural burials have occurred at various Near Eastern sites.

MAGIC

By one definition, magic is the apparent manipulation of supernatural forces to change the form of things or influence events. The Egyptians believed that magic was the "key" that enabled them to attain wisdom, and there was no real distinction between magic and religion. Magic was regarded not as low-level sorcery but as a sacred science and creative force that had existed prior to the establishment of the universe. The Egyptian word for magic, *heka*, probably meant "to control powers."

Magic existed at all levels and permeated most aspects of the society. State and private magic were not contradictory methods but were believed to influence two different areas. Through the temples cosmic magic sought by means of the daily rituals to maintain the balance and order of the universe and to prevent the return of chaos. By offering to the gods the priests attempted to renew the process of creation, ensure immortality, earthly fame, and success for the king and to bring fertility and prosperity to the land. This great temple magic (designed to preserve the world order) was regarded as an exact science and was revealed only to the elite body of temple priests.

On the other hand, private magic executed by local magicians was practiced to protect individuals against their own fears, which included sickness, harmful animals, drowning, hunger, thirst, aggression, and asphyxiation. Using simple spells, these magicians possessed secret tech-

A tomb scene (c.1450 BC) in which the owner and his wife worship a tree goddess who offers food and pours a libation of water over them.

niques and probably some basic healing skills. One of their first duties would be to try to overcome these perils and afflictions, believed to be caused by negative energy, by blocking off the negative forces.

Within the temples magical forces were believed to be present in the architectural forms of the building (which re-created the "Island of Creation"), the representations of the rituals depicted on the temple walls (which were activated by the performance of the "Ceremony of Opening the Mouth"), and the god's cult statue (which his spirit entered to receive the food offerings). The temple inscriptions placed on the temple walls or written in the great ritual books also provided a potent source of magic. By writing the sacred words or reciting the ritual spells the priests made the temple magic alive and effective.

In medical treatment magic played an important role alongside more objective methods. In cases where the cause of the illness or affliction was visible or evident scientific methods were usually employed based on observation of the patient's symptoms, but where the cause was not apparent the malady might be attributed to vengeance of the dead, malevolence of enemies, or punishment of the gods and consequently treated by magical methods. These involved the use of spells and rituals that could include dances, musical instruments to create a particular mental state, dolls or waxen images, and agents such as water, oil, wine, perfume, and incense.

Magic obviously also played an important role in funerary beliefs and customs; tomb wall scenes were magically activated, as were the tomb models, statues, and mummy, to provide the deceased with all the requirements for the next world. Special jewelry, particularly the sacred charms known as amulets, gave the owner magical protection as he journeyed to the next world.

For the living magic permeated almost every aspect of their beliefs. The colors and jewelry they wore were believed to influence their fortune, and magic even played a role in the law courts where oracles were used to obtain verdicts in some legal cases. To the Egyptians magic was the thread that linked everything, because all things were regarded as potentially animate if the correct magical procedures were performed.

The Priest-Magician

The summit of the magician's skill was to possess the ability to control the forces of nature. It was believed that they knew and could control the supernatural force that created and maintained life. The magician could use this power to achieve results in this world and in the afterlife.

Magicians were regarded as priests and scholars who could read and write the hieroglyphs, which gave them ultimate knowledge and control. They were trained for many years, and as apprentice magicians were instructed by masters at special schools and temples. In the House of Life attached to many of the temples the priest-magician would be taught to read and understand the sacred texts. Here the official Books of Magic were kept as part of the royal archive. Magic was thus an integral element of the state system, and magicians were never regarded as "strange" or abnormal. Their activities, whether for the state or for the individual, were part of mainstream belief and practice.

It was though that since they were in direct contact with the architect of the universe and knew the secrets that went back to earliest times, magicians could re-create the conditions of the time of creation. With their unique knowledge the magicians were expected to guide others along the path of wisdom. Although the events

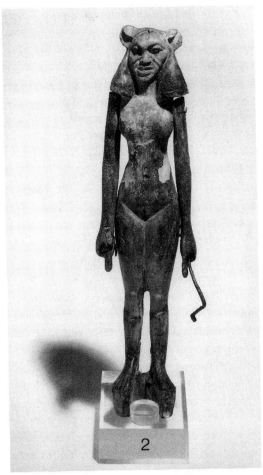

A wooden figurine representing the divine magician Beset. She has jointed arms, wears a mask, and holds two copper serpents. Found with a group of magical objects and papyri in a tomb near the Ramesseum at Thebes (c.1700 BC).

cians. One was found in a hole in the floor of a room in a house of Kahun (the pyramid work-men's town) and included a wooden, masked figurine (representing a magician in a costume with a tail) and a pair of ivory clappers. In the next room there was a full-size cartonnage mask representing the god Bes. It is likely that these items were worn and used by a local magician in some kind of ritual ceremony in which he sought to imitate Bes and take on his magical powers.

The other group was discovered in a tomb near to the funerary temple of Ramesses II at Thebes. This probably belonged to a temple priest and was of the same date as the Kahun material (Dynasty 12). It included a wooden box containing papyri; figures in glaze, stone, wood, and metal, which were probably used as substitutes for living persons once they had been magically animated; ivory wands with which magic working circles were delineated; and ivory pieces incised with figures of animals, designed to expel evil forces and capture the animals' strength and power. These two groups provide a unique opportunity to compare contemporary sets of equipment; one probably belonged to a priest-magician who practiced his art in a temple, while the other was owned by a magician who used his skills to help his community.

of an individual's life were believed to some extent to be predestined, magic could be used to influence and change the course of destiny and to avoid some of the dangers.

Magical Tools and Objects

Two interesting groups of objects have been discovered that clearly belonged to two magi-

PERSONAL PIETY, ETHICS, AND MORALS

Egyptian religious texts do not preserve any details about concepts of personal piety, ethics, and morals; most information can only be gleaned from education literature such as the

Instructions in Wisdom and the Schoolboy Letters. In addition there are the prayers of the workmen on the memorial stelae at Deir el-Medina, which provide some insight into attitudes about humility and salvation.

The Instructions in Wisdom usually take the form of an older, wise man (king, vizier, or father) addressing his son or pupils and giving them advice about standards of behavior and rules for conducting personal relationships. The earliest known examples date to the Old Kingdom, and it is evident that the Egyptians had already developed an ethical code that was believed to have been divinely authorized. On the "First Occasion" (the time of creation) it was thought that all the elements for a civilized existence, including ethics and laws, had been handed down from the gods.

The earliest extant example of a wisdom instruction is accredited to Prince Hardedef, the son of Cheops, builder of the Great Pyramid. Hardedef may indeed have been the actual author of the piece, as he was later revered as a sage and probably received a personal cult. The text is addressed to his son, Au-ib-re, whom he advised to build his life and career wisely for the future.

The best-known wisdom text is attributed to Ptah-hotep, a vizier of Dynasty 5. His text includes thirty-seven maxims emphasizing the importance of obedience to one's father or superior and extolling the virtues of modesty, humility, self-control, truthfulness, tact, and good manners. It also provides guidance on how to deal fairly and generously with superiors, peers, and inferiors. Not only did this text seek to offer advice on good conduct but it was regarded as a model of fine language and literary expression. In the Instruction for Kagemni (which is set in Dynasty 3, although it probably dates to Dynasty 6), King Huni tells his vizier to write down his own wisdom and experience for the benefit of his children, among whom is the future vizier Kagemni. Again it offers advice on how to pursue a successful course in life.

By the New Kingdom new instructions were still being composed as an important literary genre, but they reflected the changes in society, particularly the emphasis on middle-class rather than aristocratic values. In the Instruction of Any, a minor official addressed his son; a new element is introduced in the epilogue where the son questions his father's advice. This would never have occurred in the earlier texts, but here it is used to encourage a discussion between father and son, although the father's advice is finally accepted.

In the Ramesside Period the final stage of development is reached in this type of literature; individual modesty and humility are now considered to be more important than wealth and success. Wisdom texts were still being composed as late as the Ptolemaic Period; one example is the Instruction of Ankhsheshonqy, a priest of Re at Heliopolis. Here the advise is set in the context of a story that relates how Ankhheshonqy, through a series of incidents, became implicated in a plot to kill the king. Although innocent, he was sent to prison, where he had time to consider his thoughts and set down his personal wisdom for his son's benefit.

In addition to the accredited authors of wisdom texts there were also men whom later generations regarded as sages and revered for their knowledge, wisdom, and embodiment of the true values of the society. A famous example was Amenhotep, son of Hapu, who lived in the reign of Amenhotep III. As the royal architect he was responsible for constructing some of the great Theban monuments, including the Temple of Luxor and the king's own mortuary temple of which only the Colossi of Memnon (the massive statues once flanking its entrance) still survive. Amenhotep was also in charge of the great estates of Princess Sitamun, the king's daughter and wife.

Amenhotep was so important that he received the unique honor of being given his own mortuary temple at Thebes (these were usually only built for kings), which was granted a perpetual royal endowment. He was worshiped there and at other temples and locations. One aspect of his cult is evident at the temple at Deir el-Bahri; there he was regarded as a god of healing, and the sick visited his sanatorium in the hope of obtaining a cure.

Thus, although personal piety and ethics were expressed in different ways, it is evident that the Egyptians had a deeply personal awareness of their relationship with the gods and of the need to live according to clearly defined principles and standards. Their "ideal" person not only existed in literature; occasionally he was identified as a living being (for example, the sages Imhotep, Hardedef, and Amenhotep, son of Hapu) and was consequently deified and worshiped.

MONOTHEISM AND THE CULT OF THE ATEN

In the reign of Akhenaten (Amenhotep IV) toward the end of Dynasty 18, radical changes affected Egyptian religious beliefs and customs. Amenhotep IV, son of Amenhotep III and Queen Tiye, turned the cult of the Aten into a form of solar monotheism based on the worship of the life force present in the sun and imposed this doctrine on his subjects. Although each line of kings had previously adopted one deity as royal patron and supreme state god, there had never been an attempt to exclude other deities, and the multitude of gods had been tolerated and worshiped at all times.

The Aten is first mentioned in the Middle Kingdom when, as the sun disk, it was merely one aspect of the sun god Re. However, in the reign of Tuthmosis IV it was identified as a distinct solar god, and his son Amenhotep III established and promoted a separate cult for the Aten. There is no evidence that he neglected the other gods or attempted to promote the Aten as an exclusive deity.

There is no single source of evidence for the cult's beliefs and doctrines, but the famous Hymn to the Aten, found inscribed on tomb walls at Akhetaten (Tell el-Amarna), described the god as the creator of all living things. The sun disk was the visible symbol of the god; this represented the Aten's real essence, which was its beneficent and universal creative force expressed through the light and warmth of the sun. The other element in the doctrine was the role of the king (Akhetaten), who had a divine nature and acted as the god's sole representative and agent on earth. This concept restored the kingship to a status it had enjoyed in earlier times.

Although at first scholars believed that Atenism was a new set of beliefs promoted by Akhenaten, it is now generally accepted that some elements (such as the god's role as universal creator of mankind, animals, birds, and plants, and his fatherhood of foreign peoples as well as the Egyptians) were present in earlier cults, particularly that of Amen-Re. In the New Kingdom such ideas were promoted to unite the peoples of Egypt's empire under one supreme god. But Akhenaten did introduce one entirely new concept that was alien to traditional Egyptian religion—the belief that the Aten was the only god and that all other deities should be obliterated.

Amenhotep IV spent the early years of his reign at Thebes where he lived with his queen Nefertiti and their growing family of six daughters. At first he allowed the traditional deities to continue, but near the Temple of Karnak (Amen-Re's great cult center) he erected several buildings including temples to the Aten. These were dismantled by his successors and used as infilling for new constructions in the Temple of Karnak. When these were dismantled in modern times for restoration of the temple, some 36,000 decorated blocks from the Aten buildings were revealed; archaeologists were able to use a computer to assist them in piecing together many elements of these relief scenes and inscriptions.

The relationship between the king and priesthood of Amen-Re soon deteriorated, however, and in year 5 of his reign Amenhotep IV took decisive steps to establish the Aten as an exclusive, monotheistic god. He disbanded the priesthoods of all the other gods, obliterated the divine names from the monuments, and diverted the income from these cults to support the Aten. To emphasize his complete allegiance to the god the king changed his name from Amenhotep to Akenaten ("Servant of the Aten"), and Nefertiti took the additional name of Nefernefruaten. Akenaten then moved from Thebes and established a new royal residence and political and religious capital at a site midway along the Nile. He claimed that the god had chosen this place, which, as a virgin site, had no associations with any traditional deities. The royal court and a nucleus of professionals and craftsmen now began to establish a city there, and it was given the name "Akhetaten" ("Horizon of the Aten").

Hastily constructed, the city covered some eight miles of land on the east bank of the river, while on the west bank land was set aside to provide crops for the population. The whole area was encircled with fourteen boundary stelae inscribed with the king's conditions that governed the establishment of the capital. The city included palaces, a records office, administrative headquarters, military barracks, and houses for the officials and craftsmen; several temples built to honor the Aten were a most important feature. Behind the city in the eastern cliffs rock-cut tombs were constructed for the courtiers and officials, and in a distant wadi (dry valley) a tomb was prepared for the royal family.

The cult of the Aten was vigorously promoted by the king and the court circle, but it probably gained little external support. It could not offer any moral philosophy or popular mythology to attract ordinary people, and it could not replace the comforting prospect of the afterlife, which Osiris had promised, with any valid alternative. Once again the belief was probably promoted that eternity could only be attained through the king's bounty rather than through divine worship and observance of a moral code during life.

At Akhetaten, a special art form developed that is unique in its representation of the human figure. This may have been based on Akhenaten's own physical abnormalities (although the only evidence for these is provided by reliefs and statuary, since his body has never been found). Each figure is shown with an elongated face and head, slanting eyes, and a malformed body with an emaciated neck and pronounced breasts and thighs. This may indicate that the king suffered from a disorder of the endocrine glands, and these features were then extended to representations of all human figures to emphasise that the king's abnormalities were in fact the perfect form, since he was the god on earth. Another interpretation suggests that this was simply a new and experimental art form encouraged by the king to mark a complete break with the traditional art that was so closely associated with abandoned religious ideas. The term "Amarna

Art" is often used for this experiment; indeed, the site itself is frequently referred to as Tell el-Amarna (its modern name).

Akhenaten apparently produced no male heirs (although one theory proposes that he was Tutankhamun's father), and this undoubtedly contributed to his failure to ensure that his religious innovations continued after his death. Later generations regarded him as a heretic who ruled without the traditional gods' approval, and the temple closures and disbanding of the priesthood would have had dire effects upon the country's economy and employment. Atenism never gained popular support and probably had little direct effect on people's religious beliefs. When Akhenaten's successors reversed his experiment and returned to the traditional gods, the population was largely unaffected. Under Tutankhamun the court went back to Thebes and the pantheon of gods was reinstated.

The motives behind this religious "revolution" have been much discussed. Was Akhenaten a visionary who believed that he was prompted by revelation to take these steps to advance the cult of the Aten? Or were his aims politically inspired in that he tried to restore the status and influence of the kingship by introducing a "new," omnipotent god who was represented on earth by the king? Was he a political opportunist who merely carried to their conclusion the trends and reforms initiated by his father and grandfather, thus attempting to resolve the age-old threat posed to the kingship by the power of Amen-Re and his priesthood? By thus attempting to define and separate his "religious" and "political" motives, however, perhaps we are imposing modern concepts that are not applicable to that age.

LINKS WITH OTHER RELIGIONS

Foreign Gods

From earliest times the Egyptians incorporated foreign deities into their own pantheon so that they became part of the Egyptian system. It is possible that Osiris, god of vegetation and king of the dead, may have originated as a human ruler who led tribes into Egypt from elsewhere—possibly Syria, part of Asia Minor, an area of Africa, or Libya. Similarly Horus may have been the supreme god of a group who perhaps entered Egypt in the Predynastic Period; Punt, Arabia, or Mesopotamia have been suggested as possible homelands. Horus later became the patron and protector of the first rulers of Egypt. The cult of the sun god Re may also have been introduced from elsewhere in the late Predynastic Period, possibly from Arabia, Crete, or western Asia. In later communities, such as the pyramid workmen's town of Kahun (Dynasty 12), evidence indicates that there was a foreign presence, although the extent of this and the degree to which the local religious beliefs and customs were influenced remains uncertain.

LIBYAN AND NUBIAN DEITIES

During the New Kingdom, the establishment of an empire brought the Egyptians into direct contact with the religious beliefs and cults of many other lands. Previously religious influences had mainly come from three areas: Libya, Nubia, and lands to the north. Egypt and Libya probably derived a number of common features from a general North African culture, and some early Egyptian deities such as Neith, goddess of hunting, and Ash, the personification of the desert, may have had Libyan origins. In Nubia, where Egypt had always pursued a policy of colonization emphasizing its own superiority and introducing cultural as well as military and political innovation, the deities were nevertheless incorporated within the Egyptian pantheon so that they could be brought under the control of the pharaoh. As early as the Old Kingdom the Nubian bird god Dedun was included among the Egyptian gods and associated with Horus.

ASIATIC DEITIES

From the Middle Kingdom onward Egypt's contact with Palestine, Phoenicia, and Syria increased and by the New Kingdom exerted considerable influence in this area. In religion as in other matters there was a cross-fertilization of ideas, although the pharaoh's role as protector was now extended to other peoples in Asia who came under his control. The cult of the state god Amen-Re as the creator of all men was promoted by the Egyptians, but the chief gods of other lands and areas retained control over their local populations, and temples that the pharaohs built in Asia Minor were usually dedicated to these gods.

Some foreign gods were adopted by the Egyptians in order that the Egyptian worshipers could acquire their additional strengths. Some Syrian gods were now introduced into the Egyptian pantheon and may have been worshiped in Egypt by both foreign residents and Egyptians. These gods were represented with Egyptian clothing and attributes and their temples within Egypt followed the Egyptian pattern. Foreign residents probably also worshiped their own gods at household shrines. Cults of Ba'al, Astarte, and Reshep were established at Memphis, and of 'Anat, Astarte, Hurun, and Seth at Pi-Ramesse; similarly Hurun was worshiped at Giza and Ba'alaat in the Fayoum. At the royal workmen's village of Deir el-Medina Asiatic gods included Reshep (a war god) and Qudshu, 'Anat, and Astarte (fertility goddesses). This may indicate the presence of some foreign residents among the workforce, but by including foreign deities in their own pantheon the Egyptians ensured that their followers could continued to worship their own gods within Egypt without displaying disloyalty to the state gods. Also, once the foreign gods were incorporated they could not provide a rallying point for the immigrants outside the Egyptian system.

Selected for their warlike attributes, their fertility, or healing powers, these Asiatic deities had some importance and influence. For example, a statue of the healing goddess Ishtar of Nineveh was sent by the Mitannian king, Tushratta, to the Egyptian court of Amenhotep III in an attempt to cure his ailments.

It is difficult to determine the extent to which Egyptian gods penetrated the societies of Syria/Palestine since the source material is limited and fragmentary. Although there is no evidence that Egyptian gods entered the Syrian pantheon, there are some Egyptian forms of local deities, such as Ptah-south-of-his-Wall who was the Great Chief of Askelon. At Byblos in Phoenicia there was a temple dedicated to Hathor as "Lady of Byblos," and at Gaza there was a temple to Amun. Also, Egyptians visiting Ugarit and Beth-shan set up stelae there to local gods.

Contact between Egypt and Syria probably occurred at several different social levels during the New Kingdom. There were marriages and diplomatic alliances between the royal courts and exchanges between diplomats and envoys; also, some ideas may have been spread through itinerant artisans, mercenaries, and even prisoners of war. There is no direct evidence of Egyptian influence on the temple architecture or rituals in Syria/Palestine, and any exchange of deities and religious beliefs probably occurred on a largely superficial level and had little real impact on the customs practiced in either region.

Egyptian Texts and the Bible

Egypt dominated the political arena for many centuries, and it is, therefore, not surprising that aspects of this civilization permeated the beliefs and customs of neighboring and successive cultures. Christianity and Judaism were fundamentally different from Egyptian religion in that they are considered to be scriptural religions —based on God's revelation to mankind —whereas Egyptian religion was founded on ritual and cultic practices. However, associations between Egyptian texts and the Old and New Testaments have been traced, and it is probable that some biblical elements were derived from Egyptian beliefs. Egyptian wisdom instructions may have directly influenced biblical texts, and some parallels have been drawn between the instructions and the sentiments expressed in the books of Proverbs, Ecclesiastes, Song of Solomon, Psalms, and Job. The Instruction of Ptah-hotep may have had an impact on the Book of Proverbs, but the closest parallels in style and content occur in the later instructions (particularly those of Amenemope) and Proverbs. This text was composed in the Ramesside Period (c.1250 BC) when Egyptian influence on the Israelites was probably at its height. The author of Proverbs possibly had direct access to the instruction of Amenemope, although it is conceivable that they both derive from a lost source.

Other similarities have been noted between the Hymn to the Aten (which was inscribed on a wall in the tomb of Ay at Tell el-Amarna) and Psalm 104 in the Bible. The hymn expresses the doctrine of Atenism and emphasizes the king's attempt to make the god unique in Egypt and other lands. Passages in the hymn and in Psalm 104 underline a close association of ideas, describing the divine role as creative and sustaining. Again it is not clear if direct borrowing occurred between these two texts or if they were both derived from a common source.

Nubia

Egypt's cultural influence on neighboring societies reflected to some extent the pattern of political control. There had always been a policy of direct colonization of Nubia to the south, and Egypt's religious impact was very strong there. When a line of rulers from the southern city of Napata conquered and briefly ruled Egypt in the eighth century BC (Dynasty 25), they already worshiped the god Amen-Re at Napata who had been introduced from Egypt earlier. When they were driven back to Napata following the Assyrian invasion of Egypt the Nubians continued to practice this religion. With the eventual decline of the Napatan kingdom the rulers established another capital at Meroë (situated between the Fifth and Sixth Cataracts on the Nile). Here they inherited and developed elements of the pharaonic culture, and although direct contact between Egypt and the southern kingdom had now ceased the Meroitic civilization displayed many features that were strongly influenced by Egypt. These included their religious beliefs, gods, temples, art, and funerary customs. While pharaonic culture was undergoing profound changes in Egypt, the Meroitic kingdom preserved the final stages of many of these ideas during the period between the sixth century BC and the fourth century AD when Aeizanes of Axum destroyed Meroë.

The Hellenistic and Roman Worlds

In Egypt itself, political institutions and cultural influences underwent profound changes in the period when the country was ruled by the Greeks and then by the Romans following the conquest by Alexander the Great in 332 BC (the effect of this change of rule on various religious traditions is considered in the following section). But it is possible that traditional Egyptian beliefs about the divinity and role of the pharaoh may have directly influenced Alexander's own concepts.

Egyptian ideas and images may also have been transmitted through the Old and New Testaments and thus become embedded in early Christian belief. There would probably have been an even more direct route for this transmission to Christianity through Egypt's influence on the Hellenistic world. The concept of the Trinity, although biblical in origin, may have derived something from the Egyptian divine triads. The ideas of death, rebirth, and resurrection, as well as the Day of Judgment, which occur in the Egyptian Myth of Osiris may have had some association with later beliefs, and links have been suggested between the Isis cult and Mariolatry. Alexandria, the great center of Hellenism, would have provided a channel for Egyptian traditions to come into contact with early Christian beliefs.

Apart from Christianity, aspects of Egyptian religion were carried abroad through the Roman Empire. Isis, Egypt's great mother goddess, received widespread acclaim when the Isis-Osiris Mysteries were celebrated in Rome and Corinth, and she was worshiped as far north as the Danube region, Germania, and Britain. She not only preserved her original role as the devoted wife of Osiris and protective mother of Horus but acquired new aspects as a goddess of seafarers and the controller of destiny.

Surviving Traditions

Some ancient traditions still survive in modern Egypt. These include the Festival of Sham el-Nessim which marks the start of spring in the same way that the Festival of Khoiakh did in antiquity. Families celebrate this out-of-doors, exchanging gifts of colored eggs to reassert the renewal of the vegetation and the annual rebirth of life. Another modern festival, Awru el-Nil, takes the form of a national holiday; at this celebration of the inundation of the Nile flowers are thrown into the river. In ancient times a festival was held annually to mark the inundation, and prayers were offered to ask for a good flood (neither too high nor too low) which would ensure ample crops and general prosperity. Other modern ceremonies reflect ancient funerary customs. Forty days after death and burial the family of the deceased will take food to the grave, and this is then distributed among the poor who have gathered there. This occasion, known as el-Arbeiyin, retains elements of the ancient service performed at the time of burial when relatives gathered at the tomb and at the conclusion of the burial rites shared the funerary meal. The forty days that still elapse between death and el-Arbeiyin probably reflect the period that was set aside for mummification procedures in ancient Egypt. Another early tradition is probably preserved in the modern annual family visit to the grave when special food is brought which is then given to the poor.

RELIGION UNDER THE GREEKS AND ROMANS

When Alexander the Great conquered Egypt in 332 BC, he was welcomed by the people as their savior from the burden of Persian domination and the effects of ineffectual native rulership. The ensuing period of domination by the Ptolemaic Dynasty and then the Roman emperors, however, did little to improve the lives of most Egyptians.

During this time Egypt experienced many changes in aspects of its civilization, including religious beliefs and customs. Increasing numbers of Greeks settled in Egypt, but there was little attempt to integrate the gods of both peoples although some Greeks eventually adopted some aspects of Egyptian religion. The state, however, attempted to introduce certain cults with the aim of uniting the two peoples. The Ptolemies who established this dynasty were not entirely secure in their claim to rule Egypt; therefore, they established an official dynastic cult to justify their rulership. The earlier Egyptian practice of deifying and worshiping the dead king as one of the royal ancestors now became a cult of the living rulers.

Serapis

Ptolemy I also created a new god, Serapis, to unite the Greeks and Egyptians. The god had a Greek appearance but was given an Egyptian name, and some of his features were based on the Apis bull, an Egyptian deity worshiped at Memphis. Serapis was tolerated by the Egyptians perhaps because of the long association between the Apis and the Egyptian god of the dead, Osiris; similarly, his appearance made Serapis acceptable to the Greeks, and with royal support the cult attracted many adherents. This artificially created cult, however, never achieved any fundamental religious unity between the Greeks and the Egyptians.

Importance of Egyptian Religion

In their own cities and communities within Egypt the Greeks worshiped their own gods and built shrines to Zeus, Apollo, Demeter, and Aphrodite. From the third century BC, however, the political climate began to change in favor of the Egyptians, and Egyptian religion became increasingly important. Their religious beliefs were pervasive because the gods had been worshiped for many centuries and, unlike Greek deities, they offered the promise of eternal life in a clearly envisaged hereafter. Even the animal cults that the Egyptians promoted to emphasize their national loyalties during the foreign dynasties were sometimes adopted by the Greeks. One example was Suchos, the crocodile god of the Fayoum, whom both Egyptians and Greeks worshiped.

Some native Egyptian gods such as Isis and Amun were taken by traders and administrators to Greece, the Greek islands, and Asia Minor. Under the Romans Serapis reached the Black Sea, Sicily, and south Italy, while the cults of Osiris and Isis also became widespread. Isis continued to be worshiped until the fifth century AD, long after the arrival of Christianity. These gods retained popularity because they guaranteed individual immortality and combined a sense of mystery with their own almost human characteristics.

One aspect of Egyptian religion that both the Greeks and the Romans sought to promote and perpetuate was the idea that the Ptolemaic rulers and the Roman emperors were also pharaohs within Egypt. This gave them the claim of ownership over the land and its people, a right that most of them exercised unscrupulously and with considerable zeal and that enabled them to extract economic benefits. As pharaoh, however, it was necessary for the ruler to build and repair the temples and promote the interests of the Egyptian gods and their priests. The Ptolemies decreed substantial concessions to the temples and regarded them as a vital element in the state. By comparison there were probably few large Greek temples outside Alexandria.

The Romans also recognized the need to gain the Egyptian priests' support, and they built new temples at several sites. The best-preserved examples of Egyptian temples dating to the Greco-Roman Period are found at Edfu, Esna, Denderah, Kom Ombo, and Philae. In the early years of Ptolemaic rule the kings had merely made additions to existing temples at Luxor, Karnak, and the Theban funerary temples, but they later built new monuments. These continued the earlier architectural traditions of the Pharaonic Period with only minor variations. Each temple had a series of courts, halls, and a sanctuary that were all reached through a main gateway. They were all built to a single plan and essentially repeated the same architectural and decorative features. Temples of this period, however, also introduced some new features including screen walls to separate the forecourts from the inner areas, roof apertures instead of clerestory lighting in the hypostyle halls, and the addition of a birth house (mammisi) where the god's birth was celebrated.

Tomb Building

During this period the Greeks and Egyptians followed separate customs in building tombs. Ptolemaic burials for Greeks in Egypt are found in the cemeteries at Alexandria, Naucratis, and in the Fayoum. There is almost no evidence of fusion between Greek and Egyptian styles in these tombs. At Alexandria little evidence survives of the Egyptian burials, but elsewhere New Kingdom tombs were reused for multiple burials. These were entirely Egyptian with continued use of body coffins, mummification, and hieroglyphs. More attention, however, was paid to embellishing the outer casing of the mummy than to the decoration of the tomb or the provision of funerary goods. One particularly interesting example of Greek influence on an Egyptian tomb still survives at Tuna el-Gebel, the necropolis of the city of Hermopolis. Here in the tomb of Petosiris (high priest of the temple of Thoth in the reign of Ptolemy I) there is some evidence that, to some extent, Egyptian and Greek art and religion had fused, but such examples are rare because the underlying Greek and Egyptian concepts were so different.

Mummy Panel Portraits

One important area where Egyptian beliefs and practices united with those of the Greeks and Romans is in the painted panel portraits that were now placed over the faces of the mummies. Intermarriage and increased links between the native and immigrant populations had led some Greeks and Romans to adopt certain Egyptian funerary beliefs and the associated practice of mummification. The painted panel portraits, head and chest covers, painted burial shrouds, and cartonnage or wooden coffins accompanying the mummy all demonstrate this hybridization and exhibit new or changed forms.

Most panel portraits date to the Roman Period from the first half of the first century AD to the fourth century, when they were gradually abandoned because of decline in the practice of mummification. They are reminiscent of paintings found on the walls of houses at Pompeii, but in Egypt their funerary use and the climate have ensured that some have survived. They provide the most important single collection for the study of ancient portrait painting. The painting style and technique are truly innovative because, unlike the pharaonic face masks, which represented idealized rather than individual faces, these were undoubtedly personal portraits. They also introduced new artistic techniques and conventions such as shading, highlighting, perspective, and depth from the Classical world. Inside the elaborate outer casings, however, the mummies were often poorly preserved. This provides evidence of a steep decline in the embalmers' skills and also perhaps of a rise in the number of clients who now chose to have their bodies mummified.

CHRISTIANITY IN EGYPT

The arrival and spread of Christianity in Egypt brought about profound and irreversible changes in many aspects of the society. Effectively, it drew to a close the ancient religion that had underpinned so many facets of the civilization including writing, literature, architecture, and art.

The Egyptians eagerly adopted Christianity, which reached them as early as the first century AD, probably entering the country through Alexandria. Brought there from Jerusalem by relatives and friends of the Jewish community the new faith promoted ideas such as disinterest in worldly goods and the need for mutual support,

that found an immediate response among the masses. The poor readily adopted these concepts while the wealthy continued to follow the traditional religions.

Initial hostility to Christianity, however, came not from other faiths but from the Romans who regarded it as a subversive movement because it did not acknowledge the divinity of the emperor. Under the Romans there was a systematic persecution of the Christians; Decius in AD 50 ordered severe persecution of the Christians at Alexandria, and Septimius Severus's edict in 204 prohibited Roman subjects from embracing Christianity. Diocletian was regarded as the instigator of further persecutions in Egypt that occurred around 303 and lasted for ten years.

These events, nevertheless, only encouraged the Egyptian population to embrace Christianity as an expression of their antagonism toward the Roman state, and by the end of the second century Christian communities were flourishing in Alexandria and Lower Egypt. Constantine I (the son of St. Helena) was the first emperor to give support to Christianity. He stopped the persecutions started under Diocletian and issued the Edict of Toleration in 311; further measures were introduced to restore the property of churches and to make public funds available to them. Theodosius I completed the establishment of Christianity as the empire's official religion. He was baptized as a Christian soon after his accession, and his edict (384) formally declared Christianity to be the official state religion. He also ordered the closure of temples dedicated to the old deities; there followed a widespread persecution of pagans and heretics and systematic destruction of temples and monuments in Egypt. The last traces of the old faith, however, were only finally removed

A woolen border, perhaps from a tapestry hanging, representing a female theatrical mask and floral garlands. This is the only known example of this subject depicted on a textile, although it is common in mosaic. This piece may not have been woven in Egypt but imported there from elsewhere. Late third century.

in the time of Justinian (c.540) when the temples on the island of Philae were closed.

The particular contribution that Egyptian Christianity made to the faith was the idea of physical retreat from the world in search of spiritual values. These ideals were first pursued by hermits who went to live in desert caves and later by religious communities in specially built monasteries. The church in Egypt, however, formed a sect that broke away from the rest of Christendom when, at the Council of Ephesus (451), the Egyptian clerics rejected the commonly held doctrine that Christ combined a human and divine nature.

Strong Christian communities still survived after the Arab invasion of Egypt in the seventh century AD, particularly in the south and around Thebes. The term "Copt" (derived from the Greek *Aigyptios*, which became *Qibt* after the Arab invasion) was first used in Europe in the sixteenth century to distinguish the Christians in Egypt from other Christians. Before that it had described all inhabitants of Egypt. Today the Copts (Egyptian Christians) have their own patriarch and form an important and substantial minority in the country.

The language of the Copts, Coptic, still survives today in the liturgy of their church. It was last spoken in Christian villages in the seventeenth century, but Arabic has gradually replaced it as Egypt's main language and script. Coptic played an important role, however, in the decipherment of hieroglyphs and the associated scripts hieratic and demotic. The earliest Coptic manuscripts date to the third century AD. The Gospels and Old Testament were translated into Coptic for the Egyptian population, and other important works include the writing of St. Antony (251–356) who lived as Egypt's first hermit in the desert east of Aphroditopolis.

This change in religion and language profoundly affected other aspects of the culture. Until then Egypt's culture had drawn its inspiration from pharaonic and Hellenistic traditions, but new and distinctive art forms now emerged. At first the non-Christian themes still tended to be emphasized, but by the fourth and fifth centuries Christian influences can be seen in the paintings, sculpture, and textiles that once adorned the churches, monasteries, and houses. In particular the ideal climatic conditions of Egypt have preserved quantities of woolen and linen textiles that supply information about religious vestments, burial garments and wrappings, secular garments, and household furnishings.

The territories of the Roman Empire, divided into eastern and western sections in 305, were ruled from Constantinople and Rome, and Egypt was allocated to the Eastern Empire. This period of Roman rule and the predominance of Christianity within Egypt were both brought to an end by the Arab conquest in 641, when Islam was introduced as the country's new religion.

READING

State Religion

Morenz 1973: general account of religion; Frankfort 1961: a discussion of some aspects of the religion.

Gods and Goddesses

Watterson 1984: introduction to Egyptian deities.

Temples and Temple Art

David 1981: study of the Egyptian temple, explaining its architecture and ritual use; Schafer 1974: the principles of Egyptian religious art.

Priests

Sauneron 1960: general but scholarly account of the Egyptian priesthood.

Religious Rituals

David 1981: describes how temples worked as ritual units; Blackman 1953: description of myth and ritual in Egypt.

Religious Artifacts

Aldred 1971: explains the magical-religious significance of jewelry and amulets.

Creation Myths

Lichtheim 1973: translations of some of the myths; Faulkner 1969: translation of the Pyramid Texts (the Heliopolitan cosmogony); Morenz 1973: discussion of the meaning and significance of the myths.

Household Gods and Domestic Worship

David 1986: the lives and worship of the pyramid workmen; Černý 1973: the lives and religious customs of the royal necropolis workmen.

Magic

Jacq 1985: general discussion of magic in Egypt; Pinch 1994: study of Egyptian magic.

Personal Piety

Lichtheim 1973: translation of wisdom texts; Gunn 1916: study of personal prayers at Deir el-Medina.

Monotheism

Aldred 1988: general account of the reign of Akhenaten; Redford 1984: assessment of the motives and personality of Akhenaten; Martin 1974, 1989: study of the royal tomb at Amarna; Mercer 1939: translation of the amarna tablets.

Links with Other Religions

David 1986: includes discussion of possibly foreign religious practices at Kahun; Černý 1973: comments on foreign deities worshiped at Deir el-Medina; Blackman 1916: discussion of links between ancient Egypt and modern Nubia; Murray 1921: ancient and modern festivals; Wainwright 1949: survival of pharaonic customs in west Africa.

Religion under the Greeks and Romans

Bell 1953: study of religion in this period; Bowman 1986: general sections on religion in this period.

Christianity

Watterson 1988: general introduction to Christian Egypt; Bowman 1986: historical account of post-pharaonic Egypt, including aspects of Christian Egypt; Worrell 1945: description of Egyptian Christians.

5

FUNERARY BELIEFS
AND CUSTOMS

IMPORTANCE OF THE TOMB

Because tombs and temples were built of stone, evidence relating to burials and state religious customs has survived better than evidence relating to domestic buildings, which were constructed primarily of mud brick. This tends to present an inaccurate and partly misleading view of Egyptian society, perhaps placing undue emphasis on its preoccupation with death and preparation for the afterlife. Nevertheless, funerary beliefs and customs were obviously extremely important and influenced many of the concepts and developments of the civilization.

Central to Egyptian mortuary practices was the belief that life continued after death. Although this at first applied only to the king, it was assumed by the Middle Kingdom that all worthy people could aspire to individual immortality. The classes maintained somewhat different views about the location of the afterlife and what they would experience there, but everyone planned to prepare a burial place that had the function not only of protecting the body but also of providing a location to which the owner's free-roaming spirit could return to obtain sustenance.

The Egyptians believed that the burial site was a home for the spirit, and in the mastaba tomb this idea was developed so that the features of a house—reception area, bedroom, storerooms—were reproduced. Indeed, the dead were believed to have the same needs as the living—a home, possessions, and food and drink. These were supplied for the deceased by means of a tomb, funerary goods, and a funerary offering ritual.

The provisioning of the tomb was also regarded as essential to the owner's continued existence after death. A man's heir was expected to bring food and drink to his tomb on a daily basis to feed his spirit (ka). His descendants inherited this obligation to bring the offerings to the tomb chapel and present them to the owner by means of the funerary ritual. Accompanied by the recitation of prayers, they were offered on a flat altar table. It was believed that the essence of their sustaining qualities would be absorbed through the mummy or the owner's statue on behalf of his spirit.

This obligation, however, became a burden to later generations. As tombs grew increasingly neglected, it was feared that the ka would experience starvation. Other means of securing a food supply were sought, and a ka servant was often employed. This priest had the duty of presenting the offerings, and the tomb owner set aside an area of land in his estate from which the produce would supply perpetual offerings for his tomb and also payment for the ka servant and his descendants who inherited this commitment. Again, however, duties were often neglected, and the Egyptians resorted to magic.

Wall-scenes within the tomb re-created a pleasant hereafter for the deceased and included representations of food production (harvesting, butchering, brewing, and baking) and offering rites. They were later augmented by statues and models that were shown engaged in similar activities. All these inanimate figures would, it was believed, be activated by a special ceremony carried out at the funeral. Once the life force entered them, they would be able to serve the owner. There was also an offering list inscribed within the tomb that provided an eternal substitute menu for the deceased; this was intended to lessen his reliance on food brought by relatives or the ka servant.

Concepts of the Afterlife

The Personality

The Egyptians' concept of the personality was complex and had a direct influence on their belief in immortality. It was probably formulated early in the Old Kingdom. Some elements were believed to function only in life, while others were regarded as immortal. The body was the essential link between the deceased and his former earthly existence, since it was regarded as a means of supplying him with food and drink for spiritual sustenance in the afterlife. Mummification was developed so that the body could be preserved and remain recognizable to the deceased's spirit. In case the mummy was damaged or destroyed, statues of the owner and magical spells were placed in the tomb to act as substitutes and to enable the deceased to receive food and drink. During his lifetime other elements such as his name (which was written on his mummy or statue to confirm its identity) and his shadow (considered to be the focus of his procreative powers) were regarded as integral parts of the personality.

KA

Some elements were directly related to an individual's immortality. The most important, the *ka* (spirit), was the person's life force, which acted as his guide and protector from birth onward. During life this was sometimes regarded as his double and thought to incorporate all the qualities and characteristics that make an individual unique. Essentially, it was the "self" or personality. On death the ka separated from the body and became the immortal spirit of the owner.

The ka nevertheless still retained a vital link with the preserved body and depended on the food offerings brought to the tomb. In art representations it is shown either as a human figure with upraised arms or as a pair of upraised arms. To ensure an individual's immortality, it was essential that the link between the living and dead was maintained. Correct performance of the funerary rites and continued provision of the material needs of the deceased, especially food and drink, were vital to enable the deceased to attain immortality. In order that the deceased could regain his life force and in order to restore the senses to his body so that he could continue to function and receive his offerings, the funerary priest performed special rites at the burial. Known as the Ceremony of Opening the Mouth, this involved the priest touching the mummy, tomb statues, and figures in the wall reliefs on the mouth, hands, and feet with an adze to restore the life force to them.

BA AND AKH

Another immortal element was the *ba* (soul), represented as a human-headed bird. This force had the ability to leave the body after death and travel outside the tomb to favorite haunts of the deceased. Force believed to help both the living and the dead was the *akh*; this supernatural power was also represented with a bird form.

The Changing Eternal World

With the "democratization" of the afterlife that occurred from the Middle Kingdom onward, it was believed that everyone could expect an individual eternity if they led a good life. The

A stone "false door" from a tomb at Saqqara (c.2500 BC), inscribed with the name and titles of the owner. The false door was supposed to enable the spirit of the deceased owner to enter his tomb at will, so that he could take possession of his mummy and absorb spiritual sustenance from the food offerings.

nature of this afterlife and where it would be spent, however, varied according to the earthly status of the individual.

By the beginning of the Old Kingdom there was a firm conviction that the king would ascend to the heavens when he died and pass his eternity sailing in the sky in the sacred bark; he would be accompanied in this boat by the gods and he himself would become fully divine, finally joining his father, Re, the sun god. Other Egyptians could only experience a vicarious eternity through the king's bounty: His family and the nobility were provided with tombs, funerary possessions, and endowments through royal favor; the craftsmen who prepared and decorated the king's tomb and funerary goods gained immortality through their participation in his burial; and the peasants who labored on his pyramid also hoped for a share in the god-king's eternity.

By the Middle Kingdom a less rigid idea of this royal celestial hereafter continued for the kings, but now wealthy people and even the peasants anticipated individual resurrection and immortality. Those who could afford to prepare and equip fine tombs hoped to pass at least part of their eternity there, enjoying the benefits provided by the tomb goods.

Wall scenes, models of servants, magical inscriptions, and other equipment were all designed to give the tomb owner the opportunity to continue the influential and comfortable lifestyle he had enjoyed in this world. Special sets of figurines (ushabtis) were even placed in the tombs to relieve the owners of the agricultural labors they would otherwise have to undertake in the underworld. The tomb was regarded as the house of the deceased and included a burial chamber and an offering chapel where the food offerings could be brought by the family or the ka priest. A false door was provided in the tomb structure to allow the deceased's ka to pass from the burial chamber to partake of the offerings.

With the increased influence of the god Osiris from the Middle Kingdom onward, it was believed that all worthy persons could spend eternity in the kingdom of Osiris. This was envisaged as a place of lush vegetation, a mirror image of the cultivated land of Egypt, that was situated somewhere below the western horizon or on a group of islands. This kingdom is sometimes called the "Fields of Reeds," and the inhabitants were believed to enjoy eternal springtime, unfailing harvests, and no pain or suffering. The land was democratically divided into equal plots that rich and poor alike were expected to cultivate. This situation was welcomed by the peasants, but the rich tried to avoid this eternity of agricultural labor by providing themselves with lavish tombs and equipment. These three main concepts of the afterlife—eternity spent in the sky, in the tomb, or in the Fields of Reeds—largely reflects the hopes and aspirations of the royalty, the wealthy nobles and middle classes, and the peasants and continued long after the Middle Kingdom, although the conditions found within these eternal worlds were to some extent regarded as interchangeable.

THE SUN CULT AND THE PYRAMIDS

The cult of the sun god Re dominated the religious beliefs and practices of the Old Kingdom. The Nile and the sun were the two great life-givers of Egypt, and the sun, with its regular appearance at dawn and withdrawal at sunset, was regarded as an eternal and self-regenerating force. Many myths developed about the sun: Re was regarded as the great creator of life in the Heliopolitan cosmogony, and he also featured prominently in the Egyptian concept of the universe. The daily pattern of the sun's life, death, and rebirth was seen as the model for the king's own life, death, and resurrection.

Re may have entered Egypt from elsewhere, brought in by early immigrants in the Predynastic Period, but he soon assimilated the cult center, Iwnw (Heliopolis), and some aspects of the character and appearance of an earlier deity, Atum. As early as Dynasty 2, each king proclaimed his allegiance to Re by adopting the title "Son of Re." The god became the patron of royalty throughout the Old Kingdom, and his priesthood at Heliopolis held great power. According to the mythology developed at Heliopolis, Re-Atum had created the world. Re played an important role in the Pyramid Texts and in creation mythology and probably influenced the architectural development of the pyramid form.

It was during Dynasty 5 that the god's cult and his Heliopolitan priesthood reached the zenith of their power. The kings of this dynasty patronized the cult to an unprecedented degree and may have owed their accession and support to Re's priesthood. For the first time they incorporated the title "Son of Re" into the official royal titulary.

Some elements of the historical truth surrounding the beginning of Dynasty 5 may survive in the Westcar Papyrus, which preserves much of the story of "King Cheops and the Magicians." This text emphasizes the divine origin of the line, the role of Re in fathering these kings, and their pious actions in building temples for the god and replenishing his altars. They revived the practice of pyramid building, moving their cemeteries to Abusir and Saqqara, but these monuments were inferior in their construction to those of earlier dynasties.

Instead, the kings devoted their resources to building solar temples at Abu Ghurab. These were probably modeled on the much earlier original sun temple at Heliopolis (which has never been discovered). This seems to have consisted of a series of enclosures leading to a wide, paved open-air court containing a rectangular podium, which probably represented the primeval mound of creation. A squat obelisk (the benben) was mounted on top of the podium; this represented a sun ray and acted as the god's cult symbol. It was the central feature of the temple and probably influenced the form and development of the true pyramid.

The Step Pyramid at Saqqara, the first stone monument, had started out as a mastaba tomb but then underwent a number of design changes to reach its final form as a stepped structure. Its architect may have intended that the greater size of this burial place might deter tomb robbers, although it is also possible that it reflected some association with a star cult. The evidence of several transitional pyramids shows how the step pyramids were ultimately transformed into true pyramids with smooth, sloping sides. Again, these changes may have been introduced as practical and architectural developments to give the pyramids greater security, but they may also have been influenced by mythology. One interpretation is that the pyramid represented the mythological Island of Creation where the first god had alighted and life had come into existence. As such it would have been regarded as a place of great spiritual potency where the king's life could be renewed. From the pit grave through to the mastaba tomb, step pyramid, and finally true pyramid the concept of the "mound" is evident, whether in the pile of stones marking the pit grave, the superstructure of the tomb, or the structures of the step and true pyramids.

The true pyramid, however, was probably closely associated with the sun cult, and the transition from step pyramid to true pyramid may mark a change from the predominance of a star cult to that of the sun cult. In the ancient texts the word used for the true pyramid, *mer*, is nowadays translated as "place of ascension." The pyramid may have been seen as a means of access for the deceased king buried inside to reach heaven and join Re and the other gods on their celestial journey.

Similarly, this "ramp" would have allowed the king to return to his burial place to receive his eternal food offerings. A possible explanation is that the pyramid form was regarded as a sun's ray, forming a link between heaven and earth along which the king's spirit could travel. The full-size pyramid was perhaps a variant form of the benben, the sun god's cult symbol at Heliopolis, which took the form of a pyramidion or small pyramid placed on top of a squat obelisk.

TOMBS AND TOMB ART

In some periods royal burials were accommodated in pyramids, but nobles and officials had tombs. There were variations in design over the centuries, but two basic architectural types developed and survived—the mastaba tomb and the rock-cut tomb.

Mastaba Tombs

At first the mastaba tomb was used for royalty as well as for nobility, but when the kings began to build pyramids at the beginning of the Old Kingdom, the nobles and officials retained and developed the mastaba tomb. These were now grouped around the pyramid to form "royal courts." The tomb's main functions were to house the body and the funerary goods and to provide an earthly location where offerings could be brought to sustain the owner's spirit. The belief that the tomb was a house for the deceased where he could continue to exist after death prompted the development of certain architectural features.

The mastaba tomb had a superstructure above ground and a substructure below ground. The superstructure was rectangular and bench shaped, hence the term used by Egyptologists: *Mastaba* is the Arabic word for "bench shaped." In earliest times (from c.3400 BC) it was built entirely of mud brick. This continued into Dynasty 4, but there was increasing use of stone: The core was now built of solid masonry or of rubble contained within a bench-shaped wall, and whereas the outside of the superstructure had once been covered with a mud brick paneled facade, this was now often replaced by smooth limestone facings. The superstructure marked the location of the tomb and protected the burial and also provided a place where food offerings could be brought. It housed the offering chapel or chamber (equivalent to the reception area in domestic architecture) where the family or priest brought the food offerings, and the *serdab* (closed room), which contained the owner's statue through which his spirit could absorb sustenance and benefit from the offerings. There were also two false doors set into the east wall; decorated with relief sculpture, these provided the owner's spirit access to the offerings and emphasized the appearance of the tomb as a dwelling place.

The substructure housed the burial chamber and was the equivalent of the domestic bedroom. There was also sometimes a second chamber to accommodate the burial of the

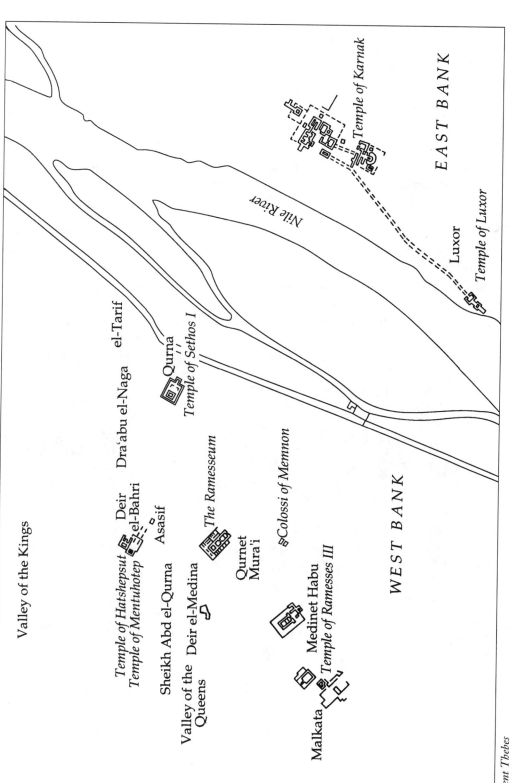

Valley of the Kings

Temple of Hatshepsut
Temple of Mentuhotep
Deir
el-Bahri

Dra'abu el-Naga

el-Tarif

Sheikh Abd el-Qurna

Asasif

Qurna

Temple of Sethos I

Valley of the
Queens

Deir el-Medina

The Ramesseum

Qurnet
Mura'i

Colossi of Memnon

Malkata

Medinet Habu
Temple of Ramesses III

Nile River

WEST BANK

Temple of Karnak

EAST BANK

Luxor

Temple of Luxor

Ancient Thebes

owner's wife, and there were storage areas for goods and possessions. Access to the chambers was provided by shafts or stairways, and various devices were developed to attempt to protect the burial and funerary goods against robbers. These included deeper access routes, blocking internal doors with stone or bricks, or filling the shafts and stairways with gravel and rocks. The Egyptian name for the tomb was Hwt Ka ("House of the Spirit").

Rock-Cut Tombs

Although rock-cut tombs had begun to appear by the end of Dynasty 4, it was in the succeeding dynasties that they became widespread. Some were constructed at Giza, but the most important development was in the provincial districts along the Nile where they were built in the desert cliffs for the provincial governors, who had assumed semi-independence. The rock tombs continued to flourish during the First Intermediate Period, a time of civil war between the provincial rulers, and also survived for nonroyal, wealthy burials during the Middle Kingdom.

Each rock tomb cut into the mountainside or cliffs which border parts of the Nile in Middle or Upper Egypt included a portico with columns or a terraced courtyard which led into a columned hall. All the architectural features were cut out of the natural rock. The hall gave access to a small room or niche that contained the tomb owner's statue, and offerings were presented here on his behalf. The burial chamber lay beyond the offering chapel, and access was frequently provided through an opening cut in the floor of the chapel.

By the New Kingdom the kings themselves had abandoned pyramids in favor of rock-cut

Tomb scenes (c.1400 BC) show women mourning, bending down in front of the mummy which is supported by the priest and stands at the tomb entrance (right). The women's grief is expressed by their torn dresses and by rubbing dirt into the forehead (left).

tombs in a bleak valley (Valley of the Kings) on the west bank opposite Thebes. Some queens and royal princes were buried in rock-cut tombs in the nearby Valley of the Queens, while the tombs of many courtiers and officials were scattered across several areas of the same necropolis. A king's tomb usually consisted of a series of stairways and corridors interspersed by one or more rectangular halls that descended to a pillared hall. This hall contained a sarcophagus (stone coffin) that accommodated the burial. Several storerooms for the funerary goods led off of this chamber. The tombs in the Valley of the Queens were similar and sometimes only slightly less elaborate. Nonroyal tombs typically consisted of an open rectangular courtyard behind which lay an inverted T-shaped offering chapel cut into the rock. A hidden shaft located at the rear of the chapel or in a corner of the forecourt led down to one or more subterranean chambers which accommodated the burial and tomb goods. Within the T-shaped chapel there was a niche at the far end that housed statues of the owner and his wife and sometimes a false door.

oped over the centuries, the main principles of tomb art remained the same. But when tombs were built in areas that did not have easy access to good quality stone, the artists developed techniques for painting scenes directly onto plastered surfaces prepared on top of mudstone walls. While nonroyal tombs of all periods were decorated with scenes of daily life, royal tombs in the New Kingdom depicted representations from the funerary "books" to enable the king to overcome the dangers he would encounter as he passed into the world of the dead.

The two-dimensional art that decorates the walls of tombs and temples exhibits some puzzling features. Executed solely for reasons of sympathetic magic (so that the owner could "use" them) rather than for visual impact, these reliefs represent "conceptual," or "aspective," art rather than "perceptual," or "perspective," art. Heinrich Schafer's observations (AD 1919) on this art enabled him to identify its main principles (although the Egyptians themselves left no account of these), and his work remains the basis of modern interpretation of such religious scenes.

Wall Art

The introduction of stone for building and facing the offering chapel in the early Old Kingdom provided wall surfaces that could be carved and painted, and from Dynasty 3, the fully developed wall composition was in use, showing a large figure (the tomb owner) dominating a series of horizontal registers occupied by subsidiary figures. The purpose of these scenes, which represented aspects of food production and everyday pastimes, was to provide the owner with a series of activities that he could magically activate for his own benefit and enjoyment after death. Although some minor variations devel-

TOMB GOODS

To provide the deceased with the requirements for the afterlife—clothing, food, jewelry, cosmetics, tools, weapons, domestic utensils, and many other items—the body, even in the earliest graves, was surrounded by a selection of such funerary equipment.

Later, when pyramids were built for royal burials and stone or mud brick tombs accommodated the wealthy nobility, preparations became more elaborate. Mummification was introduced

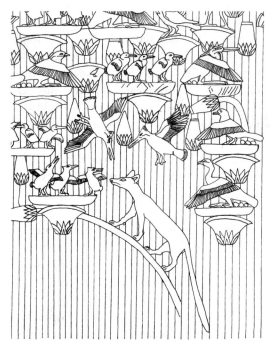

A tomb scene in which a civet hunts birds in the marshes. The composition and detail of the scene demonstrate the artist's ability to observe nature and convey his impression of the flora and fauna in an original way.

centered around the absolute power of the king or the supremacy of his patron god Re (closely linked with the pyramids of the Old Kingdom). Osiris (believed to have been a human king who was murdered and subsequently resurrected at the behest of a divine tribunal as god and judge of the underworld) now received widespread worship because he offered his followers their own chance of personal immortality.

This democratization of religious and funerary beliefs in the Middle Kingdom led to an immediate desire for men and women to supply and equip their tombs with a lavish range of goods. All those who could afford to prepare in this way for the afterlife now purchased a variety of tomb goods, and no other period perhaps preserves such a range of funerary items. These were stored in chambers in the tombs.

In the New Kingdom the kings abandoned pyramids for their own burials and chose instead to prepare tombs in the desolate area known today as the Valley of the Kings. The only royal burial of the New Kingdom to have survived here virtually intact until its discovery in 1922 was that of Tutankhamun, and his funerary equipment has provided much evidence about the preparation of a royal burial of this period.

Nonroyal tombs of the New Kingdom continued earlier traditions with their painted wall reliefs and tomb goods. In those burials that have survived destruction or looting by robbers there is evidence of increased luxury and a more cosmopolitan awareness—both legacies of Egypt's new status as a great empire builder and center of international diplomacy and wealth.

Later Egypt's gradual decline is again reflected in the burials, although magnificent treasure has been discovered in the royal tombs of Dynasty 21 at Tanis. In the final years when Greeks and Romans established their rulership over Egypt and many made their home there, they frequently adopted at least some of the

for the upper classes in order to preserve the body in a form that would be recognizable to its owner's spirit. The interior walls of the nobles' tombs were decorated with registers of carved and painted scenes of everyday existence—especially the production of food—which the Egyptians believed could be activated by magic for the owner's benefit and enjoyment after death. Since the two main cults associated with death and resurrection at this time were those of Re (the sun god) and Osiris (the god of the underworld), their mythology and associations had a profound effect on contemporary funerary beliefs and burial customs.

With the political downfall of the Old Kingdom and the rise of the First Intermediate Period and then the Middle Kingdom, the Egyptians sought a new set of beliefs, one not

Egyptian funerary beliefs and customs. Thus we find the Classical art of portraiture introduced and used to produce painted likenesses of individuals; probably executed in the owner's lifetime, the portrait was hung in the house and then, at death, cut to size and placed over the face of the owner's mummy. These panel portraits replaced the stylized, mass-produced coffins and masks of earlier times and brought Egyptian funerary customs and Hellenistic techniques together in a unique way.

By now, however, there was a general cynicism about the advisability of providing tomb equipment, since it would almost inevitably be robbed; instead, the outer casings of the mummies became even more elaborate. Jewelry was now often symbolized, either molded in the cartonnage and gilded and inlaid with glass to represent semiprecious stones or simply painted onto the owner's panel portrait.

Coffins

Coffins were used to protect the dead from earliest times. Reed matting and pottery "box" coffins occur in predynastic and early dynastic burials, but from c.3400 BC when the mastaba tomb was introduced for royalty and nobility the burials incorporated a rectangular wooden coffin. This was probably regarded as a house for the deceased. During the Old Kingdom, stone coffins (sarcophagi) were introduced into the wealthiest burials, but it was in the Middle Kingdom that the typical "nest" of coffins became much more widely available. Most middle-class burials now included them as a major element of tomb equipment. It was customary to have two coffins.

THE RECTANGULAR COFFIN

Rectangular coffins were usually made of wood and decorated with painted scenes on the exterior surfaces, although royalty and the great nobles sometimes supplied themselves with stone coffins whose decoration imitated the main features found on the wooden ones. The

A linen and stucco cover from a mummy. Painted with the representation of a young boy, this was used for a child's burial. Early second century AD.

inside the coffin to look out at the food offerings brought to the tomb. On some examples there were also paintings of food so that, in addition to the menu contained in the coffin inscriptions, the owner would have an additional source of magical food.

THE ANTHROPOID (BODY) COFFIN

During the Middle Kingdom the anthropoid coffin was placed inside the rectangular coffin. Later in the New Kingdom a nest of two or even three anthropoid coffins replaced the rectangular and anthropoid set.

The earliest body coffins were made of cartonnage (a kind of papier-mâché made from papyrus and gum) or wood, but by the Middle

A painted panel portrait of a man, originally placed over the face of a mummy. It probably represented a likeness of the owner and is a fine example of this genre of funerary art. It was discovered, with many similar portraits, in the Ptolemaic Period cemetery at Hawara (c.200 BC).

A gilded cartonnage mask from a mummy (Ptolemaic Period), showing simulated jewelry (a bead collar) and a winged headdress.

decoration consisted of horizontal lines of inscription (the so-called Coffin Texts, which were magical spells designed to assist the deceased in his passage to the next world; these were adapted for nonroyal use from the Pyramid Texts placed in the pyramids of the Old Kingdom to ensure the king's eternity) and brightly painted geometric designs. These designs represented the facade of a palace or house, probably emphasizing the idea of the coffin as a dwelling place for the deceased. On the east or left side of the coffin there was also a painted pair of eyes, intended to allow the mummy

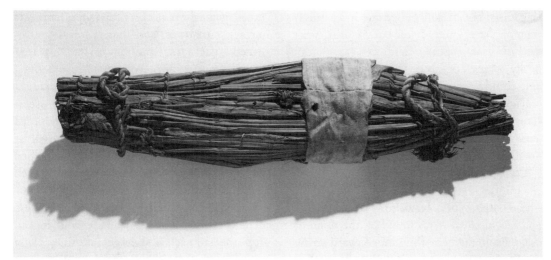

A reed coffin (from Gurob, c.1450 BC), tied with ropes at either end; it contains the naturally preserved body of a baby. Such poor burials are relatively rare because they have not survived as well as wealthier examples.

Wooden coffin from Tarkhan (c.2500 BC), with a domed lid; this represented a dwelling-place for the dead. Such coffins replaced the earlier basket coffins or skins for the burial of wealthy persons.

FUNERARY BELIEFS AND CUSTOMS

Kingdom wooden coffins became increasingly commonplace. Later, some body coffins were made of stone or pottery and even (usually for royalty) of gold or silver. It is thought that the body coffin originally developed from the cartonnage masks used in the Old Kingdom, which were placed over the head and face of the mummy both to protect it and to act as a substitute if the mummy was destroyed.

A typical anthropoid coffin has the shape of a mummy; features painted on the outside —bead collar, girdle, bandaging, and jewelry— represent the real items found on the mummy inside. From the New Kingdom onward scenes of gods, the weighing of the deceased's heart on his Day of Judgment and of his resurrection, as well as inscriptions from the funerary "books," are also included. The deceased's name and titles are inscribed in the texts to identify his ownership, but most coffins were mass-produced and the facial features are stylized rather than portraits of the owners. A wig or head cover is painted on the head; the eyes are often inlaid with obsidian and alabaster; and the wooden false beard and uraeus (snake) on the forehead indicate the status of the deceased as an "Osiris." This meant that he had passed the moral examination at the Day of Judgment and was therefore regarded as an embodiment of Osiris, god of the dead.

Although there were variations in style over hundreds of years, the basic aims of the anthropoid coffin—to protect the body and provide a substitute for the deceased—remained unchanged.

Canopic Jars

Mummification involved the evisceration of most of the body's organs from the abdominal and chest cavities. The viscera were then pre-served by means of packing them in a dehydrating agent (natron), and they were either returned as packages to the body cavities or placed in containers (made of wood, pottery, or stone), known today as "canopic jars." (The name is a misnomer—early Egyptologists wrongly associated them with the Greek legend of Canopus, a helmsman of Menelaus, who was buried at Canopus in the Delta where he was worshiped in the form of a jar.) There were four jars in each set, and they were dedicated to a group of demigods called the "Four Sons of Horus". These included Imset (human-headed), who looked after the stomach and large intestine; Hapy (ape-headed), responsible for the small intestine; Duamutef (jackal-headed), in charge of the lungs; and Qebhsennuef (hawk-headed), who controlled the liver and gallbladder. In turn these deities were protected by the goddesses Isis, Nephthys, Neith, and Selket.

In the earlier examples of the Old and Middle Kingdoms the four jars were supplied with stoppers carved to represent human heads (probably to symbolize the tomb owner), but from Dynasty 18 onward the stoppers were in the form of four different heads—human, ape, jackal, and hawk—symbolizing the Four Sons of Horus.

Canopic Chest

Some sets of canopic jars were placed in wooden canopic chests; the exterior sides and lid were brightly painted with lines of hieroglyphic inscription, representations of false doors, and a pair of painted eyes. They were in effect miniature coffins, and these features were present to allow the deceased to gain access to and be reunited with his viscera in the next life. For the same reason the chest was sometimes placed in a niche in the east wall of the burial chamber to be in the line of vision of the mummy.

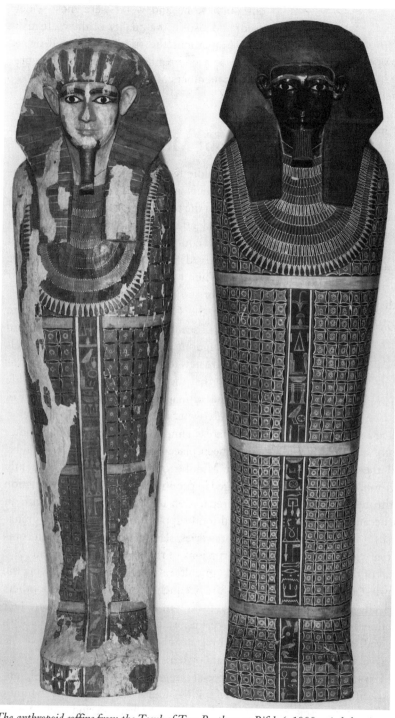

The anthropoid coffins from the Tomb of Two Brothers at Rifeh (c.1900 BC), belonging to Khnum-Nakht (left) and Nekht-Ankh (right). They represent mummiform figures of the deceased, with headcloths, false beards, "broad collars," and body wrappings decorated with geometric designs that imitate textiles. The vertical column of inscription supplies the funerary menu to ensure the continued survival of the owner.

Soul Houses

In the Old Kingdom it was customary to place a circular, stone offering table or rectangular slab or platter in front of the stela in the tomb for the owner to receive his food offerings. By the Middle Kingdom, however, this became of secondary importance and was incorporated as a courtyard in the pottery model house (known as a "soul house"), which now became part of the tomb equipment. In effect these soul houses were funerary offering tables, but because of their design they also supply us with information about the period's domestic architecture, which is often difficult to obtain from other sources.

The design of these model houses varied, but most have a two-storied portico, a flat rooftop reached by a staircase from the ground level, and a cooking area in the courtyard at the front of the house.

Tomb Statues

It became the custom to place a statue or statuette of the owner in his tomb. In the early Old Kingdom only royalty and the great nobility were able to make this provision. Gradually the practice spread downward through society, and by the Middle Kingdom it became widespread throughout the middle classes.

Most nonroyal tomb statuary is not life-size; it was believed that the ritual of the opening of the mouth, performed by a priest at the tomb on the day of burial, would magically restore the life force, original size, and functional abilities of all models and figures in the wall scenes in the tomb.

Most examples, produced in large numbers, were only identified with a specific owner once his name had been inscribed on the statue. There is great variety in style and in materials (although stone and wood were most widely used) and also in the quality of the craftsmanship. Sometimes the statue of a tomb owner would be accompanied by other statues representing members of his family.

Servant Models

In the Middle Kingdom democratization of funerary beliefs and customs resulted in a great increase in the tomb goods made available to all who could afford to purchase them. Tombs were now equipped with a variety of servant models carved in wood and painted with realistic details. They were often based on the subject content of the carved and painted wall scenes found in the Old Kingdom nonroyal tombs. These wall scenes continued in the Middle and New Kingdom tombs, but the servant models provided a new dimension; with the scenes it was believed that they could also be brought to life by means of magic to provide for the needs of the tomb owner in the next world.

Whereas simple servant models had sometimes been placed in the Old Kingdom tombs, by the Middle Kingdom they were frequently arranged in groups, engaged in food production and preparation to provide the owner with an eternal food supply. We find models of granaries, breweries, slaughterhouses, and even complete versions of the owner's house, estate, and herds; agricultural activities such as plowing the fields are frequently represented, and others include fishing in the river. In addition to their funerary importance they also supply us with fascinating details of the daily activities of the great landowners and their servants.

A special category consists of the model figurines of soldiers found most frequently in tombs of the First Intermediate Period and Middle Kingdom when civil strife and local warfare between powerful rulers were widespread. These models, fully armed with miniature weapons, were intended to protect the tomb owner against his enemies in the next life.

USHABTIS

A special category of servant model is known today as a *ushabti* or *shabti*, and many examples can be seen in museum collections. During the First Intermediate Period there emerged the idea of the kingdom of Osiris—a realm for the dead where everyone would be required to undertake menial and agricultural labor irrespective of their rank. To avoid this obligation the wealthy began to supply themselves with model agricultural workers (ushabtis) to undertake forced labor. Introduced in Dynasties 9 and 10, they continued in use throughout most of Egypt's history; their size and quality of manufacture often provide an indication of the political and economic status of the country at any specific period.

Each tomb set included hundreds of figurines (it is sometimes said that one was provided for each day of the year), and there were also "overseer" figures to keep the ushabti workers under control. The ushabtis are represented as mummiform figures, and they carry hoes, mattocks, and baskets painted or carved on the body; they are frequently inscribed with the owner's name and a magical formula indicating their willingness and readiness to undertake tasks for the deceased. The overseers are shown with flared skirts, and they each carry a whip.

The material, style, size, decoration, and inscriptions show minor variations throughout the dynasties, and examples made of wax, baked clay, wood, stone, and metal have been found, but faience—introduced for ushabti manufacture in Dynasty 18—became the most popular material. In the later periods ushabtis were often mass-produced in clay molds, but there was a revival in quality in Dynasty 26 when some superb figurines were produced.

The origin of the word *ushabti* probably came from the Egyptian verb *wesheb*, meaning "to reply" or "answer"; as "answerers," the ushabtis responded to the daily call to forced labor on behalf of their owner.

Dolls and Concubine Figures

It is sometimes difficult to determine if figurines placed in tombs were intended as toys to entertain a child in the next world or if they had a different function as symbols of fertility and of rebirth after death. Examples of "dolls" are particularly problematic; some may have been playthings, but the "paddle dolls" introduced in Dynasty 11 (flat, wooden, paddle-shaped figures whose painted decoration greatly enlarged and emphasized their sexual organs) obviously had a different purpose.

Later, there were also "concubine figures" made of wood, stone, or pottery and often decorated with inlaid eyes and elaborate, detachable wigs (also a sexual symbol in ancient Egypt). As well as the fertility/rebirth aspect of such figures, they were probably intended to cater by means of magic for the tomb owner's entertainment in the same way that the servant models supplied his food.

Model Boats

By the Middle Kingdom an essential feature of tomb equipment was the wooden model boat. This was often produced with great attention to detail and included linen sails and oars and deck cabin and crew, all carved and painted appropriately. The most important reason for including a model boat in the tomb was to allow the deceased owner to make a pilgrimage to Abydos, the sacred city of Egypt where Osiris, god of the dead, was believed to be buried. Such a journey, it was thought, would enhance the dead person's chances of resurrection and eternal life.

Some people supplied their tombs with several model boats, and the wealthy nobility even had complete model fleets that included a variety of craft such as long-distance boats, funerary barks, and fishing vessels. These obviously had different purposes—to allow the deceased to travel, to convey him from his home on the east bank of the Nile to the cemetery in the west, or to augment his food supply. As with the servant models the magical funerary rites were expected to give these boats the full size and operational ability of the originals.

Stela

In nonroyal tombs of the Old Kingdom the owner was provided with an offering list and an autobiography inscribed on the interior walls. The autobiography summarized his life and characteristics; it included his official rank and titles so that in his afterlife he could justify his claim to continue in high office. The text laid great emphasis on his worthiness and virtues but omitted any reference to his failures or sins, thus presenting an insight into the standards of behavior required at that time. These are of additional use to the Egyptologist in providing information about family relationships and Old Kingdom ranks and titles.

The offering list, which became the main feature of the nonroyal tomb of the Old Kingdom, was a formal inscription that asked for benefits on behalf of the deceased in the next world (especially food and drink) and also requested that he be well received there. It developed a specific formula asking for the offerings either through the agency of Anubis, the jackal-headed god of embalming, or through the king's bounty. Called the *Hetep-di-nesew* formula ("a boon which the king gives"), it was later used on wooden coffins of the Middle Kingdom. The essentially magical formula was designed to provide access for the deceased to the next world and to supply all his material needs there.

The offering list and the autobiography had reached their most complete forms in the tombs of Dynasty 6, but later in the Middle Kingdom they emerged in the form of a stela. This was a stone block, often round topped, carved with a scene of the deceased offering to the gods. The inscription included the autobiography, which featured the main events of the owner's life, as well as prayers that praised the kings and gods. Some stelae were large, but most were small or medium sized, and many were set up by ordinary people in their tombs or at centers of pilgrimage such as Abydos as personal memorials. Many stelae survive today, partly because of the large numbers produced but also because stone—a durable material—was used for most of them. Some wooden examples have also survived.

OSIRIS AND GODS OF THE DEAD

Since the Egyptians were much concerned with death and the afterlife, several gods were attributed with special powers to assist them in this area. The most important was Osiris who, from the Middle Kingdom, dominated funerary beliefs and practices.

Origins and Evolution of Osiris

No extant account of the myth of Osiris survives in Egyptian literature; the earliest, most complete version exists in the writings of the classical author Plutarch (AD 50–120). Other sources for Osiris include the Pyramid Texts and some late temple inscriptions. Plutarch's myth describes Osiris as an early human king who brought civilization and agriculture to Egypt. Murdered by his jealous brother Seth, his body was dismembered and scattered, but Isis, his sister and wife, collected and magically reunited his limbs. Posthumously conceiving Osiris's son, Horus, Isis hid and reared the child in the Delta marshes. Once grown Horus set out to avenge his father's death and engaged Seth in a bloody conflict. Their dispute was brought before a divine tribunal whose judgment favored Horus and Osiris. Resurrected, Osiris became king and judge of the dead in his underworld realm, while Horus (with whom every king was now identified) became ruler of the living. Seth, regarded as the "Evil One," became an outcast.

Osiris probably originated as a vegetation god personifying the phases of the agricultural year with the annual life, death, and rebirth of the vegetation. He was regarded as the life giver and source of fertility. The annual Festival of Khoiakh celebrated his death and resurrection and was closely associated with the accession, coronation, and jubilee of the living king. From this role Osiris acquired his functions as ruler of the underworld and divine judge, expressing the wider concepts of victory over evil and conquest of death.

In the Middle Kingdom democratization of religious beliefs and funerary customs was closely associated with Osiris's ability to offer immortality to all his followers, rich or poor. Entry to his kingdom was now dependent on

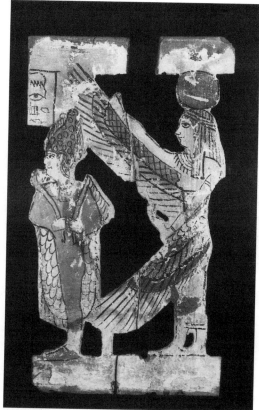

Painted wooden figures (c. 600 BC) of Osiris (left) and his wife Isis (right), who protects him with her wings. As god of the dead, he is shown as a mummiform figure wearing a feathered crown and holding the royal insignia of crook and flail.

correct burial procedures and a successful trial before the divine judges. At this "Day of Judgment" the deceased faced a tribunal of forty-two gods and was required to recite the Negative Confession, declaring innocence of any serious offense during life. His heart weighed in the balance against the feather representing truth, and if he lied his heart would weigh against him. If he was innocent and his heart balanced the feather he was declared "true of voice" and, reunited with his soul, passed into the eternal kingdom of Osiris. If found guilty his heart would be thrown to a composite creature called the "Devourer" and he lost any chance of immortality.

Through his vegetation role Osiris came to be regarded as a corn god. He may also have had associations with deities in other countries, such as Adonis, Tammuz, and Dionysus. He was always represented as a mummiform, dead king wearing a long white cloak and the crown of Upper Egypt and carrying a crook and flail. His face was sometimes colored black or green to symbolize his powers of regeneration. His two major cult centers were Busiris in the Delta and Abydos, Egypt's greatest religious city. Pilgrimage to Abydos to enhance the chance of eternity became essential for all worshipers who could make the journey.

Other Gods of the Dead

An earlier god at Abydos was Khentiamentiu, the "Foremost of the Westerners," an important deity in the land of the dead. When Osiris arrived at Abydos in Dynasty 5, he supplanted and adopted some of the characteristics and attributes of Khentiamentiu. The oldest known god of Abydos, Wepwawet, had himself been supplanted by Khentiamentiu. Wepwawet (the name means "Opener of the Ways") was believed to lead the dead to the underworld. Represented as a jackal with a grey or white head, Wepwawet may have been worshiped originally as a wolf god at Abydos; at Lycopolis ("Wolf City," modern Assiut), another important center for his cult, he definitely received worship as a wolf.

Osiris also had close funerary associations with other gods. At Memphis he first acquired funerary characteristics when he became identified with Sokar, the ancient local deity of the dead who was usually represented as a hawk and regarded as guardian of the Memphite necropolis. Sokar was himself amalgamated with Ptah when the latter became principal god of Memphis. By the end of the Middle Kingdom a composite deity, Ptah-Sokar-Osiris, had been created. In later times a wooden figure of this god, with a hollowed base that contained a papyrus of the Book of the Dead, was often placed in the tomb.

Under the Ptolemies a new god, Serapis, was introduced in an attempt to provide a deity whom both Greeks and Egyptians could worship. Serapis combined elements of the Greek gods Zeus, Asklepios, and Dionysus and of Osiris and the cult of the sacred Apis bull of Memphis. Serapis was a god of fertility and of the underworld, but he never received full acceptance by the Egyptians.

Other members of the Osirian family also played funerary roles. Isis, wife of Osiris, was a universal mother goddess with a reputation as a great magician. With Nephthys, Neith, and Selket, she protected the body; these goddesses stood at the four corners of the sarcophagus, and Isis also had the task of guarding the deceased's liver (an organ particularly revered). Isis and her sister Nephthys were the chief divine mourners and protectors of the dead. Nephthys, although the sister-wife of Seth, nevertheless supported her other siblings, Osiris and Isis, in the conflict and helped Isis to reassemble and wrap the body of Osiris and then to mourn for him. She also protected the sarcophagus and the canopic jars. And according to one myth Nephthys's union with Osiris (who mistook her for Isis) produced the god Anubis. Worshipped at Cynopolis in Middle Egypt, Anubis was the great funerary god and judge of the dead prior to Osiris's prominence. Originally the royal god of the dead, Anubis's role was eventually extended. He had embalmed and wrapped the body of Osiris, and he subsequently performed this duty for all the dead. Anubis was represented as a jackal and became the patron of embalmers. Jackals were frequent scavengers in cemeteries, and by deifying the animal the Egyptians may have hoped to appease and prevent him from molesting the dead. In the afterlife Anubis was also the guardian of the balance at the Day of Judgment, and he read the scales and reported the deceased's fate to the tribunal.

Horus, the legitimate son of Osiris, in his form as Harsiesis (Horus-son-of-Isis) was also a protector of the dead. He was helped by the demigods known as the "Four Sons of Horus" (Imset, Hapy, Duamutef, and Qebhsennuef) to guard the viscera removed during mummification. They in turn were protected by the four goddesses Isis, Nephthys, Neith, and Selket.

MUMMIFICATION

The term *mummy* is used to describe a naturally or artificially preserved body in which desiccation of the tissues has enabled it to resist putrefaction. There are examples of such bodies in several countries, although originally *mummy* (derived from the Arabic or Persian word *mumia*, meaning "bitumen," or "pitch") was only used to describe the artificially preserved bodies from Egypt.

Human remains are indefinitely preserved in a number of ways in different countries. Natural environmental conditions such as dryness of sand in which the body is buried, heat or cold of the climate, or absence of air in the burial are major factors in this unintentional type of preservation. Sometimes these natural conditions were enhanced intentionally to achieve the preservation of the body. True mummification, however, is an intentional method using a process of sophisticated and intrusive techniques. Egyptian mummies provide the best example of this method.

The geography and environment of Egypt produced conditions that led at first to natural, unintentional mummification. The dead were buried in shallow pit graves on the edge of the desert, and the combination of the sun's heat and the dryness of the sand ensured that the body tissues became desiccated before decomposition occurred. In c.3400 BC, however, advances in building techniques led to the introduction of tombs with brick-lined burial chambers for the upper classes. The environmental conditions that had previously ensured preservation were now absent, and the bodies rapidly decomposed. But religious beliefs required that the body should be preserved and recognizable to the owner's spirit (ka) when it returned to the tomb for sustenance.

A period of experimentation now took place. There was an attempt to re-create the bodily shape by covering it with fine linen and then coating it with stucco plaster to preserve the contours; breasts, genitalia, and facial features were emphasized by molding and painting in the details. Underneath the bandages, however, the body still decomposed, and these attempts produced nothing more than a skeleton with a wrapped and molded structure.

There is some evidence that there had been earlier attempts to use natron as a means of dehydrating the skin, but the first real confirmation that true mummification had been used dates to Dynasty 4 (c.2600 BC). A box containing the viscera of Queen Hetepheres, mother of King Cheops, was found in her tomb at Giza. When these packets were analyzed, it was shown that natron had been used. From this period until the Christian era (some 3,000 years), true mummification was practiced in

Egypt. Introduced for royalty, mummification gradually became available for all who could afford it, and in the Greco-Roman Period it became widespread. It was never universally available, however, and most poor people continued to be buried in shallow graves in the desert.

For a detailed description of the embalming process, see "Mummification Techniques" in Chapter 10.

RECENT EVIDENCE: THE EXCAVATION OF TOMB KV5

Despite the continuing problems posed by environmental conditions, theft, and vandalism, archaeology still reveals tombs and funerary goods of great significance in Egypt. The discoveries of the royal tombs of Tutankhamun at Thebes (1922) and of the rulers at Tanis (1940s) have provided new evidence about royal funerary beliefs and customs. From 1988 to 1990, Kent Weeks, an American archaeologist, and his excavation team began to clear Tomb KV5 in the Valley of the Kings at Thebes (Luxor) and have been able to show that this was the burial place of some of the sons of Ramesses II.

This tomb may be the one referred to as the "tomb of the royal children" in the Turin Papyrus, which deals with the tomb robberies in the later reign of Ramesses III. The tomb was located in 1987–88 by the Theban Mapping Project, an American study established in 1978 to prepare a survey of the entire Theban necropolis.

KV5 (Kings' Valley Tomb 5) is situated about 40 meters (131 feet) to the northeast of Ramesses II's own tomb. The early English traveler James Burton was the first to identify the name of Ramesses II carved on the entrance jamb of KV5, and various other travelers and scholars had noted the tomb's existence. Howard Carter, who discovered and excavated Tutankhamun's tomb, partially cleared and subsequently reburied the entrance to KV5 in 1922.

Geophysical surveys and clearing operations enabled the Theban Mapping Project to relocate the tomb in recent times. Considerable damage had been caused to the interior by flash floods, by the heavy tourist bus traffic that used the nearby asphalt-paved parking area, and by a sewer line that had been laid some years ago from the Valley of the Kings rest house. The sewage pipe had subsequently leaked, releasing hot, moist air into the tomb. Nonetheless, continuing careful excavation of the tomb and the production of detailed drawings, plans, and photographs of the interior chambers of KV5 are gradually revealing the survival of a surprising amount of carving and wall painting.

A program is in progress to systematically clear, clean, and chemically treat the walls and, where necessary, to rebond them to the stone. The archaeologists are seeking further information about the physical extent of this tomb and hope to be able to identify which royal sons were interred there. Since the tomb was apparently initially constructed for someone else, the excavators may also be able to determine the identity of the original owner. The human mummified fragments that have been discovered to date are also very important because of their potential for biomedical studies and for DNA identifications relating to the royal family.

READING

Concepts of the Afterlife

Budge 1911: discussion of myths and evidence relating to Osiris; Griffiths 1966: account of possible origin and characteristics of Osiris; Mercer 1952: translation and commentary on the Pyramid Texts; Perry 1925: discussion of the sun cult; Badawy 1956: the role of the mastaba tomb; Morenz 1973: general account of Egyptian religion.

The Sun Cult and the Pyramids

Edwards 1985: comprehensive account of Egyptian pyramids; Reisner 1942, 1955: study of burials in Giza necropolis; W. Stevenson Smith 1958: a well-illustrated account of the art and architectural forms of the Old Kingdom; Lauer 1976: description of the excavation of the Saqqara necropolis.

Tombs and Tomb Art

W. Stevenson Smith 1958: op cit; Aldred 1949: description of art forms in Old Kingdom; Davies 1900–1901: the wall decoration of two important tombs; Iversen 1955: explanation of the Egyptian canon; Lange and Hirmer 1956: classic account of history of Egyptian art; Schafer: sets out the principles for interpreting the art; W. Stevenson Smith 1946: account of Old Kingdom sculpture and art; Wilson 1947: the role of the artist.

TOMB GOODS

Winlock 1955: description of models from tomb of Meket-Re. (Also worth consulting are the series of catalogs produced by museums, especially the Cairo and British Museums, and Petrie's series on Edwards's collection, University College London.)

Gods of the Dead

Otto 1966: account of Osiris and Amun; Griffiths 1970: translation and commentary on Plutarch's myth; Griffiths 1966: op cit; Budge 1911: op cit; Watterson 1984: survey of Egyptian gods; Černý 1952: account of many aspects of religion.

Mummification

Herodotus 1961: account of mummification techniques in Book II; Smith and Dawson 1991: classic account of techniques, based on evidence of examination of mummies; Harris and Wente 1980: scientific study of radiography of royal mummies; Lucas 1962: chapter on techniques and materials used in mummification; Cockburn 1980: survey of mummification worldwide; David and Tapp 1992: includes description of mummification procedure as well as scientific investigation of a mummy.

The Excavation of Tomb KV5

Weeks 1992: discussion of the Theban Mapping Project and excavation of KV5.

6

ARCHITECTURE AND BUILDING

ARCHITECTURAL DEVELOPMENTS

In predynastic times the Egyptians had huts and shrines built of reeds and plant materials. They buried their dead in shallow sand graves. From c.3400 BC, they began to use sun-dried brick to construct great tombs for the ruling classes, and palaces and shrines were also now enclosed by brick walls. Gradually stone was introduced as a building material, and tomb walls and entrances were lined with dressed blocks of stone. In Dynasty 3 the vizier Imhotep designed a unique burial monument for Djoser—the world's first pyramid and earliest extant stone building.

The Old Kingdom witnessed the first great period of architecture and building, when pyramid complexes, fields of mastaba tombs, and solar temples were constructed at vast expense. By this time it had become the custom to build with stone, to ensure that these great structures would last for eternity. However, domestic buildings—palaces, houses, fortresses, record offices, and administrative headquarters—as well as lesser tombs were made of mud brick and wood with stone doorways and recesses, for it was not important that domestic buildings should survive forever. Because these structures are less well preserved we have a rather uneven impression of many aspects of Egyptian civilization. It is known, though, that most architectural forms and decoration had already been established by the Old Kingdom, and as with many other aspects of the civilization, subsequent changes were essentially superficial.

The surviving architecture reflects the availability of various building materials: Good quality timber was rare, stone was accessible throughout Egypt, and Nile mud was readily converted into mud bricks. Mathematical knowledge and simple equipment enabled the architects to produce plans and sketches to enable these great monuments to be built. They had the use of the plumb bob, cubit, square, measuring line, leveling staff, and a primitive theodolite; tools were made of flint, hard stone, and copper or bronze since iron was not used in Egypt until the Late Period (c.750 BC) after the Assyrians had conquered the country.

The builders' construction equipment was also limited: Brick and earth ramps, wooden

A selection of stone, copper, and bronze knives from Kahun (c.1890 BC), showing that metal and stone tools continued to be used alongside each other. The flint knife (center row, right) has a handle of fiber and cord.

sledges and rollers, and ropes and levers enabled them to move vast quantities of stone and to erect monumental buildings. The secret of their success lay in the skill and patience of the workmen and their obvious ability to work as members of an effective gang. Although the numbers of conscripted labor used for the heaviest work may have been considerable, the corps of professional craftsmen was probably quite small. Certainly in the Old Kingdom, and probably at other times, religious fervor and the belief that their efforts were contributing to the king's (and, therefore, their own) chance of attaining eternity must have inspired their efforts.

Initially the Egyptians' knowledge and expertise went into constructing their tombs and temples, but it was subsequently utilized for improving their living conditions. Preparation for death and worship of the gods accounted for the expenditure of much of the national wealth and resources, and after several generations the burden became too great for society to bear, as occurred, for example, at the end of the Old Kingdom. Not only was each king expected to build his own tomb and support the tombs of his favored courtiers and officials but he was also required to restore and renovate the monuments built by his predecessors.

Nevertheless, the tombs and temples were vitally important because they represented in stone the magical concepts and rituals of the religion. Each temple symbolized not only the place of creation but also the god's house and was regarded as a microcosm of the universe; its rituals ensured the continuation of the world, the king's success, and the fertility of Egypt. Similarly the pyramids and tombs represented the dwellings of the dead where they would be able to experience resurrection and rebirth. Therefore, despite the expense and labor involved in constructing these monuments, it was inconceivable that they would ever cease to be built and maintained.

ARCHITECTS AND ARTISANS

Few details have survived of individual artists and architects, as their work was mostly anonymous. Fortunately, information can be gained from some tomb biographies in which a man's titles and position are recorded and, occasionally, the fact that he was responsible for the construction or decoration of a particular monument is noted. There were administrators with titles such as "Chief-of-Works"; the Scribes of Thoth (the god of learning) who oversaw the building plans and programs; and technicians who executed the work. Construction and decoration of a tomb or temple was carried out by craftsmen who worked together under a master; they included quarrymen, sculptors, painters, carpenters, and metalsmiths.

One particularly famous architect, Imhotep, was remembered by later generations, not for his role as the designer and builder of Djoser's Step Pyramid at Saqqara but because he was credited with the foundation of medical science. A man of obscure origins he became Djoser's vizier and held the titles of "Hereditary Prince," "King's Sealer," and "Royal Carpenter and Mason." He was also regarded as a sage, and in one of the Songs of Harpers the author writes, "I have heard the words of Imhotep and Hardedef, who both speak thus: 'Behold the dwellings of those men, their walls fall down, their place is no more, they are as though they had never existed.'" Indeed Imhotep is attributed with authorship of the oldest Instructions in Wisdom (which have not survived), and he apparently advised the king successfully on many matters including actions to be taken following a seven-year period of famine.

The Egyptian historian Manetho credits Imhotep with the invention of building in stone; the Step Pyramid complex at Saqqara, the world's earliest known stone building, incorporates many architectural innovations and new building materials and techniques. This is Imhotep's only surviving heritage, however, since the literary and medical texts attributed to him have never been discovered, and the location of his tomb remains unknown.

In later years Imhotep was greatly renowned and worshiped by Egyptians and Greeks as their god of medicine. Many bronze figurines have survived from this period showing him as a seated, shaven-headed priest who holds an unrolled papyrus on his knees as the symbol of his wisdom and knowledge.

All draftsmen followed the traditions that had been laid down for architectural designs and wall decorations. The "Scribe of Forms" drew up the design; one example, made of stucco on wood, preserves the remains of a draftsman's grid with the figure of the king positioned on one side while on the other there are artist's studies for hieroglyphs. Magic underpinned the architectural and decorative plans of any monument, and architects and designers were governed by these rules when they positioned architectural features and scenes. The construction of a temple, royal funerary monument, or nonroyal tomb was either ordered by royal command or as a favor from the king for the owners of private (nonroyal) tombs. Then the "Overseer of Works" and the master craftsmen, heeding the magical requirements and the physical layout of the land, decided upon the orientation of the monument (using astronomical observations)

and determined how they would deal with any building problems; they also organized the sequence and performance of rites associated with the foundation and construction of the monument. They played both a religious and practical role, which underlined the importance of their contribution.

THE ROYAL WORKFORCE

Documentation discovered at the royal necropolis workmen's towns at Kahun and Deir el-Medina provides insight into the royal labor force's terms and conditions of service. In general these were quite favorable owing to the workers' unique status and contribution to the royal after-life.

Anatomy of a Work Gang

Documents found in the rubbish heaps at Deir el-Medina indicate that the gang of craftsmen engaged in constructing and decorating the royal tomb may have numbered 120 men as a full complement, perhaps at the start of a reign when a new tomb was inaugurated, but fell to a lower number as the tomb progressed. These figures are based on the records of grain rations supplied to the men.

The gang was divided into a right and left side, and men were usually permanently attached to one side, although they could be temporarily or permanently transferred as the need arose. Each gang contained different categories of workmen; the most important—the chief workmen—numbered two, each controlling one side of the tomb. They directed the workmen and acted as their representatives in dealings with the authorities. They also settled disputes and sat on the local law court (kenbet) which handled the community's legal problems. At the site they supervised the tomb materials and took charge of the wood and colors supplied by the authorities as well as distributing new tools, wood, clothes, oil, and wicks to the workforce as required.

Each gang had two deputies who supported the chiefs; the deputies also had legal and administrative responsibilities, helped the chief and the royal scribe with investigations and inspections, and assisted with the distribution to the workforce of their rations—bread, fish, wicks, timber, and charcoal for fuel, gypsum, oil, and jugs of beer. There were also tomb guardians who protected the stock of tomb materials, sat on the local court, inspected tombs, and escorted prisoners and suspects. Each tomb had two doorkeepers conscripted from outside the gang who acted as messengers and couriers for the workmen. Male servants carried water and food for the workmen, cut wood, made gypsum for coating the tomb walls, made pots, and washed clothes. Women slaves were also attached to the gang. They were provided by the king to grind the workmen's grain rations into flour on grindstones in the village.

The administrative duties associated with the tomb were carried out by two royal scribes. They kept records of the workmen's activities and wages, payments received for the workmen, tools and commodities issued to the community, and the workers' reasons for absenteeism. Chiefs and scribes formed the three or four "captains of the tomb" who were collectively responsible for the workmen's behavior. There were also the police (Medjay) of the tomb who ensured the site's safety.

Wages and Labor Relations

The records supply information not only about the composition and responsibilities of the gang but also about promotion procedures and wages. There seems to have been a policy of paying men at two levels: Those supporting wives and families had a higher wage than bachelors who, as young men, received training as stonemasons, carpenters, sculptors, or draftsmen. They either succeeded their fathers to become members of the royal gang or were recruited from outside. Places were limited, and there were more workmen's children than available vacancies; this led to intense competition with fathers attempting to persuade the chiefs to appoint their sons. This was done by means of flattery and bribery with presents, mostly of wooden furniture.

Wages were paid on the twenty-eighth day of each month for the following month. Basic payment was in grain (emmer wheat for flour and barley for beer) authorized by the vizier and drawn from the king's granary by the royal scribe. The government also supplied fish, vegetables, water, wood for fuel, and pottery; there were less regular payments of cakes, ready-made beer, and dates and bonuses of salt, natron, sesame oil, and meat for special occasions such as festivals. Some clothes were also supplied. The payments generally exceeded requirements, and the community could barter some of these goods with other people for different products. Workers also enhanced their income by producing fine quality goods for the homes and tombs of the wealthy.

Deir el-Medina was generally a prosperous community when the government payments were regular, but if crop failures or other demands depleted the granaries and the wages were delayed, the workers and their families experienced hardship. There were frequent complaints about these delays in Dynasty 20, and when the food was still not forthcoming the workforce withdrew its labor. The first record of a major strike occurred in year 29 of Ramesses III's reign (c.1158 BC), and there were shorter strikes in later reigns, the last being recorded in year 13 of Ramesses X. Documentary evidence from Kahun, an earlier workmen's town, however, indicates that such disputes probably occurred before and may have been a feature of industrial relations since the Old Kingdom. Because work on the royal tomb had special significance and it was essential that the tomb should be completed so that the king could pass safely to the afterlife, the royal workforce had considerable bargaining power with the authorities. They were obliged to find the means of supplying the rations, and the strike action was inevitably successful.

There were, however, other reasons for delay in completing the royal tomb. Records indicate that absenteeism from work was commonplace; on occasions, the whole gang absconded to undertake unofficial duties for the chiefs and scribes—such as decorating their tombs. The attendance register gives other reasons for absenteeism, including illness, nursing other workmen, preparing the body of a deceased member of the community for burial, attending funerals, offering to the gods, attending festivals, undertaking household repairs, and even quarreling with one's wife, brewing beer, and getting drunk!

Living Conditions

The workmen lived with their families at Deir el-Medina but spent their working days in the Valley of the Kings, sleeping overnight in huts nearby. Remains of these camp buildings have been found at both Deir el-Medina and Amarna. The men worked continuously for eight days and returned to their homes on the ninth and tenth days. Each day in the Valley of the Kings, they worked two four-hour shifts with a lunch break at noon. In addition to their six days of rest each month, however, there were sometimes other free days in the work week and frequent official holidays and religious festivals as well as unofficial extended "weekend breaks" and time taken off to prepare their own tombs.

In the workmen's absence, when they were at the royal tomb site, the life of the community in the town was organized by the women; they were responsible for bringing up their families and supervising the household and the slaves who ground the grain. Other residents who lived permanently in the town included retired men, the sick, men on special duties associated with the law courts and religion, and the servants.

BUILDING MATERIALS AND TECHNIQUES

Brick

Stone was used to build tombs and temples, but dried bricks were employed for all domestic dwellings, since Nile mud can be easily fashioned into the required shape and then dried in the sun. Kiln-baked bricks appeared c.600 BC, but most bricks were unburned. Scenes in the tomb of the vizier Rekhmire at Thebes (Dynasty 18) illustrate the process of manufacturing the bricks, and at Kahun the excavator W. M. Flinders Petrie discovered a wooden mud brick mold.

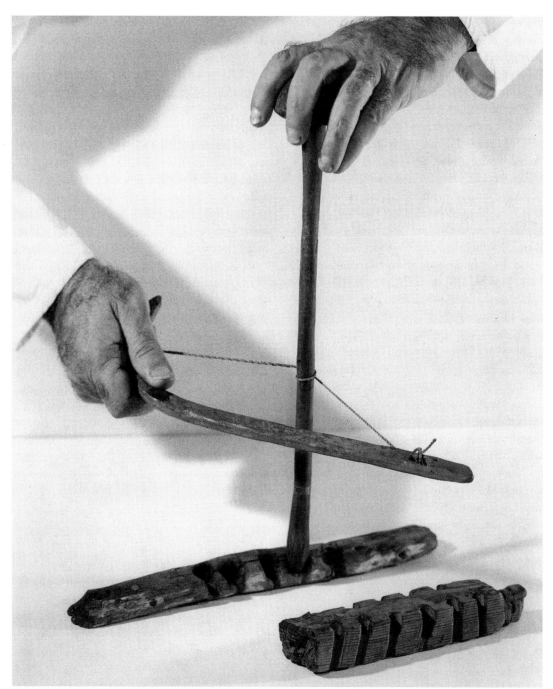

This firestick from Kahun (c.1890 BC) was the first fire-making tool ever found in Egypt. It is essentially a bow drill with four parts: Heavy pressure was exerted on a conical stone drill-cap that pushed the wooden firestick down into the hole in the wooden matrix; by simultaneously pressing down the firestick and pulling the bow drill, the operator caused sparks to ignite at the matrix. A spare matrix is shown (front right).

Construction commenced as soon as the required number of bricks was produced. The bricks, often concave to provide stability, were built up alternately in one or two layers with the broad side facing outward first and then the narrow side, unlike the modern custom of placing all bricks in each row so that the broad side faces outward. Pieces of wood, even complete tree trunks, were sometimes incorporated into large brick buildings to give them strength. Nile mud mixed with potsherds was also used as a mortar in the brick buildings.

Wood and Wooden Pillars

In earliest times trees were relatively abundant in Egypt, and wood was probably widely used for building. By the historic period, however, local woods became scarce and not very serviceable; they were used for the production of weapons, domestic articles, ordinary coffins, and statuettes. Local sycamore, palm trees, willow, acacia, and thorn trees met these needs, but the Egyptians had to go abroad for better timber. From at least as early as Dynasty 2 they traveled to Byblos to obtain cedars from Lebanon, which could be used for ships, the best coffins, flag masts on pylons, and large temple doors.

An important architectural feature of later stone buildings owes its form to the initial use of wood for this purpose. The pillar was originally devised as a wooden prop, needed to support the roof even in mud or wooden buildings. It was fixed at the base in a lump of clay so that it had a firmer hold on the ground, and where the roof beam rested on it at the top a board was placed between the pillar and the beam to divide the weight. In the later stone columns these features were retained as a round base and square abacus. Wooden pillars were decorated around the top with bunches or garlands of flowers and buds, which developed into the flower- and bud-form capitals of later stone columns.

Stone

Egyptian carpenters were no doubt skillful, using mortises and joints from the time of the Old Kingdom, but it was the masons who were the outstanding craftsmen; they carried the mastery of stone to perhaps unequaled heights. Masons could not only carve limestone with delicate reliefs but also carve and polish hard stones such as granite and diorite; they were especially adept at dealing with deficiencies in the available material.

Fine white limestone, used for the pyramids and best mastabas, was obtained from the Tura quarries near Memphis. Alabaster came from quarries south of Tura in the Wadi Gerrawi, and sandstone—the least destructible building material—came mainly from Gebel es-Silsila. Red granite was brought from the quarries at Aswan, while black granite was transported from the Wadi Hammamat between Coptos and the Red Sea, a journey of two or three days from the Nile.

In the Aswan quarries it is possible to observe the places from which obelisks (upright stones placed at the entrance to temples) were cut. Obelisks often weighed hundreds of tons, and the largest (over a thousand tons) still lies in an unfinished state in the Aswan quarry. There are various theories about the methods of quarrying, transporting, and erecting the obelisks. Evidence at Aswan indicates that to remove the stone the masons probably chiseled holes into the rock to a depth of about six inches and then forced wooden wedges into these holes before moistening them with water so that the wood swelled and caused the rock to split. The obelisk could then be chiseled out and transported by river to the site of the temple, where it was finished.

Tools

Craftsmen's tools were generally simple. In addition to tomb scenes illustrating craftsmen at work, some rare examples of tools have also been found. At Kahun W. M. Flinders Petrie discovered a caster's shop that still contained metal tools and earthenware molds for metal casting. He also found masons' tools and wooden pieces used in stoneworking near the royal monuments at Lahun. At Kahun metal and stone tools both continued to be used alongside each other for appropriate tasks.

Carpenters generally used copper or bronze tools, but stonemasons employed both stone and metal implements. Stone tools included flint axe and adze blades, knives, scrapers, and flakes; the adze blades were fitted with wooden handles. Metal tools were now used for stone facing, however, and the masons could cut and work stones that ranged from soft limestone to granite and basalt. Analysis of the Kahun metals has shown that the metalsmiths were adept at judiciously adding certain alloys to metals to make them suitable for particular tasks; they also tempered them and thus were probably able to produce tools of required strengths to deal with all these stones.

Other masons' tools found at Kahun included wooden wedges and clamps (flat pieces of wood with expanding ends) to hold stones in place, as in pavements. There were also stone and clay plummets and wooden offset pieces that were used for facing the stone blocks.

TOMBS AND PYRAMIDS

From earliest times the Egyptians believed that people continued their existence after death, and the burial place (grave, tomb, or pyramid) was designed to protect the body and provide a location to which the deceased owner's spirit could return at will to partake of food and other offerings. In the first Neolithic communities of the Badarian Period, the graves were situated away from the living communities, at the edge of the desert. They were mostly oval in shape and contained single burials, although some held two bodies. The body, wrapped in coarse matting or placed in a coffin of woven twigs or in an animal skin, lay a few feet deep in the sand. Such graves were probably marked by a small pile of sand or stones placed on top of the burial.

Early Tomb Development

THE MASTABA

By c.3400 BC (Nagada II Period) the burial customs had changed, and although the pit graves continued in use for the poorer classes a new type of tomb was introduced for the ruling class. (This new, marked distinction between the burials of the rulers and the masses may indicate an ethnic or racial distinction, perhaps the result of foreign incursions.) The new type of tomb—known today as a mastaba—set the pattern for wealthy burials in the Archaic Period and Old Kingdom. Rectangular in shape with four sloping sides, the mastaba tomb was at first built of mud brick, but later it resembled the pile of stones used to mark the location of each predynastic tomb. Those built as early as Dynasty 4 actually consisted of heaps of stone covered with a casing of sloping flat blocks. The burial chamber, cut in the rock, was reached by means of a shaft that led down from the roof of the mastaba. In the earliest examples the interior walls were lined with matting or strengthened with wooden planks, but in early dynastic times this had developed into a wooden coffin or a wood-paneled chamber. The wooden coffin (which eventually entirely replaced the custom of placing the body in a reed mat) was placed in a recess cut into the side and floor of the burial pit.

Apart from this substructure below ground, there was a superstructure within the stone-cased walls above ground. This housed the tomb goods and accommodated the tomb chapel, where offerings were brought as eternal supplies for the deceased. The interior walls of the chapel were decorated with scenes of the everyday existence of the owner and of food production and harvesting so that his soul would never experience hunger.

Throughout Dynasty 1 the substructure was deepened and enlarged in an attempt to protect the funerary goods from robbers. The size of the tomb was increased, and a staircase was built onto the east side of the superstructure; this led directly down to the burial area and was an additional security feature, since it could be blocked with stone slabs. It also provided an easier route for transporting the increased number of tomb goods. At this time two important tombs—those of Enezib and Queen Herneith—were built; these possessed features that may have formed the basis for the building designs ultimately found in the first step pyramid at Saqqara.

By the end of Dynasty 1, the substructure continued to be enlarged and deepened, but the storerooms, once situated in the superstructure, were now discontinued. Funerary goods were placed in the burial chamber, although the food and drink offerings were kept in subsidiary rooms. The tomb structure itself became more elaborate, but the quantity of funerary goods diminished. A large, rectangular stone coffin, which sometimes contained a wooden coffin, was now used.

The external walls of the mud brick mastabas were originally covered with recessed brick paneling that as a decorative feature simulated the facade of contemporary palaces. This again disappeared, however, toward the end of Dynasty 1. The recesses in the paneled facade were translated into niches that perhaps acted as false doors in the superstructure to allow the deceased's spirit to gain access to the storeroom inside. When the storage rooms were discontinued the recesses were reduced to two in number, situated at the east end of the mastaba. One was now the false door to the tomb and the other formed a subsidiary entrance.

Burial structures developed and became more elaborate throughout Dynasty 2, but by the end of the Archaic Period mastaba tombs had become standardized for the rulers and nobility. Toward the end of the Old Kingdom, when the king's power declined and nobles seized their own opportunities, they increasingly prepared their tombs near their own homes instead of at the base of the king's pyramid. The nobles now preferred to be buried in rock tombs cut into the steep cliffs fringing the river in Middle and Upper Egypt. It was probably the stepped, layered brick superstructures of the earlier mastabas, however, that formed the inspiration for the Step Pyramid at Saqqara and later pyramid constructions.

Pyramid Construction

STEP PYRAMIDS

The Step Pyramid at Saqqara consists of a series of superimposed mastaba tombs of decreasing

An early twentieth-century photograph showing the Great Sphinx (which may represent Chephren's own facial features) and the Great Pyramid built by Cheops at Giza. Scholars and travelers have regularly visited Giza over the centuries.

size. It was constructed at the beginning of Dynasty 3 by Imhotep, the royal architect, for King Djoser and was originally designed as a mastaba but later extended upward to incorporate six steps. Below ground level there is a deep shaft that allows access to a series of corridors and rooms where Djoser and his family were buried. This pyramid retains the two main areas of a mastaba tomb: the superstructure and substructure. It has been suggested that step pyramids were associated with a star cult, whereas the later "true" pyramids were symbols of the sun god.

The Step Pyramid at Saqqara was only the central feature in a vast complex surrounded by wall of white limestone (which may have imitated the wall around the king's palace). The complex was planned as a single unit, and it is unique; there is no known precedent for any of the buildings, and the overall scheme was never repeated. The complex displays many interesting features: The craftsmen were novices in the use of stone for large monuments since mud brick, wood, and reed had been used for earlier religious buildings, and there is evidence of experimentation with different forms. Stone fluted and ribbed columns imitated the bundles of reeds and wooden pillars found in earlier buildings, and uncertain if free-standing columns would hold up the roof the builders designed engaged columns to give added support; also, small stone blocks rather than the massive pieces found in later constructions were employed here to imitate the mud bricks used in earlier tombs.

TRUE PYRAMIDS

It was perhaps a religious change from a star cult to the sun cult that prompted the transition from step pyramid to the true, or smooth-sided, pyramids. It is possible to trace this development in a number of pyramids. Several stepped or layered pyramids are known; for example, the Meidum pyramid was originally designed as a small step pyramid, which was subsequently extended to incorporate seven or eight superimposed layers. When the steps were infilled with local stone and the sides of the pyramid were faced with white limestone, it became a true pyramid.

It is believed that the smooth-sided angles of the true pyramid form may have symbolized the sun ray which provided the king's soul with a means of access to heaven. The first building planned from its inception as a true pyramid was the northern pyramid at Dahshur; its southern neighbor (both were probably built for King Sneferu) was planned as a true pyramid, but perhaps because of anxiety over the original angle of its sides, the angle of incline was later sharply decreased just beyond halfway up the monument's height, producing a bent, or blunted, effect.

It was at Giza, however, that the pyramid complex reached its classical form. Cheops (Khufu) chose this dramatic site—a slightly elevated plateau—which provided him with the opportunity to build an unrivaled monument with surrounding space for subsidiary buildings. He not only constructed the Great Pyramid; sufficient evidence remains of the adjacent minor pyramids, boat pits, and mastaba tomb fields for his relatives and courtiers to convey something of his original scheme. His son Chephren (Khafre) and grandson Mycerinus (Menkaure)

also built pyramid complexes at Giza, and in Chephren's burial we can see the fully developed elements of the classic complex: a pyramid for the royal burial; adjoining mortuary temple for the burial rites and subsequent rituals to provide the king's eternal food supply; and a covered causeway that joined the mortuary temple to the valley building where the king's body was first received on its final journey. The valley building lay at the river's edge and was also the place where the eternal supplies would have been landed and unloaded. It was possibly also used for embalming and purification rites.

Building Methods

Little is actually known of pyramid construction methods and work practices, although there are many theories. It has been suggested that the peasants, occupied for most of the year irrigating the soil and cultivating the land, may have been summoned to work at the pyramid site for three months annually, when the inundation placed much of the soil underwater. Paid in kind, this work would have kept them from starvation and also occupied them so that they did not cause political or social problems.

It is generally accepted that construction of a pyramid involved the laying of individual courses of stone from the center outward, building the inner core of local stone and using Tura limestone and occasionally granite for the outer casing, which was smoothed from the apex downward once the pyramid was finished. There has been much discussion, however, over how the stones were lifted from the ground to the required height or level and then moved into place. Brick ramps may have been used; lengthened and raised as each course was laid, the stones would have been dragged up these, possibly on sledges. Remains of such ramps have been found at a couple of sites, but the effort involved in building these would have been very great. An alternative theory (although no archaeological evidence has yet been found to support this) is that they constructed girdle ramps around the four sides of the pyramid.

TEMPLES

The foundation of a temple was an important and sacred event (few were built in each reign). At the start of Egypt's history probably only one type of temple was built at sites throughout the country. Records kept in temple archives provided information about the stages of temple construction so that there was conformity between those erected in the Old Kingdom (which were themselves probably based on plans of predynastic shrines) and those put up thousands of years later in the Greco-Roman Period.

Construction Rituals

The first known reference to an actual foundation ritual occurs in association with the Old Kingdom solar temples when the rites of "Stretching the Cord" and "Setting out the Four Sides of the Enclosure" are mentioned. The rite of Stretching the Cord (staking out the ground) occurs in Dynasty 2 and almost certainly goes back to predynastic times. Its earliest depiction is in two scenes on a gate jamb at Hieraconpolis (reign of Khasekhemui). This was the first phase in laying out the ground plan when the axis on the plan was marked on the ground with a twelve-knot cord. In one scene the king holds a stick or mace and stands before his people; facing him are four ranks of smaller figures who

also hold sticks. In the next scene the king and the goddess Seshat are shown hammering boundary poles into the earth.

The subsequent rite was that of "Releasing the Cord," when four stakes and a length of rope were used to determine the size and position of the temple. Next, the land on the four sides of the site was hacked up with a hoe; this created trenches that would hold the foundation blocks. Pits were excavated in the trench in the positions where the blocks would be placed. The bricks were then manufactured, and the trench was filled with a mixture of sand and sherds to protect the walls against water infiltration. Foundation deposits containing small models of tools and implements were next inserted at various points under the walls, and four bricks (or sometimes more) were put at the corners of the building, representing a very ancient rite. The king then whitewashed the building with *besen* (probably chalk) as a form of purification. At some point heads of a bull and geese were also placed in the ground.

Once the temple was finished the building was consecrated, and the temple and its enclosure were named. The god Tanen performed this ceremony which magically brought the temple to life so that it could be handed over to its resident god. The naming of the temple enabled it to protect the god, which was the main purpose of these rites. The god was finally invited by Tanen to enter and take possession of his sanctuary. The mural scenes in the temples that depict the foundation and consecration rites usually occur together, but in the Temple of Sethos I at Abydos they were placed in different parts of the building. Their inclusion in the building was meant to impart magical protection to the temple.

The position of a temple was probably fixed astronomically on the previous night by orientating the south axis of the temple from north to

Part of the facade of the Great Temple (c.1290 BC) built by Ramesses II at Abu Simbel. This rock-cult temple was dedicated to Ptah, Amen-Re, Re-Harakhte and Ramesses II and was discovered by the traveler J. L. Burckhardt in AD 1813. It was moved to a new location between 1964 and 1968 as part of the UNESCO Salvage Campaign.

south between the constellation of the Great Bear and Orion. The ritual was said to be performed by the king who was accompanied by Seshat, Ptah, and Khnum. Seshat, the "Lady of Builders," was a very ancient goddess whose duty was to help the king measure out the ground plan of the temple and reckon the measurement of the building. Sometimes she was replaced by Thoth, god of science, or Ptah, god of crafts, but usually Ptah and Khnum, a creator god, were primarily concerned with the physical construction of the temple.

The kings appear to have shown a great personal interest in these foundation ceremonies. They would almost certainly have performed the rites in person at each temple, particularly the staking out of the constructional diagram of the plan. They would have been assisted by priests impersonating Ptah and Thoth and possibly the queen representing Seshat. The founding and establishing of the gods' temples was one of the king's most important duties, in return for which he received Egypt as his inheritance.

The temple consecration was repeated every year on New Year's Day to give new life to the buildings, its scenes, and all its furnishings and equipment. At the conclusion of the consecration, and once the purification of the temple was completed, a meal was prepared for the craftsmen who had built and decorated the god's mansion and for the priests who served the deity.

Building Methods

The actual construction methods can be deduced, although no records have survived; nevertheless, plans must have existed in the past. Great skill was required to erect these monumental buildings: cutting and dressing stones, placing the huge blocks in position, and raising the columns, capitals, architraves, and ceilings.

They had a well-trained, coordinated workforce although their equipment was simple. In addition to the problems of construction on site, however, the blocks had to be carried on barges and transported by river and then finally dragged across land on rollers. Once the construction had been completed the craftsmen began the arduous tasks of sculpting and painting the reliefs on the walls, columns, and ceilings, thus creating a superb and appropriate dwelling for the god.

TOWNS

Tombs and temples provide most information about ancient Egypt because they were built of stone to last for eternity. They are well preserved, and most have not been built over in succeeding periods; their wall scenes and the objects buried in the tombs provide a wealth of information about daily life as well as religious and funerary practices. The towns (settlement sites) are also very important, but many of these no longer exist because they were all built of mud brick, which did not fare well under the alluvial mud of the yearly inundations or was removed for use as fertilizer by many generations of local people. Therefore, settlement sites have not been studied in as much detail as the tombs and temples, and it is difficult to correctly assess the number and size of towns that once existed.

Patterns of Urban Development

Some archaeologists claim that there was no widespread true urban development and that walled cities with different building levels and continuous settlement did not exist throughout the land. The strong, centralized monarchy established at the start of Dynasty 1 removed the need, it is argued, for walled towns, and deserts and mountains protected the people from external threats. Egypt was thus able to use most of its resources for constructing tombs (especially the king's burial monument) and temples rather than for fortified towns. This contrasted markedly with the parallel early civilization in Mesopotamia where the city-state was the most important element dominating the society, and there were continuing conflicts between the city-states. In Egypt, however, towns were possibly only built in those areas where products entered the country or along the east-west trade route linking the Red Sea and the oases in the Western Desert. Otherwise, there were perhaps only a small number of towns situated along the Nile; each nome (district) had an urban center that housed the local administrators and officials and their families; and there was the royal capital which accommodated the residence of the royal family and was also the seat of government. The location of the capital varied from one period to another, and there were also other royal residences, which the kings visited periodically, around the country. All these towns housed not only the officials but all the other people—craftsmen, traders, and farmers—who were needed to feed and service the community. This state of relative nonurbanization, it is claimed, continued until the New Kingdom.

According to an alternative view, however, Egypt had an ordinary pattern of urban development rather than just these scattered towns. Certainly when the Greeks arrived they remarked that there were thousands of towns and villages. Centers would have developed in a number of ways: In many cases the predynastic villages developed to become capitals of nomes;

new villages sometimes grew up; there were new locations for temples and royal residences; and there were military colonies at the forts and fortresses and royal workmen's towns to house the necropolis workforces and their families. There were three major capital cities—Memphis, Heliopolis, and Thebes—and, it is claimed, even in the Old Kingdom there were also walled towns of various types and sizes such as Edfu and Abydos. Some were administrative centers, and others were centers of worship that had a national importance. The geographic location of a town or the economic activity of a community sometimes dictated their growth and development, but others were specifically created by the government to house the personnel associated with temples or other monuments. Again, in addition to the officials and their families, craftsmen and agricultural workers lived in these settlements to supply the community's needs.

The inundation dictated the location of the towns, which were concentrated on mounds and hillocks formed by the alluvial deposits and on the dykes. They were continuously rebuilt on former constructions that were demolished and leveled, and certainly in the long-established towns there was no logical order or real attempt at town planning. This practice of rebuilding at the same site over many generations makes it very difficult to study their town planning principles, but a few sites that were built for a particular purpose and occupied for a limited period have remained sufficiently intact to enable us to examine their methods. These include the towns built for the royal necropolis workers (Kahun, Deir el-Medina, and the special village at Tell el-Amarna) and the capital city of Akhetaten (Tell el-Amarna). The latter demonstrates that this city at least had an overall plan: Three distinct areas—residential, the palace and temple district, and administrative headquarters—were linked by three almost parallel main streets. The villas belonging to the wealthy were arranged to good advantage and occupied prime sites, but the poorer dwellings were built randomly between them.

The question of the quantity, importance, and spread of towns remains in dispute, but it is evident that two main types of urban development emerged. There was the natural and unplanned growth of towns, which evolved, for economic, administrative, or religious reasons, from the predynastic villages; and there were planned towns, initiated for particular purposes in specific locations. The latter were occupied for the duration of the project but were subsequently abandoned because there was no continuing need for them. Since they were not leveled and rebuilt for continuous occupation, some have survived in a better state than the great cities of Memphis or Thebes. They include several royal workmen's towns.

Towns for Necropolis Workmen

For building the pyramids and royal temples the Egyptians used a labor force made up of conscripted peasants and professional craftsmen and architects. No details survive of how the conscripts were controlled and managed, but they were probably temporarily housed in barracks near the building site. Purpose-built towns, however, were constructed to accommodate the craftsmen and their families for the duration of the project, and three of these have survived in a good state of preservation. Unlike most towns these were not used and rebuilt over many centuries, so their original plan and buildings have survived. Although these towns were constructed at different periods, they shared a common functional purpose and have certain physical and environmental features in common.

The earliest that has been discovered and substantially excavated to date is Kahun (although there were undoubtedly other examples in various locations built over a wide time span), constructed for the work force engaged on the pyramid at Lahun (Dynasty 12) for King Senusret II. Another town survives at the site known as Deir el-Medina whose occupants built and decorated the royal tombs of the New Kingdom (Dynasties 18 to 20) at Thebes. As part of Akhetaten (Tell el-Amarna), a capital city built specifically to accommodate the king's religious innovations, a third workmen's town was established to house the craftsmen engaged in constructing and decorating the city and its associated tombs toward the end of Dynasty 18.

The three towns were built to a predetermined plan that was unimaginative but methodical; none had developed from a previous random settlement. There was a brick enclosure wall that confined the workmen and their families to a particular location. The sites were all on the desert's edge, chosen because of proximity to the royal burial site and also because isolation ensured that their inhabitants (who had knowledge of the location and construction of the royal tombs) could be guarded. They were enclosed communities that were allowed as little contact as possible with the outside world so that their knowledge would remain secret. At Amarna and Deir el-Medina (which was occupied for several hundred years), however, random growth of houses occurred outside the boundary wall initially used to limit the physical extent of the community. Isolation and the security of these towns were considered more important than a readily available water supply, and water had to be brought some distance from the river and stored in jars at the site.

The town walls enclosed a series of alleyways laid out on a grid plan with parallel rows of regular terraced houses for the workforce and, at Kahun and Deir el-Medina, the addition of special houses for the officials. The towns varied in size—Kahun had 100 houses, Amarna had 74, and Deir el-Medina had 140. Although the towns were similar, each had some unique features in terms of its concept and development and also with regard to the objects that have been discovered there. As a group, however, they provide a unique insight into early town planning and the daily lives of these special communities.

Kahun, built (c.1895 BC) to house the pyramid and temple officials and craftsmen and their families, was excavated by William M. Flinders Petrie in the late nineteenth century. Rectangular in shape and designed by a single architect who was almost certainly the builder of the Lahun pyramid, Kahun was arranged in two sections within its enclosure wall. These were built at the same date, but the eastern part housed the wealthier quarters while the workmen's houses were concentrated in the western area. Kahun is uniquely important because it was the first example of Egyptian town planning to be uncovered by archaeologists and the possessions of the people had been left behind in the houses. This provided an unparalleled opportunity to study articles of everyday use, which were so rarely preserved in comparison with the objects placed in tombs. Some of these demonstrate specific technological developments. The discovery of written documents at Kahun has also enabled scholars to study legal, medical, veterinary, and educational practices in the town, which was continuously occupied for about 100 years. There is evidence that some of the residents were of non-Egyptian origin. The reason for desertion of the site remains unclear.

Deir el-Medina housed the royal necropolis workmen and their families for some 450 years while royal tombs were being constructed in the Valley of the Kings. Tombs of these families discovered nearby have also been excavated. Although personal possessions have not been uncovered in this town as at Kahun, a wealth of documentation has survived in the adjacent rubbish heaps. These records have supplied information about the legal and religious organization of the community. They show that the people enjoyed considerable autonomy. They also show many details of the workforce's conditions of service including the successful industrial action they took when their food rations were not paid.

At Amarna the workmen's town was divided internally into two sections, but these did not reflect a class segregation as at Kahun. Domestic objects discovered here have not been as numerous as at Kahun, but they do indicate the use of the same type of tools, household equipment, and toilet objects. Again, there is not the same wealth of inscriptional evidence as at the other sites, but Amarna is of unique religious interest because the finds in this village indicate that the workforce continued to worship traditional deities although they were building a city dedicated to the monotheistic cult of the sun disk (Aten). The workmen's town was probably only occupied for about twenty years.

PALACES

Palaces, like houses, were built of mud brick and fragile materials, and consequently only a few examples have survived. These include the palaces of Sethos I at Abydos, Ramesses II at

Qantir, Merenptah at Memphis, and Amenhotep III at Malkata, Thebes. The palaces at Tell el-Amarna are the ones that provide the most complete source of evidence, since there was only one level of occupation at this site.

The kings each had several palaces in different parts of the country that they visited regularly. Some palaces were built near temples such as those of Ramesses II and Ramesses III on the west bank at Thebes. The palace of Ramesses III at Medinet Habu features a towerlike structure uncharacteristically built of stone, which has ensured that this part has survived while the remainder of the mud brick palace has not. This residence was known as the "Pavilion of Medinet Habu."

The king's palace was called *per-aa*, meaning "great house," and this was also the title used for the ruler himself—pharaoh—from the New Kingdom onward. The main palace had a double function: It was the king's residence and also the administrative headquarters of the government. These buildings were very large with many rooms and were divided into two main sections. The outer wide walled enclosure contained the state rooms including corridors, courts, and porticos, while the inner area, a narrow and elaborately decorated building that lay at the back of the enclosure, housed the king's apartment, chambers belonging to the royal family, and the harem. A main door and two side doors led into the antechamber of the state apartments. Above this was a wide, open balcony (known as the Window of Appearances) that overlooked the street where the king and his family showed themselves to the people. The balcony was lavishly decorated with gold, lapis lazuli, and malachite and provided a place from which the king could inspect the tribute piled up below and the slaves who were paraded before him. It was also the place where he could hand out honors and collars to favorite courtiers as a mark of recognition for their services and achievements.

Behind the three antechambers were the staterooms. In the Broad Hall, which featured many columns, the king held his council meetings and had audiences with the chief government officials. There was also the King's Room, where access was allowed only to his sons, close friends, and the governor of the palace—the lord chamberlain—a prince or close personal servant of the king who controlled the royal residence.

A feature of both palaces and houses in Egypt was the inclusion of an area that we designate as a "harem." This special part of the master's house, however, was not a place of restriction. It was an area reserved for the women where they carried out their own activities and undertook the early education of their children. In addition to the harem there were dining halls, bedrooms, and a kitchen. There were also royal residence towns, visited periodically by the king, where queens and other women lived; these towns are known to have existed at Memphis and Gurob (in the Fayoum, where the king went for hunting), among other places. (At Gurob the women and their female servants produced high-quality textiles, including the royal garments, on a large scale.) These considerable communities were administered by a male bureaucracy that included a director, scribes, tax collectors, traders, and guards.

Colorful, attractive wall decorations and elegant furnishings lent both sophistication and comfort to the royal homes. The state apartments, with their columned halls, would have provided impressive settings for audiences with the king. It was regarded as a great honor to enter the god-king's presence, and people who had this privilege recorded the fact with considerable pride in their tomb inscriptions. Etiquette before the king was strictly observed.

There was a particular order in which these men were allowed to approach the king; this order was jealously guarded by the officials who presented them. In earlier periods the nobles kissed the ground in front of the king when they approached him. In the New Kingdom they simply bowed, with their hands held at their sides or raised in acclamation. Servants, however, continued to kiss the ground whenever they saw the king. In this period the councillors also addressed their ruler with an introductory eulogy when they discussed business with him. The palaces, with their impressive chambers, would have been appropriate settings for such formal audiences.

HOUSES

Relatively few examples of houses have survived. Houses were built of perishable materials, and they were also continuously leveled and rebuilt over the centuries so that the original plans and structures have been lost. There are a few surviving towns, however, that were built for a specific purpose, occupied briefly, and then abandoned so that there was only one level of occupation. From these—Kahun, Deir el-Medina, and Amarna village (all royal workmen's towns), and Amarna (the capital built for king Akhenaten's monotheistic cult)—it is possible to study the architecture of the houses. Additional information is derived from illustrations of houses in tomb scenes and models of houses placed in the tombs, which sometimes include gardens with representational trees and pools. There appear to have been two main types of houses: the townhouse, which existed in the long-established cities as well as in the purpose-built towns, and the villa, situated where there was sufficient space to incorporate a garden. The houses, constructed of mud brick, were similar to those found today in modern country villages throughout Egypt.

All Egyptian houses were quite dark. The use of glass for windows was unknown; small, sometimes barred windows were set high into the walls of some main rooms or, as at Deir el-Medina, small holes were left in the roof construction to provide some light. Doors would also have been left open to increase the natural light supply, and in the larger houses open and partly colonnaded courts brought sunlight to the inner living areas. Natural light was augmented by the use of lamps and wicks.

Villas

Villas, exemplified by those uncovered at Amarna, sometimes included small chapels in their gardens for family worship. Wealthy houses had rooms on two stories plus a basement for storage. The master greeted his guests in a columned reception hall located on the ground floor, with access provided from the main door. This was furnished with low divans where the guests could relax. The bedrooms and women's quarters formed the private area of the house, which was often situated on the first floor. At the front of the house there was frequently a terrace facing north where the owner could sit in the evenings. In the larger villas the conical silos, stables, kennels, storerooms, servants' quarters, and kitchens were located in an area of the garden. These houses also had bathrooms and lavatories, and they were generally furnished to provide a luxurious lifestyle.

At Kahun houses had reception areas, women's quarters, a washing/bathing room, a kitchen, cellars, and circular granaries. Some of the officials who were associated with the administration of the pyramid or temple lived in large houses. Five mansions were built along the north wall and followed one plan. Leading from the street to the south, a doorway with a stone lintel (facing a doorkeeper's room) gave access to the house. Behind it there lay three separate means of entry to the rooms beyond, which visitors would take according to their individual business; thus, these houses were used for both the owner's private and public activities. At the left-hand side of the entrance, a passage led to the offices and rooms of the male servants and guests.

In the center of the house, reached by a large passage from the main entrance, a group of private chambers opened onto a four-pillared hall; behind this was a reception hall, partly colonnaded and partly open to the sky, where the master met his guests. Private chambers used only by the owner and his family led directly off this hall; these included the master's own colonnaded court with a sunken tank for washing, which was used by the family—possibly in connection with their domestic worship.

From the main entrance a third passage on the right-hand side led to several small rooms and another columned hall, which had direct access to the main reception hall. This comprised the women's quarters, and it was the most private area of the house. Generally, each mansion had large, cool rooms and a roof supported by stone or wooden columns set in stone bases. These columns were fluted or ribbed with capitals decorated with plain abaci or the palm leaf motif. The houses were inwardly centered, with halls and chambers where the outside heat and dust of the street could be forgotten.

Workmen's Housing

By contrast, in the streets of workmen's terraced houses, each dwelling had either four or seven rooms (depending on their location within the town). The rooms were grouped together, with one entrance to the street. Built of mud brick, they had one story; the flat roof was probably used for sitting out or sleeping and to store fuel and straw, since a series of steps provided access to this area. Some houses were roofed with a barrel vault of brickwork (indicating that the arch was already in common use), but most roofs were built of beams of wood supporting poles onto which bundles of reeds or straw were lashed; the inner and outer surfaces were subsequently coated with mud plaster.

Semicircular arches of brick spaced with chips of limestone formed the doorways, and wood was used for door cases, thresholds, doors, and door bolts. In each block of houses the design followed a repetitive scheme, and the dwellings were obviously built to meet precise official requirements. The roofs over the larger rooms were supported by octagonal, wooden columns set in stone bases, and the inside walls of the best rooms were mud plastered and decorated. In the kitchen there were conical, brick granaries plastered on the inner and outer surfaces and frequently arranged in pairs; the cooking fire was generally located at one side of the room in a depression in the floor.

In the Amarna village the workmen's houses followed a uniform design with an outer hall, living room, bedroom, and a kitchen that gave access to the roof. Two distinct types of brick were used in construction, perhaps indicating that the government had supplied proper mud bricks and an architect to build the enclosure wall and the foundation courses of some houses and that subsequently each family provided its own materials, including inferior bricks or rough stones.

At Deir el-Medina the houses were all arranged in blocks of terraces. The earliest were built entirely of mud brick, but later ones had stone or brick basements and stone walls topped with mud brick, and stone was used for some of the thresholds. They had one story, and the flat roofs were constructed of wooden beams and matting. Stone or wood was used for the door frames, and on the door jambs and lintels hieroglyphic texts painted in red assisted in the identification of the occupant.

These houses all opened directly off the street and had four rooms. First, there was an entrance hall with a brick structure resembling a four-poster bed, which was decorated with painted figures of women and Bes, the household god of marriage and happiness. This may have been an altar for domestic worship or a "birthbed." Niches in the wall held painted stelae, ancestral busts, and offering tables, and the room probably served as a domestic shrine. Off the entrance hall was the main living room. Here, the roof level was higher and one or more columns supported it, allowing small windows to be set high in the walls to provide some light. There was also a low, brick platform that was used as a bed or divan. One or two other rooms lay behind and probably provided a sleeping area or storage space, and finally at the rear of the house there was a kitchen. This was walled but open to the sky and contained storage bins, a small brick or pottery oven for baking bread, an open hearth, and an area for grinding grain. There was a staircase leading from the first, second, or fourth rooms that gave access to the flat roof, and some houses had underground cellars that were used for additional storage.

The government apparently built all the houses within the original enclosure of the town and assigned them to particular tenants, but gradually occupancy became hereditary and families passed on the tenancies from one generation to the next.

DECORATION: RELIGIOUS AND SECULAR

Tombs and Temples

In buildings with a religious purpose, the decoration of the walls and ceiling was largely dictated by principles of sympathetic magic. The main aim was to enable the owner (god, king, or tomb owner) to magically reactivate the content of the scenes so that they could continue to experience and enjoy these activities throughout eternity. A ceremony known as the "Opening of the Mouth," performed by a special priest who, with an adze, touched the mouth, hands, and feet of the figures sculpted and painted on these walls, was believed to bring these scenes to life.

Although there was some variation in the wall decoration of nobles' tombs over the centuries, the pattern essentially included scenes of offerings being presented; activities on the owner's estate such as harvesting, agriculture, herding cattle, tending wild and domestic animals, dairy farming, and netting birds; and the owner's leisure activities such as hunting birds, fishing in a papyrus marsh, hunting animals in the desert, listening to music and singing, playing games, and banqueting. The preparations for the owner's funeral were often depicted and frequently included scenes of craftsmen preparing tomb goods.

During the Old Kingdom, from Dynasty 5, the Pyramid Texts were inscribed on the interior walls of pyramids to provide the king with magical protection and supply him with spells that would give him every means of access to heaven. In the New Kingdom, the kings' tombs at Thebes were decorated with scenes of rites taken from the sacred books, thus providing an illustrated record of the journey of the sun god through the underworld where he fought evils and demons. These were present to help the king defeat the dangers encountered in his own passage from life to the hereafter. In the queens' and princes' tombs, the scenes again focused on the successful completion of their final journey and on their relationship with the gods.

In the temples, the wall scenes depicted the rituals once performed in various areas of the building (thus ensuring their continuation) or historical events such as the king's coronation or the foundation and consecration of the temple.

Dwellings

In the palaces and houses, there was greater freedom and opportunity to develop the architectural features found in the stone temples and tombs. In the palaces at Amarna and Thebes there is evidence of their richly painted interiors; rural scenes and details adorned the walls, floors, and ceilings. The Ramesside palaces also provide evidence that faience tiles and rosettes were used as inlays in friezes and borders. In the king's bedroom, flowers were placed around his bed as additional decoration.

There is also evidence that people painted scenes and designs on the interior walls of their houses. At Kahun the inside walls of the best rooms in the houses were often plastered with a layer of mud. Plasterers' floats were discovered there; the larger float, made of wood, was used to apply the rough coat of plaster, and the smaller, lighter one was employed for the facing coat.

Sometimes a series of colored borders was painted on top of the plaster with a dark color or black at the bottom. Three to five feet above this, black and red lines were painted on a white background above which the wall was given a yellow wash. In two of the workmen's houses there were wall scenes; one showed a representation of an apparently unique building with columns, while the other illustrated a large house. The outside of the lower half of the house is shown, but for the upper level the wall is cut away to give a view of the interior where the master is waited upon by his servant.

At the New Kingdom royal workmen's town of Deir el-Medina, the more affluent occupants plastered and whitewashed the outside walls of their houses and painted their doors red. Interior walls were either whitewashed or decorated with murals, and the columns, door surrounds, and windows were painted (yellow and blue were particularly favored). Unlike at Kahun the furniture and household goods did not survive at Deir el-Medina, but scenes on the walls of the houses show the items that were once in use. These included stools, tables, headrests for sleeping, chests, boxes, baskets, and jars.

The ornamentation found in the brick buildings drew on the forms found in stone monuments, inspiration from the natural world, and the buildings, domestic goods, and everyday scenes observed around them. Sometimes an element of house furnishing or decoration itself provided the basis for ornamentation: Some patterns found in decorative details in brick buildings and in the stone architecture were derived from the designs of the brightly colored woven reed mats that were hung on walls.

READING

Architects and Artisans

Hurry 1926: an account of Imhotep; Edwards 1985: full description of the Step Pyramid at Saqqara.

The Royal Workforce

Černý. 1973: discussion of the workforce and their conditions at Deir el-Medina; Bierbrier 1982: a popular, general account of the town.

Building Materials and Techniques

Lucas 1962: definitive account of ancient Egyptian materials and industries; Forbes 1956–66: detailed studies of ancient technology; Hodges 1970: studies of technology in the ancient world with clear illustrations; Petrie 1917: excavator's catalog of tools and weapons found at various sites in Egypt; Petrie 1927: excavator's catalog of objects of daily use illustrated by examples from various sites.

Tombs and Pyramids

Emery 1961: general account of civilization in the Archaic Period; Emery 1949, 1954: scholarly account of Archaic Period tombs; Reisner 1936: survey of the development of the early tombs; Edwards 1985: definitive study on the pyramids and their development with chapter 8 on construction; Smith 1958: study of Egyptian art and architecture; Badawy 1977: discussion of pyramid construction; Neugebauer 1980: discussion of pyramid orientation.

Temples

David 1980: study of the ritual use of the Egyptian temple with section on foundation and consecration rites; Fairman 1945: scholarly article on the consecration of the Temple of Horus at Edfu.

Towns

Kemp 1977: study of the early development of the Egyptian town; Fairman 1949: article on town planning in Egypt; Trigger, et al. 1983: account of the social history of ancient Egypt.

Towns for Necropolis Workmen

Černý 1973: op cit; Bierbrier 1982: op cit; David 1986: general account of Kahun; Petrie 1890, 1891: reports of the excavations at Kahun; Kemp 1978–80: reports of the excavations at the workmen's village at Amarna.

Palaces

Trigger, et al. 1983: some discussion of palaces as administrative centers.

Houses

David 1986: op cit; Černý 1973: op cit; Kemp 1978–80: op cit; Kemp 1976: discussion of the city of Tell el-Amarna.

Decoration: Religious and Secular

David 1980: discussion of ritual scenes and decoration of the temples; Edwards 1985: references to the Pyramid Texts; David 1986: op cit; Černý 1973: op cit; Bierbrier 1982: op cit.

7

WRITTEN
EVIDENCE

CONTRIBUTIONS TO EGYPTOLOGY

Modern understanding of Egyptian civilization is greatly enhanced because it is now possible to read its extensive religious and secular literature. This became feasible because of the efforts of Jean-François Champollion and other scholars in deciphering hieroglyphic and other Egyptian scripts. The ability to read and translate the language enables accurate interpretation of the ancient evidence.

Archaeology can only provide a narrow view of a civilization. Although excavated material provides indications about the structure and beliefs of a society, the lack of written evidence greatly limits our understanding of the community. Knowledge of the literature, however, has enabled scholars to assess Egypt's rich legacy (transmitted through Hebrew and Greek sources) in establishing the foundations of Western civilization. Present knowledge of the civilization, based on literary as well as archaeological evidence, can now be compared with the often ludicrous conclusions reached by Classical, medieval, and Renaissance scholars (who were writing before the texts had been deciphered) about the significance and meaning of such monuments as the pyramids and about the purpose and function of the hieroglyphs themselves. It was through decipherment that Egypt ceased to be regarded merely as a land of magnificent monuments and quaint customs.

Since most surfaces of monuments and artifacts were inscribed, the ability to read the texts allowed scholars to reassess and correctly interpret the purpose and significance of monuments and artifacts. The Pyramid Texts illuminated understanding of the pyramid complexes and Old Kingdom royal funerary customs; tomb inscriptions provided information about rituals, religion and magic, genealogies, social and economic systems, and arts and crafts; and temple inscriptions gave details of the rituals and ceremonies once performed within these buildings and added to knowledge of mythology, religion, and political history.

Wisdom texts and votive hymns supply our only insight into Egyptian wisdom, piety, and personal ethics, and these, together with the surviving schoolboy exercises and letters, preserve some details of the educational system. Similarly the Aten hymns and those that predate them provide the only doctrinal evidence relating to the solar monotheism that developed under King Akhenaten. The significance of Amarna and other centers of Atenism would be even more difficult to interpret from only the archaeological evidence without these extant writings.

Knowledge of medical science in Egypt would also be severely limited without access to the medical papyri, which preserve case studies and treatments. Other sources of evidence are limited to a relatively few examples of surgical instruments from the later periods, a wall scene at the temple of Kom Ombo that may depict a set of surgical instruments, and evidence of deformity and disease in the mummified remains and in the portrayal of some servants and workers in the tomb scenes. Information from settlement sites (towns and villages) is less abundant than from tombs and temples, but archives of papyri found in town sites often provide the most important information about secular, urban activities and encompass education, legal and administrative matters, and medical practices.

Knowledge of the political history of Egypt, its chronology, and correlation with events in other areas of the Near East is also enhanced by textual evidence. This includes historical records that provide important military details and king lists in temples that supply the chronological order of rulers and were used by early historians such as Manetho.

In one area, literary sources not only augment the archaeological evidence but present an entirely different viewpoint. Some texts in the Pessimistic Literature question the accepted traditions and emphasize the benefits of life in contrast to the uncertainty of death. Whereas archaeology presents the view that the Egyptians were convinced of the existence of an afterlife for which they prepared with elaborate tombs and funerary goods, the literature provides an alternative, skeptical, questioning approach that must alter any assessment of the Egyptians' religious beliefs and aspirations.

The wealth of literature that survives is due not only to the ideal environmental conditions that have preserved the writing materials but also to the Egyptian idea that all writing was a sacred and divinely creative act that would renew the powers of the gods and kings. Thus, writing was a state function undertaken in special areas of the temples, and great effort was devoted to education. In particular the scribe or learned man enjoyed an unequaled status and respect in society because of his ability to perform this sacred duty.

EGYPTIAN LANGUAGE AND WRITING

Hieroglyphs

The origin of the ancient Egyptian language and writing system is obscure because of its extreme antiquity. Fortunately, the development of the language and writing can be deduced through various stages and scripts from the many surviving inscriptions. The earliest script used for writing the language, known today as "Egyptian hieroglyphs" or "hieroglyphs," was in use before 3100 BC. Hieroglyphs (which literally means "sacred carvings") were developed from pictures of objects or things (pictographs), and they always retained their pictorial form. In fact, the ancient Egyptians never developed a truly alphabetic system in which each symbol, sign, or letter represented a simple sound in the language. By c.3100 BC, however, and perhaps earlier, there was already in use a fully comprehensive language system expressed in the written form with its own syntax, grammar, and vocabulary.

Hieroglyphs continued to be used, simultaneous with other writing systems, for inscriptions on papyrus, wood, and stone for over 3,000 years, often employed for formal or religious purposes. The classical stage of the language, known today as "Middle Egyptian," developed during the Middle Kingdom (c.1900 BC) when some of the finest literary texts were composed. Modern students of Egyptian hieroglyphs are introduced to the language and script by learning Middle Egyptian. The last known hieroglyphic inscription (AD 394) in Egypt survives on one of the monuments originally constructed on the island of Philae and now rebuilt on the neighboring island of Agilkia.

PICTOGRAPHS

The Egyptian system grew out of pictographs—simple drawings of objects that prehistoric peoples knew and saw around them, which they used as symbols to represent the words for the objects in their particular language. Such pictographs would also be visually recognizable to people who had a different language (for example, people with different languages would all recognize that a pictograph of a man represented a man), but they would not be able to identify from the pictograph the correct word for "man" in another language. Although pictographs can convey the meaning of concrete objects (house, man, fish, to eat), they cannot express more abstract ideas (emotions, thoughts, beliefs) nor tenses of a verb and nuances of the language.

PHONOGRAMS AND IDEOGRAMS

To expand and develop their ability to write their language the Egyptians, at an early stage, introduced a system that combined phonograms and ideograms. Phonograms are "sound signs" and represent the individual sounds which make up the words in a language. In effect they "spell out" each word. The important difference between phonograms and pictographs is that, whereas pictographs can be recognized and understood by people who speak different languages, phonograms (although they can be pictorial in form) represent sound values in a particular language and can only be understood by people who know that language. For example, in hieroglyphs one use of the phonogram depicting an owl is to convey the sound "m."

There are three types of phonograms in hieroglyphs: uniliteral or alphabetic signs, where one hieroglyph (picture) represents a single consonant or sound value; biliteral signs, where one hieroglyph represents two consonants; and triliteral signs, where one hieroglyph represent three consonants. There are twenty-four hieroglyphic signs in the Egyptian alphabet and these are the phonograms most commonly used. But since there was never a purely alphabetic system, these signs were placed alongside other phonograms (biliterals and triliterals) and ideograms.

Ideograms are "sense signs" that pictorially convey the meaning of a word; they are never pronounced. They were often placed at the end of a word (spelled out in phonograms) to clarify the meaning of that word, and when used in this way we refer to them as "determinatives." This assists in two ways: The addition of a determinative helps to clarify the meaning of a particular word, since some words look similar or identical to each other when spelled out and written down only in the phonograms; and because determinatives stand at the end of the word they can indicate where one word ends and another begins.

Hieratic and Demotic

Although hieroglyphs continued in use for the whole of Egyptian history, two cursive scripts (hieratic and demotic) were developed from the hieroglyphic signs to provide increased speed in writing, particularly for business and literary texts.

HIERATIC

Hieratic appeared in the earliest dynasties as a contemporary writing form in parallel use with hieroglyphs. It continued in use until c.800 BC when it was gradually replaced first by a new cursive script ("abnormal hieratic") in southern Egypt and then by demotic. Each hieratic character was a simplification of a hieroglyphic sign, but it is possible to identify an early hieratic text from a later one because the script developed over the centuries and is marked by changes in the way the signs were written and grouped together. Both hieratic and hieroglyphs could be written either vertically or horizontally. Until the Middle Kingdom it was commonplace to arrange hieratic in vertical columns; it later became customary to write it horizontally. Hieroglyphs could be written from right to left or vice versa (the direction in which the hieroglyphs should be read is indicated by the direction in which the pictographs of humans, animals, or birds face—if they face left the inscription reads from left to right, and vice versa). In hieratic, however, the direction of writing was always from right to left.

Whereas hieroglyphs frequently fulfilled a monumental function and were carved on stone, hieratic was written on cheaper materials such as papyrus, wood, leather, or ostraca (inscribed pottery sherds or stone flakes). From hieratic inscribed on papyrus, however, there developed another script—cursive writing on stone —which appears on stelae left in the quarries by masons and travelers. Hieratic was used for many purposes: There were religious texts (hence its name meaning "sacred writing"), magical texts, letters, administrative and legal documents such as accounts, wills, reports, and lists, as well as literary and scientific texts. It was regularly employed for writing on papyrus with a brush (made from a reed with a frayed tip) and black or red ink (which indicated where a new paragraph began). Use of the brush was eventually replaced (third century BC) by a stylus (a sharpened reed with a fine point), which substantially changed the appearance of the signs.

DEMOTIC

From c.700 BC another cursive script was introduced. This was used for business, legal, and literary documents for nearly 1,000 years, although hieratic was retained alongside it mainly for religious texts, and hieroglyphs continued to be used for inscriptions on stone. This new development in the language and writing of Egypt is known as "demotic" ("popular writing"), a term that Herodotus first used for it. It incorporated new and distinct grammatical

forms as well as a new vocabulary. Demotic was apparently derived from a type of Egyptian spoken originally in the Delta, and although the earliest writings in this script are lost, it apparently spread southward when the princes of Sais (a Delta town) conquered the rest of Egypt and established Dynasty 26. Although demotic is derived from business hieratic and therefore ultimately from hieroglyphs, it has many complications and is relatively difficult to read and translate.

Coptic

The final stage of the Egyptian language —known as Coptic—developed when Egypt became a Christian country. The Copts (Christian inhabitants of Egypt) retained their language, which incorporated ancient Egyptian dialects, and wrote it down in Greek alphabetic characters with the addition of a few new signs taken from demotic to express Egyptian sounds that did not occur in Greek. The use of Greek characters enabled writers to produce the full pronunciation of the ancient Egyptian language because Greek had vowels, whereas the Egyptian scripts expressed only the consonants. The ancient Egyptian language and scripts had been replaced as the official language by Greek following the conquest of Egypt by Alexander the Great in 332 BC and subsequent rulership by the Ptolemies. Greek was now employed for administrative purposes, although the native population continued to use their own language, and formal and religious texts were still inscribed in hieroglyphs on temples and elsewhere.

Coptic played an important role in early Christianity in Egypt, and from the third century AD it became the medium for the translation of the books of the Old Testament and the Gospels, and, during the third and fourth centuries, versions of the heretical Gnostic and Mannichean writings. A key factor in the development of Egyptian Christianity was the strength of the national church, which at the Council of Ephesus (451) adopted the Monophysite belief and separated itself from western Christianity. At the same time, there was also a widespread growth of monasteries throughout the country. Religious art and literature flourished against this background, and important Coptic writings were produced by St. Athanasius (c.293–c.373) and monks such as St. Anthony (251–356) and Pachomius (286–346).

Although the Arab invasion of Egypt in the seventh century and the introduction of Islam brought radical changes, strong Christian communities still survived, particularly in the south and around Thebes. Arabic became the official language of the country, but Coptic was retained as the language of the Christians for many centuries. The great scriptoria at the monasteries were closed by the tenth century, but Coptic influences remained strong in villages of southern Egypt until the fourteenth century. Today, Coptic is still used for the liturgy of the Coptic Church, although the language of modern Egypt is Arabic.

In historical terms Coptic played a very important role in the decipherment of hieroglyphs, since it provided a link between the ancient language of Egypt and the Classical and later European traditions. As Christianity grew and spread throughout Egypt knowledge of ancient Egyptian, written in hieroglyphs, hieratic, or demotic, was finally lost, and Coptic remained the only link with that past.

However, until it was recognized that Coptic had developed directly out of those earlier scripts, it was of little use in deciphering hieroglyphs. Once it was identified as the final stage of the language, it became important in illuminating aspects of Egyptian grammar and vocabulary.

Notable studies in the Coptic language were produced by the Jesuit scholar Athanasius Kircher (1602–80), although he is perhaps best known for proposing the erroneous symbolic theory of hieroglyphs that regarded individual signs as symbols. Knowledge of Coptic also helped Johan David Akerblad (1763–1819) in his work on the Egyptian scripts, and Thomas Young (1773–1824) correctly proposed a close association between hieroglyphs and Coptic. Jean-François Champollion (1790–1832) began his illustrious academic career at age sixteen by reading a paper to the Grenoble Academy in which he claimed that Coptic (which he had learned, together with Hebrew, Arabic, Syriac, Chaldean, Sanskrit, Zand, Pali, Parsi, and Persian, to prepare himself for the decipherment of hieroglyphs) was the same as the ancient language of Egypt, although it was written in different characters from the ancient scripts of hieroglyphs, hieratic, and demotic. Following the decipherment of hieroglyphs Coptic continued to assist scholars in their attempts to unravel the scripts and grammar of the ancient Egyptian language.

Pronunciation

It is not generally known how the Egyptians pronounced their language. Over the 3,000 years that it was used there would have been many changes and variations. Coptic (the final stage of Egyptian) can provide some clues regarding the pronunciation of individual words, since it conveys vowel sounds through the Greek characters (whereas hieroglyphs, hieratic, and demotic only preserve the consonants in each word). However, since Coptic was in use only at the end of the period when

Egyptian was spoken, it cannot reflect the many changes and variations in grammar and pronunciation that would have occurred during that time.

Nevertheless, Egyptologists need to be able to refer to words orally, so a convenient method of pronunciation has been developed in which scholars use a generally accepted (although artificial) system of vocalizing the words. This addition of vowels, however, may bear little resemblance to the way in which the ancient Egyptians actually pronounced the words.

Scholars of different nationalities also need a common system for identifying and transcribing individual hieroglyphs before they translate them into their own language. Thus, they first transliterate the hieroglyphs (turn them into modern written characters) before they translate a text.

DECIPHERMENT OF HIEROGLYPHS

As Christianity gradually spread through Egypt, knowledge of the ancient Egyptian language written in hieroglyphs, hieratic, and demotic disappeared, and the key to understanding it was lost. Over the centuries scholars theorized about the nature of the language but reached the erroneous conclusion that the hieroglyphic signs still visible on the temple walls must have had a purely symbolic function and reflected mystical doctrines. It was not realized that the hieroglyphs conveyed a language with its own grammar and vocabulary. After the Renaissance, as travelers again began to visit Egypt, interest in hieroglyphs was revived and Coptic manuscripts

began to be imported into Europe. Some advances were now being made in the study of Coptic, particularly by Athanasius Kircher (1643). Although there had been earlier theories about the nature and meaning of hieroglyphs (the Greek writers Horapollo and Chaeremon were among the first), it was Kircher who became the best-known exponent of the symbolic theory of hieroglyphs. Unfortunately, his attempts to decipher and read hieroglyphs (found on the obelisks that had been removed from Egypt to Rome and elsewhere during the period of Roman rule) added nothing to further the study, since he continued to regard the individual hieroglyphs as symbols.

The Rosetta Stone

A new era began when the Rosetta Stone was discovered in the Nile Delta during Napoleon Bonaparte's expedition to Egypt. In 1799, as the French were gathering stones to strengthen the ramparts for their coastal defenses against the British navy, the officer in charge of the exercise, Lieutenant Pierre François Xavier Bouchard, was shown a stone inscribed with three horizontal panels of text. Realizing it might be of importance he sent it to the institute that Napoleon had founded in Cairo.

As it turned out, the impact of the Rosetta Stone on the decipherment of hieroglyphs was crucial. This black basalt stone carried an inscription in three scripts—Greek, hieroglyphs, and demotic. Scholars soon realized that the three texts contained the same content. Since the section in Greek could be understood and readily translated the Stone provided an unparalleled opportunity to attempt a decipherment of the hieroglyphs and demotic.

Translation of the Greek showed that the text was a decree by the priesthoods of Egypt in honor of King Ptolemy V Epiphanes (196 BC) issued in Greek, the official language of Egypt; hieroglyphs, the ancient sacred writing; and demotic, used as a legal and business script. Originally set up in Memphis, the stone had been moved to Rosetta on the Delta coast at an unknown period. As a condition of the British success over French troops in Egypt, the Rosetta Stone was ceded to Britain in 1801 and was brought to England, where it was placed in the British Museum as a gift from King George III.

Initial attempts to decipher the hieroglyphs and demotic on the Rosetta Stone were unsuccessful, since the scholars still attempted to use the old symbolic theory. Some progress was made by Silvestre de Sacy (1758–1838), who declared, in 1802, that certain sign groups in the demotic corresponding to the names of Ptolemy and Alexander could be readily identified in the Greek. Johan David Akerblad also made significant steps toward the decipherment of the demotic text, which he set out in his *Lettre à M. de Sacy* (1802). However, it was the work of Thomas Young and then Champollion that enabled the hieroglyphs to be deciphered.

Thomas Young was an English physician and physicist with wide-ranging interest. He made several important discoveries regarding the Egyptian texts. First, he recognized that some demotic characters as well as linear hieroglyphs and hieratic, were derived from hieroglyphs. This was significant because it showed that demotic was not an entirely alphabetic script—as Akerblad had claimed—and it recognized for the first time that Egyptian texts used alphabetic and nonalphabetic signs alongside each other. He (and other scholars) also made the important claim that the Egyptians enclosed royal names in ovals (cartouches). Using the parallel Greek text he was able to identify the royal names of Ptolemy and Berenice (on another similar royal decree) and to attribute the sound values in those names to the hieroglyphic signs within the cartouches. He identified thirteen signs in these two names of which six were found to be correct, three were partly right, and four were wrong. This short list, however, enabled him to read the name of Ptolemy correctly in the hieroglyphs. He also correctly proposed a close relationship between hieroglyphs and Coptic; he began a comparison of Greek, demotic, and hieroglyphs; and he concluded that demotic was a cursive form of hieroglyphs.

Young's publication *Remarks on Egyptian Papyri and on the Inscription of Rosetta* (1815) set out his ideas on translating the demotic text on the Rosetta Stone. Financial problems and ill health led Young to withdraw from Egyptian studies, but his contribution to the decipherment of hieroglyphs was considerable, and it has been suggested that he did not receive due recognition for his work. Honor for achieving the breakthrough was eventually awarded to the French scholar Champollion.

Jean-François Champollion, born in Figeac, France, was a prodigious child, and an early visit to the mathematician Jean-Baptiste Joseph Fourier, who had been one of the scholars to accompany Napoleon's expedition to Egypt, may have inspired Champollion's interest in hieroglyphs. He prepared himself for the task of decipherment by learning at least nine oriental languages before he was seventeen. Ultimately his studies were rewarded with success, and in 1831 the first chair in Egyptian history and archaeology was created for him at the Collège de France.

At first he supported the theory that hieroglyphs were purely symbolic in purpose, as had been proposed by earlier scholars. He set out this view (which opposed Young's claim that some signs were alphabetic) in his *De l'écriture hiératique des anciens Égyptiens* (1821), concluding that Egyptian was not alphabetic. However, he later adopted the alphabetic approach favored by Young and found that considerable progress could then be made in deciphering the royal names.

A major turning point came in September 1822. He was studying copies of an inscription from the temple at Abu Simbel and, using the phonetic principles already established by Young and himself, he was able to identify the name of King Ramesses II. This made him realize that the Egyptians not only used hieroglyphs phonetically to write the names of foreign rulers such as Ptolemy and Berenice but also wrote the names of their own kings in the same way. Thus, for the first time, he understood that many hieroglyphs were in fact truly phonetic and not symbolic and he set out his conclusions in his famous *Lettre à M Dacier . . . relative à l'alphabet des hieroglyphes phonetiques (1822)*.

This was a landmark in his research, but not all scholars accepted his ideas, and there also continued to be a dispute about the extent of his appropriation of Young's initial discoveries. In 1824 Champollion published *Précis du système hiéroglyphique*, which showed that Egyptian combined both phonetic and ideographic signs. This breakthrough in understanding the writing system allowed Egyptian to be read and translated as readily as any other language. He formulated his major discoveries in such later works as *Grammaire* (1836–41) and *Dictionnaire* (1841–44); most scholars only acknowledged and accepted his system as a true analysis as late as 1837. Champollion's discovery opened a new chapter in the historical study of ancient Egypt; henceforth, the literature as well as the architecture and artifacts could be properly studied.

THE ART OF WRITING

The idea of writing may have been introduced into Egypt from Mesopotamia (the "Land between Two Rivers"—the Tigris and the Euphrates—which occupied approximately the region of modern Iraq). A people known as the Sumerians arrived in Mesopotamia c.3500 BC and established a civilization based on the concept of the city-state. One major achievement was the establishment of a writing system based initially on pictures of things or objects (pictographs). The Sumerians engraved these pictographs with a reed stylus on clay tablets. Because these writing implements produced lines and wedge-shaped impressions on the wet clay, the pictographs soon became stylized. Eventually this method of writing was used for the languages of other civilizations that developed later in the same region—Akkadian, Babylonian, and Assyrian. This writing system is known as "cuneiform." Extant cuneiform texts predate those from Egypt perhaps because writing occurred first in Mesopotamia, but possibly because the Sumerian writing material (clay) was more durable than the Egyptian (papyrus and wood).

It has been argued that the "Dynastic Race" may have introduced the concept of writing to Egypt from elsewhere, perhaps Mesopotamia, in c.3400 BC. If the Egyptians did receive the idea of writing from outside, however, they quickly adapted if for their own purposes and used their own images from the world around them for their pictographs. Examples of the earliest Egyptian hieroglyphic writing found on slate palettes (c.3200 BC) indicate that the writing system was already fully developed and that the earliest hieroglyphs represented Egyptian and not Mesopotamian objects.

Once they had developed their writing system the Egyptians adopted an almost obsessional preoccupation with the written word: They covered almost every monumental wall surface with hieroglyphs, and objects as well as papyri often carry a text written in hieroglyphs, hieratic, or demotic. Since the Egyptians regarded hieroglyphs as an art form as well as a means of conveying language, they devoted themselves to the skills associated with the production of hieroglyphs. Many of the pictorial signs reflect the natural beauty of the land and represent its flora and fauna.

Texts are found not only on the outer walls or areas of monuments where they would impress the viewer but also within the innermost chambers and on funerary goods, which were intended to remain buried forever. The main purpose of writing was not decorative, and it was not originally intended for literary or commercial use. Its most important function was to provide a means by which certain concepts or events could be brought into existence. The Egyptians believed that if something were committed to writing it could be repeatedly "made to happen" by means of magic.

Scenes and inscriptions in tombs and temples were intended to be ceremonially activated, or "brought to life," through the ritual of "Opening the Mouth," which was performed during the burial ceremony at the tomb or at the consecration of a temple. Gradually, writing (even hieroglyphs) developed secular uses, but the idea that the written word had intrinsic magical properties was never lost.

Monumental Inscriptions

Monumental inscriptions occur on the walls of pyramids, tombs, and temples. From Dynasty 5, the Pyramid Texts were placed on interior walls of pyramids to ensure the safe passage of the king to the next world; walls in tomb offering chapels and burial chambers were decorated with autobiographies of the owners (often inscribed on stelae), offering texts, funerary hymns, and hymns to the sun; and temple walls were covered with horizontal registers of scenes and inscriptions showing the rites performed there for the gods and dead kings, as well as formal, historical inscriptions and great festival texts that sometimes preserve the hymns sung to praise the gods at these events.

Inscribed Objects

Texts were also inscribed on objects placed in the tomb. The Coffin Texts (to ensure the successful passage of the deceased to the next world) and other divine or magical inscriptions appear on wooden, stone, or cartonnage mummy cases. Magico-religious texts also decorated tomb furniture and equipment (made from a variety of materials including wood, metal, pottery, ivory, and faience) to ensure that the object would function for the tomb owner in the next world. His name was often written on the object to ensure eternal ownership. The scarab (usually made of faience) placed over the heart of the mummy usually carried the spell to prevent the heart witnessing against its owner at the Day of Judgment. Ushabtis—model mummiform figurines intended to relieve the owner of agricultural duties in the next world—were inscribed with the owner's name and a spell confirming they would undertake these duties. Inscribed objects also occurred in domestic contexts and in temples: Shrines and statues bearing their owners' names were placed in temples so that they could receive the god's bounty.

WRITING MATERIALS

Egyptian texts in hieroglyphs were inscribed on stone, wood, and papyrus and in hieratic and demotic, on papyrus, wood, leather, and ostraca.

Papyrus

The material most widely associated with writing in Egypt is papyrus. The word is derived

A painted wooden stela (c.1450 BC) with a curved top. It shows figures of the goddesses Isis (left) and her sister Nephthys (right) adoring the djed pillar, which represented Isis's husband, Osiris. Stelae were set up in tombs and elsewhere to commemorate the deceased owner and ensure his continued existence and sustenance.

from the Greek *papyros*, which is believed to come from the Egyptian word *papuro* meaning "the royal," as manufacture of papyrus was a state monopoly. This tall plant (*Cyperus papyrus* L.) grew in abundance in Egypt, particularly in the marshlands of the Delta. Although at first it covered large areas of the river valley as well and formed part of the natural vegetation, it was later managed and harvested in cultivated fields. In addition to producing a writing material from it, the plant was also used to make ropes, mats, boxes, sandals, and small sailing craft.

PROCESSING

From predynastic times the fibrous pith of the plant was used to manufacture a writing material. It has been possible to identify the various stages of production. In the first stage, the stalk of the plant was sliced into pieces and the pith was cut out and beaten with a hammer to produce wafers. These were arranged side by side and crosswise in two layers and were then beaten into sheets. Then the individual pages were stuck together in the same way to form a standard roll of twenty pages; sometimes the rolls were stuck together as required to provide an even longer writing surface. After drying in the sun the full strip was rolled up with the horizontal fibers on the inside. This was the "recto" that would be written on first.

RELIGIOUS AND SECULAR USES

Papyrus was relatively expensive to produce and was generally used for religious and more important secular documents. The most common and cheapest writing materials were ostraca and pieces of wood. These were often used by schoolboys for their letters and exercises, and some school texts found on papyrus also occur on these cheaper writing materials, supplying scholars with an additional source for knowl-

A tomb scene showing scribes writing on papyrus; their scribal palettes are placed on their sides, and each has pushed his spare reed pen behind his ear. The hieroglyphs give the name and titles of the tomb owner.

edge of words or phrases damaged or destroyed in the papyrus version.

As a major source of textual evidence, papyri preserve a wealth of literature: the "funerary books" to ensure the owner's safe journey to the afterlife; school exercises and copies; model letters; hymns and prayers; wisdom instructions; folk tales; love poems; educational and scientific texts; magical and medical prescriptions; and legal and administrative records.

The Egyptians exported papyrus as a writing material to other areas of the ancient world. The Greeks and Romans adopted it and used it for their own administrative and literary texts; classical accounts of Egypt such as those of Plutarch or Herodotus were written on papyrus. Its use undoubtedly preserved vast quantities of inscriptions allowing the survival of information about administrative, legal, religious, medical, and literary aspects of pharaonic Egypt. The Greek residents of Egypt in later periods also used papyrus as their main writing material. Egypt's ideal climatic conditions have preserved the largest quantity of Greek papyri of all that have survived from antiquity. In particular thousands of papyri written in Greek and Egyptian have been recovered from the Greek settlements in the Fayoum, providing a detailed account of life in these communities.

Writing and Incising Tools

Inscriptions were carved (or sometimes painted) on walls or written on the other materials. Fine quality stone was selected for temples and the best tombs; the masons used copper or bronze chisels to carve the stone for the walls and hardened stones to incise the hieroglyphs. Scribes' writing equipment has also been discovered. This consisted of a case (usually of wood) to hold reed pens, a palette with cakes of paint (usually one black and one red), and a water flask for mixing the paint. Very rare examples of slate ink trays have also been found. The pen (a thin reed with a frayed tip) was eventually replaced by the stylus (a sharpened reed with a fine point) in the third century BC. Texts were usually written in black paint, the red being reserved to mark the beginning of a new paragraph, a total in sets of accounts, certain types of punctuation, or the names of evil beings.

LIBRARIES

Private and Town Libraries

The Egyptians stored their papyri in several ways. Personal collections were kept in jars or boxes in the home. Some private libraries have been found at Thebes, and papyri were also placed in tombs—these included not only the magico-religious "books" intended to safeguard the owner's journey to the next world but documents that the owner had used in his everyday work (such as the collection of a lector priest found, together with his magical artifacts, in his burial in the precincts of the Ramesseum at Thebes). The refuse heaps of the royal workmen's village at Deir el-Medina, Thebes (New Kingdom), have also revealed a wealth of documentary evidence about the community, including records of working practices, magical texts, folk tales and myths, psalms, dream interpretations, and literary copies. In an earlier royal workmen's town, Kahun (Middle Kingdom), the town's archive has revealed documents associated with the local administration, legal, medical, and veterinary matters, conditions relating to the royal workforce, and religious and educational texts.

Temple Libraries

There were also libraries and scriptoria in the temples where books were written and stored. The papyri of a priestly library at the town of Tebtunis in the Fayoum have been discovered; these include literary, religious, and scientific documents. Also, a list of the titles of books kept by the priests occurs in inscriptions carved on the walls of a small chapel in the Temple of Edfu.

The temple had no role as a center of communal worship; it was primarily the residence of the god, but it was also often a place of higher education where specialist priests had charge of various branches of learning including liturgy, astronomy, astrology, and the interpretation of animal cults. The scribes, trained in the use of the written language, held priesthoods and received their instruction in the temples. One school has been found among the buildings surrounding the temple known as the Ramesseum at Thebes, and excavation of the nearby rubbish heaps has revealed the schoolboys' discarded writing tablets.

The physical act of copying ancient texts and composing new ones was believed to maintain and renew the vigor of the king and gods. This magico-religious concept of writing inspired the almost unparalleled wealth of literary texts found in Egypt. It was also the reason why these activities were carried out in special areas of the temples so that they would contribute to the overall spiritual potency of the temple.

THE HOUSE OF LIFE

The "House of Life" appears to have been an area of the temple that acted as a library, scriptorium, and higher teaching institution, where the sacred writings were produced and stored and where instruction was given. Medical and magical texts as well as religious books were probably compiled and copied there. Sometimes this institution may have been situated within the temple itself, but elsewhere it was probably located in one of the buildings within the temple precinct. Very little is known of its administration or organization, but it is possible that every sizable town had one. They are known to have existed at Tell el-Amarna, Edfu, and Abydos.

The House of Life seems to have functioned primarily as a scriptorium that was supplied with its own scribal equipment. They were sometimes, although perhaps not always, associated with the temple library. The scribes of the House of Life were the "servants" or "followers" of Re (the sun god); since this deity possessed the creative power to maintain life, it was appropriate that the scribes were believed to have the ability to express this creative power in their compositions. Since the House of Life was associated with spiritual rebirth, it was also linked to Osiris, the god of the dead and resurrection. The activity of composing and copying texts, it was believed, would assist the god's resuscitation at his yearly festival.

The presence of particular architectural features in some areas of the temple may assist in the identification of the location of the scriptoria and libraries. At Edfu and Philae there are library rooms with niches in the walls that were probably used for storing scrolls; similar niches in a hall in the Temple of Sethos I at Abydos may indicate the same use for that area. The Abydos hall also has a ceiling carved and painted with astronomical signs and symbols. A room with a similar ceiling has been found in the Ramesseum (Temple of Ramesses II) at Thebes, but this has no wall niches. Possibly the rooms at Edfu and Philae were used as libraries while the Astronomical Room at the Ramesseum was a scriptorium, and the hall at Abydos fulfilled both functions.

It would seem that the House of Life had both a practical use and a deeply religious significance. Its very title may reflect the power of life that was believed to exist in the divinely inspired writings composed, copied, and often stored there. This power conferred the ability to resuscitate the dead, and as the prototype of all dead men the god Osiris was likely to gain most benefit from the potency of these compositions. In one ancient text the books in the House of Life are claimed not only to have the ability to renew life but actually to be able to provide the food and sustenance needed for the continuation of life.

SCRIBES

One concept survived virtually intact from the Old Kingdom and was emphasized further in the New Kingdom: that the scribe—the educated man—held a position in society that no other profession or trade could equal. The ability to write gave the scribe (the Egyptian term for scribe means literally "he who writes") his rank and power. He had access to all the highest posts in the bureaucracy and directed and supervised everyone else.

Duties and Privileges

The papyri recount his many duties and privileges. In the Satire on Trades (First Intermediate Period) an unusual text has survived that takes the form of instruction from Khety to his son Pepy. Khety is a man of humble origin who conveys the benefit of his experience to Pepy, who has the good fortune to be placed in the Residence School among the sons of the magistrates. Khety instructs his son in the duties and rewards of the scribal profession and is anxious that he should become a scribe and escape the toil associated with all other trades. Describing how all other work is subject to supervision and its own hardships, the excellence and status of the scribe's profession are extolled in contrast.

From this and other sources it is evident that the scribe's duties included imposition and collection of taxes, keeping accounts, keeping army records, and controlling the law courts. Perhaps most important were the duties associated with composing and copying religious and other texts in the temple scriptoria, because the scribe thus became directly involved with the religious act of creating and reviving life. Scribes received their own instruction in the temples; some held priesthoods and taught students.

The scribes were the mainstay of Egyptian society for thousands of years and established and maintained the standards for ordinary people. There were many advantages for a scribe: Often they did not pay taxes; they were not required to undertake heavy labor or agricultural duties; and they were not responsible to a supervisor, since they themselves controlled and supervised the various trades and professions. They were well fed and wore the finest clothes, and wherever they went they were given respect and honor. The profession included not only royal princes whose statues, particularly in the Old Kingdom, represented them as scribes but also minor officials who oversaw many aspects of Egypt's extensive bureaucracy.

The scribe was not expected to be merely a recorder of facts. There emerged the idea that he should be an educated, cultured man who could express himself in writing and speech and who could influence others. He had a love of learning, of books, and of intellectual pursuits, and the scribe's special training and education separated him at an early age from the rest of the people. Because he enjoyed the benefits of this profession, however, he was also expected to exercise high standards of behavior and to protect the interests of the weak with impartiality. This code of behavior was handed down to future generations through the Instructions in

Wisdom (teaching manuals), letters, hymns, and prayers that are preserved in the school exercises.

Thoth, the Patron Deity

All scribes had the same patron deity, Thoth. Represented as an ibis, Thoth was the god of wisdom, learning and writing, and magical formulas. He was worshiped throughout Egypt as the lunar god, but Hermopolis was his particular cult center. The Greeks later identified him with their god Hermes, and he was known by the name Trismegistos. At Hermopolis Thoth was the chief deity in a creation myth that featured an ogdoad (group of eight gods). As well as the ibis, he was associated with the baboon and is sometimes shown in this form. Thoth was the divine secretary responsible for inventing writing and recording laws and annuals; he also had control over numbers and the divisions of time, and he calculated the years and the calendar.

Because of his knowledge of writing he had power over the divine words, and through speech he played an important role in the creative process. Since he knew the formulas for healing the sick, he also acted as patron of magicians, and some of the medical books were attributed to his authorship to give them proper authenticity. He had knowledge of secret wisdom and thus held a position of considerable importance among the gods. He was often shown as an ibis-headed deity standing with his scribal palette and pen; as clerk of the divine court he recorded the outcome of the interrogation faced by the deceased on the occasion of the "Weighing of the Heart." His many duties and powers reflected the important role that the scribes themselves held in directing and administering Egyptian society.

EDUCATION

The Egyptian system of education is not clearly defined in the papyri, but it seems that most children, boys and girls, whatever their social status, received some kind of education up to a certain age. Until age four, most children were under the control and guidance of their mothers and probably lived in the women's quarters of the house. They were expected to be obedient and to show great respect to their mothers. After this age, though, supervision of their education was assumed by their fathers, and a child was generally expected to follow his father's trade or profession. (At this point, a girl's formal education generally came to an end.) Some boys, therefore, attended the village school while others pursued courses at specialized schools; those intended for the priesthood and associated professions or the civil service received an academic education. Royal tutors taught some of the nobles' children together with the king's offspring, and future officials for the home and foreign services attended special training schools. Despite this hereditary pattern in the professions, some children of humble origin were able to receive education alongside the sons of the wealthy and powerful and to pursue important careers. However, education was not free, and each family was expected to pay in kind; in country areas they would have offered the produce of the land.

School Curriculum

The curriculum at the schools included sports such as swimming, boating, wrestling, ball games, and shooting with bows and arrows as well as formal instruction. For those intending to pursue further education emphasis was placed on writing (which was taught to train the character) and also mathematics. Corporal punishment was considered a desirable means of correction for laziness and disobedience.

The Egyptian educational system was famed in antiquity because it attempted to create a person who not only possessed scientific or scholarly attributes but could also exhibit self-control, good manners and morals, and who would be a useful member of society. These concepts are set out in the Instructions in Wisdom, which provide one of the main sources for current knowledge of moral and ethical education in Egypt. This system of creating a "whole person" was highly regarded and praised by the Greeks in later times.

From age fourteen, sons of farmers and craftsmen followed their fathers into the fields or became apprentices. Education for girls was elementary, and apart from some of the princesses, it is unlikely that they pursued further education. However, boys intended for careers as scribes (including doctors and lawyers) or civil servants were sent to temples or centers of administration where they would each receive personal tuition from a senior official. In addition to reading, writing, and the study of literature, specialist subjects such as foreign languages for future officials of the diplomatic service and mathematics for the architects and engineers of the home civil service were taught. The students, thus enrolled as junior scribes, were instructed by teachers from a variety of backgrounds: Some were scribes of the royal treasury of pharaoh's workshop; one is known to have come from the royal stable. At the temples, priests with a wide range of knowledge instructed the pupils, probably within the area known as the House of Life. It is nowhere stated that the students had to take examinations, but their teachers certainly complained about their laziness and drinking bouts!

Training took the form of copying out long compositions that were then corrected in the margins by the master. The exercise of copying out these texts, taken down by the students in dictation, had two purposes: It enabled the pupils to acquire reading and writing skills and an understanding of grammar, vocabulary, and composition; and the texts, selected for their moral content, helped to form a boy's character.

In the Old and Middle Kingdoms higher education had been mainly directed toward the nobility and upper classes and had concentrated on the Instructions in Wisdom. By the New Kingdom, however, the increasingly structured and organized education and training of scribes had been expanded to include the middle classes. New Instructions in Wisdom reflecting the social and educational concepts of that period were added to those of the Old and Middle Kingdoms, and the Schoolboy Exercises (mainly dating to the Ramesside Period, c.1250 BC) have also survived. They are copies of moral compositions and letters, designed to give inspiration and guidance, which provide information about the contemporary social and religious background. They also preserve texts that have not survived elsewhere and, in some cases, are the only source for important, much earlier texts. However, there are difficulties in translating these, since the boys frequently misunderstood what they were copying and made many mistakes. Although the masters corrected these exercises, they concentrated on the handwriting rather than the content of the passages. Also, since these texts date to the time of Egypt's empire, the inclusion of foreign names and words added to the pupils' difficulties.

Some of these model compositions were preserved on papyri, but excerpts of the texts were also found on ostraca, which schoolboys used as a cheaper writing material and then threw into garbage piles. Inscribed writing boards and tablets have also been found. At the Ramesseum (the mortuary temple built by Ramesses II at Thebes) large numbers of inscribed shards have been recovered from the nearby rubbish mounds. They were discarded by pupils of the school, situated within the temple precinct, when they had finished their writing exercises. The inscriptions indicate that there were set texts that the pupils copied out; these may have been important passages that they were expected to know.

Teaching Aids

Although the educational system is not clearly defined in any of the papyri, two main literary sources preserve the concepts and teaching methods that were employed.

THE INSTRUCTIONS IN WISDOM

The Instructions in Wisdom, or wisdom literature, provided advice couched in terms of didactic or contemplative concepts handed down by a sage to his charges or a father to his son. They give us some idea of the ethics and morals that formed the basis of educational instruction. The earliest known instruction is attributed to Hardedef, a famous sage of the Old Kingdom. Both the Instruction of Ptah-hotep and the Instruction for Kagemni probably originated in the Old Kingdom. The Instruction of Ptah-hotep was attributed to a vizier of King Isesi of Dynasty 5, and the tomb of an official of the same name has been discovered at Saqqara (although the text was probably actually composed later toward the end of Dynasty 6, c.2185 BC). The Instruction for Kagemni was set in Dynasty 3 and addressed to the son of King Huni. There was a vizier named Kagemni who lived several hundred years later, but again the composition

probably dates to Dynasty 6. Both of these texts survive on a later papyrus (Papyrus Prisse, Middle Kingdom, c.1900 BC), which is now in the Bibliothèque Nationale in Paris.

The instructions generally reflect the stability of the social order as it existed in Dynasty 6 and embody the values and virtues of Old Kingdom society. They refer to well-known rulers and historical figures of that era, and authorship of these texts is attributed to famous sages and viziers. The Instructions in Wisdom counsel caution in speech, prudence in friendship, and good behavior in the houses of others and at the table. They recommend modesty and specify correct behavior toward peers, superiors, and inferiors. The advice is practical and seeks to ensure advancement in life and to promote the skills required in good leaders.

Although most instructions are presented as guidance from a royal or noble sage, in one text (the Satire on Trades) a man of humble origin advises his son, who has gained a school place among the magistrates' children, to aspire to a career as a scribe. He highlights the advantages and compares the benefits of this career with the hardships and problems encountered in all other trades and professions.

By the New Kingdom the instructions underwent further changes and were now directed at the sons of the expanded middle classes. In the Instruction of Any a minor official addresses his son and eulogizes middle-class rather than aristocratic values. The culmination of these wisdom texts appears in the Instruction of Amenemope (composed in the Ramesside Period, c.1250 BC) in which a new attitude and emphasis are demonstrated—material wealth and achievement are still regarded as the legitimate goals of a righteous life, but the true ideal is now a man who is humble in his dealings with gods and men. Wealth and worldly status no longer have supreme significance: The new ideal man is expected to be honest even if his wealth is limited. In the earlier texts correct and modest behavior was deemed to bring personal advancement, but it is the inner qualities of endurance, self-control, and kindliness that are now considered most important. Other themes present in the Old Kingdom texts such as the superiority of the "silent" man over the "heated" man are developed further, but there are also marked changes in attitude. Individual humility before the god is now emphasized, and an important innovation is the idea that no man can hope to achieve personal perfection because only the gods are perfect. Another interesting aspect of Amenemope's text is the parallelism that has been observed between some of its passages and those found in the biblical Book of Proverbs.

Schoolboy Exercises

Another important source for our understanding of the educational system are the Schoolboy Exercises of the Ramesside Period (c.1250 BC), which are known from numerous papyri and ostraca. Schoolboys were taught writing and grammar by copying out a variety of highly regarded texts, but the Egyptians also attempted to form their children's characters by exposing them to the moral concepts found in these works. They included hymns, prayers, the Instructions in Wisdom, and letters. There were also business and legal documents, and the pupils gained wide experience in different types of literature.

Some of the texts were taken from early periods such as the Satire on Trades and Instruction of King Amenemhet I composed in the Old and Middle Kingdoms. New compositions were also copies as models. Some of these works arose from the school system itself, and they reflect the process of education and the pupil's relationship with his teacher. These texts composed by teachers and pupils became models that later generations copied for their own inspiration. They include three main themes: the teacher offering good advice to his pupil and encouraging him to work hard and reject excessive pleasure; praise for the scribal profession and its superiority over all others; and the grateful student praising his teacher and wishing him health and happiness. An important aspect of scribal activity was letter writing, and some of this advice is presented in the form of model letters exchanged between teachers and pupils; these sometimes insert the names of individual teachers and students.

Model compositions are preserved on documents such as Papyrus Anastasi and Papyrus Sallier, which came from Memphis; they emphasized respect for the teacher, advised the pupil to follow a scribal career, and provided a warning against strong liquor and girls. Another particularly famous text is preserved in Papyrus Lansing, where a scribe has compiled selected passages to produce a "book" of model compositions for students' use. In Papyrus Chester Beatty IV the text considers the value of the scribal profession and claims that the only immortality a man can ever achieve is through his writings, since there is no conclusive evidence for the existence of an afterlife. This indicates a profound skepticism and disregard for the supposed benefits conferred on the deceased by his tomb and funerary goods.

One concept of the educated man that survived virtually unchanged was that he held a position in society that no other profession or trade could equal. Education was used to create an elite class, but the scribes, who enjoyed the benefits of this sytem, were also expected to exercise the highest standards of behavior and to protect with impartiality the interests of the weak and less fortunate. This code of behavior preserved in the texts was passed down through the generations.

ANCIENT EGYPTIAN LITERATURE: RELIGIOUS

Most major advances in Egyptian civilization were first introduced to assist religion (particularly funerary practices) before they were applied to secular needs. The earliest examples of writing (hieroglyphs) are found in religious contexts. This probably reflects the purpose for which they were first used, but it must also be recognized that they may have survived because they were carved on stone, whereas any secular writings of the same date, even if they existed, would have been inscribed on perishable materials such as papyrus and wood.

Old Kingdom

The first extant important texts date to the Old Kingdom. They include the Pyramid Texts, Instructions in Wisdom, and creation myths, but in addition to these state or royal inscriptions there are also nonroyal or "private" examples. Inscriptions were used to identify and augment the pictorial content of the wall scenes in nobles' and officials' tombs. There were also the autobiography and offering list in the nonroyal tomb to ensure the status of the deceased owner in the next world and his eternal food supply. The autobiography recorded the owner's official rank, titles, and details of family relationships so that he would continue to hold high office in the next world. It gave a summary of his life, emphasizing his virtues and high standard of behavior but omitting any details of his sins. The offering list, one of the earliest examples of a formal inscription, became an important element in the Old Kingdom tomb. It included a basic offering formula (the *hetep-di-nesw* meaning "a boon which the King gives") that asked for food and other offerings through the agency of the god Anubis or the king's bounty. It provided the deceased with a magical source of sustenance throughout eternity. This became a standard feature of the funerary equipment for hundreds of years. Later, it was often inscribed on a stela (a stone block); these were produced and set up by ordinary people as memorials.

Middle Kingdom

The Middle Kingdom was the greatest period of literature, when the classical form of hieroglyphs, known today as Middle Egyptian, was developed. The literature of this era reflected the added depth and maturity that the country now gained as a result of the civil wars and upheavals of the First Intermediate Period. New genres of literature were developed including the so-called Pessimistic Literature, which perhaps best exemplifies the self-analysis and doubts that the Egyptians now experienced. The formal magico-religious funerary inscriptions continued, but because of the democratization of religious beliefs these were now used by many people across a much greater social spectrum.

The Pyramid Texts, once the strict preserve of royalty and designed to ensure the king's afterlife in the heavens, were now adapted for nonroyal use. Written on the coffins of all who could afford them, these now became the Coffin Texts. They incorporated spells and the offering list designed to ensure the continuation of the deceased in the next world. There were also new forms introduced into the wisdom literature. This, as well as the formal historical inscriptions, now emphasized the king's role as an all-powerful human ruler who had reunited

Egypt rather than his status as a god. In the Instruction of King Amenemhet I even the assassination of the king could be mentioned because royal power was again firmly established. In addition to this formal moral propaganda, the new vehicle of the short story—designed to entertain public audiences—was used to convey propaganda supported by the state.

New Kingdom

New Kingdom literature, developed in a period when Egypt had founded an empire, displays a more cosmopolitan approach. This is expressed in texts that seek to promote the great state god, Amen-Re, as a universal creator and in the inscriptions carved on temple walls and elsewhere that relate the king's military victories in Nubia and Syria. The walls of cultus and mortuary temples are covered in scenes with accompanying inscriptions depicting the rituals offered to the gods and kings and the great festivals as well as coronation and temple foundation and consecration ceremonies. These inscriptions also include hymns sung at the festivals.

In the New Kingdom, deep rock-cut tombs replaced pyramids as royal burial places, and scenes within the tombs in the Valley of the Kings represent the dangers that the owner encountered and had to defeat in his journey to the next world. The accompanying inscriptions provide magical spells to enable him to overcome these barriers. In the tombs of courtiers and officials the wall scenes and accompanying inscriptions illustrate the daily existence of the owner, which he hoped to re-create in the afterlife. He was also supplied with a papyrus roll inscribed with the Book of the Dead (and sometimes other similar magical texts), which was intended to ensure his safe passage into the next world. These formed the final development of the Pyramid Texts and Coffin Texts now made available to many people.

The Schoolboy Exercises from the late New Kingdom preserve wisdom texts, prayers, and hymns to gods, as well as a new genre—model letters between teachers and pupils emphasizing moral and ethical standards. These texts sometimes form the only extant copies of important earlier works. In general both in the new wisdom texts and in votive hymns from the royal workmen's village of Deir el-Medina there is greater personal awareness and humility in the relationship expressed between an individual and his god.

During the Amarna Period at the end of Dynasty 18, the hymns to the Aten express the concept of solar monotheism that the king now attempted to introduce. They incorporate some earlier ideas but also express in an unprecedented way the idea of the Aten's exclusive nature and role as a creative and caring universal deity. Passages in these hymns and in some other New Kingdom texts have been shown to have close associations with some biblical verses.

Later Periods

During the last millennium of Egypt's history there was a complex pattern of conquest, decline, native resurgence, and final destruction and incorporation within the Roman Empire. These changes produced their own effects upon personal beliefs and attitudes; widespread uncertainty and personal distress replaced the old values and certainties, forcing people to seek new solutions and personal salvation. The idea that a virtuous life would ensure a blessed eternity was less readily accepted. Instead, people placed more reliance on obtaining divine help to attain happiness. In this uncertain world the literature reflects the widespread insecurity.

On one hand there were nationalistic trends, such as the revival of earlier Egyptian forms in the art and literature under the native rulers of Dynasty 26. Scribes studied and faithfully reproduced the style and content of earlier texts, since it was believed that power and prestige could be derived from such works. Some monumental inscriptions were even written in Middle Egyptian. Under the Ptolemaic and Roman rulers existing Egyptian temples were refurbished, and new ones were built. These copied the wall scenes and inscriptions of New Kingdom temples so that the foreign kings could now claim that the Egyptian gods accepted them as legitimate rulers, thus allowing them to take advantage of the same rights and privileges. Because of their relatively late date these temple inscriptions are well preserved and provide extensive material about rituals, festivals, and other ceremonies, although some of the texts are written in Ptolemaic Egyptian, a late and specialized form of hieroglyphs that is still not fully understood.

Many other earlier types of literature such as funerary autobiographies, historical accounts of decrees and military victories, and some Instructions in Wisdom survived into these later periods. The wisdom texts incorporated some new ideas and were now written in demotic.

ANCIENT EGYPTIAN LITERATURE: SECULAR

Egypt had a very old national literature that was not affected by any significant outside influences during its formative period. It promoted the historical and military achievements of the kings and attempted to ensure their worldly success and continuation after death. Although many major advances including literary forms were introduced for religious purposes before they were put to secular use, as early as 2000 BC the Egyptians produced "entertainment literature" with no primary religious, political, or commercial purpose. They cultivated literature for its own sake and displayed a highly developed sense of form and style. Not only do literary texts extend over a time span of some 3,000 years, but they preserve a wide range of subject matter.

Historical Inscriptions

Historical texts often occur in religious contexts (tomb or temple walls), although the content is primarily concerned with the king's military exploits. Since the New Kingdom was the period of greatest activity in warfare and empire-building, it is not surprising that most of these texts date to this time. The earliest military undertaking of the New Kingdom was the expulsion of the Hyksos, and the most significant account of this occurs in the tomb autobiography of Ahmose, son of Ebana, at el-Kab. This relates the events of his career as a professional soldier in the service of King Amosis.

The extensive campaigns and conquests of two kings of Dynasty 18 in Nubia and Syria/Palestine were recorded in two great historical inscriptions: the Annals of Tuthmosis I, preserved in carvings on the walls of two halls behind the sixth pylon (gateway) in the Temple of Amun at Karnak, which provide an annual record written in a factual way; and the Poetical Stela of Tuthmosis III, a hymn of victory and triumph proclaiming the king's dominion over his empire. The hymn was carved on a black granite stone discovered in one of the courts of Amun's temple at Karnak and is composed as a speech delivered by the god.

Later in the New Kingdom the Ramesside rulers fought against the Hittites in an attempt to reestablish the empire, and their exploits are again enshrined in historical inscriptions. The campaign of Ramesses II to Kadesh on the Orontes is recorded in two main accounts, the Bulletin (repeated in multiple copies on temple walls) and the Poem (repeated eight times on temple walls and also in two hieratic papyri). The Poem is the first known example of an epic in Egyptian literature; earlier poems had been used for celebration rather than narration. Later Ramessides also inscribed accounts of their campaigns on temple walls: Ramesses III's successes against the Sea Peoples decorate the walls of his mortuary temple at Medinet Habu and provide important historical information.

Entertainment Literature

The New Kingdom was also a time of prosperity and sophistication when entertainment literature was developed for the enjoyment of the leisure classes. Two main genres emerged—the popular story and the love poem.

POPULAR STORIES

Storytelling had existed in the Old Kingdom and had developed into an art form by the Middle Kingdom with such classics as the Story of Sinuhe. The popular story known as King Cheops and the Magicians is preserved in the Westcar Papyrus, which dates to the Hyksos Period (c.1600 BC), though its content places it in the Old Kingdom. Unlike other tales intended to educate and inform the upper and middle classes, the style and language of this text indicate that it would have belonged to Egypt's popular tradition, passed on orally by public storytellers traveling from town to town. Although it was expressed in popular terms, the story had specific political and religious propagandist aims: to justify to a wide audience the claim of the earliest kings of Dynasty 5 to rule Egypt by emphasizing the divinity of their birth. The story uses a technique found in other propagandist texts: It takes the form of a prophecy, although written after the events it describes, and thus seeks to justify the actions of a particular king or line of rulers.

Events of the Middle Kingdom are reflected in the famous Story of Sinuhe, often regarded as the greatest masterpiece of Egyptian literature. Composed as an autobiographical text intended for the tomb, it relates the events in the life of a man called Sinuhe. It may in fact be a true story, and it was so popular that it became a classic copied by generations of scribes. Some of these numerous but fragmentary inscriptions have survived, but the major existing copies can be found on two papyri in the Berlin Museum and a large ostracon in the Ashmolean Museum in Oxford, England. The story seems to accurately represent true historical events of the Middle Kingdom; it relates Sinuhe's flight from Egypt to Palestine, his adventures there, and his eventual return to Egypt to die and be buried. The text characterizes Sinuhe as an individual with feelings and emotions and has succeeded in engaging the reader's sympathy over the centuries.

The popular story was further developed in the New Kingdom: New ideas were added, the narrative grew longer and more complex, and allusions appeared that indicated the Egyptians' more cosmopolitan outlook and exposure to many foreign influences and experiences. Sometimes the tales have an "exotic" location or show an awareness of foreign peoples and events. They frequently have mythological backgrounds or settings; some are entirely concerned with gods' activities, and in others, even if the locations and characters are human, events occur in a fantasy world where animals can speak and humans have almost divine powers.

Among the mythological tales are the Story of Horus and Seth, which retells an earlier account of the conflict between these two gods, and the Destruction of Mankind, which relates how human evil aroused divine wrath and resulted in the partial destruction of mankind. Some stories, such as The Doomed Prince, have both divine and human elements; in this tale the prince was threatened by three fates at birth, and the actions he and his father took to try to avert his death are recounted. In the Tale of Two Brothers a conflict between two gods is translated into the human sphere and related as a quarrel between two brothers. Although the world in which they functioned retains some supernatural qualities, the story basically seeks to explore human feelings through the two main characters and their actions.

Other tales have a historical background; for example the Capture of Joppa relates an incident in the Palestinian campaigns of Tuthmosis III. Another example, the Story of Wenamun, differs from the others in that it appears to describe actual conditions and events that existed at the end of Dynasty 20 (c.1080 BC). It is a tale of misfortune and failure set in a period of Egypt's decline when prestige had been lost and Egyptians traveling abroad (in this case, Wenamun) encountered many difficulties. As a vivid and realistic account of a trading voyage in the eastern Mediterranean, it is an important social and historical document.

LOVE POEMS

Unlike the popular story love poetry has no apparent history in Egypt before the New Kingdom. The extant poems are contained in four texts (Papyrus Chester Beatty I, Papyrus Harris 500, the Turin Papyrus, and the Cairo Museum Vase). They were written as short "songs," and many may have been sung, each perhaps being followed by the playing of a musical instrument. Each poem is presented as a monologue by a man or woman describing the speaker's feelings and emotions. These were not spontaneous poems, which were then later written down, but sophisticated literary pieces using a range of composition techniques that represent a specific and apparently innovative art form. There is great emphasis on associating the emotions of love with an acute awareness of the beauty of the landscape, and there are many allusions to trees, flowers, gardens, and water. In the poems the lovers frequently refer to each other as "my brother" or "my sister," but this does not indicate any familiar relationship; these were simply terms of endearment.

Although short stories continued to be composed in later periods, the love poetry seems to cease at the end of the New Kingdom.

CLASSICAL AND LATER AUTHORS

As a province of the Roman Empire, Egypt was a safe and interesting country to visit. Its ancient sites and civilization attracted many "tourists" from other parts of the empire, including several famous classical authors. Their firsthand accounts remained the main source for the study of ancient Egypt until hieroglyphs were deciphered in the eighteenth century. When they visited Egypt most of the monuments were in a better state of preservation than they are today, and many of the ancient traditions and customs were still being practiced. Following are the most important Classical accounts.

Herodotus

Regarded as the "Father of History," Herodotus was the first writer who attempted to separate fantasy from reality. His work, *The Histories*, gives an account of the conflict between Persia and Greece, but Book II, called "Euterpe," digresses from the main theme and provides an account of Egypt's geography and history. It is the first comprehensive study of Egypt by a foreign observer that has survived intact, and it was based on his firsthand observation of the monuments and on "facts" and evidence obtained from priests and other people whom he met there.

Born at Halicarnassus in Asia Minor between 490 and 480 BC, Herodotus traveled widely. He visited Egypt in c.450 BC during the period of Persian domination and probably reached the First Cataract on the Nile. His travels may have been less extensive, however, since he provides more information about the Delta than the South and omits any detailed references to the monuments at Thebes.

He describes in detail the Giza pyramids (correctly identifying them as royal burial places); Lake Moeris and the Labyrinth in the Fayoum; Memphis; and the temples at Sais and Bubastis in the Delta. He also speculates about the source and inundation of the Nile and considers plants and animals, especially the strange behavior of the hippopotamus, ibis, crocodile, and mythical phoenix.

Enthusiastic about the Egyptians' peculiar customs, Herodotus also discusses religious beliefs and customs, festivals, magical rites, dream interpretation, and animal cults. He remains the most important literary source regarding the procedure of mummification, and modern scientific studies have mostly confirmed his statements.

Nevertheless, there have been criticisms of some of his "factual evidence," which, it is claimed, was obtained from informants who were either ignorant or who consciously misled him. But despite shortcomings and possible inaccuracies, his account remains a most important source, and its new approach to reporting and assessing information influenced other Classical writers. He was one of the few authorities trusted and quoted by medieval and Renaissance writers.

Diodorus Siculus

Diodorus Siculus was a Greek writer who lived in the late first century BC and visited Egypt briefly in c.59 BC. He discusses this firsthand experience in the first book of the twelve volumes of his *Universal History* in which he considered aspects of ancient Egypt. He also relied heavily on earlier writers such as Herodotus, Hecataeus of Abdera, and Agartharchides of Cnidus. He covers many of the same topics as Herodotus including mummification, but he provides additional facts. Other subjects include the Osiris Myth, animal worship, the cult and burial of the dead, administration, law, education, medicine, the flora and fauna, and the cause of the Nile's inundation. The work includes many inaccuracies and lacks Herodotus's originality and entertaining style, but it is still an important source for those periods when other evidence is scarce.

Strabo

General interest in Egypt during the Roman Empire prompted Strabo to devote the last of the seventeen volumes of his *Geographia* (which amassed a wealth of facts about the

Roman world) to Egypt. He also provided other details about Egypt in his other works.

Born at Pontus, Strabo (64 BC–AD 22) lived at Alexandria in Egypt for some years. In 25–24 BC he accompanied the Roman prefect Aelius Gallus on a journey probably as far south as the First Cataract. He visited the tombs at Thebes in 27 BC and the nilometer at Elephantine and also commented on the Colossi of Memnon (the massive statues that once flanked the entrance to Amenhotep III's mortuary temple at Thebes). Although his "facts" should be treated with caution, the geographical details he provides are generally considered to be accurate. Alexandria and the Delta are described in most detail, and he includes a topographical list of ninety-nine towns, settlements, and resources. He refers to major monuments such as the pyramids, tombs, and temples and comments on religious cults.

Some details have assisted modern investigation. Strabo's description of an avenue of sphinxes leading to the Serapeum (the burial monument of the Apis bulls) at Saqqara enabled the archaeologist Auguste Mariette to correctly identify the site 2,000 years later.

Pliny the Elder

The account (*Historia Naturalis*) of this Roman author (23–79 AD) provides some useful information about Egypt mainly drawn from earlier writers. He comments on human inventions and material objects not manufactured by man; mummification; and monuments within Egypt as well as those (such as obelisks) that the emperor had ordered to be removed and set up in Rome. He was one of the first Roman writers to describe the Great Sphinx at Giza.

Plutarch

This Greek writer (c.50–120 AD) concentrated on one aspect of Egyptian religion in his *Moralia*, providing the most complete version of the famous Egyptian myth of Osiris and Isis (*De Iside et Osiride*). This relates how Osiris defeated his wicked brother Seth, describing the eternal conflict between good and evil and the ultimate triumph of life over death. There are many references to the myth in Egyptian papyri and on tomb and temple walls, but no extant Egyptian version survives. Plutarch's account of the story, although it may provide a viewpoint that differs in some respects from the lost original Egyptian tradition, nevertheless made the myth available to scholars in medieval and Renaissance Europe.

Medieval and Later Writers

The Classical authors provide a unique view of Egypt, and despite their shortcomings they remained the most reliable source for studying ancient Egypt until Champollion deciphered Egyptian hieroglyphs. However, there are accounts by travelers who visited Egypt in medieval and later times that add their own views and some fragmentary knowledge.

In the early years after Egypt became a Christian country, few travelers reached the sites. The earliest account of a European making the journey survives in a manuscript discovered in Tuscany in 1883. The traveler, Lady Etheria, was a nun from Gaul who visited Egypt between 378 and 388 to identify sites known from the Bible. She apparently saw Alexandria, Tanis, and the area around Thebes.

When the Arabs conquered Egypt in 640, there was little knowledge or interest about the ancient past among either the indigenous inhabitants or the new invaders. Nevertheless, travelers still visited the country: Some, such as Bernard the Wise, who was there in 870, and Rabbi Benjamin ben Jonah of Tudela in Navarre, who traveled in 1165–71, were not Muslim. The most important account of this period, however, is by an Arab writer. Abd' el-Latif, a doctor from Baghdad who taught medicine and philosophy in Cairo, visited Giza and Memphis in c.1200. His observations on the monuments provide a different perspective (as he was not Christian), and he visited the sites at a time when Europeans were absent because of the Crusades.

With the end of the Crusades, Europeans were able to travel to the Near East more easily, and conditions improved in Egypt when it became a Turkish province after the invasion by Selim I in 1517. Merchants, diplomats, pilgrims, and travelers now enjoyed greater freedom and safety to move around Egypt, and the Renaissance also encouraged a new interest in the philosophies and heritage of the ancient civilizations. From this period until Napoleon Bonaparte's expedition to Egypt in 1798, there were many Europeans who came either to view and record the monuments or to collect coins, manuscripts, and antiquities for royal or wealthy patrons. Some officials at embassies and consulates in Egypt began to act as local agents to acquire collections of antiquities, and foreign collectors eventually sought and gained permission from the Turkish rulers to excavate their own sites and to remove the antiquities. It was at this time that several of the great private collections were made; these later became the foundation of important national collections, particularly in France, Italy, and England.

Classical accounts of Egypt were now augmented by firsthand descriptions provided by contemporary travelers. Interesting narratives include George Sandys's account of his travels in the Mediterranean and Egypt (*Sandys' Travels*, 1621), Richard Pococke's *Travels in Egypt* (1743), and Frederick Nordern's *Voyage* (1755), which contained excellent plans and drawings of the monuments. The great eighteenth-century traveler James Bruce visited Egypt in 1768, and his memoirs, published in five volumes (1790), included a description of his travels in Egypt as he attempted to reach the source of the Nile.

Later publications include the great epigraphic studies of the monuments undertaken by expeditions from various nations; accounts of excavations such as G. B. Belzoni's *Narrative of the Operations and Recent Discoveries within the Pyramids, Temples, Tombs and Excavations in Egypt and Nubia* (1820); and Gardner Wilkinson's volumes *The Manners and Customs of the Ancient Egyptians* (1835), which was the first serious study to use Egyptian evidence rather than Classical accounts as primary source material. From the middle of the nineteenth century tourism in Egypt became increasingly popular, and a wealth of books inspired and encouraged Europeans to take a Nile journey. David Robert's publications, with magnificent lithographs of drawings he had made of the monuments in the Holy Land, Egypt, and Nubia, and F. Frith's photographic record (*Egypt and Palestine*, 1858–63) brought information about the sites to many readers. Amelia B. Edwards's *A Thousand Miles Up the Nile* (1877) was a very popular account of her own river journey that described the monuments and customs she observed.

THE EXACT SCIENCES

Mathematics and Measurement

Mathematics served basically utilitarian purposes in Egypt and does not seem to have been regarded as a theoretical science. Only a few mathematical documents survive, including four papyri, a manuscript on a leather roll, and two wooden tablets; the most famous is the Rhind Papyrus.

The ancient Greeks considered the Egyptians skilled in mathematics and astronomy, but Egyptian geometry and arithmetic were primarily used for practical applications. The Egyptians are not credited with the abstract thought associated with algebra and equations, which were probably invented by the Babylonians, but they could construct pyramids, obelisks, and rock-cut tombs. This demonstrates that they knew how to draw up plans, obtain accurate measurements, and devise methods for transporting materials and raising and setting in place very large blocks of stone.

The arithmetic was clumsy yet effective in being able to yield correct results. The Egyptians used a decimal system of counting. For cardinal numbers they used the powers of ten (corresponding to units, tens, hundreds, and thousands, etc., in the modern system). Vertical strokes indicated the numbers from 1 to 9, while phonetic signs were used for 10, 100, and 1,000; a finger represented 10,000, a tadpole was 100,000, and a kneeling god upholding the sky with his raised arms expressed 1 million. The highest numbers would be written first, followed in order by the lower numbers, ending with the units. Thus, for 1,364 there would be one "thousand" sign, followed by three "hundred" signs, followed by six "ten" signs, and then four units. The numerals were placed after the noun, which usually took the singular form (i.e., year 18 = 18 years). The ordinal numbers (first, second, third, etc.) followed the noun, and if the noun was feminine the ordinal would take a feminine ending (e.g., lord first = the first lord).

The Egyptians used addition and subtraction as their basic arithmetical system. They did not have any multiplication tables but used fairly complicated methods of multiplication and division. They either multiplied or divided by ten or, where this was not possible, they had a system whereby they multiplied or divided by two.

The Egyptians also represented some fractions and proportional parts, but they usually only wrote fractions in which the numerator was one (e.g., one-eighth), although occasionally the fractions two-thirds, four-fifths, and five-sixths are also found.

Although their methods were somewhat tortuous, they could calculate the area of a square and a rectangle (by multiplying its length by its width), and they could measure the surface of a trapezoid. Most significantly, however, they devised a method of calculating the area of a circle according to the length of its diameter, which they obtained by constructing a square, the sides of which were equal to eight-ninths of the diameter. As well as being able to assess the angle of a pyramid they could measure the volume of a pyramid, a truncated pyramid, and a cylinder —a skill which helped them to construct pyramids and columns.

The Egyptians also faced logistical problems in other areas. They had to evolve systems to measure estates of land so that they could calculate taxes and to organize and distribute food and other supplies to large workforces and to the army. For area measurements they used the *setat* (100 square cubits), the land mile (1,000 square cubits), and the *atour* (a square with sides each of one lineal atour).

Thus, the Egyptians certainly possessed an organized system of mathematical knowledge, but they used practical experience rather than reasoning skills to solve problems. Although they started with elementary concepts, they soon developed systems that coped with some complicated arithmetical and geometrical problems, and they made use of fractions.

Calendar

The Egyptians developed a calendar based on the natural cycle of the agricultural seasons. It was divided into three main periods: the inundation season (*akhet*), which lasted for one-third of the year; the sowing and growth of the corps (*perit*); and the harvest (*shemu*). These three seasons each consisted of 120 days and were divided into 4 months of 30 days; at an early date 5 extra days were added to the calendar to bring the yearly total to 365 days. The inundation never occurred on a fixed date each year, so the Egyptians chose another natural event that would be readily visible to mark the beginning of each year. This was the appearance or rising of the Dog Star, Sirius (Egyptian: Sopdet; Greek: Sothis). The calendar of 365 days was actually too short, a fact that would have become evident after each four successive years, but they did not choose to solve this by adding an extra day every four years.

The civil (calendar) year and the agricultural year were closely interwoven; in fact, the start of the civil year coincided with the beginning of the agricultural year. In addition, years were counted from the beginning of each reign; therefore, year 6 of Tuthmosis III refers to the sixth year of his reign. Records and historical documents were kept in terms of each king's reign.

Astronomy

The Egyptians were also noted astronomers who distinguished between the "imperishable stars" (the circumpolar stars) and the "indefatigable stars" (the planets and stars not visible at all hours of the night). They used stellar observations to determine the true north and were able to orientate the pyramids with great accuracy, although the later cultus and mortuary temples were not given an exact orientation. Each temple was possibly aligned toward a star that had a particular association with the deity resident in that building. Despite these astronomical observations, however, the Egyptians believed that the earth was flat suspended in the midst of a circular ocean; the upper half of this represented the sky while the underworld, the dwelling place of the dead, was situated in the lower part of the circle.

THE ROYAL TITULARY

From the Old Kingdom onward, each king adopted a royal titulary that included five names. Certain aspects of the titulary emphasized features common to all rulers, such as the fact that all kings were protected by the goddesses of predynastic Egypt known as the "Two Ladies" and that each ruler was the incarnation of the god Horus.

Other parts of the titulary underlined the particular strengths and qualities of each ruler. Two names were each written within a "cartouche." This appears in hieroglyphic texts as an oval loop formed by a double thickness of rope with the ends tied together at one end of the oval. Originally, the loop of the cartouche was depicted as a circle, but because most names written within the cartouche were quite long the circle was stretched out to form an oval. The Egyptian word for a cartouche, *shenew*, was derived from the verb *sheni*, meaning "to encircle." By enclosing the royal name the *shenew* symbolized the role of the king as all powerful ruler of everything that the sun encircled. The word *cartouche* was originally used by the French to translate the concept of a tablet of stone, wood, or metal containing a royal name, but it has now become a generally accepted Egyptological term. When Thomas Young and Jean-François Champollion realized that each royal name in hieroglyphic texts was inscribed within a cartouche, it enabled them to compare the Greek and Egyptian names for the rulers on the Rosetta Stone and achieve a breakthrough in deciphering hieroglyphs.

The five names of the titulary are as follows:

The Horus Name   Often written within a rectangular frame surmounted by the falcon god Horus, this probably represented the king's palace. Horus was the first divine patron of royalty, and this name represented the king as the deity's earthly incarnation.

The Nebty Name   *Nebty* was the Egyptian word for the "Two Ladies." This name expressed the king's special relationship with Nekhbet (vulture goddess of Upper Egypt) and Edjo (cobra goddess of Lower Egypt). Once the supreme divine patrons of the two predynastic kingdoms (c.3400–3100 BC) with capitals at Hieraconpolis and Pe, the Two Ladies continued to protect the king of Egypt after unification in c.3100 BC and were, therefore, included in the titulary.

The Golden Horus Name   The significance of this name remains uncertain. Although it may express Horus's victory over Seth in the Myth of Osiris, another interpretation claims that it symbolizes Horus and Seth as reconciled enemies and lords of Egypt.

The Prenomen   Each king adopted the prenomen as a religious name on his accession to the throne. From Dynasty 5 onward the prenomen and nomen were both written inside cartouches. The prenomen was always immediately preceded (in front of the cartouche) by the title *nesew-bit*, meaning "he who belongs to the sedge and the bee." The sedge represented Upper Egypt and the bee was the symbol of Lower Egypt, so the title meant "King of Upper and Lower Egypt." The prenomen usually incorporated the name of the sun god Re, the patron of royalty in the Old Kingdom (e.g., User-maet-Re).

The Nomen   Enclosed within its own cartouche, the nomen was usually the king's name before his accession, and therefore several kings within a family often have the same nomen (e.g., Tuthmosis, Amenhotep). The title "son of Re" stood immediately in front of this cartouche.

The full titulary was only used in formal inscriptions; otherwise, only the prenomen, sometimes accompanied by the nomen, was used to identify a king.

Today, rather than literal translation of the royal names (e.g., "Thoth-is-born"), the prenomen and nomen are usually left in their Egyptian forms (e.g., Tuthmosis). Modern books may vary in their transliteration of royal names (e.g., Amenophis or Amenhotep; Sesostris or Senusret). Some authors retain the Grecized form of a name as it occurred in the historical account of Manetho (e.g.,

Amenophis, Cheops, Sesostris) whereas others prefer to use forms based directly on the hieroglyphs (e.g., Amenhotep, Khufu, Senusret). Because vowels are absent in hieroglyphic texts and our knowledge of the pronunciation of Egyptian is therefore imperfect, modern vocalization of these names also shows some variation.

READING

Egyptian Language and Writing

HIEROGLYPHS

Andrews 1981: general account of decipherment of Rosetta Stone; Clayton 1982: includes assessment of decipherment of hieroglyphs in understanding modern rediscovery of Egypt; Watterson 1986, 1993: introduction to Egyptian grammar; Zauzich 1992: basic principles of Egyptian hieroglyphs; Faulkner 1964; hieroglyphs/English dictionary; Gardiner 1966: classic hieroglyphs/English grammar with sections on transliteration and pronunciation; Hooker 1990: development of ancient writing; Ray 1986: the earliest writing in Egypt; Gardiner 1916: contribution of hieroglyphs to the Semitic alphabet; Millard 1986: development of the alphabet.

HIERATIC AND DEMOTIC

Andrews 1981: op cit; Clayton 1982: op cit.

COPTIC

Khs-Burmester 1967: Coptic liturgy; Drescher 1946: Coptic texts referring to Saint Menas; Pagels 1982: Gnostic gospels; Till 1961: Coptic grammar.

DECIPHERMENT OF HIEROGLYPHS

Clayton 1982: op cit; David 1993: includes story of decipherment; Andrews 1981: importance of Rosetta Stone; Baines and Málek 1980: brief account of decipherment.

Writing Materials

Erman 1927: includes account of writing materials.

Libraries

David 1981: includes account of House of Life at Abydos.

Scribes

Williams 1972: scribal training.

Education

Lichtheim 1976: includes account of education. Gardiner 1931: includes Schoolboy Exercises; Lichtheim 1976: includes Schoolboy Exercises.

Ancient Literature: Religious

Lichtheim 1973, 1976, 1980: anthology of Egyptian literature; Erman 1927: anthology of Egyptian literature; Pritchard 1969: includes texts relating to the Old Testament; de Buck 1935–61: translation of Coffin Texts; Faulkner 1969: translation of Pyramid Texts; Mercer 1952: translation of Pyramid Texts; Davies 1903–08: inscriptions in tombs at el-Amarna; Sandman 1938: Amarna Period texts; Allen 1960: translation of Book of the Dead.

Ancient Literature: Secular

Lichtheim 1973, 1976, 1980: op cit; Erman 1927: op cit; Blackman 1932: selection of stories; Gardiner 1935: stories in hieratic papyri in British Museum; Breasted 1906–07: translation of historical records; Simpson 1973: translation of stories; Kitchen 1975–90: texts from Ramesside Period.

Classical and Later Authors

Griffiths 1966: discussion of Osiris myth; Griffiths 1970: translation and commentary on Plutarch's myth; Africa 1963: discussion of accounts of Herodotus and Diodorus Siculus about Egypt; Waddell 1940: translation of Manetho; Loeb Classical Library series: original texts with English translations of Herodotus, Diodorus Siculus, Strabo, Pliny the Elder, and Plutarch.

The Exact Sciences

Peet 1923: account of Rhind Mathematical Papyrus; Peet 1931: general account of mathematics.

The Royal Titulary

Gardiner 1966: includes account of royal titulary.

8

THE ARMY
AND NAVY

THE MILITARY: HISTORICAL BACKGROUND

Egypt was the least warlike country in the ancient world. The geography and natural resources of the country provided protection and food; therefore, it was not necessary for the Egyptians to fight would-be conquerors or promote wars to assist the economy. Until the New Kingdom there was no professional army, only a part-time, nonprofessional national army partly raised through conscription. But the Hyksos domination during the Second Intermediate Period made the Egyptians aware of the need for an aggressive policy toward their neighbors.

Although there had always been a national army and a warlike tradition and the soldiers were well drilled and organized, the Egyptians were reluctant to fight abroad because they feared that they might die and be buried outside Egypt without the appropriate rites. Therefore, as early as the Old Kingdom the army recruited foreign mercenaries, a practice that increased in later years.

The kings were traditionally the chief warriors of the state from the time when King Menes (Narmer) conquered the north and established a united kingdom. Gods such as Seth, Sekhmet, and Montu were regarded as patrons of warfare who helped the king achieve his victories. The king personally led his troops on campaigns, and according to some accounts such as the description of the exploits of Ramesses II at the Battle of Kadesh the king was depicted as the sole conqueror who vanquished his enemies single-handedly. Temple scenes and inscriptions commemorate the pharaoh's campaigns, battles, and victories and show him as a mighty hero. Kings acted on behalf of the gods in overcoming Egypt's enemies with the main purpose of restoring cosmic order over chaos.

There were many potential enemies including the Hyksos, Libyans, Nubians, Sea Peoples, Ethiopians, Assyrians, Persians, Greeks, and Romans who attempted to penetrate Egypt's borders; there were also foes such as the Mitannians and Hittites whom they encountered in conflicts abroad. Civil wars also broke out between local princes or governors in the periods when centralized control collapsed.

Nevertheless, by the middle of Dynasty 18, the kings had established Egypt as the major military power in the area with an empire reaching from the Euphrates River to southern Nubia. It was the first empire in the region, but there was no centralized system of officials and it was much smaller than the later Assyrian and Persian Empires. Nubia was effectively ruled as a colony of Egypt, but in Syria/Palestine a different system of administration was adopted. The local governors or princes were left in charge of their own conquered cities, but the Egyptians ensured that only those who followed their line were given control. To underline this policy the children or brothers of these vassal rulers were removed to Egypt where they became hostages, educated as Egyptians.

By the reign of Tuthmosis IV there was a marked change in policy. Both the Egyptians and their chief enemy, the Mitannians, realized that neither could prevail and permanently expel the other from northern Syria. Therefore, they made peace, and this policy was continued by the next ruler, Amenhotep III, who was heir to the vast domains and great wealth of Egypt's empire at its zenith. Warfare was now replaced by peace and diplomacy.

Ties between Egypt and Mitanni were strengthened still further by the marriage of Amenhotep III to Ghilukhepa, the daughter of the Mittanian king Shuttarna. Later,

Tadukhepa, another Mitannian princess, was also sent to Egypt to marry the same king. Correspondence between the two royal courts showed concern for each other's welfare—when Amenhotep III became sick in his old age, the Mittanian ruler Tushratta sent an image of the goddess Ishtar to aid his recovery.

During the long reign of Amenhotep III and partly as the result of the subsequent actions of his son, Amenhotep IV/Akhenaten, however, Egypt's power abroad declined. Increasingly, the vassal princes in Palestine began to loosen their ties with Egypt and to move toward the new power in the area, the Hittites. In Dynasty 19, Sethos I and Ramesses II had to reestablish Egypt's influence in the area by launching a series of military campaigns. By the reign of Ramesses III, Egypt had adopted a defensive policy, fighting against a new threat posed by the coalition of Libyans and Sea Peoples.

In general, nonetheless, the Egyptian army (and the navy as its supporting force) reached its zenith during this period, the New Kingdom, when an aggressive rather than a defensive policy was pursued abroad. The empire that they established was loosely organized and had a relatively benign approach. The Egyptians were never really a nation of conquerors, however, and other more warlike peoples eventually seized power: A series of conquerors—Ethiopians, Assyrians, Persians, Greeks, and Romans —succeeded in defeating their forces and occupying their country. The superior weapons and more advanced military strategies of the foreigners were key factors in these victories. Nevertheless, Egyptian weapons, models of soldiers placed in the tombs, battle scenes and inscriptions, model and full-scale boats, and excavated fortresses have provided a wealth of information about Egypt's armed forces and military policy.

EARLY EXPEDITIONS

As early as the Old Kingdom there was a national army with a loosely organized military hierarchy, permanent forces that undertook specialist duties, and additional conscripted troops who could be raised when the need arose. It was only after the Hyksos domination that the Egyptians considered it necessary to adopt an aggressive military policy to prevent future invasion of their country. In earlier times, however, they were not threatened by their neighbors and did not seek to conquer and impose their rule over other lands. When punitive expeditions were necessary to subdue border incursions or when military force was needed to underpin trading expeditions, district governors (nomarchs) were requested to raise temporary troops from their own locality to assist the king. These were conscripted from the peasants. The national army, a relatively small core of permanent soldiers, was generally used for peaceful expeditions such as collecting produce from neighboring countries, for escorting the minerals from the desert mines, for cutting and carrying blocks of stone at building sites, or for duties such as guarding the palace or policing the desert frontiers.

Byblos

Some of the expeditions went to Byblos on the Syrian coast. This city's association with Egypt lasted from early dynastic times until the Ptolemaic era. The rulers of Dynasty 2 imported cedar through Byblos; the first Egyptian object discovered there that can be dated accurately is a fragment of a stone polished vase inscribed with the name of a Dynasty 2 ruler, Khasekhemui. By the Old Kingdom contact between

Egypt and Byblos was well established: In Sahure's pyramid complex at Abusir there were reliefs showing ships returning from Syria, possibly from an expedition to obtain timber. Aboard these ships are depicted sailors; some are bearded foreigners, but they appear to be visitors or envoys rather than bound captives as they lift up their arms to praise the Egyptian king. Stone vessels inscribed with the names of Old Kingdom kings Teti and Unas have been excavated at Byblos. They were probably brought to Byblos by Egyptian traders as offerings to the local goddess, the "Mistress of Byblos," whom they identified with the Egyptian deity Hathor.

During the First Intermediate Period when Egypt was preoccupied with civil wars, the trade with Byblos fell away. Under the kings of Dynasty 11, however, this was revived, and during Dynasty 12 close ties were once again established. Although Byblos was never an Egyptian colony, there was a strong Egyptian influence; the local ruler used an Egyptian title that meant "hereditary prince" or "governor," and goods and jewelry found at Byblos were either imported from Egypt or made locally in imitation of Egyptian styles.

Sinai

Expeditions were also sent by boat to the Wadi Maghara or Serabit el-Khadim in Sinai; inscriptions on the rocks at Wadi Maghara indicate that the Egyptians traveled there from Dynasty 1 through to the Late Period. This area provided them with turquoise and copper. As well as the mining communities, there were also trading centers that attracted merchants from far afield who came in search of turquoise.

The transportation of precious commodities back to the Nile Valley involved dangers for the soldiers who accompanied these expeditions. There were skirmishes with various desert tribes, and punitive expeditions were organized during the Old Kingdom to stop acts of aggression by these nomads (the "Sand Dwellers").

Nubia

The Egyptians sent early expeditions to the south to gain access to building stone and gem stones and later to gold. People from this region were also engaged to work for the Egyptians as soldiers and in the mines and quarries. In order to maintain control over this area the Egyptians of the earliest dynasties annexed the region that lay north of Elephantine (Aswan) and fixed the frontier at the First Cataract. Djer, a king of Dynasty 1, led his army as far south as the Second Cataract, and by the Old Kingdom an increasing number of commercial expeditions were sent to Nubia, supported by the militia. Tombs, cut into the cliffside at Aswan, belonging to the governors of Elephantine contain inscriptions with interesting details about these expeditions. During the First Intermediate Period this contact with the south was interrupted, but the rulers of Dynasty 12 colonized Nubia and conquered the country as far as Semna, which lay south of the Second Cataract. Senusret III was famous for his conquests in Nubia, and he and a predecessor, Senusret I, safeguarded the new frontier with a string of fortresses built between Semna South and Buhen at the Second Cataract.

Punt

The Egyptians also sent expeditions to Punt, a region situated somewhere to the southeast of Egypt, probably on the east coast of Africa near the southern end of the Red Sea. Their relationship with the people of Punt was similar to their contacts with Byblos. Regular expeditions were sent there to negotiate with the local inhabitants for the highly prized commodities of myrrh trees, packed in baskets for planting in temple groves in Egypt, and ebony, ivory, leopard skins, and baboons.

The Egyptians traded with Punt from at least Dynasty 5, but there may have been even earlier expeditions. They appear to have established a trading route between Byblos and Punt going via Egypt. Ships used for these voyages were known as "Byblos ships" and were built at a place on the Red Sea coast (probably near the modern Wadi el-Gasus). Expeditions set out from here for Punt, but when they returned they had to disembark and their produce was loaded onto donkeys so that it could be taken overland to the Nile Valley.

Western Desert

Finally, to the west of the Nile Valley there lies a string of oases that the Egyptians controlled. In Dynasty 6, when a Nubian chieftain attempted to gain control of one of these, peace was restored by Harkhuf, the governor of Elephantine. The Egyptians recruited soldiers from the oases but also used them as a place of banishment for criminals. Beyond the oases lay Tjehenu, a desert area inhabited by a number of tribes including the Tjemhu, Tjehnya, and later the Meshwesh and Libu.

THE PROFESSIONAL ARMY

After the Hyksos domination of Egypt in Dynasties 15 and 16, the native kings who ruled the country in Dynasty 18 had become very aware of the need for a professional, national army. For the first time the rulers of the New Kingdom were determined to create an outstanding military power that would be able to fight off any future attempts by foreign groups to dominate Egypt. This army, probably started by King Amosis I, was organized on a national basis with professional soldiers as officers. This replaced the earlier arrangements when governors had conscripted soldiers from the local population whenever the king decided to fight or undertake expeditions. One of the main ambitions during Dynasty 18 was to establish and retain an empire, and this underpinned the need for development in the army and navy.

Sources for our knowledge of this army include wall scenes in Dynasty 18 tombs; chariots found in the tombs of Tuthmosis IV, Yuya (a leading soldier and father-in-law of Amenhotep III), and Userhet (scribe under Amenhotep II); reliefs on the chariot of Tuthmosis IV; paintings on the lid of a wooden chest belonging to Tutankhamun; and reliefs on walls in the city of Tell el-Amarna and in the temples of Abydos, Beit el-Wali, the Ramesseum, Karnak, and Abu Simbel. There is also literary evidence, such as the Edict of Horemheb, which provides details about the organization of the army.

Organization and Recruitment

The pharaoh was commander in chief and led the army in major campaigns; however, princes or minor officials were usually in charge of less important expeditions. The vizier (chief minister) was also minister of war, and he was advised by an army council. The army was broken down into divisions of about 5,000 men in the field;

each was named after a principal god. Divisions consisted of infantry and chariotry and were under the command of either the king or one of the princes. Before battle the king was advised by the senior officials who made up the council of war.

In the Middle Kingdom the infantry consisted of two main groups—older foot soldiers and younger, less experienced men. In later times the pattern changed: The infantry included recruits, trained men, and specialized troops. During Dynasty 18 some recruits were drawn from Nubia, and prisoners of war began to be enlisted from the reign of Amenhotep III onward, a practice that was continued under the Ramesside rulers of Dynasty 19. In later periods there were many foreigners in the army, but in the New Kingdom it was customary to recruit soldiers by conscription so that, in the reign of Ramesses II, the proportion of the population who was forced to take up military service numbered one man in every ten.

In addition to conscription there were men who chose the army as a profession, and during the Ramesside Period the upper classes included many military officials. Military service for them offered rapid wealth and promotion, and officers were selected from these professional soldiers. Also, since the king believed that he could rely on the army he created important palace officials from their number such as the tutor to the royal children. Other incentives to join and remain in the army included the opportunity to gain great wealth by acquiring booty taken during the campaigns—and the law also ensured that land given by the king to his professional soldiers could only be inherited by their sons if they also joined the army. Conscription, recruitment of foreign soldiers, and inducements to join the army all helped the Egyptian rulers to build a professional army that could establish and control an empire. This was no mean feat since the Egyptians were essentially peace loving.

CHAIN OF COMMAND

From the titles held by the soldiers it is possible to deduce that the lowest commander was known as the "Greatest of Fifty." Above him was the standard-bearer who was in charge of 200 men and then another commander of slightly higher rank who led 250 soldiers; his superior was the captain of the troop. The commander of the troop may have controlled a brigade, several regiments, or a fortress; he was responsible to the overseer of garrison troops who answered to the overseer of fortresses (there were two, one each for the Nubian frontier and the Mediterranean coast). Then there was the lieutenant commander who acted as a senior officer, general administrator, and military commander; his superior was the general (overseer of the army) who in turn reported to the king.

THE CHARIOTRY

As well as an infantry, there was also the chariotry, which had probably been introduced into Egypt under the Hyksos. This was divided into squadrons, each of which had twenty-five chariots and was commanded by a "Charioteer of the Residence." Each chariot had two wheels and was drawn by two horses; it carried two men —the driver and a fighting soldier who had bows and arrows, a shield, sword, and javelin. The "First Charioteer of his Majesty" probably drove the king's chariot and wielded great power; his other duties included traveling abroad, probably to acquire stud horses. In addition to this method of increasing the breeding stock the Egyptians may have captured horses during their foreign campaigns. Another important position was held by the royal stable master who was in charge of the royal training stables. Other stable masters were responsible for feeding and exercising the horses. There was no cavalry, perhaps because the horses were not strong or large enough to carry a rider.

SPECIAL FORCES

There were also specialized troops. The "Braves of the King" were an elite fighting force who led attacks, and the 'w'yt were garrison troops, on service at home or abroad, who sometimes acted as household troops for the king. Then there were the "Retainers," whose exact role remains obscure; they may have functioned originally as a royal bodyguard, but in the middle of Dynasty 18 they were in charge of issuing rations to troops, and by Ramesside times they acted as letter couriers.

The Edict of Horemheb (end of Dynasty 18) implies that the army was divided into two corps (in Upper and Lower Egypt) when they were at home; each was led by a lieutenant commander who was responsible to the general. They garrisoned frontier forts, dealt with riots, escorted royal processions and public celebrations, and perhaps provided unskilled labor for public building works.

MILITARY PERSONALITIES

Some individuals have left records of their particular contributions to the armed services in Egypt. All kings were commanders in chief of their troops, but some were especially famous as strategists or warriors. Apart from the early conquerors such as Scorpion and King Menes (Nar-mer) who used military force to unify Egypt and create a nation, others were notable for their actions against foreign threats. During the Middle Kingdom Senusret III extended Egypt's control over Nubia and completed a series of fortresses there to subjugate and control the local population. Seqenenre Ta'o II, Kamose, Amosis I, and Amenhotep I fought bravely during the conflict between the Theban rulers and the Hyksos to expel the Hyksos and then to establish the foundations of the Egyptian Empire in Palestine. Under the later kings of Dynasty 18 this policy was extended, and under Tuthmosis I, Tuthmosis III, and Amenhotep II the Egyptian frontiers were fixed in southern Nubia and as far north as the Euphrates River. During Dynasty 19, Sethos I and Ramesses II had to reestablish Egyptian influence in Syria/Palestine. Finally, Ramesses III, Egypt's last great warrior king, fought a vital although defensive battle to prevent the Sea Peoples from entering the Delta.

Commanders

Most of the royal achievements are recorded in scenes and inscriptions on temple walls. Scenes and inscriptions in nonroyal tombs, however, sometimes provide additional information. At el-Kab there are two rock tombs of particular interest. One belonged to Ahmose, son of Ebana, a warrior who served under Amosis I, Amenhotep I, and Tuthmosis I. His father had served under the Theban prince, Seqenenre Ta'o II. A long inscription on the tomb walls at el-Kab records the life and deeds of Ahmose and relates his actions as an admiral in the war fought to expel the Hyksos. Fighting for Amosis, he accompanied the king when he sailed north to attack the Hyksos. As a reward for his bravery, he was promoted from one ship to another; he also received male and female slaves on several occasions and the award of the decoration "Gold of Valor" for his actions in battle. It is clear that although he was transported by ship, he fought as a soldier on land, thus emphasizing the role of the navy as "soldiers at sea," or land troops transported via water. Ahmose took part in the seige of a Hyksos fortress and of the town of Sharuhen in southwest Palestine.

In a neighboring tomb at el-Kab belonging to a relative, Ahmose Pennekheb, there is another biographical inscription that relates this man's military actions fighting for Amosis and Amenhotep I. These two relatives from el-Kab both fought bravely with Amenhotep I in his campaign to reestablish supremacy in Nubia.

Later in the New Kingdom there were several interesting tombs built for military commanders. That of Amenemhab on the west bank at Thebes includes scenes of the customary funerary and banqueting scenes. Amenemhab was commander of the troops under Tuthmosis III and Amenhotep II, and the scenes show him in Tuthmosis III's presence, presenting tribute-bearing Syrians; in the long, accompanying inscription Amenemhab describes the part he played in the Asiatic campaigns of Tuthmosis III. In another Theban tomb, belonging to Horemheb, an army officer under Tuthmosis IV, there are wall scenes showing the tribute being brought by Nubians and Syrians and also the recruitment of soldiers.

Mercenaries

The use of mercenaries was important in the Egyptian army. In the Old and Middle Kingdoms the army consisted of the militia of the individual nomes or districts, co-opted when required to assist the small national standing army. In the New Kingdom, however, merce-nary troops became a significant element in the new professional army. The Medjay (from tribes of Nubian nomads) were engaged to serve in the army and in the internal police force; onetime prisoners of war or enemies, such as the Sherden and Libyans, also became Egyptian soldiers. Numerically, they were so significant that chiefs or captains were appointed to control them and direct their work. In fact, by the late New Kingdom, foreign mercenaries probably formed the major part of the Egyptian army. Even in the reign of Amenhotep IV (Akhenaten) the king's personal bodyguard included Nubians, Libyans, and Syrians. From the end of Dynasty 18 down to Dynasty 20, foreign officers and troops were given preference over native troops. Considerable numbers of conquered soldiers from the coalition of Sea Peoples and Libyans (the Sherden, Kehek, and Meshwesh) entered the Egyptian army from Dynasty 19 onward. They fought under their own chiefs within the Egyptian army, and in the wars of the Sea Peoples and Libyans against Merenptah and Ramesses III members of some of these tribes fought on both sides. Later, the descendants of these Libyan mercenaries became the rulers of Egypt in Dynasties 22 and 23. In the period from Dynasty 26 to 30 the Egyptian kings employed mercenaries from Greece and Caria to support their rule and to introduce new ideas and techniques into the army and navy.

THE POLICE FORCE

The police force was not part of the army. It existed to uphold the established order as handed down by the gods and to protect the weak against the strong. The rural police had many duties. They guarded farmers against theft and attack and used persuasion and even physical force to make the peasants pay their taxes. Tomb scenes show how punishment was exacted for nonpayment or cheating: The culprit was forced to lie prostrate on the ground and was beaten by the policeman. They generally upheld order and ensured that troublemakers were sent away from local communities.

Other police forces patrolled the desert frontiers using dogs to hunt out troublesome nomads or escaped prisoners. In Dynasty 18 the Medjay (Nubian nomads who had been known to the Egyptians as early as the Old and Middle Kingdoms) were enrolled in the Egyptian police force and given the duty of protecting towns in Egypt, especially in the area of western Thebes. During an earlier period the Medjay had been engaged as mercenaries in the Egyptian army when they helped to expel the Hyksos; now working as policemen they were well organized and quickly became absorbed into Egyptian society.

At Thebes the records of the royal necropolis workmen's town at Deir el-Medina provide details of the Medjay's role as guardians of the royal tomb during its construction. There were probably eight of them; their main duty was to secure the safety of the tomb, and they were responsible to the mayor of western Thebes. The Medjay were also required to ensure the good conduct of the workmen and to protect them whenever necessary from dangers, such as the Libyan incursions that threatened the community in the late New Kingdom. The Medjay's other duties included interrogating thieves, inflicting punishments, inspecting the tomb, acting as witnesses for various administrative functions, and bringing messages and official letters. Sometimes they were asked to help the official workforce and assist with the transport of stone blocks.

Although the Medjay were closely associated with the community at Deir el-Medina, they never resided in the village; they lived on the west bank between the Temple of Sethos I at Qurna and the Temple of Ramesses III at Medinet Habu. Nor were they buried in the royal workmen's cemetery. This distinction may have existed to ensure that they kept their independence and could be impartial in their dealings with the community. The police force of the west bank was certainly involved in capturing thieves who participated in robbing the royal tombs. In the reign of Ramesses X documents record that sixty people were arrested on suspicion of this crime. Some were local people, but others came from neighboring areas; most were low-ranking officials (including priests and scribes), and they were probably helped by their wives, who were also arrested. The stolen property was sold, but one thief was displeased with his share and consequently reported his comrades to the police.

The police undoubtedly played an important role in bringing people to justice and maintaining law and order. They were allowed to inflict beatings on culprits as a normal punishment for minor offenses, but Egyptian society was essentially law abiding and the police were not regarded as an unduly aggressive force. Their duty as guardians and protectors was at least as important as their punitive role.

FRONTIERS

Protecting the frontiers of Egypt was considered to be one of the Pharaoh's greatest duties, undertaken as an act of reverence for the chief state god. The king was not only the ruler of

Upper and Lower Egypt; he was also overlord of the Nine Bows, a confederation of peoples and lands whom the Egyptians mention from earliest times. This amalgamation included the people who inhabited the region just south of Aswan as well as those who dwelt in the west and in the oases of the Western Desert; those who occupied the "empty land" to the east; and the sailors driven by storms toward Egypt's Mediterranean coast. In effect, this confederation included the Nile Valley and all the tribes and peoples with whom the Egyptians came into contact on all their borders.

In the Old Kingdom when Egypt first became a powerful state, the country was relatively secure from outside attack, but later the reality changed. The natural barriers and boundaries defined the extent of the country during the Old Kingdom, and in later periods when the Egyptians lived through difficult times, they were again reduced to these confines. The natural barriers were the First Cataract on the Nile at Aswan, the deserts to the east and west of the Nile Valley, and the Mediterranean coast to the north. At times these frontiers were under attack from many peoples.

When the Egyptians tried to cross the Eastern Desert into the Isthmus of Suez they met various "Asiatic" tribes. Some, such as the Mentiu, were desert dwellers in Sinai who had spread into southern Palestine. They were closely associated with the 'Aamu who had originated in Syria. The Egyptians through their encounters differentiated between the 'Aamu, the desert dwellers, the nomads, and the city dwellers who lived beyond this eastern frontier.

To the west of the Nile Valley there were the inhabitants of the oases that stretched out along the edge of the desert; these were controlled by the Egyptians who also recruited soldiers there. Beyond the oases lay the land of Tjehenu (Libya), which had always had close associations with Egypt and supplied them with donkeys,

oxen, sheep, and goats. They were occasionally enemies (as when the people of Tjehenu joined the cause of the Sea Peoples in the late New Kingdom) but more often acted as allies of the Egyptians.

Egypt extended its boundaries to the south from the natural frontier at the First Cataract, annexing and colonizing the land and controlling the people by building a string of fortresses. In the north the Mediterranean at first provided Egypt with a formidable protective barrier, but later the Egyptians established trade with lands beyond the sea. By the New Kingdom the Egyptians sent campaigns to Syria/Palestine accompanied by ships carrying troops and baggage, which sailed along the coast of Syria/Palestine. Also, the onslaught of the Sea Peoples against Egypt during the time of Ramesses III was launched from the sea.

The Egyptians used various means of patrolling and controlling these frontiers, including military fortifications in Nubia across the northeastern approaches and in the region of Mareotis in the western Delta. Deserts and the frontier posts were patrolled by special police forces. The police, who were not connected to the army, patrolled the east and west desert highways accompanied by their dogs to hunt out lurking enemies or criminals. These forces sought out those who were escaping justice, protected caravans from raiders, and monitored the movements and actions of the nomadic tribes.

Customs posts at the frontiers recorded movements of people and reasons for their journeys as well as detailing the number of letters that envoys carried. At these posts customs were levied on goods, and travelers were required to complete border formalities. This was a slow procedure. Those seeking entry to Egypt included people, driven out by famine in their own countries, who wished to resettle or to buy grain; those seeking asylum; and those wishing to return from exile. There were also ordinary travelers.

As well as these fixed geographical boundaries there were the more fluid frontiers of the Egyptian Empire, which at its peak stretched from Nubia to the Euphrates River. Military campaigns, followed by construction of fortresses or by local diplomacy to bring vassal states under Egyptian influence, were the prime measures undertaken to establish and maintain these frontiers.

DEFENSIVE AND MILITARY ARCHITECTURE

The Egyptians soon developed their early building skills to enable them to construct artificial fortifications. There were different types of defense works: Fortresses guarded the frontiers, small forts were built on desert hills, and there were other buildings across the countryside that acted both as prisons and surveillance posts (the Egyptian word for "prison" and "fortress" was the same). In temple and other scenes there are "fortress cartouches" in the shape of crenellated ovals, each surmounted by the head and shoulders of a bound prisoner, with the name of the foreign enemy written inside the cartouche. They are arranged in rows, and the Egyptian king is shown holding bunches of cords attached to the cartouches, thus indicating his conquests of these peoples. Early royal residences were similarly built with high, enclosing mud brick walls, but they were rectangular in plan and were decorated with the design of a paneled facade.

Another style of fortress used by both Egyptians and Palestinians in earliest times was oval and had rounded buttresses.

During the Middle Kingdom, Egypt first began to build extensive fortifications on the frontier with Nubia. Senusret III was responsible for the extension or construction of at least eight of these forts situated on islands and promontories between Semna South and Buhen. At Semna he blockaded the right bank of the river with a great fortress, portions of which have survived. These immense mud brick buildings were sixteen to twenty feet high and had double-tiered walls. Semna, with an irregular ground plan, had many projecting corners and was protected on the outside by a wall that incorporated a change of direction in the line of its slope. This was intended to make the use of scaling ladders by the enemy more difficult, since much longer ladders would be needed to climb a wall with a change of angle. A similar device is shown in a Middle Kingdom tomb scene at Beni Hasan, where a fortress with a change in the angle of the wall is depicted. The Middle Kingdom fortresses also had parapets and balconies and sometimes ditches and ramps. During the New Kingdom the number of Nubian fortresses was increased by the addition of new buildings intended to defend Egypt's extended area of influence. These centers were manned by military and other personnel who not only ensured that Egypt retained control of the region but also introduced Egyptian customs and traditions.

Another weak point in Egypt's defense was in the east of the Delta where the Wadi Tumilat (the old land of Goshen) ran from the center of the Delta to a break in the string of the Bitter Lakes. This was a place of strategic importance requiring defense against the Asiatics. A fortress had existed here from at least as early as the Middle Kingdom when Amenemhet I built the castle called the "Wall of the Prince." This was garrisoned so that the soldiers could constantly guard against the enemy. A later adage that a king built a continuous wall from Pelusium to Heliopolis is probably an exaggerated description of these castles.

During the New Kingdom, when the Egyptians came into contact with fortifications in Asia, they quickly adopted an Asian style of fort, the "migdol." This had a crenellated outer wall, a keep, and turrets. In the Temple of Ramesses III at Medinet Habu the stone gateway is designed as a copy of the simple form of the Syrian migdol.

In the Egyptian account, told in words and pictures on the pylons of the Ramesseum, of Ramesses II's encounter with the Hittites at Kadesh, there is a description of the Egyptian camp pitched by the division of Amun. The soldiers placed their shields side by side to construct a four-cornered enclosure to which there was only one entrance; this was fortified with barricades and defended by four infantry divisions. A large tent at the center of the enclosure accommodated the king, and this was surrounded by the officers' smaller tents; between these and the enclosure wall the ordinary soldiers, their animals, and the transport vehicles were housed. These included war chariots, two-wheeled wagons for the baggage, horses, oxen, donkeys, and the king's tame lion.

In the later campaigns when Ramesses continued his fight against the Hittites, he was mainly engaged in storming fortresses built close to the towns in Syria/Palestine. There are several representations of these buildings: They all had the same basic form, with strong gates that gave access to a lower story featuring battlements above and widely projecting balconies on each of the four sides; there was a second, more narrow story above with similar balconies and barred windows. The Egyptians still succeeded in taking these fortified buildings, however, breaking down the gates with their axes and using scaling ladders to climb the walls to the first story; meanwhile, they protected their backs with their shields and used their daggers against the enemy. The inhabitants are shown taking refuge in the second story, but as soon as they saw the Egyptians approaching they begged the king for mercy, and some tried to help the women and children escape by letting them down over the wall.

Throughout the New Kingdom the Egyptians expanded and added to the protection of their kingdom by building fortresses along their frontiers and garrisoning them with troops and by constructing forts along the most important strategic routes to Libya and Palestine. Although natural barriers—the sea and deserts—protected Egypt, a few points of access remained particularly vulnerable, especially the Nubian frontier and the northeastern and northwestern boundaries with Palestine and Libya. Here, it was always necessary to use fortified defenses and soldiers to keep the enemy at bay.

BATTLE STRATEGY AND TACTICS

The Mitannian Campaigns

Temple scenes and inscriptions as well as autobiographical inscriptions in tombs of serving soldiers provide details of campaigns and battle tactics. Temple inscriptions record the expeditions of Tuthmosis I and Tuthmosis III in Syria/Palestine and describe their actions to control the expansion of the Mitannians in that

Part of the wall reliefs at the Ramesseum, Thebes, that depict Ramesses II's famous Battle of Kadesh. This was the mortuary temple of Ramesses II (c. 1240 BC).

area. On his first campaign Tuthmosis III defeated a coalition of Syrian princes at the fortified town of Megiddo; this victory was the basis of his future expansion in Syria/Palestine. In all he led seventeen campaigns in Syria to drive the Mitannians back across the Euphrates and establish his power there. A key policy in his assault on the Syrian hinterland was the preliminary subjugation and provisioning of harbors along the Palestine/Syria coast to support and supply his troops. For the crossing of the Euphrates in his eight campaign (year 33), boats were built in the coastal port of Byblos and then transported overland on ox drawn wagons.

Ramesses II at Kadesh

There is a detailed account (in several versions) of Ramesses II's tactics at Kadesh in year 5 of his reign. He led his army across the Egyptian frontier at Sile and then marched for a month to reach the height overlooking the city of Kadesh some fifteen miles away. His army was split up into four divisions and named after gods—Amun, Pre, Sutekh, and Ptah. The army waited, ready to attack, and early the next morning Ramesses led the Amun division forward to surprise Kadesh. Two Bedouin who said they had deserted the service of the Hittite king gave Ramesses false information that the Hittites were far away in the land of Khaleb. Ramesses and his bodyguard therefore marched ahead of the rest of the army and set up camp about six miles from the ford northwest of Kadesh. Several miles behind was the division of Pre, followed by the division of Ptah, with the division of Sutekh bringing up the rear. The king, with only his bodyguard at hand, should have waited for these troops to reach him, but he soon realized that the Bedouin had lied to him and that the enemy was actually near at hand hidden to

the east of Kadesh. They now advanced on Ramesses, cutting through the division of Pre, and the king quickly sent his vizier to bring forward the division of Ptah.

The Egyptian account claims that Ramesses, single-handed and surrounded by Hittite troops, now exercised his own skill and enterprise to throw them into the river Orontes. The text of one of the Egyptian inscriptions that relates these events (known as the "Report") and the accompanying scenes on the temple walls suggests however that it was the young troops who arrived just in time from the land of Amor who saved the Egyptian position by attacking the Hittites from the rear. Ramesses probably did display great valor (the Hittite ruler even sent him a letter praising his bravery), but the Egyptian accounts generally give a one-sided and probably not entirely accurate version of events. Records found at Bogazköy (the Hittite capital) inscribed on clay tablets imply that the Egyptians returned home after a strategic defeat. There is probably some truth and exaggeration in both accounts since Ramesses did have further military successes in Hittite territory after the Kadesh encounter.

Style of Warfare

In general, however, the Egyptians did not really develop any true art of warfare. When enemies such as the Syrians, Hittites, and Libyans took refuge within fortified towns and areas, the Egyptian policy was to starve them into submission and then to enter the stronghold by using ladders and breaking down the gates. As early as the Old Kingdom the scaling ladder was already in use, and by the Middle Kingdom they employed the battering ram and protected themselves against the enemy's projectiles by means of a type of hut. They do not seem to have had siege engines, however, and never developed war techniques to the same standard as the Assyrians.

In open territory soldiers engaged in hand-to-hand combat. The fallen enemy were numbered in a count and offered up to the king: Their heads, hands, or penises were cut off and piled up to be presented to the royal herald. Generally, the battle convention was that the Egyptians suggested a specific day for battle, and if the enemy was not ready the encounter was postponed. Their enemies did not always observe these rules, however, and sometimes launched surprise attacks as in Ramesses II's encounter with the Hittites at Kadesh.

Fighting was obviously severe on many occasions, and soldiers sustained dreadful wounds. One example is provided by the mummy of Seqenenre Ta'o II the Theban ruler who played a major role in expelling the Hyksos from Egypt. Evidence of an axe wound is clearly visible in his skull. Also, in a tomb near the funerary monument of King Mentuhotep Nebhepetre at Deir el-Bahri the badly mutilated bodies of sixty Egyptian soldiers have been discovered. Nearly all have severe wounds on the top of their skulls, and it is likely that they perished while attacking a fortress or town. The king probably acknowledged their contribution to his victory by having them buried near his own tomb.

An important aspect of training recruits was their participation in competitions and contests watched by the king and his nobles. Scenes in mastaba tombs show young men engaged in javelin throwing and wrestling contests, and in a tomb at Beni Hasan there is a continuous series of scenes showing two wrestlers. They are engaged in actions and movements that according to modern experts closely follow the current rules of this sport.

WEAPONS AND EQUIPMENT

There was little difference between the weapons of Egypt and her neighbors in Africa and Palestine during the time from the Archaic Period to the Middle Kingdom, and the equipment underwent few changes. In predynastic times the throwstick was exhibited in war dances, but in fact it was only used for fowling in the Delta marshes. During the Old and Middle Kingdoms soldiers used a sling or bow for long-distance fighting. There were different types of bows, and the Egyptian version had one curve while the Nubian type had two. For close combat fighting, soldiers used spears, daggers, maces, and axes, which were made of beaten cooper or stone with wooden handles. By Dynasty 12, bronze was beginning to replace copper, but there were few changes in the weapons. It was the Egyptian custom to retain stone and metal tools and weapons alongside each other if they still suited a particular purpose. This innate conservatism meant that they never gained superiority in weaponry over their neighbors. To defend themselves foot soldiers had rectangular shields made of wood and covered with leather. Curved at the top, these had developed from the shields made from turtle shell that were used in predynastic times.

Both scenes and objects provide information about weapons. Generally, traditional style weapons of proven ability were favored. For example, the Egyptians continued to use the tang type axe (this became common in the Middle Kingdom and had a convex cutting edge attached by tangs to the haft) when other people had introduced the socket type axe (in this, the blade was attached to the handle by means of a socket). Over the years, however, some changes were introduced: Axe blades became shorter with a more narrow edge, as exemplified by those depicted in the hands of infantrymen on the lid of the wooden chest in the tomb of Tutankhamun and those used by soldiers of Ramesses II in a wall relief in the Temple of Karnak. Arrows were made of reed, and arrowheads were fashioned from bronze.

Foreign Innovations

Innovations were introduced from Asia during the New Kingdom and later. The first of these occurred at the end of the period of Hyksos domination. Although the Egyptians used their traditional weapons in the wars to drive out the Hyksos, they subsequently adopted some of the Hyksos's military equipment for their own use, which made an impact on their military organization and tactics over the next few centuries.

The Hyksos had obtained new skills and war techniques from the north in their attempt to overcome the Egyptians toward the end of their overlordship of the country. These included advancements in metalworking skills; construction of a particular type of fort that was very large with an earthen wall surrounded by a moat; the introduction of the horse-drawn chariot; weapons such as the khepesh sword and composite bow; and protective armor.

The khepesh (sickle sword), similar to the curved sword used by the Asiatics, was probably introduced from Canaan. It became part of the Egyptian weaponry from the New Kingdom and is shown in temple scenes presented by the gods to the king as a promise of victory over his enemies. The Egyptian chariot was also similar in design to the Canaanite chariot and was probably introduced to Egypt from Canaan. The Hyksos first used horses and chariots in their conflict with the native Egyptians at the *end* of their time in the country, and there is no con-

vincing evidence that they employed them before that.

It has been argued, however, that it was easy for the Hyksos to invade Egypt because they used the horse drawn chariot. The chariot has been claimed to be of Aryan origin since technical terms associated with it are said to be of Indo-Aryan origin. The Hyksos included numbers of Hurrians, an Aryan people who came from the Caspian Sea region. Both horses and chariots were known in Mesopotamia, however, long before the Hurrian influence reached there. There is no conclusive evidence that the Hurrians were a major element in the "Hyksos invasion" or that the horse drawn chariot was introduced directly to Egypt from anywhere other than Canaan toward the end of the Hyksos domination.

Egyptian chariots that have been found in New Kingdom tombs are made of pliable wood covered with leather. The earliest had two four-spoke wheels, but by the reign of Tuthmosis IV (middle of Dynasty 18) the Canaanite influence had disappeared and they usually had six-spoke or, more rarely, eight-spoke wheels. In the reign of Ramesses II a further innovation provided the chariot with a special quiver for hurling javelins.

Armor and Equipment

In early times soldiers wore a leather triangular apron over a short kilt as a protective garment. Coats of mail introduced in the New Kingdom were rare in the middle of Dynasty 18 and were worn only by the king. Archaeologists have discovered a set of bronze corselets in the Theban palace at Malkata. Under the Ramesside kings soldiers wore a leather or cloth tunic covered with metal scales.

Soldiers probably did not wear helmets before the Late Period except for the Sherden (a group of foreign mercenaries), who had real helmets and were equipped with long swords and round shields, all part of their own original war dress. (Generally, the Egyptians allowed their foreign mercenaries to use their own weapons, thus maximizing the army's capacity to kill and wound the enemy. For example, in the great battles of the New Kingdom the Egyptians used chariots, arrows, swords, and axes while the Nubians fighting for them brandished hardwood clubs and the Sherden mercenaries used long swords.) The king is often shown wearing the Khepresh, or Blue Crown, in the New Kingdom, which is usually misidentified as the royal war helmet. It was in fact a crown that symbolized victory rather than a helmet worn in battle.

Other army equipment included scaling ladders, which are depicted in scenes of military attacks when the soldiers scale the walls of enemy towns or forts or force entry through gates. There is no evidence that battering rams were used on campaigns in Syria-Palestine, perhaps because it would have been difficult to transport them from Egypt on such long-distance campaigns. The army had a substantial support system which enabled it to assemble and administer supplies at home or abroad. This was the responsibility of military scribes who acquired supplies from local governors en route when the army was campaigning abroad. They also made detailed lists of booty taken after the battles. Donkeys and ox drawn wagons provided transport on foreign campaigns. Ramesses II used ox drawn carts and pack animals, including mules, when he fought at Kadesh in Syria, and for Tuthmosis III's campaigns wheeled ox carts transported boats built at Byblos on the Syrian coast overland to the river Euphrates.

There is little evidence relating to weapons and equipment after the New Kingdom, but there were apparently no major innovations. Later, Greek mercenaries brought some changes to the weaponry, but the conservative Egyptians continued to use bronze weapons well into the Iron Age. Egypt's lack of native iron deposits and an unwillingness to change meant that the Assyrians, who had good resources of iron and new weaponry, were eventually able to establish their own empire and conquer Egypt.

CAMPAIGNS

Nubia

Nubia, the land to the south of Egypt, consisted of Wawat (Lower Nubia), which stretched from Elephantine (Aswan) to the Second Cataract, and Kush (Upper Nubia) between the Second and Fourth Cataracts. The Egyptians used Nubia as a corridor to gain access to the region's goods and to the exotic products of central Africa. King Djer's name appears in a rock carving at Wadi Halfa accompanying a battle scene; this indicates that military campaigns had reached the Second Cataract as early as Dynasty 1. By the Old Kingdom, inscriptions in the tombs of local governors at Elephantine describe an increasing number of official trading expeditions supported by military force. In Dynasty 6 the local governor Harkhuf describes his expedition to Yam (whose chieftain had tried to seize control of one of the western oases). This journey was probably undertaken partly by river and partly overland using donkeys; he brought back incense, ebony, ivory, oil, panther skins, and oxen and also a dancing dwarf to entertain the young king of Egypt.

ANNEXATION

These expeditions ceased during the First Intermediate Period because of Egypt's own internal conflicts, but the new rulers of Dynasty 12 were determined to conquer and colonize Nubia. As early as the Archaic Period the Egyptians had established their southern frontier at Elephantine (Aswan) at the First Cataract. Senusret I now launched a ruthless campaign to conquer and occupy Lower Nubia in year 18 of his reign. He was able to annex the region so that Egypt controlled the land between the Second and Third Cataracts and thus ensured their access to local supplies of gold, copper, granite, diorite, and amethyst.

Senusret III, a successor, is best remembered for his activity in Nubia where he consolidated the annexation of the whole area. There had been conflicts in the region during the reigns of his two predecessors, so in year 8 of his reign and on at least three other occasions Senusret III led campaigns to Nubia. He cut a new channel in the First Cataract near the island of Sehel, allowing him to reach Nubia through a navigable waterway that linked Upper Egypt and Lower Nubia. His domain now reached as far as Semna at the southern end of the Second Cataract where the frontier was now fixed, but the Egyptians exerted influence even beyond this. To safeguard their possessions here, he established a string of brick fortresses, as Senusret I had done too. At least eight, built or extended by Senusret III, were situated on islands and promontories and lay between Semna South (at the frontier) and Buhen (at the northern end of the Second Cataract). They provided an effective defense system. Senusret III was deified and worshiped in Nubia in later times in commemoration of the vital role he had played in making Nubia part of Egypt.

When the Middle Kingdom declined, however, the Nubians broke away and established their own kingdom. They helped the Hyksos when the Egyptians tried to expel them, and the repossession of Nubia became a top priority for the rulers of Dynasty 18. Tuthmosis I campaigned there in year 2 of his reign; this is recalled in an inscription on a rock near the island of Tombos above the Third Cataract and also in the biographical inscription of his commander, Ahmose of el-Kab. Tuthmosis I eventually took Egypt's control of Nubia to its farthest point when he campaigned beyond the Fourth Cataract.

Tuthmosis III continued the subjugation of Nubia and established the most distant major outpost at Napata near the Fourth Cataract. With these great advances many fortresses established in the Middle Kingdom had now lost their military significance, and so the rulers of Dynasty 18 built additional forts including those at Sai, Sedeinga, Napata, and Sulb.

Once the military campaigns had reestablished Egypt's domination of Nubia, further rebellions were prevented by the introduction of political measures. The whole area south of Nekhen in Upper Egypt as far as the southern limits of Egyptian influence (between the Fourth and Fifth Cataracts) was placed under the control of a viceroy, the "King's Son of Kush." One of his duties was to oversee the construction of great temples, often cut out of the rock, at Beit el-Wali, Gerf Hussein, Wadi el-Sebu'a, Amada, ed-Derr, and Abu Simbel; these temples were designed to impress and intimidate the local population.

Egyptian power in Nubia was at its height during the New Kingdom, and the Nubians accepted their part as a colony of Egypt, sending annual tribute of gold, ostrich plumes, leopard skins, animals, precious stones, and slaves. The few minor revolts led by a desert tribesmen were quickly subdued by expeditionary forces.

THE NUBIAN DYNASTY

After the Ramesside kings of Dynasty 20, the administration of Nubia through the viceroys continued for some time, but ultimately a separate kingdom emerged in the south ruled from its capital, Napata. This preserved many aspects of Egyptian civilization including the worship of the god Amen-Re. When Egypt itself was split and ruled by a number of princelings in Dynasties 22 and 23, Piankhy, the son of a Napatan chieftain, marched northward to attack these rulers. A large stela dating to year 21 of Piankhy's reign is inscribed with the account of this conquest, giving details of his seizure of the cities and the resultant slaughter and capture of prisoners. He returned to his southern kingdom where he was buried in a pyramid at Kurru, but his successor Shabako went back to Egypt to continue the fight. Established as the first Nubian pharaoh, Shabako ruled the whole of Egypt, and his successors formed Egypt's Dynasty 25.

The dynasty's greatest ruler, Taharka, was finally driven out of Egypt by the Assyrians. He escaped to Napata in the far south where he eventually died and was buried in a pyramid at Nuri. His successor Tanuatamun again claimed the joint kingship of Nubia and Egypt and briefly regained Egypt from the Assyrians and their vassals. The native vassal rulers appointed by the Assyrians, however, soon established themselves as the new kings of Egypt and founded Dynasty 26, thus bringing the Nubian overlordship to an end.

Syria/Palestine

During the First Intermediate Period the 'Aamu ("Asiatics" or Bedouin) infiltrated Egypt through the northeastern border. These incursions had not ceased by the start of Dynasty 12, and it was necessary for Amenemhet I to construct the "Walls of the Ruler" (perhaps a line of fortresses) in this area to repel the Asiatics.

Some of the 'Aamu, many of whom apparently lived in Egypt in later years, may have entered the country at this time as prisoners of war. Generally, however, the Egyptians seem to have enjoyed good relations with their northern neighbors during Dynasty 12. These contacts were mainly based on trade, but there were also military encounters. The stela of Nesoumontou indicates that he campaigned under both Amenemhet I and Senusret I against the Asiatics. Later, Senusret III and his troops reached as far north as Sekmem (probably the district of Shechem in Samaria); details are preserved in the stela of Sebekkhu who fought in this campaign.

During the New Kingdom Egypt's military relations with her northern neighbors were dominated by activities against the Hyksos (early Dynasty 18), conflict with the Mitannians (mid-Dynasty 18) and the Hittites (Dynasty 19), and then the arrival and repulsion of the Sea Peoples (Dynasty 20).

In Dynasty 18, the first important steps were taken to establish the Egyptian Empire. The Theban rulers Seqenenre Ta'o II, Kamose, and Amosis I had acted to expel the Hyksos from Egypt. According to inscriptions in tombs at el-Kab Amosis I besieged and took the Hyksos fortress of Avaris and then, over a three-year period, besieged the town of Sharuhen in southwest Palestine so that the Hyksos would have no base for a return attack. This seems to mark the extent to these Theban rulers' campaigns in Palestine. Amenhotep I has left no record of his activities in Asia, but he seems to have pursued and extended his father's policies rather than merely attempting to restore Egypt's earlier border. Possibly, he took preliminary action in Palestine that laid the foundation for Tuthmosis I's new, aggressive policy.

THE MITANNIAN CAMPAIGNS

The next few reigns were concerned with establishing Egypt's empire. Ethnic movements in the Near East had created a power vacuum, and a new force—the kingdom of Mitanni—now became one of Egypt's major contacts, first as an enemy and then as an ally. Mitanni now occupied the land of Naharin (between the rivers Tigris and Euphrates) where the Hurrians (originally from the region south of the Caspian Sea) were ruled by an aristocracy of Indo-Aryan origin.

When the Mitannians attempted to push southward they became a major threat to Egypt's military ambitions to establish the northern boundaries of its new empire at the Euphrates. The main arena of this conflict was northern Syria; however, the petty princedoms and city-states that occupied Palestine and the rest of Syria were also drawn into the confrontation as the two powers rivaled each other in attempting to make them vassals or client-states.

Tuthmosis I led the first major offensive in Syria, taking an expedition across the Euphrates into Naharin (this means the "River Country"; the names Naharin and Mitanni are synonymous in Egyptian texts). A commemorative stela set up there records that the king killed many of the enemy and also took prisoners. Tomb inscriptions at el-Kab supply other details: The king returned through Syria and celebrated his success with an elephant hunt in the region of Niy.

His son, Tuthmosis II, also campaigned in Palestine and took many prisoners, but his grandson, Tuthmosis III, was the greatest of all Egyptian warrior kings. While his stepmother, Hatshepsut, ruled Egypt, Mitanni had gained influence over many of the vassals in Syria/Palestine. Tuthmosis III was determined to halt this process and to drive the Mitannians back beyond the Euphrates.

He waged a total of seventeen campaigns in Syria against Mitanni, and some of the most important successes of these campaigns are recorded in the wall scenes and inscriptions in the Temple of Karnak and on two stelae, one in his temple at Napata (Gebel Barkal) and the other from Armant.

The king evidently regarded his success in capturing Megiddo (a fortified town overlooking the Plain of Esdraelon) as a very important achievement in his long-term strategy. He launched this campaign in year 2 of his reign and faced a rebellious coalition of princes of Syria/Palestine led by the prince of Kadesh, a city on the river Orontes. Tuthmosis III marched first to the city of Gaza and took it before proceeding to Megiddo. Here, the princes and the ruler of Kadesh faced Tuthmosis III, but his personal bravery and clever tactics ensured that the Egyptians routed the enemy, although they then had to endure a seven-month seige to take the city.

A feature of Tuthmosis III's military organization was the subjugation and provisioning of the harbors along the Palestine/Syria coast so that they could be used to support Egyptian campaigns in the hinterland. Although the coalition of princes had been subdued, Mitanni still posed a great threat to Egypt, and in the eighth campaign in year 33, the Egyptians pushed forward to cross the Euphrates and to defeat the Mitannians. The Egyptians crossed the river by using boats that had been built at Byblos on the Syrian coast and then taken overland on wheeled wagons drawn by oxen. Several sources recount this victory including the stela that Tuthmosis III ordered to be inscribed and set up at Napata. On his return journey Tuthmosis III hunted elephants at Niy and revisited the city of Kadesh, which had been destroyed in year 30.

EGYPTIAN HEGEMONY

Egypt was now the greatest military power in the area and received lavish gifts from Assyria, Babylonia, and the Hittites. The Egyptian Empire, now firmly established, reached from southern Nubia to the Euphrates River. Amenhotep II, son of Tuthmosis III, tried to emulate this success. In year 3 of his reign he led his first campaign against the district of Takhsy near Kadesh. He crossed the river Orontes and eventually reached Kadesh, where the princes and their children were obliged to take oaths of allegiance to the Egyptians. Amenhotep II then went target shooting and hunted game in the forest before taking prisoners and booty back to Memphis. He undertook a smaller campaign in year 9, but he was the last king of Dynasty 18 to pursue an aggressive military policy. Recognizing that neither could permanently expel the other from northern Syria the Mitannian and Egyptian rulers ultimately made peace. This marked a profound change in the relationship of the two countries and in the power struggles of the whole area.

THE HITTITES

The Hittites were the next major threat to Egyptian supremacy. A vigorous king, Suppiluliumas, attacked Mitanni, and its king, Tushratta, was murdered. His kingdom was split apart by internal troubles and foreign intervention, and the Mitannians were no longer able to hold sway. During the later years of Dynasty 18 and in Dynasty 19 the Egyptian kings had to face and fight the Hittites.

The major campaigns of Sethos I (Dynasty 19) are recorded in scenes on the north and east walls in the hypostyle hall in the Temple of Karnak. In year 1 of his reign he took his troops along the military coast road from Egypt to Palestine and probably reached the southern end of the Phoenician coast. A second campaign returned there, and Sethos I then continued along the coast and inflicted an attack on the town of Kadesh. Problems in the western Delta brought him back to fight the Libyans, but he returned to Syria in years 5 and 6 to face the Hittites and to briefly take possession of the land of Amurru and the town of Kadesh. This conflict was brought to a conclusion by a treaty with the Hittite king in which the Egyptians agreed to allow Amurru and Kadesh to return to Hittite control. The Hittites respected Egyptian influence, particularly in the Phoenician coastal towns.

Sethos I tried to reinstate Egyptian control of Palestine and temporarily regained authority over part of Syria. His strategy mirrored the actions of pharaohs in Dynasty 18: He led his forces to Canaan (Palestine) and took control of the coastal towns so that he could launch attacks into the hinterland (central and northern Syria).

His son, Ramesses II, continued this policy. In the Great Dedicatory Inscription in the Temple of Sethos I at Abydos (a monument which Ramesses completed) it is recorded that Ramesses began his campaigns to Syria in year 4 of his reign. The first "Campaign of Victory" reached the "Dog River" (Nahr el-Kelb), which lay a few miles beyond the site of modern Beirut. The following year he set out to try to repossess the town of Kadesh on the river Orontes which Sethos I had briefly taken from the Hittites.

The account of this battle is preserved in an epic poem repeated in eight inscriptions in the temples of Karnak, Luxor, Abydos, and the Ramesseum. There is also a shorter account (the "Report," or "Bulletin") preserved in these temples (except Karnak) and in Ramesses' temple at Abu Simbel. These all describe the king's valor and brilliance in battle and claim that he gained a single-handed victory. Records preserved on clay tablets at Bogazköy, the Hittite capital, however, present a different version of the conflict. They suggest that the Egyptians returned home after a strategic defeat, but both versions probably preserve an element of the truth since Ramesses II had further military successes elsewhere after Kadesh and was able to subjugate revolts in the Palestinian city-states and penetrate further into the Hittite territories.

Both the Egyptians and Hittites realized, however, that neither could become the outright winner. It was always difficult for the Egyptians to retain control over these distant areas, and in year 21 of his reign Ramesses II signed a peace treaty with the Hittite king Khattusilis III. Separate copies of the treaty have survived in the two capitals of Thebes and Bogazköy. The Egyptians and Hittites were equal partners in the treaty and entered into a pact of brotherhood and perpetual peace. It was both an offensive and defensive alliance, and the two parties agreed not to attack each other's territories, to recognize a mutual frontier, and to have a joint defensive pact against other aggressors with the ability to extradite refugees from each other's country. The alliance was to continue even after the death of either ruler, and the treaty was to be witnessed and approved by the gods of both countries.

The Egyptians and Hittites now became firm friends and allies; friendship developed between the royal households and their members exchanged cordial letters. Finally, in year 34 of his reign a Hittite princess traveled to Egypt to become the wife of Ramesses II. She was warmly welcomed and was soon elevated to the status of Great Royal Wife. Later, another Hittite princess may have joined the Egyptian royal family.

This change in the relationship between the Egyptians and the Hittites effectively brought to an end Egyptian military ambitions to control an empire in Syria/Palestine. The problems of ruling and controlling lands far from Egypt and the gradual but inevitable decline of the pharaoh's own powers forced the Egyptians to reverse their earlier policy of expansion in this area.

THE NAVY

The navy was an extension of the army. Its main role was to transport troops and supplies over long distances, although on rare occasions it engaged in active warfare. The sailors were not actually a separate force but acted as soldiers at sea. The two services were so closely associated that an individual could be promoted from the army to the navy and vice versa. During Dynasty 18 the navy played an important role in the Syrian campaigns, when Egypt was establishing and consolidating an empire, and again in Dynasty 20 when the Egyptians repelled the Sea Peoples and their allies. Essentially, however, in wartime the navy was regarded as a transport service for the army and a means of maintaining the bases that the army had set up; in peacetime it made a significant contribution to the development of trading links.

Inscriptional evidence provides useful details about the navy. The record left by Kamose, the Theban prince who helped to expel the Hyksos, relates that vessels were used as mobile bases for military operations in driving out the Hyksos. A wall relief in the Temple of Ramesses III at Medinet Habu also indicates that ships were used for fighting as well as for transport. There is also the personal account of Ahmose, son of Ebana, in his tomb at el-Kab, describing his service in the navy during the early part of Dynasty 18. Reliefs in Hatshepsut's mortuary temple at Deir el-Bahri, Thebes, provide a vivid, illustrated account of the great expedition to

Punt via the Red Sea, which occurred during this queen's reign. The Gebel Barkal stela is inscribed with the information that ships were built every year at Byblos on the Syrian coast and sent with other tribute to Egypt. Thus, the Egyptians were able to take possession of a regular supply of excellent vessels even though their own country was deficient in building timber.

Byblos also played an important part in supplying the boats that Tuthmosis III took overland to cross the river Euphrates in his campaigns against the Mitannians. He also used ships during his sixth campaign to Syria/Palestine to transport some of his troops to the coastal area, and in his next campaign he sailed along the coastal cities of Phoenicia where he proceeded from one harbor to the next, subduing them and demanding supplies for his troops for their next onslaught. Subsequently, these harbors were regularly inspected and equipped to ensure that they would provide support for the king when he marched inland to extend his attacks against the Mittanians. Even when Egypt's power declined in the late Dynasty 18, these Syrian ports still apparently flourished.

In addition to these coastal bases, the Egyptians also developed their naval center at home. One dockyard called Perw-nefer was built near Memphis and was probably the chief port and naval base during the reigns of Tuthmosis III and Amenhotep II in Dynasty 18. Ships sailed to Palestine and Syria from this port.

There is also inscriptional information (the Edict of Horemheb, Nauri Decree of Sethos I, and Elephantine Decree of Ramesses III) regarding the legal rights possessed by fleets belonging to temples or private individuals.

Organization

Most information about the organization of the royal navy comes from the Nauri Decree and various biographies of officials. These indicate that the recruits ($w'w$) were professional sailors, often the sons of military families. They usually served on warships. At first they were assigned to training crews directed by a standard-bearer of a training crew of rowers, and then they progressed to join the crew of a ship. No exact information is available about the number in each crew, but this appears to have varied from ship to ship. Scenes in some tombs at Thebes show the sailors clothed in special leather loin cloths (two kinds apparently existed).

On board the sailors were responsible to the commander of rowers; his superior was the standard-bearer. Navigation, however, was under the control of the ship's captain and the captain's mates. Their overseer, the chief of ship's captains, probably commanded several ships. Above the standard-bearer was the commander of troops, a title usually held by older men; this seems to have been an appointment with land-based duties rather than active seagoing duties. At the pinnacle of the naval hierarchy were the admirals, responsible to the commander in chief (the crown prince), who in turn answered directly to the king. Promotion could be either to a higher rank or to a larger ship, and sometimes a man was transferred from a ship to an army regiment. In some inscriptions it is not always clear if the text refers to a ship or to a regiment.

Conditions of service for soldiers and sailors must have varied greatly, and some literary texts describe the miseries of their lives. In contrast to the tough physical conditions they often had to endure, however, there were compensations. In the New Kingdom they enjoyed many rewards including access to booty from campaigns, income from their estates, exemption from taxes, and in some cases royal rewards of gold for their bravery.

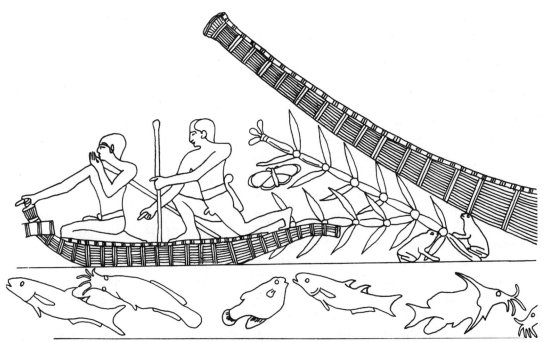

A tomb scene (c.2500 BC) showing men in a papyrus skiff. The river is depicted in cross section so that a rich harvest of fish can be represented, providing the sailors with a good catch with which to feed the tomb owner.

The army and navy eventually included both Egyptian professional fighters and foreign mercenaries such as Nubians, Syro-Palestinians, and, toward the end of the New Kingdom, Libyans and Sea Peoples.

Ships and Seafaring

Ships used by the Egyptians have aroused great interest. Sources for our knowledge include inscriptions, detailed representations on tomb walls, pottery model boats placed in tombs, and rare examples of original ships such as the solar bark found at Giza. A technical vocabulary has also survived with details of the various types of boats and their equipment.

The Egyptians were skillful sailors and navigators who had extensive experience with the Nile, canals, lakes, and the sea. The earliest boats were papyrus skiffs for Nile transport, but even in predynastic times elaborate ships with oars and cabins were being built, and there was early trade with other lands. Evidence suggests that a variety of craft were developed for different purposes: There were squat transport ships incurved at prow and stern: long ships; funerary barks to transport the dead across the Nile to the necropolis or to make the journey to Abydos, sacred city of Osiris, or for sailing in the heavens; and barges to transport animals, corn, or stone.

In the New Kingdom, specialist warships were built and several innovations were introduced. After that time, the fleet did not alter much until Dynasty 26 (c.600 BC) when new features were introduced by the Greek and Phoenician mercenaries whom the Egyptians employed. In the New Kingdom, however, the so-called Knpwt (Byblos) ships and Keftiu

(Cretan) ships played their part in the Egyptian navy. The Byblos ships may have been specially built in Egypt to go to Byblos on the Syrian coast, or this term may refer to some ships that were made at Byblos and other Syrian coastal towns. It is possible that these were modeled on ships that were captured by Tuthmosis III during his Syrian campaigns and subsequently used as the nucleus and prototype for his own navy. Although it is known that two Syrian ships were captured during his fifth campaign, however, these were probably taken for their cargoes rather than as technical prototypes. Even before the reign of Tuthmosis III the Egyptians had been sailing along the Red Sea to Punt for centuries; they had a long established reputation as excellent seafarers and traders, and they had constructed wooden seagoing ships since early times. It is likely that the name "Byblos ship" indicated its use for traveling to Byblos rather than its place of origin. Also, the Keftiu ship (often translated as "Cretan ship") was probably the term for a type of vessel rather than any reference to its place of origin or source of influence.

Pits resembling the shape of boats have been found in early cemeteries alongside some royal tombs. These were probably the predecessors of the famous pits discovered in 1954 adjacent to Cheops's pyramid at Giza. One of these pits has been opened and the contents carefully removed and reconstructed by staff from the Cairo Museum. The pit contained a boat, dismantled into pieces for burial in antiquity, that is now housed in a glass museum alongside the Great Pyramid. Over 130 feet long and made of carved pieces of cedar bonded with small cords, this complete vessel is one of the great sights in Egypt. The second pit will be opened in due course and may contain a similar bark.

The purpose of these funerary vessels is uncertain. One explanation is that they were included among the royal funerary equipment to provide the king with the means to sail the celestial sea in the company of the gods during his afterlife. They may have been funerary barks, however, used to transport the king's body to his burial place on his last journey. The Giza example provides evidence of great skill in shipbuilding techniques early in the Old Kingdom.

During the Pharaonic Period boats were used for religious and funerary purposes, transporting festival crowds and funerals; for the transport of cargo around the empire (which stretched from Syria to Nubia) and beyond to Punt via the Red Sea; and for military exploits both to fight the enemy and to support the army by transporting soldiers and equipment. There were permanent dockyards inside Egypt as well as at Byblos on the Syrian coast where ships were built for Egyptian campaigns. Wood from Egypt and imported timbers from Lebanon, sent via Byblos, were used in the Delta dockyards.

The ships, sometimes 200 feet in length, were well built and had decks and cabins. In earliest times several large planks lain on each other were held together by pegs or ropes and then caulked with resin. Oars used to propel these vessels were arranged in a bank on either side; in the stern a single oar was mounted to act as a rudder, or two large oars were placed in the fork of the stern posts, and one or the other was raised by means of a rope to steer the ship. The vessel also had a trapezoidal sail.

Within Egypt and Nubia the Egyptian troops were transported by boat. In Egypt's relations with its northern neighbors the Syrian coastal town of Byblos was of great importance, and Egypt's close association with its inhabitants from Dynasty 2 down to the Ptolemaic Period was only interrupted when Egypt faced internal problems. Coniferous woods were imported from Byblos and environs (sea pine and parasol pine) and also from northern Lebanon (firs and cedars). The rulers of Byblos not only traded with the Egyptians but provided them with support and ships for their military campaigns.

Sea journeys were also undertaken to the land of Punt. This district, known as the "Terraces of Incense" or the "God's Land," was where the Egyptians sought incense for use in their temples. Egypt's relations with Punt, which probably go back to the early dynastic period, may have involved some military coercion on the part of the Egyptians rather than reflecting a true trading partnership between equals. (See Chapter 9 for a discussion of trade with Punt.)

The Egyptians were clearly excellent sailors both on the Nile and when they traveled to other lands. Their greatest naval victories over their enemies occurred not abroad, however, but when they were forced to protect the mouths of the Delta against the Sea Peoples and their allies in the late New Kingdom.

Sea Battles

From earliest times the Egyptians engaged in naval conflict. The famous Gebel el-Arak knife, which was found in Egypt and dates to the Predynastic Period, has scenes carved on its ivory handle that depict some kind of armed conflict in which a sea battle is fought out between ships that have been identified as Egyptian and Mesopotamian types. This may represent an attempt to invade Egypt, or one stage in that conflict for which one possible entry route would have been across the Red Sea and into the Eastern Desert before passing into the upper part of the Nile Valley.

There were later naval conflicts between vessels and their crews, for example, when the Egyptians captured two Syrian ships during the fifth campaign of Tuthmosis III. In the later years of the New Kingdom, however, the Egyptians fought classic sea battles against an enemy referred to as the "Sea Peoples" in the inscribed records of the conflicts preserved on the temple walls at Karnak and Medinet Habu. They were a confederation of peoples or tribes who attacked Egypt during the reigns of Merenptah and Ramesses III. They probably came from several different homelands, but after the turn of the thirteenth century they were apparently driven southward, perhaps by hunger and displacement. Some groups, however, were known in earlier times, and one—the Sherden—fought as Egyptian mercenaries in the reign of Amenhotep III.

Some Sea Peoples fought as allies of the Hittites against Ramesses II and his troops at the Battle of Kadesh. It was their increased and repeated pressure, however, together with Assyrian attacks, that eventually overthrew the Hittite kingdom. The Sea Peoples then attacked Cyprus and the coastal cities of Syria before moving down through Palestine and joining Libyan tribes to form a coalition that attacked Egypt from the west. They intended to invade the Egyptian coast and then to establish a new homeland in Palestine and the Egyptian Delta. They brought their families and possessions with them, transported in oxdrawn carts. Ramesses III finally defeated them when he blocked their entry by land into Egypt by deploying his garrisons in Palestine; simultaneously, he destroyed their fleet in a sea battle fought in one of the mouths of the Nile.

During the earlier reign of Ramesses II the Sea Peoples had been pressing down into Asia, the Aegean area, and Libya, while a coalition of Libyan tribes— the Tjemehu, Tjehenu, Meshwesh, and Libu—were possibly driven by hunger to invade and settle in Egypt. Ramesses II dealt with these incursions by building a series of forts along the western coast road, but the threat was renewed during the reign of his son Merenptah.

After the long reign of Ramesses II, his thirteenth son Merenptah was faced with several major crises. In year 5 of his reign (c.1231 BC) there was an attempted Libyan invasion. Driven by hunger to raid the western Delta, a coalition of Libyan tribes (the Libu, Kehek, and Meshwesh) joined forces with the Sea Peoples who now approached Egypt from the Aegean Islands and the eastern Mediterranean seeking new homes. They included the Sherden, Sheklesh, Lukka, Tursha, and Akawasha, and they brought their families, cattle, and personal possessions with them.

This coalition, led by a Libyan prince, engaged the Egyptians just northwest of Memphis. Merenptah mobilized his army and after a six-hour battle achieved complete victory. The Egyptians recorded that they took over 9,000 prisoners and large quantities of booty; they also killed many of their enemies, and the Libyan prince fled back to his own people in disgrace.

This conflict is recorded in several Egyptian sources, including inscriptions in the Temple of Karnak and on a stela from Athribis and the famous Israel Stela. This granite stela usurped from Amenhotep III was set up in Merenptah's funerary temple at Thebes. It is important not only because it records this conflict but also because it contains the only known reference in Egyptian texts to Israel. It indicates that Israel was already in existence early in Merenptah's reign, thus implying that the biblical Exodus must have occurred at an earlier date, perhaps in the reign of Ramesses II.

The danger posed by the Sea Peoples was temporarily halted, but under Ramesses III it reached a climax. He was the last great warrior king of Egypt although he was forced to pursue a defensive rather than an active policy. In year 5 of his reign he faced a coalition including the Libyan tribes of Sped, Libu, and Meshwesh who were again seeking land in the Delta. The king completely defeated them and took captives who were forced to become laborers in Egypt.

In year 8, however, there was an even greater threat when a confederation of Sea Peoples (including the Sheklesh, Sherden, and Weshwesh, who all occur in earlier records, and the new groups known as Peleset, Tjekker, and Denen) attacked Egypt. They planned to settle in Syria, Palestine, and the Egyptian Delta and once again brought their families, possessions, and ox carts.

This time the action involved a double attack mounted from the sea and land; one group marched down the Syrian coast, accompanied by their families, while a considerable fleet escorted them offshore. Ramesses III mobilized his garrisons in Palestine to hold off the land attack while he prepared his main troops in Egypt. At the same time the Egyptian fleet trapped the enemy ships in one of the mouths of the Nile and destroyed them. In the mortuary temple of Ramesses III at Medinet Habu there is an important record, preserved in wall reliefs and inscriptions, of his conflict with these enemies. Details of this victory are recorded in the scenes rather than the inscriptions, providing a unique depiction of a naval battle. Various stages of the engagement are shown in one picture: Egyptian soldiers attack the enemy from the deck of their ship while opposite them an enemy vessel is held in the vice of grappling irons. Its crew is in disarray, and two fall into the water. Another enemy ship is attacked by a shower of arrows shot from the land. The inscriptions record that a net was prepared to trap the enemy. When they entered the river mouths they were caught in it and butchered to death.

These pictorial representations show the Egyptian fleet returning home with numerous bound captives; one seeks to escape but is taken by a soldier on the bank. Thus, the invaders were utterly defeated and the incursions of the Sea Peoples were arrested. Some of the attackers such as the Meshwesh managed to remain in Egypt, however, and became soldiers for the Egyptians. Eventually they were rewarded for their services with gifts of land, and a descendant of this group became the founder of Dynasty 22. Other tribes—the Peleset and Tjekker—remained and settled in Palestine where they eventually supplanted Egyptian sovereignty.

Ramesses III faced a final conflict in year 11 when he again defeated a Libyan coalition of Libu, Meshwesh, and five other unnamed tribes who tried to overrun the Delta. Supported by his forces at the frontier forts, the king engaged in a land battle and expelled the coalition, killing more than 2,000 and taking many prisoners and much booty. The commander of the Meshwesh was captured and killed. The danger of direct invasion by these people was thus eliminated, but their arrival in the region had a profound effect on Egypt and her neighbors.

THE SEA PEOPLES

The term *Sea Peoples* is used collectively in the inscriptions on the temple walls at Karnak and Medinet Habu to describe the confederation of peoples or tribes who attacked Egypt during the reigns of Merenptah and Ramesses III. They are also mentioned in cuneiform records, Greek legends, and in the Great Papyrus Harris, the most extensive state archive ever discovered in Egypt, which most likely formed part of the king's funerary temple archive. It was probably compiled by order of Ramesses IV to record the benefactions that his father, Ramesses III, had bestowed upon the god's temples and to list the events of his reign. It was apparently written on

the day of his death to ensure that he was accepted by the gods in his afterlife.

The Sea Peoples probably came from different homelands in Asia and were forced, perhaps by hunger and other factors, to exert increasing pressure at first against the Hittite kingdom, which was overwhelmed, and then against the coastal area of Syria/Palestine. Finally, they reached Egypt but were repulsed by the Pharaoh's troops, although some remained and settled in the Delta and in Palestine. Other groups probably established themselves in the Mediterranean lands and islands. Some of their names are similar to, and have therefore been tentatively identified with, later peoples who lived in this area.

The Akawasha One group, the Akawasha, supported the Libyans in attacking Egypt in year 5 of Merenptah's reign. They are not represented in Egyptian temple reliefs, but inscriptions indicate that they were circumcised because their hands rather than their genitals were amputated and piled up for presentation to the Egyptian king when the count was made of his slain enemies (presumably only complete parts—hands or genitals—were counted). There is a theory that the Akawasha may have been the Achaeans (Mycenaean Greeks); the similarity of the names "Achaean" and "Akawasha" has led to this tentative identification. But if this is true the evidence that the Akawasha were circumcised is surprising since there is no other indication that the Greeks were circumcised.

Similarly, it has been suggested that the Denen may be the Danoi of Homer's *Illiad* and that the Lukka were possibly the Lycians who lived on the south coast of Asia Minor.

The Peleset The Peleset, who fought against Ramesses III, have been tentatively identified as migrants who, perhaps in two or three stages, migrated into Palestine where they became the Philistines. They are shown in the Egyptian temple wall scenes as clean shaven, wearing a paneled kilt decorated with tassels and a chest protector made of a ribbed corselet or of horizontal strip bandages of linen. On their heads there is a circle of upright reeds or leather strips, and they carry spears and sometimes a rapier sword and circular shield.

They brought their families and possessions in wooden carts with solid wheels (Anatolian in origin) drawn by humpback cattle (such as those bred in Anatolia but not in the Aegean or Palestine). Thus, the Peleset must have had close associations with Anatolia, and they also seem to have had some connection with the Akawasha.

Theories about their homeland include the suggestion of Caphtor (because of biblical references), which can perhaps be identified with Crete or, less probably, with Cilicia in Asia Minor. Crete or Caphtor may only have been places they visited en route, however, and their place of origin may lie elsewhere. The Peleset and the Tjekker (who also finally settled in Palestine where they worked as a sea pirates out of the ports) are shown in the Egyptian reliefs wearing feathered headdresses and carrying round shields.

The Teresh and Sheklesh The Teresh or Tursha appear in the same scenes with beards and pointed kilts with tassels. Strips of linen or leather were bandaged around their chests to protect them, and they carried a pair of spears or a khepesh sword. They were circumcised and may have been the Tyrsenoi (ancestors of the Etruscans), although no evidence yet supports such an early date for the arrival of the Etruscans in their later homeland. It is possible, however, that the Teresh first traveled elsewhere, only reaching this destination much later.

In appearance the Teresh resemble the Sheklesh. Like the Sherden, Akawasha, and Teresh the Sheklesh were circumcised (their hands rather than their genitals thus appear in the representation of the enemy count delivered to the Egyptian king). Archaeological evidence in Sicily indicates the arrival of newcomers at the time when the Sheklesh were seeking a new home in the Mediterranean, and it is possible that, as the Sicels, they now reached this island and established themselves there.

The Sherden The Sherden, first mentioned in Egyptian records in the reign of Amenhotep III, were described as pirates; they served as mercenaries in the Egyptian army from Dynasty 18 onward and were rewarded by gifts of land for their service. In the conflicts with Ramesses III they fought both for and against the Egyptians, and later they were numbered among the pharaoh's bodyguard. Egyptian temple reliefs show them with distinctive helmets with a large knob or disk at the apex and projecting bull's horns. They carried round shields and two-edged swords.

They had a history as seafarers or pirates but were also probably associated with particular locations. Cyprus was perhaps their original homeland where bronze working was well established, but they may have moved on to Sardinia (according to the earliest Phoenician inscription found on the island, the name of Sardinia was "Shardan"). One theory identifies the Sherden with the bronze-working people who apparently arrived suddenly on the island between 1400 and 1200 BC and are known to have constructed the local nuraghi (stone towers). Bronze statuettes found on the island depict figures with round shields and horned helmets (but without disks) similar to the appearance of the Sherden. Also, on the neighboring island of Corsica, tombstone scenes depict warriors with banded corselets, daggers, and helmets.

The origins and eventual destinations of the Sea Peoples remain obscure, but they had a radical and far-reaching impact on the political and historical map of the area. It was a feature of their relationship with the Egyptians that some groups of Sea Peoples fought both for and against them. Although Egypt was successful in repelling their attacks, the arrival of these people probably marked the beginning of the Egyptians' slow and almost imperceptible decline.

READING

Early Expeditions

Gardiner 1961: gives a detailed account of the expeditions to Punt and Byblos.

The Professional Army

Schulman 1964: discussion of the organization and ranks in the army.

Military Personalities

Kitchen 1981: general account of the life of Ramesses II.

The Police Force

Peet 1930: account of the tomb robberies in the royal necropolis during the Dynasty 20.

Defensive and Military Architecture

Yadin 1963: general account of warfare techniques in Egypt and Palestine; Clarke 1916: a discussion of frontier fortresses; Gardiner 1916: the Nubian fortresses.

Battle Strategy and Tactics

Nelson 1913: description of Tuthmosis III's taking of Megiddo; Breasted 1903: an account of Ramesses II's tactics at Kadesh; Gardiner 1960: translation of the inscriptions describing the Battle of Kadesh.

Weapons and Equipment

Yadin 1963: op cit.

Campaigns

NUBIA

Emery 1965: account of Egypt's involvement with Nubia.

SYRIA/PALESTINE

Kitchen 1962: Egypt's foreign relations toward the end of Dynasty 18; Kitchen 1975–90: translation of inscriptions from the Ramesside period; Faulkner 1947: description of the wars of Sethos I; Kitchen 1964: comments on the wars of Ramesses II; Langdon and Gardiner 1920: the treaty between the Egyptians and the Hittites; Epigraphic Survey, Karnak 1936; wall scenes in the Temple of Karnak showing campaigns and battles; Epigraphic Survey, Medinet

Habu 1930–70: wall scenes in the Temple of Ramesses III at Medinet Habu showing the conflict with the Sea Peoples.

The Navy

Landstrom 1970: description of the navy.

SHIPS AND SEAFARING

Landstrom 1970, op cit; Nour 1960: description of Cheops's bark and its restoration; Glanville 1972: model boats in the British Museum collections; Jones 1990: study of the model boats found in Tutankhamun's tomb; Tooley 1995: an introduction to tomb models, including boats.

SEA BATTLES

Epigraphic Survey, Medinet Habu 1930–70: op cit; Edgerton and Wilson 1936: study of the Medinet Habu inscriptions and the battle of Ramesses III against the Sea Peoples.

THE SEA PEOPLES

Epigraphic Survey, Medinet Habu 1930–70: op cit; Edgerton and Wilson 1936: op cit; Wainwright 1939: account of the Sea Peoples named in the Hittite records; Wainwright 1961: description of some Sea Peoples and discussion of their possible origins; Sandars 1985: general introduction to the subject of the Sea Peoples.

9

FOREIGN TRADE
AND TRANSPORT

The Egyptians regarded their own country as the center of the world, and although they entered into commercial and trading activities with other lands to obtain commodities that were scarce or unavailable in Egypt, they apparently had no great desire to explore or travel abroad in the spirit of adventure. All their hopes and aspirations were firmly fixed within Egypt.

Their three main areas of commercial and trading activity were centered on the port of Byblos on the Syrian coast through which they obtained good quality timber; Nubia, to the south of Egypt, the source of granite, semiprecious stones, various exotic products brought up from the south, and gold; and Punt, the mysterious and as yet unidentified land to which they sailed along the west coast of the Red Sea that provided incense and myrrh for their temples. There was also less significant trade with some northern neighbors, particularly the inhabitants of Crete and other Aegean islands. Apart from Nubia, which was reached by river, the other locations had to be approached by sea; therefore, although the Egyptians were not explorers, they had to develop skills to build and sail a seagoing merchant fleet. At various times they received assistance in this from foreign mercenaries, particularly the Greeks and Phoenicians who were employed in the Egyptian navy. In the Greco-Roman Period the whole picture of trade and commerce with Egypt was substantially changed by the requirements and expectations of the country's new rulers, the Ptolemies and Romans, and also by the considerable presence in Egypt of Greek immigrants who brought with them their own commercial enterprise and expertise.

It was also the Greeks who, as tourists, first became interested in visiting the ancient monuments along the Nile Valley. Before that, few expeditions occurred purely for sightseeing, although in Dynasty 26 there was an interest in earlier buildings and inscriptions, which brought an increased awareness of the ancient monuments. Nevertheless, until the Greco-Roman Period most expeditions to tombs or temples were undertaken as tours of inspection or pilgrimages, and most traveling within Egypt was carried out for business rather than for recreational reasons.

FOREIGN CONTACTS: HISTORICAL AND LITERARY EVIDENCE

Even if the Egyptians' own travels and contact with foreign peoples and places was limited, in some of the Egyptian stories and literature events and characters are set in exotic or distant locations. Some autobiographies describe foreign expeditions; perhaps the most famous is that of the Old Kingdom governor of Upper Egypt, Harkhuf, who led four expeditions to Nubia. His autobiographical inscription carved on his tomb wall at Aswan describes these journeys and includes a copy of the letter sent to him by his ruler, the boy-king Pepy II, who expresses his excitement and eagerness to see the pygmy whom Harkhuf is bringing back for him from Nubia: "Come north to the Residence at once! Hurry and bring with you this pygmy whom you brought from the land of the horizon-dwellers, alive, fit and healthy, for the dances of the god, to please the heart of King Neferkare (Pepy II) who lives forever . . . My majesty wishes to see this pygmy more than the gifts of Sinai and Punt!" Harkhuf's account of his expeditions is a major source for knowledge of Egypt's trading

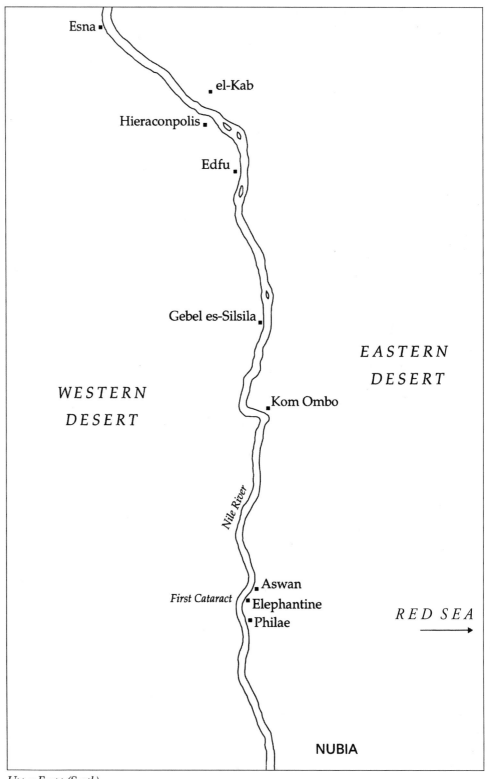

Esna

el-Kab

Hieraconpolis

Edfu

Gebel es-Silsila

*EASTERN
DESERT*

*WESTERN
DESERT*

Kom Ombo

Nile River

Aswan
First Cataract   Elephantine
Philae

RED SEA →

NUBIA

Upper Egypt (South)

relationship with Nubia during the Old Kingdom.

Several stories also provide information about voyages, expeditions, and encounters with other peoples and places. Some of these are tales of miraculous events when humans encounter supernatural powers, but others may be partly based on accounts of real events. The Story of the Shipwrecked Sailor (Middle Kingdom), preserved on a papyrus now in Moscow, describes a personal journey that an attendant relates to his master in an attempt to lift the master's spirits after he has returned from a failed expedition. The man recalls that he set out to the king's mines, sailing with a brave crew of 120 men, but a storm overwhelmed the ship and he alone survived and was swept onto an island. There he met a talking snake who told him that after passing four months on the island a ship would appear to take him home. This prophecy subsequently came true, and the man returned to Egypt where he was welcomed and honored by the king.

Another Middle Kingdom tale, the Story of Sinuhe, preserved in two papyri in Berlin and on an ostracon in Oxford, takes the form of an autobiographical text and relates the events in the life of the court official Sinuhe. He fled from Egypt at the death of King Amenemhet I for political reasons and escaped across the Delta and the Isthmus of Suez to the desert regions where the Bedouin lived. They rescued him, and he eventually became chieftain of a tribe before traveling as far as Byblos on the Syrian coast where he acquired wealth and prosperity and married the ruler's daughter. As he grew older, however, he became anxious to return to Egypt to ensure that he was buried with the correct traditions. Finally, with a decree of pardon from the new king Senusret I, he went home where he was welcomed and honored by the Egyptian ruler.

This story provides real insight into the political conditions of Dynasty 12 and the relationship between Egypt and her neighbors. It is a tale with a strong factual element and may describe a true adventure. In this respect it is similar to the Story of Wenamun (Dynasty 20) which recounts the adventures of a royal envoy sent abroad to obtain timber for the great god's sacred bark. Whereas Sinuhe was well received because of Egypt's international prestige in the Middle Kingdom, Wenamun encountered only frustrations and humiliations from foreign officials because Egypt's power had declined.

Literary sources therefore provide both "factual" and fantastic descriptions of the foreign locations to which the Egyptians traveled. In some of the stories and poems Punt in particular appears as an exotic and even romantic setting. Even in hymns there are references to Punt; in one the god Amun tells the king: "I made the lands of Punt come here to you, with all the fragrant flowers of their lands. . . . "

LAND TRANSPORT

Most traveling in Egypt was undertaken by river, but other means were needed to convey the traveler overland from the river to his destination or to cross the long distances covered by expeditions to the mines or to Nubia.

Donkey

The donkey had many uses: These animals were used for threshing corn and for transporting sheaves and were generally regarded as beasts of burden. Nobles in particular, however, did not

A wooden model of bearers accompanying a sedan chair (one method of land transportation in Egypt). The figures have jointed arms, and one holds a fan. This would have been placed in a tomb to provide the owner with transport in the afterlife. c.1900 BC.

like to ride them; in an Old Kingdom tomb there is a scene showing two donkeys supporting a sedan chair on their backs accompanied by two runners. One walks ahead of the donkey to clear the way while the other follows behind to drive the donkey and fan his master as he sits in the chair. Sometimes, a litter was carried on the shoulders of twelve or more servants; it had a seat with a canopy over it and was accompanied by men walking alongside with long fans and a servant carrying a water skin for the owner to refresh himself. Another variation of the litter had no canopy, but a servant accompanied it protecting the master with a large sun shield or umbrella. None of the tomb scenes show men riding donkeys, but one example of a donkey

saddle has been discovered. Most ordinary people, however, apparently preferred to walk.

The Litter

The litter or carrying chair was used in the Old and Middle Kingdoms to transport kings, nobles, and the statues of gods. The solid wooden wheel existed from the Old Kingdom, but it was too heavy for regular transport use over rough ground surfaces and was only employed on four-wheel carriages, which sometimes carried coffins or the god's sacred bark during his festival procession. From the New Kingdom on, the litter was apparently no longer used for general travel, although it was retained for ceremonial occasions such as transporting gods' statues.

Horse and Chariot

The horse and spoked wheel were introduced to Egypt from Asia during the Hyksos Period. Horses and war chariots had been brought into the Near East by the Aryans but were probably not used in Egypt until the end of the Hyksos reign. Horses were not usually ridden by Egyptian kings or nobility but were employed to draw light, two-wheeled chariots constructed of wood, leather, and metal that held two persons —the charioteer and the passenger.

The horse and chariot were most often used for warfare (there was a chariotry division in the army from the time of Tuthmosis III) and for transporting the royal family and nobles. Scouts and dispatch riders traveled on horseback, and there are some literary references incidating that the king and his nobles also used horses for riding, although the upper classes are never shown riding their horses and this was secondary to the horses' chariotry function. The

Egyptians greatly valued their horses, which always remained the exclusive possession of royalty and the highest courtiers. At first, horses were undoubtedly rare in Egypt, but gifts from other rulers ensured that the Egyptian studs flourished during the New Kingdom, and herds were bred and reared in the Delta.

Horses were trained to go into battle; stallions were used rather than mares, and high-spirited horses were especially prized. The great households all had their own stables and staff, but mules were sometimes preferred for drawing carriages around the owner's estate because they were easier to manage.

The Egyptians owned rich equipment for their horses. Decorative plumes placed on horses' heads were fixed into small shapes representing lions, all the metal parts of the chariot and tackle were gilded, and the straps of the harness and leather used on the frame of the chariot were often colored purple.

Two types of carriage were introduced from Palestine that became popular in the New Kingdom. The merkabot had two wheels made of wood and metal, each of which had four or six spokes; the body of the carriage, borne by the axle, consisted of a floor and wooden front and sides. The simple harness had a broad strap that passed around the chests of the two horses and was fastened to the chariot. The Egyptians had reins to guide the horses, and from Dynasty 19 onward blinders were in use. Although horses were never deified because they arrived in Egypt long after the pantheon had been established, they were nevertheless regarded as divine creatures closely associated with the king.

The merkabot, used for warfare and for traveling overland or hunting in the desert, was light and adaptable and thus became popular with the upper classes. The other carriage introduced from Palestine was the ox drawn wagon; this was used to carry baggage and particularly to transport provisions to the mines. The donkey, however, remained the most popular beast of burden in ancient Egypt; the camel is never mentioned or depicted in Egyptian sources until the Greek Period when it was first introduced to the country.

Transport of Stone and Statuary

The transportation of huge obelisks, colossal statuary, and large blocks of stone from the quarries to their final locations was an important function. Special barges were used in dry docks on the banks of the Nile, and when the inundation came these were lifted by the water and pushed along the river to their ultimate destination by a series of tugboats. It was still necessary, however, to move these huge burdens overland from the riverbank to the building site. Although some of these stone blocks were enormous, the Egyptians had only simple methods and equipment to move them. Sometimes wooden sledges on rollers drawn by oxen were used for transporting moderate-size stones along the road, but more often men were employed to pull the stones and statues. In the Old Kingdom Egyptian peasants were conscripted for this labor, but in later times they were mainly replaced by large numbers of prisoners of war and slaves.

In Ramesside times people referred to as the Habiru were employed to drag the stones for royal buildings. These workers were included in the great expedition sent by Ramesses IV to the Wadi Hammamat. Placed under three trusted commanders, the expedition had military officers, administrators, priests, stonemasons, painters, and engravers as well as 5,000 soldiers, 800 mercenaries, and 2,000 slaves. Altogether

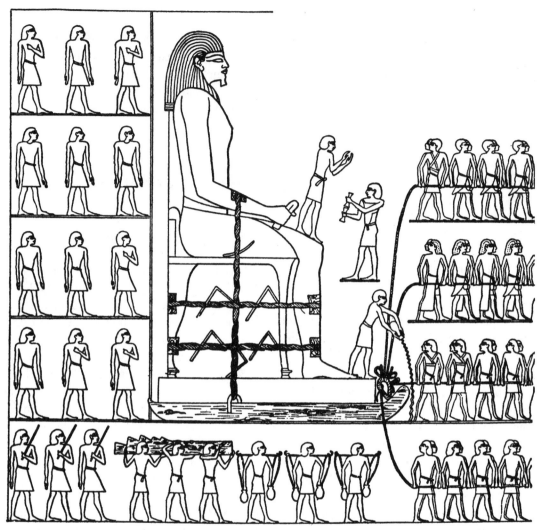

A tomb scene, c.1800 BC, showing the transportation of a colossus. Teams of men pull the colossus, which is roped to a sledge; milk is poured in front to lubricate the runners. Additional supplies are brought by men wearing shoulder yokes. In front of the statue, the foreman uses clappers to mark the rhythm for dragging the colossus forward.

the expedition numbered some 8,400 persons and was accompanied by ten ox drawn wagons to carry the food provisions.

A MOVING EXPEDITION

A Middle Kingdom scene shows how a great alabaster statue (about 20 feet high) representing the governor of the Hare nome was moved to his local temple or tomb. The statue rested on a large wooden sledge to which it was fastened by a very strong rope; pieces of leather were placed between the statue and the rope at key points to prevent the rope from chafing the stone. Four long ropes harnessed 172 men to pull this load; the overseer stood on the knee of the statue clapping his hands and issuing commands to his workforce. Another man offered incense to the statue, and a third performed the very important function of pouring milk on the ground in front of the sledge so that it would move more easily over the ground. Other men carried extra containers of milk, and the overseers with their sticks accompanied the procession to ensure that the momentum was continued.

Relatives of the governor walked at the back of the group, and the procession was met and greeted by groups of men carrying branches who accompanied their leaders; these were the governor's subjects and their presence here indicates the importance of this event for the community. Transportation of this colossus had obviously been difficult and hazardous, not least because the ground was uneven, and the inscription relates that the governor had ordered stonemasons and stonecutters to supervise young men and boys in leveling and preparing the route for the statue.

It is evident that the Egyptians used water transport whenever possible, but when they had to travel overland, other means of transport were available. To move massive blocks of stone or to send expeditions over long distances, they utilized only simple equipment but had the benefits of excellent organization and a large labor force. By the nature of its geography, however, Egypt always remained a country where it was difficult to travel around, and people probably usually remained near their own homes unless they embarked on pilgrimages to festivals held around the country or to the sacred city of Abydos to ensure their own resurrection.

WATER TRANSPORT

The Nile and its canals provided the usual means of traveling in the Delta and along the valley. The Nile, the country's natural highway, was used for transporting people and all kinds of cargo as well as for some religious processions when the god's statue was taken from one temple to another as part of a festival. Even in predynastic times these river journeys had been undertaken, and a special category of pottery known as "decorated ware" shows painted representations of boats with banks of oars that carried the god's portable shrine.

Boats on the Nile

There were many different types of boat on the Nile developed to meet a variety of needs; these ranged from the skiffs made from bundles of papyrus to the elaborate ships with cabins and banks of oars that existed back to the Predynastic Period. Ships were built for warfare, but here we will focus on those used for trade and peacetime transport.

PAPYRUS

The papyrus barks were the earliest boats built in Egypt. In effect they were rafts made of bundles of reeds bound together so that they were wider in the middle than at the ends. The smallest versions accommodated two people whereas the larger ones in which several layers of papyrus reed were bound together had space for more passengers and even an animal. The reeds were firmly held together with ropes, and a rush mat was sometimes placed on the floor. These boats, mainly used by fishermen and hunters in the shallow waters of the marshes, were propelled along with poles or short oars with broad blades. The prow lay flat on the water, and the stern stood high out of the river so that it could readily be pushed along or edged off the sandbanks.

WOOD

When they required larger boats, the Egyptians had to use wood. There was an extensive boat building industry as early as the Old Kingdom. A variety of craft was developed for which local woods such as acacia were often used. Since the Nile is difficult to navigate because of the constantly shifting sandbanks, it was necessary to build wooden ships with a shallow draft so that they did not become lodged in the sand and, to balance this, the part of the boat that stood above the water could not be built too high.

In the Old Kingdom wooden boats were propelled by wooden oars that often had a narrow pointed blade; these were fastened to the ship by a rope and held in oarlocks. Large steering oars (one or more, depending on the size of the vessel) were positioned at the helm where they were also fixed into an oarlock and held by a rope. These were used instead of a rudder at this period. Many craft also had sails.

The swiftest boats were probably built of pine imported from Syria. They were long and, unlike other vessels, their prow and stern were not raised high out of the water. They were used for transporting important dignitaries and had a cabin on deck made of plaited matting or linen where the owner could sit during his journey. The crew for these vessels included men who handled the mast and sails (when the wind dropped and the sail was lowered, the yard and mast were taken down and wrapped in the sail and placed on top of the cabin); rowers who faced the stern and pulled through the water; and a pilot who measured the water's depth with a pole and shouted instructions to the sailors and also oversaw the landing arrangements.

In addition there were large squat transport vessels that were incurved at the bow and stern. Most of the space at the ends was used for animals and goods, and most of the deck space was taken up with a main and second cabin, so the crew, consisting of three or four rowers and two steersmen, had to perform their duties in very uncomfortable conditions. Besides these boats used for transporting cattle, horses, and other commodities, there were barges for carrying grain and stones and smaller boats that were sometimes used to carry additional provisions for the larger vessels they accompanied. Some of the large freight vessels, which were too heavy to be rowed or to move without assistance, were either towed (when weather conditions prevented them from sailing) by the sailors or by tugboats steered with long oars.

By the Middle Kingdom improvements in boat building included the replacement of steering oars by a large rudder, which the helmsman operated by means of a rope and the use of a single pole mast instead of two slender masts fixed together at the top by a rope; there were also changes to the sails and rigging. From this time onward there were few innovations in the design and building of transport and merchant vessels until the Saite Period (Dynasty 26) when Greek and Phoenician mercenaries introduced new ideas. In the New Kingdom, however, the shape and size of the sail was changed, and whereas in the Old Kingdom its breadth had been less than its height, it had now reached such a breadth that it was necessary for two poles to be joined together to provide a yard that was now double the height of the mast. Also traveling boats used by the wealthy now had elaborate decoration; not only was the cabin higher but it had a front door and the walls were hung with tapestries.

Sea Ships

In addition to using river transport, the Egyptians also had seagoing craft that sailed to Byblos on the Syrian coast and along the Red Sea coast to Punt, although this appears to mark the limit of their naval activity. Ships headed for Punt are represented in scenes at the Temple of Queen Hatshepsut at Deir el-Bahri in the famous description of the expedition sent there in her reign. This fleet of five ships were sailing vessels, also fitted out with oars. About sixty-five feet in length, they were long boats with sharply pointed bows and a papyrus design on the sterns. Each had thirty rowers and very large sails and closely resembled the contemporary river boats. These so-called Byblos ships were used on coastal journeys and appear to have plied the sea route from Byblos to Punt. They traveled via the Delta through the arm of the Nile as far as Bubastis and then passed by canal to the Wadi Tumilat and across the Bitter Lakes to reach the Gulf of Suez. On some occasions they were possibly manned by mixed crews of Syrian and Egyptian sailors.

The Egyptians therefore traveled to other countries for trade purposes or, occasionally, to support the army's campaigns. They never launched major naval expeditions, however, until the Late Period when this was largely undertaken by foreign mercenaries. Again, the geography of Egypt did not encourage naval exploration or endeavors. On the Nile the cataracts made it difficult to travel south and the harbors on the Red Sea where the Byblos boats awaited the expeditions could only be reached after crossing the Eastern Desert for four days. And until Alexandria became the capital of Ptolemaic Egypt, there were no major ports on the north Delta coast that gave ready access to the Mediterranean sea routes. Nevertheless, although opportunities for foreign travel were limited, within Egypt there was a lively river traffic that flourished at all periods, with royal, temple, and private fleets moving people and goods around the country.

MAPS

Few maps of ancient Egypt (that is, plans locating particular geographical sites) have survived, but there are cosmological or star maps and mythical maps of the underworld.

At Denderah in the Temple of Hathor a map of the sky, stars, and decans (constellations) once decorated the ceiling of a terrace chapel. This "Zodiac Ceiling," now in the Louvre in Paris, has been replaced at Denderah by a plaster cast. Another relief carved on a sarcophagus now in the Metropolitan Museum in New York, shows the figure of the sky goddess Nut as she personifies the heavens. She stands with her feet on the ground and bends over so that her arms hang down and her fingertips almost touch the floor. Under her curved body between her legs and arms there is a circular representation of a map of the world. In the center there is the underworld where the gods live; this is encircled by the names of the nomes (geographical and political divisions of Egypt); and around these on the edge of the circle are the names of foreign countries. Charts of the heavens have also survived on the ceilings of some tombs and temples.

Maps of the underworld, inhabited by gods and the dead, occur in the wall scenes of New Kingdom tombs in the Valley of the Kings at Thebes and also in the various funerary "books" or papyri (on which the tomb scenes are based) that provided the deceased with a guide to the underworld. As well as supplying the deceased with spells to counteract the dangers of the underworld, the papyri also offered vignettes illustrating the underworld and sometimes giving examples of specific geographical "locations" in this mythological landscape.

There are, however, only two extant examples of maps of terrestrial locations, and they are the oldest known maps in the world. One partially preserved papyrus showing the gold mining area situated to the east of Coptos dates to the reign of Ramesses II. The other map, now in the Turin Museum in Italy, outlines two parallel valleys between mountains, which are joined together by another valley. One of the parallel valleys appears to be covered with blocks of stone and wood. Two of the mountains—each drawn with a steep point in a rather simplistic form—contain gold mines and the place where the gold was washed. One of the parallel valleys and another side pass are described as routes that led to the sea. On a third mountain there appear to be several substantial buildings as well as a shrine to the god Amun. In addition the dwellings of the miners are shown and the well of Sethos I (to whose reign this document dates) and also a great stela that he set up, possibly to commemorate the opening of this well.

TRADE OF GOODS

Domestic merchandising never became a major feature of Egyptian society. The geographical conditions of the country and the royal monopoly on the main export trade limited the development of extensive private commercial enterprise. Markets, as depicted in tomb scenes, were probably the main area of trade when food, clothes, and ornaments changed hands. As there was no coinage system until the Persian Period (c.525 BC), although by the New Kingdom metals (gold, silver, and copper) were used as the standards for valuations, barter was the means of exchange. It is probable that some merchants or middlemen (including officials) did exist, but there are few references to them. Trade only played a small part in the movement of goods

within Egypt since royal gifts provided income for the nobles and private persons were paid salaries and wages in kind.

The king and the administration decided which commodities should be traded with foreign lands, and they also controlled the mines, quarries, and vineyards. The customs barrier was positioned at the frontier, and there are references to tithes being levied at Elephantine on goods being imported from the south and also to taxes on goods coming from the Mediterranean. Greek traders who were engaged in business in Egypt from Dynasty 26 onward were obliged to enter Egypt only by the Canopic branch of the Nile.

Some foreign merchants were apparently allowed to ply their trade in Egypt. The Greeks first came to Egypt as mercenaries and enabled the Saite rulers (Dynasty 26) to gain freedom from Persian domination; during this dynasty they were allowed to found their first great commercial city at Naucratis in the reign of Psammetichus I. Egyptian protests against these Greek merchants, however, caused the king's son and successor, Necho II, to confine their commercial activity strictly to Naucratis, which functioned as a Greek city-state under Egyptian administrative control. Foreign merchants may also have operated at other sites, however, since weights and measures found at Kahun (c.1895 BC) include a number of foreign weights and measuring rods that combined the systems of measurement in use in both Egypt and Asia. They may have been brought there by foreign merchants and developed to enable them to trade with the local residents.

Foreign Commerce

Although knowledge of domestic trade is very limited, it is certain that commerce with foreign lands was always actively pursued, and the Egyptians traveled by land and sea to Nubia, Byblos, and Punt to obtain their special commodities. Egypt's political position and the lack of some basic resources constantly pushed the Egyptians to overcome the natural barriers that surrounded the country so that trade could be conducted with foreign countries.

NUBIA

Nubia was the country most readily accessible to Egypt, and from earliest times the Egyptians sent trading expeditions there. Elephantine, the island at the First Cataract (modern Aswan), became a trading center where the Nubians brought their own wares and those obtained from tribes further south to exchange for Egyptian goods. These exotic products included ivory, ebony, monkeys, and panther skins. Expeditions sent in the Old Kingdom were manned by Egyptian soldiers to ensure the safety of the venture, but during the Middle Kingdom Nubia was brought under Egyptian control and expeditions, therefore, no longer needed significant army accompaniment. Gold and hard stone were now brought from there, and although trade fell away during the Second Intermediate Period the kings of the New Kingdom completely colonized the area. From this time onward, Nubia paid annual tribute to the Egyptian king. This is represented in the tombs of various officials, including that of Huy, viceroy of Nubia under Tutankhamun, where scenes show the tribute from the area, which included gold rings, bars, gold dust in sacks, jewels, and ebony products as well as panther skins, ostrich feathers, ostrich eggs, monkeys, panthers, giraffes, dogs, and cattle.

PUNT

Another important commercial enterprise took the Egyptians to Punt on the Red Sea coast (possibly the area of modern Somalia). The products of Punt were either obtained by sending representatives to the Red Sea ports to arrange an exchange with merchants from Punt or the Egyptians sailed their own expeditions to Punt. The Egyptians had a constant demand for incense and myrrh—Punt's prime products —for their temple services and had known of the existence of this land since Dynasty 5. Expeditions had been sent there since the late Old Kingdom, but the main sources of our knowledge of trade with Punt date to the Middle and New Kingdoms. The most famous expedition is recorded in the reign of Queen Hatshepsut on the walls of her funerary temple at Deir el-Bahri. These show Egyptian envoys trading with the people of Punt through barter, exchanging beer, wine, meat, and fruit for myrrh trees packed in baskets for planting in Egyptian temple groves, ebony, ivory, leopard skins, baboons, and cattle.

The Deir el-Bahri scenes provide interesting information about this particular instance of barter and exchange, but in the accompanying inscriptions the transaction is described as payment of tribute to Egypt by the people of Punt. The illustration shows that the incense has been piled up in front of the Egyptian ambassador and his soldiers while monkeys and panthers are led forward; the Egyptian "exchanges"—daggers, axes, and necklaces—are set out on a table, and when the deal is agreed the Puntite officials are taken to the tent of the Egyptian envoy and presented with gifts of bread, beer, wine, fruit, and meat. The accompanying inscriptions attempt to explain, however, that these weapons used in barter by the Egyptians were actually an "offering" for Hathor, the goddess of Punt.

Next the goods were weighed and measured and loaded onto the ships for the return journey. In this instance these included heaps of incense, myrrh trees, ebony and ivory, gold, scented woods, incense, eye pigments, monkeys, baboons, dogs, and panther skins. They were eventually presented to Queen Hatshepsut at Thebes, and great delight was expressed particularly with the trees that were subsequently planted in the temple gardens.

SYRIA/PALESTINE

Egypt's relations with her northern neighbors were quite different. The lack of good quality timber for constructing tombs, coffins, ships, and doors had from earliest times prompted the Egyptians to trade with Byblos on the Syrian coast to obtain the cedarwood that was brought to the port from the hinterland. Expeditions already went there in the earliest dynasties, and the Byblites were obviously willing to barter and receive Egyptian goods and jewelry in payment.

Other commodities that the Egyptians needed were copper, silver, semiprecious stones, and, later, iron. Asia, on the other hand, wanted access to the African products (especially gold) on which Egypt had a monopoly and also the luxury goods that Egypt itself produced. Thus, Egypt stood at the crossroads for the exchange of these commodities from Asia and Africa. In the New Kingdom Egypt's military power enabled her leaders to seize some of these requirements as booty or to levy them as foreign tribute, but otherwise officials were still sent by the king or by the temples to conduct trade with the appropriate country.

Already in Dynasty 12 the Story of Sinuhe, which relates an official's period of exile from Egypt, demonstrates that there were close links between Egypt and Palestine and that Egyptians traveled to this area. It was only during the New Kingdom, however, that the military success of the Egyptians in Asia substantially opened up the area for trade and diplomacy, and new towns were built in the Delta as the focus of interest moved to the north.

In New Kingdom tomb scenes it is evident that gold and silver vessels, precious stones, and horses now reached Egypt. The literature indicates that many other goods, including horse carriages and accessories, musical instruments, types of drink and bread, cows, bulls, horses, and weapons also entered Egypt from Syria at this time.

THE AEGEAN ISLANDS

During the New Kingdom there were also close connections between Egypt and the inhabitants of the Aegean Islands. Courtiers' tombs of Dynasty 18 have wall scenes depicting Aegean people bringing tribute to Egypt that includes gold, silver, precious stones, copper, bronze, ivory, and distinctive metal vases of various shapes. The envoys are described as "Men of Keftiu" and "Peoples of the Islands in the midst of the Sea." The identity of the Keftians remains uncertain. Their leader is shown with the princes of the Hittites, of Tunip in Syria, and of Kadesh in a scene in the tomb of Menkheperre, high priest of Amun under Tuthmosis III (Dynasty 18). In this scene they kneel and offer tribute to Egypt; but the Keftians were not ruled by Egypt, and they visited the country as envoys and ambassadors, bringing gifts for the court and treasury and receiving goods in exchange. It is widely held that the Keftians were actually envoys sent to Egypt from Minoan Crete while the "Peoples of the Islands in the midst of the Sea" were representatives of other Aegean islands ruled by Crete.

Aegean influence is evident in Egyptian art during Dynasty 18 in vase shapes, decorative motifs, techniques of dyeing material and embroidering, and the composition of some scenes showing hunting and battle scenes. Mural decorations in the royal palaces at Malkata and Amarna may also have been carried out by Aegean craftsmen. Contact between Egypt and the Aegean peoples possibly first developed when their paths crossed in Syrian and Near Eastern ports, and there is evidence of crosscultural exchanges as early as the Middle Kingdom. Polychrome decorated pottery of Cretan manufacture (Kamares ware) has been found at several Dynasty 12 sites in Egypt; these are mainly domestic sites, and the pottery may have entered the country either through an intermediary or through trading routes or possibly it was taken there directly by Keftian merchants.

TRADING EXPEDITIONS

The Egyptians launched by land and sea both military and commercial expeditions; the latter included trading ventures and/or mining and quarrying projects. Inscriptional accounts of these expeditions provide interesting details of how they were organized and of the hardships that the participants endured.

Major expeditions were initiated by the king and placed under the leadership of princes or important officials such as royal seal bearers. If the route was by sea there were naval captains, and other officials included scribes and interpreters. There was also a considerable workforce that consisted of soldiers, conscripted laborers, and, in the New Kingdom, prisoners of war. Some expeditions went to the Sinai Peninsula to mine turquoise and copper. It seems likely that while there, they also met with merchants who had traveled from Sippar in Mesopotamia and brought lapis lazuli, which had reached them via other trading routes; they probably traded this with the Egyptians for the turquoise that was obtained locally. Thus, this

part of Sinai was a center for the exchange of precious stones as well as a mining area.

Expeditions to Punt

Expeditions were also sent to Nubia, Byblos, and Punt to obtain resources that the Egyptians lacked. Sometimes accounts of these expeditions provide details about the Egyptian views of foreign peoples and places. Punt, in particular, was regarded as a semimythical country and was used as an exotic setting for Egyptian stories and love songs. In Dynasty 11 the treasurer Henenu was sent by the king to reestablish the trade with Punt that had lapsed at the end of the Old Kingdom. Details of this expedition, preserved in an inscription in the Wadi Hammamat, are interesting. They state that Henenu was given royal instructions to go to Punt to obtain fresh incense and to fit out a Byblos ship for the journey. He led 3,000 men from Coptos to the port of Quseir on the Red Sea, following a route that was to be used regularly in the Middle and New Kingdoms. The exact route taken from Coptos is not clear, but the journey was obviously well organized. Men were sent ahead across the desert to clear a ninety-mile route and subdue the nomads: They were also required to dig fifteen wells to provide a water supply. The expedition included soldiers and artisans who were each equipped with a staff and a leather canteen and had a daily ration of two jars of water and twenty biscuits. A donkey train accompanied them, carrying spare sandals to replace their worn footwear.

The expedition marched from one water hole to the next and eventually reached the Red Sea, where the Byblos ship had been built to take the men along the coast to Punt. No details are given of this voyage, but when they returned they had to disembark and load the produce of

Punt onto donkeys to take the overland route back to the Nile Valley (at this time, there was no navigable waterway between the Nile and the Red Sea).

The best documented expedition to Punt occurred in year 9 of Queen Hatshepsut's reign; this journey from a Red Sea harbor to Punt may have taken about a month. Scenes of this expedition in the temple at Deir el-Bahri provide information about the landscape of Punt and give an almost caricatured representation of its queen. The Puntites evidently lived near the shore where their villages were partly hidden among palm, ebony, and incense trees. Their dwellings—semiconical huts —were built on piles and were reached by ladders, a device perhaps designed to protect them from wild animals and other attackers. Animals in this landscape included cattle, dogs, apes, giraffes, and hippopotamuses as well as donkeys. As the Egyptians disembarked the queen of Punt and a chieftain are shown coming to meet them. The chieftain wears a kilt and false beard, but the queen is strangely depicted; she is very large and has such physical abnormalities that her corpulence may have been due to a disease such as elephantiasis.

Another major expedition to Punt occurred in the reign of Ramesses III and is recorded in the Great Papyrus Harris. This fleet, composed of heavy transport ships and escort vessels, was apparently built and launched in Mesopotamia and sailed down the Euphrates to the Persian Gulf. It then traveled around the Arabian peninsula to Punt. Loaded up with cargo, the ships eventually sailed back through the Red Sea, landing at Quseir. At Quseir the expedition disembarked and traveled across the desert to Coptos, where it boarded other boats. These carried the men and their baggage by river northward to Pi-Ramesse, the Delta capital city.

Circumnavigation of Africa

This last expedition is the longest voyage recorded by the Egyptians before Necho II of Dynasty 26 ordered the circumnavigation of Africa. According to the king's main chronicler, Herodotus, he was responsible for initiating the canal that was constructed to provide a waterway between the Nile and the Red Sea. This increased trade and commerce, but with the advanced knowledge and naval skills of his Phoenician mercenaries, he was also able to build a fleet of triremes. The Phoenicians sailed these for him around Africa on a three-year voyage, departing from the Red Sea, going around the Cape, and then returning by Gibraltar.

The Story of Wenamun

Sometimes, however, Egyptian journeys were not so successful. The Story of Wenamun dates to the beginning of Dynasty 21 (c.1100 BC), and provides a report of a journey undertaken by the author at the end of Dynasty 20. The papyrus, purchased in Cairo in AD 1891 and now in Moscow, preserves the story almost in its entirety and provides a major literary source demonstrating the decline of Egyptian influence in Syria and Palestine at the end of the New Kingdom. The account may in fact be based on an actual report and certainly describes the geographical background with considerable accuracy.

It relates Wenamun's travels and trading experiences in the eastern Mediterranean. Wenamun was a temple official who was sent on a mission by Herihor, high priest of Amun at Thebes, to buy cedarwood from Byblos to restore the sacred bark of Amun in which the god's statue was paraded during festivals. The expedition's context was of an Egypt that no longer enjoyed great prestige abroad and that at home was suffering a nominal rulership by Ramesses XI—in reality it was controlled by Herihor in the south and by Smendes, prince of Tanis, in the north.

Wenamun took an image of his god—"Amun of the Road"—with him to enhance his prestige with foreign rulers, but the difficulties he encountered with princes and officials demonstrated that Egypt was no longer held in high esteem by other countries of the Near East. Egypt's loss of empire is reflected in this story; in earlier times any request made by an Egyptian envoy would have been readily granted. Whereas in the Story of Sinuhe, the classic literary piece set in the Middle Kingdom, Sinuhe met with great success in his travels and encounters because he came from a country that had political and economic power, Wenamun had to suffer considerable difficulties to obtain the wood, which the king of Byblos would only sell to him at a fixed price.

nean now settled in Egypt in relatively large numbers, particularly in the Delta and the Fayoum; this helped existing towns to grow in size and new ones to be established.

Under the Greeks and Romans the country prospered (although the native population probably saw few direct benefits). This was achieved in several ways. First, the irrigation system was greatly improved under the Ptolemies. Areas which were not naturally inundated required human intervention, and various water raising mechanisms were now employed, including the shaduf and two new inventions —the ox driven waterwheel (sakkiyeh) and the Archimedean screw. In the Fayoum in particular new, large areas of land were now brought under cultivation. Next, communications were much improved with the construction of new roads and canals so that people and goods could be moved around the country more easily. Furthermore, trade and prosperity were increased by the building of a canal—constructed by Ptolemy II Philadelphus and later renovated by the Roman Emperor Trajan—that joined the Nile to the Gulf of Suez.

TRADE IN THE GRECO-ROMAN PERIOD

Although Egypt was first conquered and ruled by the Assyrians and Persians, it was only when the Ptolemies and Romans came to power that significant changes were introduced in all areas of life. The Ptolemies brought political stability to Egypt, and the foundation of Alexandria as a new capital city moved the political, economic, and cultural focus to the Delta. In addition, immigrants from many areas of the Mediterra-

Prosperous Alexandria

During the Greco-Roman Period Alexandria became the most important commercial city in the Mediterranean. It had several great physical advantages including one man-made and two natural harbors. There was an extensive maritime trade with the Mediterranean and also a significant shipbuilding industry. Canals provided Alexandria with access to the Canopic branch of the Nile and thus to the Nile Valley, creating a route that enabled Egypt's domestic products to be exported through Alexandria. The Nile now became one of the world's great trading conduits, and silverware, bronze goods, lamps, pottery, glass, wine, and olive oil traveled southward beyond Khartoum. In the reverse direction the exotic products of that area —ivory, spices, gold, and myrrh—were taken north to the Mediterranean. Another route through Coptos and the Red Sea ports gave Alexandria new trading connections with India and Arabia. This link flourished in the Roman Period when a road system was developed to join the Nile Valley to the Red Sea ports.

In general Alexandria became a very wealthy city. Merchants amassed great individual fortunes, and the products of Egypt, particularly textiles, glass, papyrus, and luxury items, were welcomed in many other countries. It was Egypt's grain, however, exported through Alexandria to the Aegean, Rome, and Constantinople, that was the most significant product. Grain was brought from the Nile Valley to supply the needs of Alexandria's population, but there was a considerable surplus; this became Egypt's main export, and one of the country's main functions in the Roman Period was to supply grain to feed the population of Rome and other parts of the empire. Grain was sent to Rome in ships of the Alexandrian grain fleet on the order and under the supervision of the government.

The Nile was most effectively exploited as a trading route during the Roman Period when much of this trade was developed by Alexandrian merchants. They not only handled the government contract for shipping grain out through Alexandria to Rome and Constantinople but also undertook private ventures, importing and exporting a wide variety of goods. Greek residents in Egypt could therefore expect to enjoy many foreign delicacies including wines, honey, meat, and fish imported from the Aegean Islands and southern Asia Minor.

Impact of the Greeks

It was the Greeks under Ptolemaic rule, however, who had the greatest initial impact on the trade, industry, and commerce of Egypt. The Greeks who came to live in Egypt brought with them a tradition of trade and commerce, and soon markets were established and developed in many towns providing a wide range of goods for the local population. These commercial centers were often associated with Greek temples, which also served as the focus for the town's financial offices. Few archaeological remains of commercial buildings have survived in Egyptian towns, but evidence indicates that there were shops arranged along colonnaded streets and, in addition to established traders, there were also probably itinerant vendors.

One very important development that occurred early in the Ptolemaic Period had a profound impact on the local economy, on the movement of goods and services between different regions, and on the development of international trade. This was the rapid increase that occurred in the volume and availability of currency, because although coinage had been introduced into Egypt by the Persians after 525 BC, until now there had been relatively little coin production. The impact of coinage on Egypt's economy had not been significant before the Ptolemaic Period since much of the trade had continued to be based on the barter system.

READING

Land Transport

Shaw 1991: general introduction to Egyptian warfare and weapons and the use of land transport; Littauer and Crouwel 1979: discussion of wheeled vehicles and the use of riding animals throughout the ancient Near East; Littauer and Crouwel 1985: scientific study of the chariots and related equipment discovered in the tomb of Tutankhamun.

Water Transport

Faulkner 1940: discussion of seagoing ships in ancient Egypt; Säve-Söderbergh 1946: detailed account of the Egyptian navy in Dynasty 18; Glanville 1972: catalog of the wooden model boats in the British Museum collection; Jones 1990: description of model boats found in the tomb of Tutankhamun; Landström 1970: survey of Egyptian ships and shipbuilding throughout the Pharaonic Period.

Trade of Goods

Trigger, et al. 1983: study of the social and economic aspects of Egyptian society; Emery 1965: the contacts between Egypt and Nubia; Naville 1894–1908: study and description of the Temple of Deir el-Bahri; Lichtheim 1973: translations of Egyptian literary texts including various "travel stories."

Trading Expeditions

Gardiner 1961: description of some of these expeditions; Lichtheim 1976: translation of Egyptian literary texts, particularly the Story of Wenamun.

Trade in the Greco-Roman Period

Bagnall 1993: general study of Egypt in the Greco-Roman Period; Fraser 1972: study of Alexandria under the Ptolemies; Bowman, 1986: general introduction to most aspects of Egypt in the Greco-Roman Period.

10

ECONOMY AND INDUSTRY

THE ECONOMIC SYSTEM

The Egyptian economy was largely dependent on the fertility of the Nile. In times of peace and prosperity, when the kingdom was united and the irrigation system was effectively maintained, the economy was stable. Political strength ensured that a centralized bureaucracy was able to organize the country and to provide stockpiles of food that would offset the effects of poor inundations. Egypt was fortunately able to produce its own essentials—grain, fish, vegetables, fruit, and textiles—to provide food and clothing for its own relatively small population, and usually there was an excess that, together with gold and manufactured items such as papyrus, pottery, and luxury goods, could be traded for the wood, silver, copper, and spices that the country lacked.

The economic system was basic and relied on the annual production and immediate consumption of foodstuffs. A unique and important aspect was the continuing requirement to produce sufficient food not only for the living but also for the dead and the gods. Egypt never developed a proper commercial class partly because the economy was based on a barter system; coinage was not introduced until c.525 BC (and even then had limited use).

Economic Hierarchy

In theory the king owned all land, buildings, materials, and people, although in reality there was a system of private ownership that had developed through custom. Private property was owned by the temples, the nobles, and officials, and this diversification of wealth was increased by the king's presenting of gifts, hereditary offices, and privileges to priests and nobles and, in periods of royal weakness, by the seizures of some royal privileges by these people.

Although in theory all aspects of the economy were effectively controlled and organized by the king, in reality the pharaoh often delegated many of these duties by granting lands either to royal officials, who managed the estates on a basis of life tenure and received the estate revenues in payment, or to the temples in perpetuity. In order to cultivate the land and prepare the building materials for the great state monuments (making bricks and quarrying stone) as well as to provide the soldiers and sailors who manned the mining and trading expeditions, the Egyptians relied on the corvée system. Under this system every man (in theory) could expect to be requested to undertake these duties for the king; in practice only the poor were employed by corvée as the need arose, creating a class of serfs who were not legally "slaves" but who had few choices in their lives.

The craftsmen and artisans, however, who stood slightly above the peasants in the social hierarchy had status and enjoyed a reasonable standard of living. They included sculptors, goldsmiths, jewelers, carpenters, leather workers, masons, metalsmiths, and many others. Most craftsmen and artisans remained anonymous partly because they worked in teams. Many were organized in state or temple workshops where a range of activities were brought together under a high official. Each item was produced by several craftsmen who either worked together on the piece or passed it along the line. For complex items such as furniture or a statue the various parts were finished separately and then assembled. Each piece was presumably first designed and planned by a master craftsman, however, so that the individual workers could be given detailed instructions.

Tradition and technical skill were all important elements of this teamwork.

Above the artists were men with the title "Chief of Works" who held important positions and supervised the many aspects of designing and constructing great monuments. Sometimes architects of temples and tombs were able to claim credit for their work, and there are examples where these men managed to have themselves depicted on the walls of the buildings they had designed for royal or wealthy owners. From the inscriptions it seems that it was traditional for architects and craftsmen to hand on their skills and occupations within their own families.

Barter and Coinage

The Egyptians lacked good quality timber, copper, silver, and spices, but in exchange for them they could offer cereals, papyrus, textiles, dried fish, and various luxury items. It was the responsibility of the state to acquire these products from neighboring countries, and this was achieved in a number of ways. Kings sent royal expeditions to sources of supply such as Nubia, Byblos, or Punt, and they also engaged in warfare, which brought great rewards including booty and prisoners, although the extent to which economic considerations prompted their conquests remains uncertain. In addition, through international diplomacy, they received gifts of foreign goods from other rulers.

Both foreign trade and Egypt's own economy were based on barter since coinage was not introduced until the Persian Period (c.525 BC). The Egyptians sold goods, lent interest, paid salaries, and collected taxes using only the exchange of goods and produce, but such primitive methods of payment nevertheless seem to have enabled them to carry out quite complicated transactions.

Goods rather than treasure represented Egypt's wealth: Full granaries, flourishing herds, and ample game and wildlife were depicted in tomb scenes as symbols of affluence. Food production was essential not only to feed the living but also to offer to the gods and the dead, and the economy was primarily organized for this purpose. In addition, considerable resources were devoted to the building, decorating, and furbishing of the tombs and temples.

Although barter—a simple exchange of goods—met the society's needs in earlier times, increased trade requirements eventually brought about the introduction of an arbitrary standard by which the value of objects destined for exchange could be measured and compared. This was achieved by using a third common commodity, often wheat, as the standard, against which the products for exchange were measured and their market value was assessed accordingly. With this system, if there was a slight difference in the value of the two goods being compared, then a small amount of the standard commodity could be used to adjust the discrepancy. However, the standard commodity was generally not used at all in payment.

In Egypt from c.1580 BC all items were given a value in gold, silver, or copper to facilitate trade and commerce. Fixed weights were also introduced, but the use of a system of metal valuations—which may have been introduced from Asia—did not create a monetary system, and barter remained the sole means of trade and commerce. Both taxes and tribute continued to be paid in kind. Likewise, there undoubtedly were merchants, small traders, and even people who made loans and charged interest. However, lack of a true monetary system did not encourage the development of a national trading or commercial class, and these people apparently carried out their activities only in their own districts.

Therefore, barter continued to dominate the economy. Tomb scenes show that the collection of taxes and the reception of tribute from various districts were organized in this way, and in scenes in Queen Hatshepsut's temple at Deir el-Bahri that depict the famous Punt expedition the Egyptians and Puntites carry out their exchange of goods by means of barter.

In the Late Period, however, changes were introduced. Although most transactions continued to be carried out by means of payment in kind, a standard was still used, but it was now based not only on wheat but also on silver. At first the silver was measured in weight and used accordingly; even the Persian and Greek coins that were now available were only accepted according to their weight rather than at their face value. The concept of a monetary economy gradually began to take hold in Egypt, however, and coins—particularly where their quality and weight were completely consistent—started to be accepted at face value. The introduction of coinage with its many advantages over barter was one of the major areas of foreign influence exerted upon Egypt during the Persian Period. Nevertheless, it was only in the Ptolemaic Period that a true monetary system with significant coin production was introduced; until then barter remained the predominant method of exchange.

Weights and Measures

Egypt and Mesopotamia both developed standardized systems of weights and measures that enabled both commercial activity and building construction to be undertaken.

COUNTING AND MEASUREMENT

At an early date the Egyptians devised a decimal system of counting. Units were indicated by strokes, and tens, hundreds, and thousands were represented by hieroglyphic signs; thus, a finger was drawn to convey 10,000; a tadpole, 100,000; and a god with upraised arms, 1 million. Methods of surveying and land measurement were also well developed, and their knowledge of geometry and mathematics was used to great effect in the construction of monumental buildings.

Units of measurement were based on the distances between various points on the human body. A cubit (approximately 20 inches, or .523 meter), the largest unit, was the distance from the point of the elbow to the tip of the middle finger. This was generally divided up into smaller units: The Egyptian royal cubit consisted of seven palms; a palm was measured across the knuckles on the back of the hand and, therefore, had four finger widths. The finger width and the foot were other measurements as was the span, which was the distance from the tip of the middle finger to the tip of the thumb on an outstretched hand.

WEIGHTS

Egypt had metric weights. The standard units were the *deben* (approximately 3 ounces, or 91 grams) and the *kite* (one-tenth of the deben), which were only used for measuring metals. The other standard commodities, grain and cereals, were weighed in bushels. Set standards, measured in gold, silver, or copper, had been introduced by the Egyptians in c.1580 BC, and goods could then be measured against these. This assisted the system of barter, the main method of transaction for trade and commerce. Fixed weights were also used, and there are tomb scenes that show treasury officials weighing out the deben (in the form of gold rings) against fixed weights. Gold was extracted from the mines and was either smelted at the site or brought back as dust in bags to Egypt. For

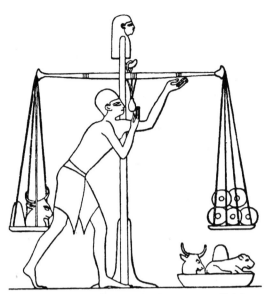

A tomb scene (c.2000 BC) in which a treasury official weighs deben (gold rings) in a balance. He uses a set of weights in the shape of animal heads to measure the dried fish ration of miners working at the copper mines in Sinai.

commercial use it was made into gold rings, which seem to have varied in thickness but had a uniform diameter of about five inches. When used in a transaction the deben were weighed and the result duly recorded in a book.

It was the international trade in metals carried out throughout the Near East that led to the need for a universal system of weights. However, although these were all based on a theoretical unit—the weight of a grain of wheat—the systems varied from one country to another. Some used multiples of the grain to make larger units, and a shekel could vary from 120 grains in one district to over 200 elsewhere. There were also larger units—the mina and the talent—which were multiples of the shekel, and these were widely used throughout the Near East.

Egyptian weights were different from those found elsewhere. Made of hard, polished stones into which the weight mark was cut, they were geometrically shaped with rounded corners and edges. In appearance and weight they were distinguishable from pieces used in other countries, and because the systems in different countries varied considerably it was necessary for visiting merchants to carry their own set of weights so that they could trade in many places.

THE KAHUN EXCAVATION

At Kahun, the pyramid workmen's village, the excavator W. M. Flinders Petrie found an interesting set of weights and measures. He maintained that they included a high proportion that were not Egyptian in origin and claimed that none of the measuring sticks was the usual Egyptian cubit. One example, a wooden rod measuring a cubit in length, conformed to the Egyptian standard, but it had one beveled edge on which cuts were marked off dividing it into six instead of the usual seven palms. In Mesopotamia the cubit had also always been used as a standard of measurement, but it was subdivided into different sections. Two other wooden rods found at Kahun were unusual in that one was divided into seven palms, but its total length was equivalent to the double foot used in Asia Minor, while the other scale was subdivided into seven and one-half spaces.

Petrie concluded that the rods combined elements of measurement systems in use in Egypt and elsewhere, and he claimed that they represented attempts by foreigners living at Kahun to imitate the local system. He also identified a significant number of foreign weights among the group found at Kahun; not one-sixth conformed to the Egyptian standard, and even those that did were made of soft materials rather than the usual hard polished stones. The Egyptians used hard stone weights in their balances that, consisting of a simple scale with two pans, were very sensitive. This collection of weights and measures was one piece of evidence Petrie used to support his theory that there was a substantial immigrant community at Kahun who lived alongside the local residents and included craftsmen, merchants, and laborers.

INDUSTRY

Religion: The Driving Force

In order to supply the needs of the gods and the dead it was inevitable that the Egyptian economy was closely linked with religious practices. Food was not only produced to provide the offerings placed at tombs and temples, but trading missions went to Punt to obtain incense for the rituals and to Byblos to acquire timber for coffins and temple doors.

The construction of religious monuments also involved industries such as quarrying, stoneworking, mining, metalworking, and carpentry. The temples, which owned mines and workshops, were effectively industrial and agricultural monopolies organized to meet the needs of their vast personnel. Furthermore, thousands of manufactured articles were produced to be placed inside the temples or tombs. The economy and industry of the country were inseparable from the religion, and unlike other societies where these were organized for the sole benefit of the living and the state, in Egypt production of goods was specifically directed first toward the gods and the dead (so that they could enjoy eternal life) and only secondly attempted to provide a good standard of living for the people. This is a vital factor in understanding how the system worked.

Craftsmen

Despite the importance of their work for the continuation of the state and the individual afterlife, craftsmen were nevertheless held in relatively low esteem apart from the scribes and officials who organized and supervised the work. The only real source of power in ancient Egypt was human labor. Unskilled manpower was used to construct and maintain the irrigation system and to build the great religious monuments. Some labor was provided by corvée duty, an obligation owed to the state by every individual (although in practice only carried out by the peasants) whose subsistence was paid by the government during the period of duty. Other members of the workforce included convicted criminals sentenced by the courts and prisoners of war.

Unskilled manpower played a significant role in several of the industries where heavy labor was needed, but there were also specialist craftsmen who from the end of the Old Kingdom began to form a middle class. They were mocked by the minor officials; although members of the same social class, these officials regarded manual labor as inferior to their own work.

Although they were all employees, craftsmen seem to have had the opportunity to undertake some private work and thus to ensure that they enjoyed a fairly comfortable living standard. Technical skills and professional secrets were handed down in the family, and sons followed their fathers within each craft or trade.

Workshops

The craftsmen did not work as independent agents. From earliest times they were employed in specialist workshops or were attached singly to wealthy households. The most important industries were either state or temple monopolies, which employed many people. In the Old Kingdom kings set up workshops at the capital (then Memphis) and there were others on estates throughout the country where craftsmen produced both essential and luxury items. Subsequently each provincial governor developed workshops in his local city, and temples also had their own production centers where goods were made for use in the temple ceremonies. Great workshops existed at the Temple of Ptah at Memphis (Ptah was the patron god of craftsmen) and at the Temple of Amun at Karnak where almost every type of craft specialization was practiced, and even local temples employed considerable numbers of craftsmen.

Tomb scenes almost always show men engaged in various arts and crafts working in specialized groups, and this is probably an accurate reflection of their physical organization. Where production of some items such as jewelry, furniture, and vases required the skills of several specialists, however, they appear to have worked near to each other and sometimes to have shared a workshop. Other workers were itinerant and moved to the required location; stonemasons would travel to a building site, boat builders erected temporary workshops along the Nile or canals, and those who mummified the dead probably set up their places in the necropolis area. Thus, the workshops were flexible in terms of their individual organization and location. Some crafts such as sculpting and goldsmithing were particularly lucrative, and the leaders of these workshops held important positions in the government. Sculptors and goldsmiths built themselves fine tombs at Memphis and Thebes; in the Theban tomb of Nebamun and Ipuky (sculptors who lived in late Dynasty 18) scenes showing carpenters, goldsmiths, and jewelers provide useful information about crafts and techniques.

Pottery

The Egyptians produced two kinds of ware: the finer quality made of faience and the commonplace pottery made of Nile mud. Pottery was widely produced because good clay was readily available in all parts of Egypt. Clay was principally used for making vessels that have a matte or slightly burnished surface and a color variation (black, red, a combination of black and red, or gray), which is the result of the material used and the process of firing. Known as "coarseware," this pottery was employed for a variety of vessels and containers with diverse forms and specialized uses including bowls, dishes, platters, goblets, pots, beer jugs, milk jugs, wine jars, oil containers, and cosmetic vases. In fact many domestic possessions were kept and stored in pottery containers, and the production of these receptacles was so extensive both in chronological and geographical terms that the study of the development of different styles and types of pottery has become an essential dating tool for archaeologists. Since potsherds were recycled as a cheap writing material they also provide a different source of evidence in that area of study.

Glazed pottery was only introduced into Egypt in the sixth century BC when Greek potters established themselves at Naucratis. There were few advances during the Pharaonic Period in the indigenous ceramic art in terms of producing either new forms or decoration. In fact pottery manufacture never rose to great heights in Egypt as it did elsewhere. The unglazed coarseware was decorated with painted ornamentation and motifs, but a different material —faience—was chosen for special objects. It is

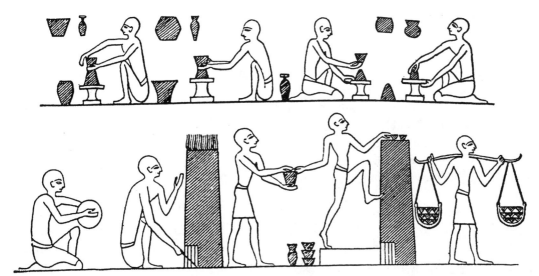

A tomb scene (c.2000 BC) that shows four men (top) squatting at low turntables, engaged in making pottery. Below, another potter (left) shapes a plate, the kiln is fired, and pottery is loaded into the kiln. Finally, a man (right) carries away the finished pots.

worth noting that the most attractive pottery vessels, covered with painted decoration, were made during the Predynastic Period before the Egyptians fully developed their considerable talents in other areas such as stoneworking and jewelry manufacture.

In addition to its use for vases and vessels the Egyptians also employed pottery for modeling and produced a variety of figurines such as statuettes of humans and animals and tomb models including soul houses, concubine figures, and ushabtis. There were also pottery canopic jars and coffins, and in the Greco-Roman Period terracotta was used extensively for manufacturing lamps and votive figures of gods.

Four stages occur in the production of pottery vessels: kneading the clay, shaping the clay into a pot, drying the vessel, and baking it. Scenes in the tombs, particularly of the Old and Middle Kingdoms, illustrate these processes, and further evidence is provided by wooden tomb models of potters' workshops. First, the clay was prepared and kneaded to the required

consistency; this was probably done by trampling on the clay. Finely chopped straw, chaff, or pulverized animal dung was added to temper the clay and reduce its stickiness.

Next, the pots were shaped. In predynastic times this was done by hand, and even in later times the manual method was sometimes employed for the very simplest vessels. One of the greatest inventions, however, was the potter's wheel which together with the brick mold was probably introduced in the earliest dynasties. There is some controversy over the exact date, but the final years of the predynastic era or the Archaic Period (Dynasty 1 or 2) have been suggested. The earliest form of the wheel was a small circular turntable that was rotated by hand on a vertical shaft or pivot with the potter using his left hand to turn the table and his right one to mold the pot. By the New Kingdom, however, a wheel was introduced that was moved by foot or turned by an assistant. This pivoted turntable with its limited momentum appears to be the only wheel known in Egypt before the

Ptolemaic Period, and handmade pottery continued to be produced alongside wheel-made ware.

The slip and wash were then applied to the pottery. For the most common slip, clay was mixed to a fine consistency and applied to the pot before it was dry. This changed the color of the pot and provided a smooth surface for the decoration to be applied. Finally, a wash of red ocher was often added to red ware to enhance its color.

The pot was then dried; some were polished with pebbles before they were baked. This final stage in the process converted the fragile clay into a hard, durable, and water-resistant material. The earliest vessels were probably baked on the ground in a mixed heap of pots and fuel covered with animal dung to keep in the heat. From this a simple pottery kiln developed with separate areas for the pots and fuel; these resembled the ovens used by bakers and appear to have incorporated a furnace underneath while the pots were placed on top of or inside the kiln.

Brickmaking

The earliest buildings were made of dried reeds; the next step, plastering these structures with clay, gave them more stability and provided an

A wooden mud brick mold (top), the first example ever found in Egypt; also, a plasterer's float (bottom right) with the remains of plaster that the workman forgot to clean off, and two wooden butterfly clamps that were used to hold stones together. From Kahun, c.1890 BC.

A scene from the tomb of Vizier Rekhmire (c.1450 BC), showing the production of mud bricks. Alluvial mud is mixed with water (left) and then packed into wooden molds. When lifted, the molds released the bricks so that they fell onto the ground where, arranged in long rows, they dried in the sun.

additional barrier against heat and cold. The invention of the brick mold, however, gave the builder much more control over his construction and his materials, enabling him to produce the correct number of bricks to the required dimensions. The mold appears to have been invented in c.3400 BC when brick architecture started to be used in Egypt for funerary monuments. Brickmaking was practiced in Egypt more than almost anywhere else, and sun-dried bricks became the most common and widely available building material since both the essential elements, Nile mud and constant sunlight, were readily available. The production of rectangular bricks of a specific size enabled the Egyptians to build walls with far greater ease and safety, and mud brick architecture remained the norm for all domestic buildings even when stone replaced brick for religious monuments such as pyramids, tombs, and temples.

THE PROCESS

Nile alluvium or mud is basically a mixture of clay and sand with small amounts of impurities; although all the cultivated land consists of alluvium, the relative proportions of clay and sand vary in different areas of the country and produce different results in terms of the suitability of the mixture for brick manufacture. There-

fore, another material such as chopped straw was often added to bind the mixture when the proportion of clay was low. Straw or chaff and animal dung acted as binders and also increased the strength of the clay.

Various sources provide information about the brickmaking process. The practice of adding chopped straw to the clay is mentioned in a New Kingdom papyrus and in Exodus, chapter 5, in the Bible. Brickmaking is illustrated by tomb models of the Middle Kingdom, the famous scene in the tomb of the vizier Rekhmire (Dynasty 18) at Thebes, and a scene in the Temple of Medinet Habu where king Taharka (Dynasty 25) is depicted carrying out this procedure. First, the mud was broken up with a hoe and then mixed with chaff and water brought from a tank; next, it was kneaded with the feet until the right consistency was achieved. Then it was taken to the brickmaker and pressed into a mold that, when lifted, allowed the brick to fall to the ground. The bricks were arranged in rows to dry in the sun and were finally placed in heaps for the builders to take to the construction site.

The sizes of the bricks varied according to their date and intended use, sometimes enabling archaeologists to date a particular building. Some wooden molds were stamped with the name of the ruling king, and stamped bricks were sometimes used in the construction of an enclosure wall, thus providing another way to date a building.

A mud brick mold was discovered at the pyramid workmen's village of Kahun, the first tangible evidence of the brickmaking industry to be found at any site. Made of wood, it is rectangular with four sides carefully fitted and pegged together; one side projects beyond the corner to form a handle with which the brickmaker could lift the mold and release the brick. Miniature models of molds have also been found elsewhere.

USES

Bricks were an effective and cheap building material for the Egyptians. Clay was readily available all over the country, and highly skilled labor was not required either to make the bricks or to use them in construction. Bricks were ideally suited to the Egyptian climate, made buildings that were warm in winter and cool in summer, and did not have to withstand any considerable rainfall. Thus, mud brick continued in use as the prime material for houses, palaces, public buildings, and fortresses. Bricks were used in buildings that incorporated the arch, such as the long vaulted storerooms associated with the Ramesseum, the funerary temple of Ramesses II at Thebes; here the vaulting was made of special flat bricks rather like tiles that had grooves to enable them to be fastened together securely.

Ancient peoples realized that bricks made from clay could be hardened by firing, and burned bricks were used in Mesopotamia and at Mohenjo-Daro in India at a very early date. A few unusual examples of burned bricks have also been found in some Egyptian tombs and in part of the foundation of a building; these can be dated to Dynasties 18 and 19. But kiln baked bricks were only introduced much later in c.600 BC for constructions at Karnak, and they did not come into general use until the Roman Period.

There was no urgency to introduce burned bricks since the dry climate enabled sun-dried bricks to last for many years. Until recently sun-dried bricks continued to be used for building houses in many villages throughout Egypt and were produced in molds that closely resembled the ancient examples.

Glazed Ware and Glass

FAIENCE

Egyptian faience is different from modern faience (clay covered with a tin enamel): It consists of a core of body material that is covered with a vitreous, alkaline glaze. It was developed in earliest times to provide a colorful substitute for semiprecious stones. The body material, often very fragile, was quartz, which was usually produced by mixing a paste of powdered quartz rock and then placing this in a pottery mold (large quantities of these were made in the form of beads, rings, scarabs, ushabtis, and other projects). Sometimes, a copper wire was placed in the mold, which, after firing, could be removed to leave a suspension hole through the middle of the object. Some faience objects, however, were not molded, and there are examples of vessels that were either wheel-turned like pottery or handmade; some other pieces were also handmade.

Next, an alkaline glaze, similar in composition to ancient glass, was applied to the object. The usual colors of blue, green, or greenish-blue were achieved by adding compounds of copper to the glaze, which was either a sodium-calcium silicate or a potassium-calcium silicate. Other colors such as violet, white, yellow, red, and black were produced by adding different ingredients. Green and blue faience were nonetheless the most popular colors because they

A pectoral (chest ornament) found on a mummy in a tomb. This fine example of cloisonné work is made of gold; the front (left) is inlaid with turquoise, lapis lazuli, and carnelian, while the same design is incised on the reverse (right). From Riqqeh, c.1850 BC.

most closely imitated the two semiprecious stones—malachite and lapis lazuli—that the Egyptian faience-makers were attempting to simulate. Once the glaze had been applied to the core, decoration was sometimes added, particularly to vessels and tiles. Designs were either painted in black onto the glaze or the surface was incised and filled with a different color glaze. Then the piece received its final firing.

The earliest faience examples occur in predynastic times. In the reign of Djoser in Dynasty 3 there are fine examples of faience tiles that once adorned the interior of his Step Pyramid at Saqqara, and faience was extremely popular with rich and poor throughout the historic period. It was used for beads and jewelry, inlays, amulets, vessels and bowls, ushabtis, statuettes, tiles, and scarabs. It continued in use until the fourteenth century AD.

Another glazed material was also produced in Egypt. As early as the Badarian Period beads were made of glazed steatite, a soft stone that is very easily carved into small objects. Since it becomes hardened when it is heated but does not decompose or fracture it makes a good base for glazing.

GLASS

Ancient Egyptian glaze and glass had the same chemical composition, but they were used for different purposes: Whereas the glaze was applied to the surface of a core of body material, glass was used to produce complete objects. The discovery of the two processes, however, was probably closely associated, although it is uncertain when glass was first used independently. Although some small glass objects were produced in the early periods, it was during Dynasty 18 that glass manufacture became important; high standards of craftsmanship were achieved which may have been inspired by contact with other areas of the Near East. The process soon declined, however, and almost disappeared from the end of Dynasty 20 onward, and glass only became popular again in the Roman Period.

From earliest times there are examples of small glass beads and amulets, but perfume jars and other vessels decorated with wavy lines, which were popular in the reign of Amenhotep III, provide the most famous examples of Egyptian glassware. The earliest glass factory found in Egypt can be dated to that reign; it was located at Thebes, but several others were built at Amarna during the reign of his son, Akhenaten. There were also other later factories, and in Roman times Alexandria became one of the world's greatest glass manufacturing centers.

Glass was produced in many colors by adding various compounds during the manufacturing process. Colorless glass occurs in objects found in the tomb of Tutankhamun and in other later examples. Glass production involved two stages: Sand and alkali were converted into a frit at a relatively low temperature, and then the frit was converted to glass in crucibles in a melting furnace at a much higher temperature. The first stage was carried out in saucer shaped pans placed on a group of cylindrical jars within the furnace, and then the material was placed in clay crucibles and heated in a special furnace. This caused the material to fuse, creating a body of clear glass. The glass was then poured into molds or made into thick rods, which were worked and cut into pieces for inlay. Evidence from the glass factories at Amarna as well as the objects themselves provides information about the various techniques employed to make beads, vases, figurines, and inlay. Blown glass was not developed until the Roman Period.

Food Processing

Food was very important to the ancient Egyptians. Although the tomb and temple scenes depict a variety of meat, fish, bread, cakes, fruit, vegetables, wine, and beer, the staple diet of most of the population was bread, beer, and some vegetables, with perhaps the addition of fish they caught themselves. Agriculture supplied the cereals, fruit, and vegetables, the great estates also provided meat and milk products, and hunting expeditions augmented the diet of the ruling classes. Butchery is depicted in tomb and temple scenes, but meat was generally a luxury that ordinary people only enjoyed on feast days, since it had to be consumed rapidly after the animal was slaughtered.

The fishing industry was well organized, and there were farms and breeding grounds, many of which were located in the Fayoum. Teams of fishermen worked in the marshes laying the trawl nets and fish traps to catch a variety of fish to tempt the palates of royalty and the nobility. Poor people were also able to enjoy the fish they caught themselves.

BREAD

The production of bread and beer was obviously of paramount importance. Bread was an essential part of every meal, and many different types are listed on the walls of tombs and temples. Although no recipe book has ever been discovered, it is most probable that these varieties were differentiated by their shapes (oval, round, or conical) and by the flours and ingredients which gave them special flavors. It is known that barley, spelt, and wheat were used and that honey, butter, milk, and eggs provided additional ingredients.

Bread making was held in high esteem. It was usually carried out at home, and from the time of the New Kingdom a wealthy household would have employed its own baker. There were also bakeries on the great estates to supply the considerable needs of the owner and his servants.

Scenes in mastaba tombs show how the bread was made. First, the grain was crushed in great mortars by one or two men who pounded it with heavy pestles. Then, to obtain a finer flour, this coarse flour was ground on a big stone or rubbed between two stones. There are tomb models showing women engaged in this work; in the Old Kingdom the woman kneeled in front of a stone placed on the ground, but in the Middle Kingdom she stood behind a hollowed-out table. This acted as the lower stone and made her work easier.

Next the flour was sieved and the dough, prepared and kneaded. The dough was made of flour, milk, and other ingredients and was either kneaded by hand or, in the larger bakeries, it was trodden by servants in a great tub. It was then fashioned into various shapes and cooked in different ways. Some cakes were fried in a large pan while others were baked on the stove. In early times the bread was baked on pottery dishes which were heated in the fire, but later in the New Kingdom a conical oven was introduced which enabled greater quantities to be cooked more quickly. These clay ovens were about three feet in height and open at the top.

BEER

Beer, the favorite drink of the Egyptians, was frequently mentioned in the ancient texts as one of the offerings made to the gods and the dead. The earliest references occur at the beginning of the Old Kingdom. There were different sorts of beer even in the earliest periods, and residues have even been found in jars of predynastic date. The classical writers also mentioned it: Strabo related that "barley beer" was peculiar to the Egyptians, and Diodorus claimed that its smell and sweetness of taste were "not much inferior to wine."

The process of brewing beer is shown in several tomb scenes, and it was apparently always closely associated with baking bread as this was an essential element in its production. There are also tomb models that illustrate various stages in the process.

The beer was prepared from well-selected, fine barley. This was macerated with water and left out in the air; it was moistened again and sieved and then ground and kneaded into a

A tomb scene (c. 2000 BC) *illustrating a bagpress. In order to extract the juice from grapes, they were placed inside a linen bag that was stretched between two posts; these were twisted to squeeze out the juice.*

dough. Next, it was lightly baked to turn it into bread and then soaked in water; dates may have been added at this stage to sweeten the mixture. Then, it was put in a warm place to allow fermentation to occur and finally squeezed through a cloth or fine sieve so that the sweet liquid could be drained off into a pot.

Various plants may have been added to the beer to flavor it, but some of these appear to have been medicinal treatments for which the beer acted as a vehicle rather than actual flavoring ingredients. Beer from Asia, imported and consumed alongside the home product, was probably a luxury item and only available in small quantities.

WINE

Wine was another popular drink of the Egyptians. Grapevines were carefully cultivated and trained over trelliswork supported by wooden forks or pillars. The grapes were picked and taken in baskets to the winepress, which consisted of a low box with a wooden framework erected over it. The box was filled with the grapes, and five or six men trampled them while holding onto the framework structure. The wine was pressed out and ran through a series of openings into large vats. The sweet juice left behind in the grapes was squeezed out by placing the grapes inside a matting sack. This was then wrung out by four men by twisting the sticks placed in the loops at either end of the matting. Finally, the wine was transferred from the vats to pottery jars, which were fastened and sealed, and scribes recorded the number of jars that had been filled. It is known that different wines were produced, but no details of special procedures have survived.

Textiles

Since the climate of Egypt made it unnecessary to wear heavy clothes, linen was the most popular fabric for daily use. Although most men of the lower classes wore a simple loincloth, kings and the wealthy are usually shown in kilts. The details of these varied to some extent but the basic garment remained the same from the Old Kingdom to the Roman Period. The upper classes sometimes added a tunic, shirt, or cloak. Women of the nobility and upper classes are shown in narrow dresses held under the bosom by two wide straps suspended from the shoulders. From the New Kingdom they also often added a cloak. Generally, for the wealthy, the clothes of both sexes became more voluminous in the later New Kingdom when transparently fine garments were worn over the basic undergarments. These contrast with the simple fashions of the Old Kingdom.

Woven fabrics have survived from the tombs, and these include mummy bandages and garments placed with the deceased. Tomb scenes from Dynasties 12 and 18 represent some of the spinning and weaving processes, and a few Middle Kingdom tomb models of weavers' workshops have survived. There is also the unique collection of textile production tools that were excavated at the Fayoum towns of Kahun and Gurob.

LINEN

Linen production was one of the most important industries of ancient Egypt. Linen was manufactured from predynastic times through to the Roman Period, and there was considerable variation in the textures produced for different uses.

Flax (*Linum usitatissimum*), grown in Egypt from earliest times, was used for linen production from the Neolithic period. Tomb scenes

A tomb scene (c. 2000 BC) showing spinning and weaving techniques. A woman spins yarn (right), and a male overseer supervises weaving (left). A horizontal loom is being used here, although some modern opinions have mistakenly interpreted this as a vertical loom, because artistic convention shows the loom in a deceptive perspective.

A selection of wooden tools used for textile production. The flax stripper (center), used to break up the tough outer fibers of the flax stalks, is from Kahun, c. 1890 BC. The loom pegs (bottom left), warp spacer (top left), and beater (top right) are all from Gurob, c. 1450 BC.

represent the gathering of flax which was pulled by hand and then drawn through a large, comb-like tool. Next, it was retted (soaked to separate the woody parts from the bast fibers), beaten with mallets, and the fibers were separated with combs. This preparation readied the fibers for spinning. It is evident that the Egyptians grew flax on a commercial scale and that it was one of their main exports to other countries during the Roman Period.

Various spinning techniques (a method of forming threads by drawing out and twisting fibers) were employed in ancient Egypt. There was simple hand spinning and three types of spindle spinning, but the distaff was not introduced until the Roman Period. Tomb scenes and models show spinning in process, and spindles, spindle whorls, and balls of thread have been found at various sites.

The next stage was weaving. There were two types of the hand operated Egyptian loom—a horizontal ground loom that was used from the Badarian Period until the end of the Middle Kingdom, and sometimes later, and the vertical loom that largely replaced it and was perhaps introduced into Egypt by the Hyksos. The ground loom consisted of two poles fixed to the ground by pegs that made the beam of the loom while the length was fixed by two other poles in the warp. To work this the weaver squatted on the ground, using a stick as a shuttle and to tighten the weft. The vertical loom consisted of an upright frame and a comb for tightening the threads. Items from Egyptian looms that have been discovered include combs, beaters, heddle rods, loom pegs, shuttles, and warp spacers.

The linen was traditionally bleached, but some textiles were colored using vegetable dyes such as madder, safflower, and indigo. There are examples of colored tapestry-woven linen such as the tunic, gloves, and girdles found in the tomb of Tutankhamun, and other textile tech-niques that have been identified include warp weave, pile, and loop techniques and embroi-dery and tablet weaving.

OTHER FABRICS

Although linen was the most popular cloth, some woolen garments were also produced. According to Herodotus, however, the Egyptians were not allowed to take wool into their tombs or temples as it was regarded as ritually unclean. Nevertheless, the Egyptians had large flocks of sheep and undoubtedly wore woolen cloaks over their linen tunics. In the Christian Period woolen garments were placed in the graves, and colored wool was woven into linen fabrics for decoration. There are several instances of wool fragments found in earlier contexts, although at least some of these may be from intrusive burials of later dates.

A child's sock, knitted in stripes of buff-yellow, green-blue, and crimson two-ply wool. There is a double start-ing row and a turned heel, and the sock is divided in two at the toe to accommodate a thonged sandal. Knitting was probably a non-Egyptian technique that was intro-duced into Egypt in the Roman Period in the form of socks. From Oxyrhynchus, late third century AD.

A pottery bowl for plying thread. From Kahun, c.1890 BC.

Herodotus states that, in Egypt in c.550 BC, King Amasis offered linen garments to several Greek temples. These were decorated with cotton embroidery; this is one of the earliest known references to the use of cotton, which must have been imported to Egypt at this time possibly from India or Arabia. It was only in the Roman Period, however, that cotton began to be manufactured in Egypt when the half-wild cotton trees that grew in Nubia provided the raw material for this industry. Silk that originated in China probably made no impact on the Egyptian textile industry until it began to be imported during the Greco-Roman Period.

Leather

Domestication of cattle, sheep, and goats and the hunting of wild animals ensured that, from early times, skins were available for clothing and as wrappings for the dead. Skins occur in predynastic graves, and hides and skins were treated with different substances to produce leather.

The most beautiful skins, particularly those of spotted animals, were greatly valued; they were never stripped of hair but were made into seat-coverings, shields, quivers, and special outfits. Less valuable skins such as those of oxen and gazelles were turned into leather and used to make a variety of objects. Coarse, fine, and colored leather was produced and turned into footwear, aprons, straps, belts, and a kind of parchment for writing.

THE LEATHER-MAKING PROCESS

In earliest times it is likely that several different methods were used for treating skins and hides; they were either simply dried or were cured by means of smoke, salt, or ocherous earths or were softened with fat, urine, or dung. True tanning, with substances containing tannin or tannic acid, was also practiced in the Predynastic Period, probably using the pods of *Acacia arabica* as the tanning agent since they contain about 30 percent tannin.

There are tomb scenes from the Old Kingdom that show various stages in the leather working process. These include the treatment of a skin in a large jar, either as a preparatory stage in the depilation, cleaning, and softening of the skin or to immerse the skin in a tanning substance. Other scenes show skin being stretched over a trestle table probably so that oil could be worked into it, cutting the skins, and making sandals and leather rope. Tools that are illustrated include the half-moon knife, awl, piercers, and a comb type tool used for stripping the flesh off a hide.

Dyed leather was produced as early as the Predynastic Period. The most popular color was red and the leather was probably dyed with madder. Yellow and green also occur, but the exact dyes have not yet been identified.

Leather was used for bags, bracelets, archers' wrist protectors, decoration for the ends of linen bands, cushion covers, parts for chariots and tackle, ropes and cords, seat covers, dog collars, wall hangings, writing material, and articles of clothing such as sandals and loincloths that were made by cutting rows of small slits, thus creating a kind of "network" material. Skins and hides were also utilized to make canopies, tents, and water carriers and to cover shields, while rawhide was employed in chariot construction, to lash the joints of furniture, and to bind blades of tools and weapons to their handles.

FOOTWEAR

Sandal making, represented in various tomb scenes and in a tomb model, is also well evidenced by surviving examples of footwear from, for example, the tomb of Tutankhamun and the town of Kahun. In the Tomb of Rekhmire at Thebes (Dynasty 18), scenes show the hide being taken from a pot where it had been softened or tanned. The skin was further prepared as men beat it with a stone and then stretched it over a wooden frame to make it supple. Next, the shoemaker put the prepared leather on his sloping worktable and cut it into soles or straps, using a knife with a curved blade and a short handle. Then, using a piercer he made holes in the skin through which the thongs would be drawn. The workman pulled these through with his teeth and fastened them with knots, thus producing the simplest form of sandal.

At Kahun the excavators discovered shoemaker's tools (a bone awl and copper piercers) as well as a variety of footwear that included aside from the customary sandals part of a slip-on shoe. Stained red, this had a leather toe-piece, with the hair turned inside, which was stitched to the sole with a leather thong. The excavator of the site suggested that this and a couple of other examples demonstrated that shoes (as distinct from sandals) were just coming into existence at this period (Dynasty 12). At Kahun, old sandals once they had worn out were apparently recycled; in some of the houses, where the doors had worn down the sockets in which they pivoted at the threshold, leather pieces (and particularly old sandals) were placed in the sockets to raise the surface.

Bone and Ivory

Animal bones, readily available in ancient Egypt from earliest times, provided a source of natural materials that could be employed in many ways. Bone can be easily splintered and carved, and from predynastic times onward it was made into awls, needles, arrowheads, harpoon heads, combs, beads, bracelets, amulets, and cosmetic containers. Bone was also inserted into some examples of inlaid eyes that were fixed into coffins, mummies, face masks, and statues, providing an alternative to crystalline limestone, opaque white quartz, or white opaque glass to represent the white of the eye.

Ivory was also extensively in Egypt from the Predynastic Period onward. Hippopotamus ivory was readily available, since the animal lived in Egypt throughout this period, but elephant ivory, also employed from Neolithic times onward, was probably imported from the south (Nubia) and later from Punt and Retenu in Asia.

Ivory, well adapted for carving, was used for a variety of objects. There were fine statuettes such as the tiny figurines of Cheops (Khufu), builder of the Great Pyramid, and beautifully carved pieces from the tomb of Tutankhamun. Many tombs included ivory objects: There was jewelry in the form of anklets, armlets, bracelets, hairpins, rings, and earrings and cosmetic items such as boxes and caskets, combs, mirror handles, fans, and ointment spoons. Luxury domes-

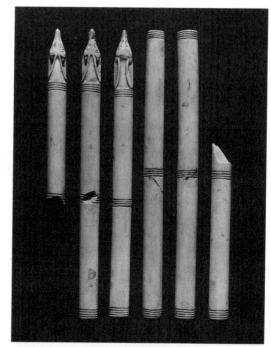

Ivory throwsticks from a tomb (c.1450 BC) were used for playing games. They are finely carved and provide a good example of ivory working techniques. Three of the sticks represent jackal heads.

tic objects included shallow dishes, inlay and legs for furniture, and vases, and there were weapons such as arrowheads, handles for knives, daggers, and harpoon heads. There are also examples of gaming boards and gaming pieces; and occasionally ivory was used as a writing material.

Ivory too was set into inlaid eyes to represent the white of the eye. It was perhaps shown to best effect, however, when combined with ebony as veneer and inlay for decorating furniture, boxes, gaming boards, and other items. Objects often made of inferior wood were covered with panels or strips of ivory and ebony. One particularly fine example is a casket from the royal treasure at Lahun covered with veneer and inlay in ebony and ivory. Outstanding pieces produced in Dynasty 18 were made for Amenhotep II,

Tutankhamun, and Yuya and Thuya, the parents-in-law of Amenhotep III.

Sometimes carved ivory objects were painted or stained, and excellent examples occur from the time of Tutankhamun. Such pieces were generally colored with red, although more rarely dark brown, black, or green were used. Red oxide of iron has been identified as the coloring agent used on some of these pieces, but otherwise the origin of the colors remains unidentified.

Plant Products

The Egyptians were skillful in their use of plants and spices, and a wealth of plant remains have survived in their tombs and rubbish heaps. These have been studied by modern botanists from various countries, and they enable us to build up a picture of the ecology, the availability of local and imported timbers, trade routes, and domestic and burial customs.

The living flora of Egypt was first studied by a Swedish scholar, Petter Forsskal, who died on a royal Danish expedition to Egypt and Yemen in AD 1763. Later, a Frenchman, Victor Loret, made a detailed study of botanical specimens from tombs. In the late nineteenth century, a German, Georg Schweinfurth, made a collection of agricultural and botanical objects that formed the nucleus of the Agricultural Museum he founded in Cairo; he also sent duplicates to the Botanical Museum in Berlin. With the discovery of the almost intact tomb of Tutankhamun at Thebes in 1922, a wealth of plant remains was recovered; these were subsequently kept at the Cairo Museum and some were identified by the Englishman Percy Newberry. A number of samples were also sent to the Royal Botanical Gardens in Kew, England.

There are other sources of information about plants and trees and their products in ancient Egypt, including wall scenes in tombs and temples, medical and other texts, mummified bodies and the plants associated with them, and the botanical texts. As yet no complete ancient Egyptian herbal has been found, although a few fragments of later papyri have survived. However, some information is provided in the work of Classical writers such as Dioscorides whose herbal, written in Greek in the first century AD, included some Egyptian plant names.

FLORAL DECORATIONS AND HOUSEHOLD PRODUCTS

The Egyptians were keen horticulturalists who grew plants and trees in their own gardens for personal pleasure and also tended them on a commercial scale to provide products for various industries. Floristry was well organized; it catered to the gods' needs in the temple rituals and provided bouquets, garlands, and collars for a variety of religious and festive occasions. Floral decorations were also worn to banquets and parties and played a part in the burial ceremony. When the mummy stood upright at the door of the tomb to receive the final rites, the relatives placed beside it a bouquet, which was probably eventually put inside the coffin. In Tutankhamun's burial archaeologists found several floral decorations inside the coffin.

Plants also had many domestic uses: Furniture, household items such as baskets, mats, and brushes, and even herb pillows were made from a variety of plant fibers and products. Plants were also utilized to keep the house free from vermin and insects. The Egyptian diet was mainly vegetarian, and plants and vegetables were cultivated for food and cooking. Other uses include the manufacture and dyeing of clothing, boat construction, the inclusion of plants and their substances in medicines and ointments, and the production of reed coffins, ropes, cords, and nets.

COSMETICS

Plants also played an important role in the production of cosmetics and perfumes and in the mummification procedure. Cosmetics included eye paints, face paints, oils, and ointmens; vegetable matter was mixed with other substances to provide eye coloring and face paints, and a mixture of vegetable oil and lime was used as a face cleansing agent.

The manufacture of oils, perfumes, and resins also relied heavily on plant ingredients, and Egyptian perfumes were famed throughout the ancient world. Different kinds of plant oils and solid animal fats were applied to the skin and hair, and fragrant substances were added to these to improve their smell. Unlike modern scents and perfumes, which are solutions in alcohol of various plants and flowers, the Egyptians were not aware of the process of distillation; instead they retained the plant odors in fat or oil, and flowers, seeds, gum resins, and other fragrant substances were steeped in oil and then wrung or squeezed in a cloth or sack, as illustrated in various tomb scenes. There is no evidence of the use of animal ingredients (ambergris, civet, and musk) in Egyptian scents and perfumes, but studies of jar contents from tombs indicate the presence of gum resin, myrrh, splinters of aromatic wood, plant products, and palm or grape wine.

INCENSE AND EMBALMING MATERIALS

The Egyptians also used incense in their religious rituals; the most important types were frankincense (olibanum) and myrrh. Frankincense is a fragrant gum resin that comes from trees of the genus *Boswellia*, which grows mainly in Somalia and southern Arabia, and from *Commiphora pedunculata*, found in the Sudan and Abyssinia. The Egyptians obtained frankincense from both Nubia and Punt. Myrrh, also a fragrant gum resin, is yielded by various species of *Balsamodendron* and *Commiphora*, which also grown in Somalia and southern Arabia.

Finally, plants and various plant derived resins and oils were used in mummification for cleansing the corpse either by injection or when it was washed down, for packing the body cavities, and for perfuming and anointing. It was intended that these plant products should assist the process of preservation, cleanse the tissues, enhance the suppleness of the skin tissue, and reduce or mask the odors associated with mummification. It is doubtful, however, that plant products made any major contribution to preserving the body or to repelling insects, but their one practical benefit may have been to partially conceal the unpleasant odors of the procedure.

Rush and Basketwork

From Neolithic times the Egyptians made use of the nonspun fibers of plants by plaiting and interlacing grasses and reeds to produce shelters, containers, clothing, and items of domestic use. They had access to young, pliable palm branches, which could be interlaced, and fibers from these were obtained by shredding, splitting, and drying the stems. Also available were the fibers of wild grasses, reeds, rushes, and papyrus, which grew in the marshes; to prepare these for use, grasses and reeds were dried and split, plant stems were cut with a sickle, and papyrus fibers were produced as a by-product of the process of making writing material. These fibers were all used to make baskets, mats, rope, sandals, boats, and sailcloth.

BASKETRY

Baskets were indispensable for storing domestic items and carrying agricultural and industrial materials. They were also used as coffins for all burials in early times and for those of the poor throughout the historic period. The principal materials were the leaves of the date palm or dom palm, grasses, reeds, and rushes.

Basket making was probably a widespread activity; it was simpler than weaving because no preparation of the fiber was needed beyond se-

lecting and cutting it into the required lengths, and no specialized tools (such as the spindle and whorl) were used. Therefore, it was widely practiced throughout Egypt as one of the first arts.

Several manual techniques were employed. Coiling, also employed in sandal making, was one of the oldest crafts; a bunch of fibers was wound into a flat coil to make the base, and then the basket was built up by wrapping the fibers spirally and fixing each row to the previous one by stitching them together with the same plant fibers. Twining involved interlacing single fibers or bunches of them on a square base; this technique is similar to primitive weaving and was often used for matting. Wrapping, another

Examples of basket making and rush work include a well-preserved fiber brush (left), a plaited rush sandal (right), and a rush basket (center). Found in the corner of a house at Kahun (c.1890 BC), this basket contained a copper bowl, chisels, and hatchets and was evidently used for transporting a workman's tools to the nearby pyramid site.

form of twining, also produced matting and involved passing a single wrapping strand around a bundle of fibers. Other techniques included matting work in which one series of fibers was used as the warp and another as the weft and plaited work in which separate plaits were made and sewn into the required shape. The coiled technique was most often used for baskets, whereas twining was employed for coffins, bags, and matting; examples of matting work have also survived. Basketworks were not generally decorated with any dyed fibers, but their shape and the natural color and texture of the plant fibers gave them an attractive appearance. In some examples, however, there is evidence of ornamental stitching and the interweaving of dyed and undyed fibers. Basketry was also used to make sieves.

MATTING

Matting was another important minor industry, and mats occur from predynastic times onward. They were used in Badarian graves either for wrapping the body or placing beneath it. Matting was found in the houses of both rich and poor; sometimes it was used as an architectural material for walls and roofs or to adorn the walls and floors of houses. Rolled-up mats were hung at open doors and could be let down as blinds to protect the interior from strong sunlight. There were imitations of matting in other architectural forms: on false doors in tombs the roll-up door blind was carved in stone, and painted decoration on the walls and ceilings of tombs copied the colored patterns found on mats. Matting was also used to make beds, seats, bags, and coffins.

Matting could be produced by means of twining, but the Egyptians also had the mat loom, which provided a transitional development between manual techniques and those required to weave fabrics. In the tomb of Khety at Beni Hasan (Dynasty 12), a wall scene shows a representation of the mat loom; it appears to be horizontal and the male weaver threads the wefts by hand over the frame. He does not use a heddle or shed. Reeds or rushes were the materials most commonly employed for matting, but palm leaves and grass have also been found.

Egypt's dry climate has ensured that these vegetable fibers have survived; as well as basketry and matting, evidence of other techniques such as rope making, netting, and sandal making with plant fibers has also been preserved.

ROPE AND NET MAKING

Rope making, using flax, rush, and palm fibers, was an important industry, and rope and cord exist from early predynastic times. Date palm fiber was most commonly used for making ropes and cords; examples of these have survived as well as tomb scenes that illustrate how they were made. In the tombs of Amenemhet and Khnumhotep at Beni Hasan, scenes depicting rope making show men twisting together by hand two cords, which are fixed to a post in the ground to increase the leverage. Next, the rope was beaten with a wooden mallet and soaked in a tub to increase its strength. Similar scenes occur in New Kingdom tombs. There were many uses for rope and cord; they were made into handles of jars, baskets, and tools, used for securing coffins and other heavy containers, and employed in shipbuilding and sailing.

Nets were produced to a high standard and for a variety of uses. They were made from string, produced using linen fabrics; string, nets, netting needles, and reels have all been discovered. Netting, a looping or knotting technique worked with a continuous thread, is illustrated in the tomb of Khety at Beni Hasan. It produced coarse nets for fishing and hunting, and finer threads were used for bags and carriers.

Papyrus

The word *papyrus* has several meanings. It can refer to the plant *Cyperus papyrus* L., which belongs to the sedge family, or to a writing material or to a particular "book" or manuscript, such as the Edwin Smith Papyrus, that exists in a museum or library collection.

In antiquity the papyrus plant grew extensively in Egypt, particularly in the Delta, although today it is only found much farther south in the Sudan. It was a symbol of renewal and rebirth, representing the primordial landscape at the time of creation, and architects used it as a form for temple columns; it also became the emblem of Lower Egypt (the flowering rush was used for Upper Egypt). Wild thickets of papyrus were often depicted in the tombs as places where the nobility could hunt and fish.

However, the Egyptians soon began to grow papyrus in cultivated fields and use it for the production of a variety of items including mats, boxes, ropes, ring stands, sails, baskets, furniture, sandals, and loincloths for the peasants, but most importantly for the production of a fine quality writing material. Scenes in tombs show men working in the fields, cutting down the papyrus stems just above the water line. They then carried these heavy bundles back to the workshops where the plants were prepared for their eventual use.

PAPER MAKING

The word *paper* is derived from the Greek *papyros*, which is believed to come from the Egyptian word meaning "the royal," because the manufacture of paper was a royal monopoly. The huge quantities of papyri (inscribed documents, letters, and records) that have survived indicate the high standard of paper making. Nevertheless, this was not the only writing material, and as it was always an expensive option, the Egyptians frequently reused papyri or wrote on cheaper materials such as potsherds or limestone fragments.

No scenes of making papyrus exist on the tomb walls, although associated activities such as gathering the plant, transporting it to the workshops, stripping and cleaning the stems, and making ropes and boats are all illustrated. Again, it is uncertain when the manufacture of papyrus as a writing material was first introduced, but there is some evidence that it already

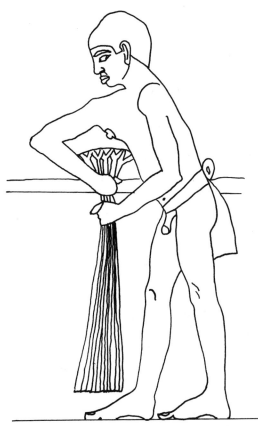

A tomb scene showing a man pulling papyrus, a plant that grew extensively in the Delta. The papyrus was subsequently processed to make a writing material, ropes, and boats. (The apparent distortion of the figure is a good example of the visual problems encountered when the principles that governed tomb art were closely followed.)

existed in Dynasty 1, and papyrus documents are known from the Old Kingdom. Paper production continued throughout the Pharaonic Period and was a major industry in the Greco-Roman era.

Although the process of manufacture is not represented anywhere, various modern studies and experiments have enabled papyrologists to reconstruct the probable stages of the procedure. The stem of the plant is triangular in section and consists of a tough outer rind and an inner cellular pith—the part that was turned into the writing material. First, the stem was cut into pieces the length of which determined the height of each "page." This was never more than 47 centimeters in order that the pieces could be easily handled. Next, the outer rind was stripped off and the inner pith was separated into thick slices. These were then laid on a table, side by side in two layers, one on top of another at right angles to each other. Next, they were beaten together for several hours, using a stone or wooden mallet, and were then probably pressed overnight. This welded them together so that they formed a homogeneous sheet of paper. After this, burnishing the papyrus could improve the surface for writing.

The individual sheets were stuck together with an adhesive; experiments have shown that although a join could be made by using only the natural juice of the pith, the results were not satisfactory as the pieces tended to separate again. A standard roll consisted of twenty pages, but it was possible to stick several rolls together, and the longest known example measures 132 feet. The piece was then cut vertically or horizontally to give the required shape and size. Finally, the strip was rolled up horizontally; the *recto*, which was written on first, was on the inside; the *verso* was on the back of the roll. Paper making was one of the most important techniques developed by the Egyptians and gave

them and the later Classical writers a convenient and easily portable writing material that has enabled their literature to be transmitted to the modern world.

Woodworking

Joiners, carpenters, sculptors, and shipwrights required woods for their work, but Egypt was not well supplied with large trees, and from the early historic period foreign timber had to be imported. Among the places that supplied wood were Assyria; the Hittite homeland; Lebanon; Naharin, the land of the Mitannians; and Punt. There the Egyptians could obtain cedar, cypress, ebony, elm, juniper, maple, oak, pine, and yew. Native Egyptian timbers used by carpenters and joiners included acacia, sycamore fig, and tamarisk as well as the wood of the date palm, dom palm, persea, and willow.

TOOLS

Woodcarving, carpentry, and joinery only became established from the late Predynastic Period when copper tools first became available for working wood. These tools are illustrated in tomb scenes and on Middle Kingdom coffins, and some examples have survived among tomb contents. Town sites such as Gurob and Kahun have also provided rare but important examples of tools actually used by local craftsmen.

There was quite a wide range of carpentry tools, which included adzes, axes, chisels, reamers and saws, awls, borers, knives, rasps, nails, bow drills, wooden mallets, and sandstone blocks for polishing. The adzes, axes, saws, and some of the chisels were all set in wooden handles; for many years copper was used for the blades but later was often replaced by bronze and finally by iron. Leather thongs were used to attach the blades to the handles.

TYPES OF WOOD

Different woods were employed for specific purposes. Sycamore and sometimes imported cedar were used when large, thick planks were required for the production of boxes, doors, tables, coffins, and large statues. If a hard wood was required—especially for tools and tool handles—the craftsmen chose tamarisk, while acacia was selected for planks and masts for boats, weapons, and some furniture. Foreign woods—apart from cedar which was used for ships, the best coffins, masts of pylons, and temple doors—were often employed for ornamental purposes, especially boxes, chairs, and tables decorated with inlaid ebony and ivory. These exotic goods were so desirable that native woods were sometimes painted to resemble the foreign ones.

THE WOODWORKING PROCESS

To produce their wares the carpenters first used a handsaw (a large knife with a toothed edge) to reduce the wood to the required size. The Egyptians employed the pull saw, the cutting edge of the teeth set toward the handle, whereas the push saw (the type used today) has teeth set away from the handle and the saw is pushed forward when it is used. Each piece of wood had to be cut singlehandedly; the wooden beam was placed upright in a simple vice and held between two posts that were firmly fixed into the ground. It was kept in place by cords and cut from the top downward. The axe and the adze were used for rough shaping, and the socket drill, worked by a bow, made smaller holes. A chisel was employed for mortises and carving; the carpenter struck the chisel with a wooden mallet. Finally, the wood was polished with a piece of fine-grained sandstone (planes were unknown in Egypt). The carpenter also utilized plummets and right-angled pieces in his work and kept his bronze nails in a leather pouch. It is probable that lathing was not introduced into Egypt until the Greco-Roman Period and that, in earlier times, handworking rather than lathe-turning was the normal method of producing items such as furniture legs.

At first the Egyptians had employed stone or flint tools for woodworking, but as metal tools were developed they were used alongside the stone implements enabling the carpenters to produce properly joined furniture. The scarcity of natural timbers encouraged the Egyptians to develop "patchwork" construction in which they joined together small or irregular pieces of wood, utilizing dowels, butterfly clamps, lashing and pegging, and tongue and groove. Although nails were used to fasten wood to metal as early as the Old Kingdom, they were only employed from Dynasty 18 onward to fix wooden pieces together.

For lashing and pegging the woodwork joints were secured to each other by means of hide or leather thongs, linen string, or copper bands. This technique was used for coffins and furniture. Mortise and tenon joints occur in many examples, including the tomb furniture of Queen Hetepheres (Dynasty 4) and that of Tutankhamun (Dynasty 18). Dovetailing is also found in examples from these tomb groups, and some other pieces indicate that dowels were also regularly employed elsewhere in the construction of coffins. Mitered joints and hinges are also represented, and some interesting boxes show how they were made secure: The box lid was usually fastened to the base by tying (and then sealing) a piece of string that was twisted around the two knobs fixed to the lid and base of the box.

From earliest times veneer and inlay were frequently employed as decoration. Inferior wood was overlaid with strips of ebony and ivory, and wooden coffins and boxes were inlaid with colored stones, faience, and glass to produce attractive designs.

Metalworking

Egyptian skill in metalworking was less advanced than in some other techniques, and they did not develop in this field as rapidly as other peoples of western Asia. This was due to the fact that local conditions did not favor metalworking: Minerals were not plentiful or easy to obtain, and there was relatively little timber for fuel. Whereas metal was preferred and used for tools and weapons in other countries, the Egyptians had developed stone and flint for this purpose from earliest times and, being innately conservative, felt little incentive to take up the new technologies.

A metalworking industry, however, gradually emerged. The principal metals in use were copper, gold, iron, lead, silver, and tin. In addition, there were four principal alloys—bronze (an alloy of copper and tin), a copper-lead alloy, electrum (an alloy of gold and silver), and brass (an alloy of copper and zinc), which was introduced at a very late date.

COPPER

Copper began to be used toward the end of the Predynastic Period and was probably introduced to Egypt from Asia. Copper ores occurred in areas such as eastern Turkey, Syria, the Zagros Mountains, Cyprus, Sinai, and Egypt's Eastern Desert. The earliest method of working copper was to hammer the small pieces of metal with rounded pebbles, but they discovered that beyond a certain point the metal became brittle and cracked. Therefore, in predynastic times, only pins, beads, and simple objects were produced from copper.

It was eventually discovered, however, that the stresses that built up within a piece of hammered metal could be relieved by heating the metal to quite a high temperature. Subsequently, the cooled metal could be hammered to a required shape until it began to harden, and then it could be reheated. This process—known today as annealing—marked an important stage in the development of metalworking techniques since it demonstrated that metals could be altered by using high temperatures.

A further important discovery indicated that metallic copper, reduced from its ores, would become molten and could be poured into molds. Special molds were gradually developed to cast metal objects; the earliest were simple and consisted of a negative cut into a piece of stone into which the molten metal was poured; the metal object was then hammered and annealed to produce the required shape. Later, two-piece molds of fired clay were introduced. Sometimes these were first molded around a carved wooden pattern that was later removed, and the two pieces were fired and joined together. The molten metal was then poured into the hollow center. Later, a clay core was included in the mold for casting objects such as socketed axes.

In the New Kingdom and later periods, the *cire perdue* (lost wax method) was introduced for casting delicate copper items such as statuettes. A beeswax model of the object to be produced was coated with clay to form the mold; this was then embedded in sand or earth, which formed a support, and was heated so that the beeswax melted and ran out of the holes in the mold. Hardened and rigid, the mold was then ready to receive the molten metal, which was poured in through the holes. Once this had cooled down,

Metal tools and five earthenware molds for bronze castings were found in a caster's shop at Kahun (c.1890 BC). The mold (left) took molten metal for the production of axes; it was lined with a coat of fine ash and clay to produce a smooth surface. The metal hatchet (right) has a break across its body, made in antiquity.

the mold was broken and the metal object was released.

The Egyptians exploited the copper mines in Sinai from Dynasty 3 onward, sending great expeditions there, but when this source began to be exhausted after the Middle Kingdom it was increasingly necessary to import copper from Cyprus and Asia. At first, and for many years, Egyptian copper ores were obtained entirely from surface deposits, employing only flint tools, but later, for underground mining, copper chisels were used to cut shafts.

BRONZE

Early bronze consisted of copper and tin, and although tin ore occurs in Egypt there is no evidence that it was worked in antiquity. Bronze—produced and used in western Asia long before it reached Egypt—was a major discovery in metalworking (probably occurring prior to 3000 BC) that marked a significant advance. The process involved adding a small quantity of tin ore to the copper ores during smelting, which yielded the harder and more easily worked metal. During the second millennium BC the Egyptians began to import bronze ingots from Asia, and gradually bronze replaced copper for industrial uses.

Experiments with methods of alloying and heating the furnace where the metals were smelted were undertaken. In early times bellows consisting of a reed or pipe attached to a bag and blown by several boys were used to increase the heat of charcoal fires, but a new type of bellows made of a pair of goatskins and operated by a man who stamped on them was later introduced. These raised the temperature of the furnace to a higher level, enabling larger scale production. Experiments adding low or high tin contents to the copper also allowed materials of different strengths to be produced for various purposes. Stone and copper tools, however, continued to be used alongside bronze ones for many years.

GOLD

Gold was found in the desert between the Nile Valley and the Red Sea. It occurred both in alluvial sands and gravels and in veins in quartz rock. Ancient workings were situated in the northern part of the Eastern Desert, around Wadi Hammamat; in the central area of the Eastern Desert; and along the Nile Valley, from Wadi Halfa to Kerma. These respectively provided the "gold of Coptos," "gold of Wawat," and the "gold of Kush." The Nubian mines of Kush, which came into production in the Middle Kingdom, continued throughout the New Kingdom and into later times.

Egyptian goldsmiths were among the most skillful and highly regarded craftsmen and produced fine jewelry, statuary, and coffins. Electrum, a natural or artificial alloy of gold and silver, was probably nearly always used in its natural state in ancient Egypt and was employed for jewelry and also for overlaying obelisks. Native silver, however, does not occur in Egypt and had to be imported from Asia. Thus, it was comparatively rare before Dynasty 18, and until the end of the Middle Kingdom it seems to have been considered more valuable than gold.

IRON

Iron was only introduced into Egyptian industry between 1000 and 600 BC, although iron ores found in the Eastern Desert and Sinai had been made into beads and amulets since predynastic times. Although the Egyptians were probably aware of the existence of smelted iron during the New Kingdom (the Hittites had developed production techniques in the fifteenth century BC), they were the last people in the area to use this technology, which was brought into Egypt several hundred years later.

Stoneworking

QUARRYING

The advent of copper tools first made it possible to quarry stone on a large scale for building purposes. Quarrying, an important aspect of the Egyptian economy and a necessary preliminary to the construction of pyramids, tombs, and temples, was one of the king's major responsibilities. In periods of great building activity, such as the Old and New Kingdoms, major expeditions were sent out by royal command to exploit the quarries, which like so many other areas of the economy were a state monopoly.

The earliest quarrying started in the north: The finest white limestone, frequently used to provide a working surface on temple and tomb walls for the carving of bas-reliefs, came from Tura (the ancient Roan, opposite Memphis). Here, it was necessary to tunnel deep to reach the best stone, and large caverns were hollowed out, leaving natural pillars to support the roof.

Alabaster came from the Eastern Desert, and the main quarry, called Hat-nub, was situated in Middle Egypt, about twelve miles from Amarna (Akhetaten). This provided ribbon alabaster, which was made into plates, dishes, and statues.

Granite was quarried around Aswan, where huge blocks of stone were roughly prepared and even dressed before they left the site for their eventual use as obelisks, colossal statues, and sarcophagi. Further south, diorite (an even harder stone than granite) was quarried as early as the Old Kingdom, but the operation was so difficult that it was discontinued after Dynasty 12. Schist deposits were found in the Eastern Desert, in the Wadi Hammamat; this stone was more easily worked than diorite and was highly prized by sculptors. Although some blocks of schist were already lying loose or were only partly attached to the parent rock and could therefore be collected rather than mined, the journey to this district was long and arduous. Schist is fragile, and the blocks not infrequently shattered into fragments as they were being transported. Nevertheless, the area was worked throughout the Pharaonic Period.

Most quarries were not worked continuously. The king dispatched a large-scale expedition when he decided to build a monument. In Dynasty 12 several expeditions were organized that included army personnel to administer the project, courtiers, artisans, and caterers. According to custom, the expedition was led by a senior official, and on one occasion in the reign of Senusret I it was recorded that the force

A diorite bowl, incised with a king's name. This is a good example of the Egyptians' expertise in stoneworking techniques; the production of stone vases reached its zenith in the earliest dynasties, but in later times their skills were concentrated on building stone monuments. c.2900 BC.

brought back 150 statues and 60 sphinxes. Inscriptions left in the quarries by the officials often provide valuable information about these ventures.

WORKING METHODS

Sufficient evidence survives in the monuments, statues, and partly excavated blocks abandoned in the quarries to provide evidence about their working methods. For sandstone and limestone, trenches were cut in the rock to isolate a block on four sides, and then wooden wedges or beams wetted with water were used to detach it from below. The masons employed stone and metal chisels, stone hammers and picks, and wooden mallets to remove the block in steps from the top downward.

Hard stone such as granite, basalt, and quartzite was probably first obtained from fallen or easily detached blocks. Only from the Middle Kingdom, when obelisks and colossal statues began to be used in monuments, did they begin to quarry stone from the living rock, using balls of dolerite for pounding and inserting wooden or metal wedges into slots that had been cut into the stone with a metal tool.

Various stages have been identified in the preparation of the stone blocks used in buildings, statuary, and the production of stone vessels. These include: pounding the block with a stone; rubbing it with stones and an abrasive powder; sawing it with a copper blade and an abrasive powder; boring it with a copper tubular drill and an abrasive powder; and drilling it with a copper or stone point and abrasive powder. The tubular drill used for boring out stone vessels is of particular interest; it consisted of a hollow tube of copper that was rolled between the hands or rotated by means of a bow. Another boring tool—the bow drill—consisted of a drill with a wooden handle and a crescent-shaped flint bit that was turned by hand. Heavy stones were attached to the drill handle to provide weight. For the production of large vessels two men were engaged in rotating the device—a process that is shown in several tomb scenes.

Egyptian expertise in stoneworking was first exemplified in the magnificent vases and vessels carved from hard stone in predynastic times, but by the Old Kingdom craftsmen had developed the skills necessary to quarry and dress large blocks of stone for monumental buildings and to sculpt the magnificent divine and royal statues that adorned their major monuments.

Jewelry

Men and women loved to adorn themselves with jewelry, and fine examples have survived from all periods, although the Middle Kingdom probably represents the greatest age of this craft. Excavations have revealed several great royal treasures, as well as the jewelry of private individuals, and there was obviously a high level of technical skill. Other sources, such as tomb scenes and temple wall reliefs, provide further information about jewelry production.

USES

The Egyptians adorned the gods' statues, the dead, and the living with jewelry, which was believed to confer certain benefits on the wearer. Amulets (magical items of jewelry) were worn to protect the owner against evil or hostile forces, and their shapes and forms—animals, hieroglyphs, images of gods, and special symbols—were believed to exert strong magical forces. The metals and stones used in the jewelry were also believed to contain magical properties. Although both the dead and the living were supplied with jewelry, the funerary pieces were often more conservative and traditional in design than pieces for the living.

Jewelry also indicated status, and kings marked important events in their reigns, such as marriage, accession to the throne, and jubilee festivals, with the production of special sets of jewelry. On some occasions, courtiers presented the king with jewelry to mark a special occasion. Jewelry was also presented to foreign powers and as gifts to favored courtiers, while certain items were given to mark the appointment of royal officials. Not only royalty and the upper classes enjoyed this display of wealth; people of all ages and classes adorned themselves with necklaces, bracelets, anklets, headdresses, belts, and rings. Earrings were introduced into Egypt from Asia at the beginning of the New Kingdom.

PRODUCTION PROCESS

The same materials tended to be popular at all periods. Gold was especially favored; first collected in the form of granules in the alluvial sands and gravel, it was later extracted from veins in the quartz rock. Electrum and silver were also used, but gold, because it did not decay or tarnish and because it reflected the color of the sun, always remained the most popular metal.

Goldsmithing was carried out in the capital city, major towns, and also in temple workshops; at Memphis the Temple of Ptah (the patron of craftsmen) was particularly famous for this work. Gold mining was a state monopoly, and gold was also levied as a tax; thus, it directly entered the state and temple workshops where it was weighed and recorded by a scribe before the master craftsmen received it. The first stage in production involved purification of the gold: The ingots were placed in a crucible and heated over an open fire. In early times, to increase the temperature, several men stood around the fire

and blew through reeds that were protected in pottery sleeves. By the New Kingdom, however, a more elaborate bellows, using a pair of goatskins attached to the reeds, had been developed. Once the gold was molten, men used tongs to lift the crucible off the fire and poured the gold into molds. Then, before it was cold, the gold was hammered on an anvil to produce plates, bars, strips, and gold wire. The introduction of the bellows and blast furnace was a major advance since it now became possible to provide very high temperatures that gave the workmen more control over their metals. Other tools were very simple and included polished pebbles to hammer the metals, possibly limestone and bronze hammers, sandstone and quartzite stones used as files, and bronze or copper tongs. The high carat gold was soft and therefore easily worked, and the results achieved with such a limited range of tools were quite outstanding. Techniques included soldering, hammering, molding, beating, and decorative processes such as chasing, engraving, embossing, repoussé, inlaying, granular and filigree work, and cloisonné.

The metals were set with semiprecious stones chosen for their colors rather than their refraction. These were brought in from the desert or from abroad: The most popular were carnelian (from the Eastern Desert), turquoise (mined in Sinai), and lapis lazuli (from Afghanistan). Other local stones included jasper, garnet, green feldspar, amethyst, rock crystal, obsidian, calcite, and chalcedony. Because there was such a demand for some of these stones, artificial copies were also produced: Transparent calcite and rock crystal were backed with colored cement, Egyptian faience was produced to imitate lapis lazuli, and by the New Kingdom colored glass was commercially produced.

The workshops appear to have accommodated goldsmiths alongside lapidaries and cutters, bead makers, and stone setters. They all carried out their tasks under joint supervision, and they were probably responsible to a chief jeweler who would have been trained both as a scribe and as craftsman and perhaps had some freedom in designing the jewelry. The crafts were handed down in families, but in some pieces of royal jewelry, especially those made during the Middle Kingdom, there is some indication of foreign influence. It is possible that highly skilled foreign jewelers were welcomed and settled in Egypt at this time.

The stones were bored and engraved by the lapidaries and then passed on to the setters. At Memphis, the center of jewelers from the Old Kingdom, dwarfs with normal-size bodies but stunted arms and legs appear to have carried out this work. Although their activities are represented in the Old Kingdom tomb of Mereruka at Saqqara, however, there are no further references to them in later periods.

Paints and Pigments

The earliest extant examples of painting date to the Predynastic Period; apart from designs on pottery, these include paintings on textiles and leather as well as the famous but now lost mural in the tomb at Hieraconpolis. The Egyptians continued to decorate their buildings and many of their artifacts with paintings throughout 3,000 years of history; the walls of tombs, temples, palaces, and houses were adorned with carved and painted scenes, and statues, coffins, funerary, and domestic items were often brightly colored while vignettes accompanying the inscriptions in papyri were also carefully painted.

Color was regarded as an integral part of an object, and the various hues were considered to have special magical properties. Particular colors were employed for different uses: Gods and goddesses were sometimes painted with green, blue, or golden skin tones, and it was traditional to represent men's coloring as reddish-brown while women were depicted with lighter, olive complexions. In the temples most of the color on the external walls has now disappeared, while the interior walls have often lost the layer of plaster that once carried the colors so that only the underlying relief carving remains. It is in the nonroyal tombs of the New Kingdom at Thebes, where the scenes were painted directly onto prepared wall surfaces as a substitute for costly carved reliefs, that the most interesting examples of painting and coloring have survived.

SOURCES

The vividness of these paintings has often prompted onlookers to inquire about the nature of the pigments employed by the ancient artists. Analysis has indicated that these were either finely ground naturally occurring minerals or were made from mineral substances. There was a limited range of basic colors, kept in the form of powdery cakes: black, blue, brown, green, gray, orange, pink, red, white, and yellow. To produce different shades the artist mixed or superimposed these basic colors.

Black pigment was nearly always a form of carbon, such as soot, carbon black (lampblack), or charcoal. For blue the artists sometimes used azurite, a naturally occurring mineral—a blue carbonate of copper—found in Sinai and the Eastern Desert. An artificial frit, however, made by heating together silica, a copper compound (usually malachite), calcium carbonate, and natron provided the most commonly used blue pigment. For brown the artists generally employed ocher or iron oxide, and green pigment was derived either from powdered malachite (which occurs as a natural ore of copper, found in Sinai and the Eastern Desert) or from an artificial frit. To produce gray the Egyptians mixed black (charcoal) and white (gypsum), and orange resulted from combining red and yellow ochers or painting red on top of yellow. Again, to obtain pink, it was customary to mix red ocher with gypsum.

For one of the most important colors—red —the artists used natural oxides of iron, namely red iron oxides and red ochers. White pigment was derived from either calcium carbonate (whiting, chalk) or calcium sulfate (gypsum). There were two different yellow pigments— yellow ocher and orpiment. Yellow ocher was plentiful in Egypt, particularly in the north and in the western oases, while orpiment was probably imported from Asia.

EQUIPMENT AND MATERIALS

The artist's equipment was simple and consisted of water pots, palettes made of shells or broken shards, and paint brushes of palm fiber and reeds. The vehicle for applying the paint to the prepared surface consisted of water and an adhesive (gelatin or glue). This technique is known as tempera painting. It was essential that the paint vehicle contained an adhesive to bind the pigments to the wall surface, and it is probable that size (gelatin, glue), gum, or albumin (egg white) were used.

The Egyptians painted on canvas, papyrus, plaster, pottery, stone, and wood. There were several types of plaster: clay, gypsum, and whiting (chalk). Sometimes the paint was applied directly to the clay plaster, but gypsum plaster was most commonly used for wall paintings while whiting was most often employed on wooded objects as a base for painting. Gypsum plaster was fairly coarse so that it covered over any irregularities in the wall surface, while whiting plaster (a mixture of whiting and glue) provided a smoother surface on smaller objects. Egyptian mural paintings are sometimes called "frescoes," but this is inaccurate; there is no evidence that the paintings were applied while the plaster was still wet, using only water as the medium.

It is uncertain how the tombs were lit to enable the artists to execute their detailed work. Lamps, developed as early as the Old Kingdom, consisted of stone or clay cups filled with oil in which a wick was placed. Although the artists probably used either these lamps or candles or torches, it is remarkable that no smoke marks remain visible on the tomb ceilings.

Mummification

True mummification—an intentional method of preserving the corpse involving several sophisticated techniques and the use of chemical and other agents—was developed by the ancient Egyptians c.2600 BC after a considerable period of experimentation. Its main purpose was to dehydrate the bodily tissues and thus prevent rapid decomposition, with the aim of preserving the appearance of the individual so that the soul could recognize the body and return to it at will. Mummification continued to be practiced in Egypt until the Christian era, although it was only available to the wealthier classes. Poor people were interred in shallow graves on the desert's edge where the heat and dryness of the sand preserved their bodies naturally. This original method of burial, universal before c.3400 BC, demonstrated that the body could be preserved indefinitely and was the Egyptians' inspiration to seek new and more sophisticated methods of mummifying their dead.

TECHNIQUES

Although there are no extant Egyptian literary accounts of how the embalming procedure was carried out, and no visual records occur (although two Theban tombs have wall scenes that show some stages in preparing and bandaging a mummy), detailed descriptions have survived in the writings of Greek historians Herodotus (fifth century BC) and Diodorus Siculus (first century BC). Herodotus describes three main methods, available according to cost. The most expensive and elaborate method (also shown by modern experiments to be the most effective) involved removal of the brain, as well as of the viscera and abdominal contents through an abdominal incision in the flank. The viscera were then cleansed with palm wine and spices and the body cavity, filled with myrrh, cassia, and other aromatic substances. After sewing up the incision, the body was dehydrated by means of natron, washed, and then wrapped in layers of bandages. The second method involved the injection of "cedar oil" into the body via the rectum and subsequent treatment with natron. The third method required an unspecified liquid to be injected via the rectum prior to treatment with natron.

From the evidence of the literature and, more importantly, the many mummies that have survived, it is clear that Egyptian mummification involved two main stages: the evisceration of the body (although this was not universally applied) and the dehydration of the tissues, using natron. Additionally, the body was anointed with oils and unguents, sometimes coated with resin, and treated with plants and plant products. Only two major refinements were added to the procedure over the course of 3,000 years: From at least as early as the Middle Kingdom the brain was removed, and this became a widespread practice in the New Kingdom; and during Dynasty 21 the body was given a plumper and more lifelike appearance by packing the face, neck, and other areas with materials such as sand, sawdust, earth,

butter, and linen, which were inserted through incisions in the skin.

Sufficient evidence exists to allow us to reconstruct the main stages in the mummification procedure. First, the family of the deceased took the body to the embalmer's workshop. The procedure lasted seventy days, although only forty days were probably required for preparation of the mummy. The remaining time would have been occupied with religious rituals.

The body was stripped and placed on a board or platform. The brain was extracted, usually via a passage chiselled through the left nostril and ethmoid bone into the cranial cavity. Using a metal hook, the brain tissue was then reduced to fragments and extracted using a spatula. Brain removal was usually incomplete, however, and some tissue was left behind. The extracted brain fragments were discarded, and the brain cavity was either left empty or eventually filled with resin or resin-soaked linen. In some mummies the brain was removed through the base of the skull or through a trepanned orbit. The eyes were not taken out; they were allowed to collapse into the orbits, and linen pads were inserted over the eyeballs or, in Dynasties 21 and 22, artificial eyes were put in place.

The body was eviscerated through an incision usually in the left flank. The embalmer inserted his hand through the flank incision and inside the abdominal cavity, he cut the organs free with a special knife and removed them from the body. Then, he entered the chest cavity by making an incision in the diaphragm and subsequently removed the thoracic organs. The heart was left in situ because it was regarded as the seat of the individual emotions and intellect. Diodorus states that the kidneys also remained in place, although no religious explanation can be offered for this. Often, evisceration was imperfect and part or all of the heart was removed with the other organs. Some mummies were not

A mummy of a young man from Hawara (dating from the first century BC). X rays have revealed that the mummy is a jumble of bones, but the outer wrappings are elaborate, featuring diagonal bandaging interspersed with gilt studs and incorporating a panel portrait that was probably a likeness of the owner.

eviscerated at all, and in others the viscera were removed through the rectum. Next, the body cavities were washed out with palm wine and spices, and then a temporary packing was inserted to assist dehydration and prevent the body wall from collapsing. This temporary stuffing probably included dry natron, packets of a natron and resin mixture, and linen impregnated with resin.

The extracted viscera were then dehydrated, using natron; sometimes, they were placed in four canopic jars that were left in the tomb, but during Dynasties 21 and 22 they were wrapped in four parcels and replaced in the abdominal and chest cavities. By Dynasty 26 canopic jars were briefly reintroduced, but in later times the viscera were wrapped in one large parcel and placed on the legs of the mummy.

The body itself was now dehydrated. It is generally accepted that natron was the main dehydrating agent, although salt or lime may have been used in some cases. Natron (a mixture of sodium carbonate and bicarbonate with natural impurities that include high proportions of salt and sodium sulphate) occurs in natural deposits in Egypt. It was used in a solid, dry state for mummification, and the body was packed with dry natron for up to forty days. This destroyed the fat and grease and dehydrated the tissues. The body was then removed from the natron bed and washed with water to remove traces of natron and other debris.

Still relatively pliable, the body was now straightened out so that it would fit into a coffin, and during Dynasty 21 the subcutaneous packing was inserted at this stage through incisions in the skin to provide a plumper form. Next, the body was anointed with cedar oil and ointments and rubbed with myrrh, cinnamon, and other fragrant substances. The flank incision was sewn up or closed by drawing the edges together and covering them with a metal or beeswax plate. The cranial cavity was packed with linen impregnated with resin, and resin or wax was used to plug the nostrils. Resinous paste was applied to the body, and the limbs and body were wrapped in linen cloths and bandages. Finally, the arms were arranged either across the chest or extended alongside the body. A special ceremony marked the conclusion of the procedure when a liquid or semiliquid resinous substance was poured over the mummy, the viscera if they were stored in a separate container, and the coffin. The family then removed the mummy and organized the burial ceremonies.

THE EMBALMERS

The persons who performed the mummification procedures were a distinct group within the society. The Greek writer Diodorus Siculus stated that there were three main classes of people who prepared the body for the funeral: the scribe, the cutter, and the embalmer or undertaker. It was the duty of the scribe to supervise the incision made in the flank of the mummy to allow the evisceration of the body. The cutter (in Greek, *paraschist*) then carried out the incision. Because of this role (which gave him direct contact with the corpse and could therefore result in his contamination by the evil spirits associated with death), the cutter was regarded as unclean and untouchable. He could never relinquish or rise above this status.

The embalmer, however, (known in Egyptian as the *wt*) belonged to the special guild or organization of undertakers and held an important and respected position within the society. The embalmer was responsible for wrapping the body in bandages; wearing a jackal-headed mask, he also impersonated Anubis, the god of embalming, during the mummification ceremonies.

The embalmers were a class of priests who perhaps also had professional associations with doctors. Evidence that supports this includes the biblical account of Joseph directing the physicians to embalm his father's body and the claim made by the Classical author Pliny that during the mummification process, the embalmers were instructed by the government to examine the corpse for evidence of the disease that had brought about the death. Also, in some cases the doctors may have consulted the embalmers prior to a patient's death. In the Ptolemaic Period, the Egyptian word for "doctor" (*swnw*) was also sometimes used to mean "embalmer."

The office of embalmer was apparently hereditary. In addition to their own duties, it seems that they also employed a workforce of coffinmakers, a separate and distinct trade that combined the skills of carpenter and painter. These men also produced the figurines and other wooden items for the tomb. It is possible that the embalmers also owned tombs in the town cemeteries that they sold to clients.

There is no specific information about the number of persons employed to prepare the mummies and participate in the funerals, but it must have been considerable. In addition to those already mentioned, other categories including lector-priests, sem-priests and "treasurers of the god" are listed in a text known as the "Ritual of Embalming" that is preserved on two papyri of the Roman Period, now held in the Berlin Museum and the Cairo Museum.

The location for the mummification procedure, with its associated religious rituals of lustration, fumigation with incense, and recitation of prayers, was a workshop known as a *wbt* ("place of purification") or alternatively as the "place of purification of the Good House." No information has survived concerning the number or location of all these workshops. It is known, however, that in some cases a small, individual embalming place was built near the tomb, but always outside the actual tomb enclosure since the mummification process was considered to be "impure" and could not be allowed to contaminate the ritual purity of the tomb itself. Archaeologists have discovered a few of these places, containing the embalming refuse that was gathered up after mummification and buried nearby.

Other workshops were situated near temples or burial grounds and accommodated many bodies. During the clearing of Queen Hatshepsut's temple at Deir el-Bahri, archaeologists found traces of such a workshop, together with the remains of natron and chopped straw that had been used to preserve and pack the bodies of priests who were prepared there for burial. The archaeologists also found the inscribed coffin of a priest in this workshop; it had presumably never been collected by the owner's family.

The embalmers—highly skilled, trained professionals—therefore had strong religious and perhaps medical associations, but they nevertheless appear to have conducted their work on an independent, commercial basis. Presumably, the most competent of these priests were entrusted with the arrangements for the preparation of the royal funerals, but there is no information on this point. It is evident that in all mummification procedures, the embalmers supervised all the stages. However, the unpleasant, potentially dangerous, and "impure" activities associated with making the incision and removing the viscera were carried out by a group of social outcasts who may have included convicted criminals.

READING

A number of studies provide useful accounts and detailed bibliographies of ancient technology. These are Hodges 1970; Singer, Holmyard, and Hall 1954, 1956; Forbes 1964–72; and Lucas and Harris 1962. Further specific bibliographies are provided below for some of the sections.

The Economic System

Trigger, et al. 1983: discussion of Egypt's economic structure; Petrie 1926: discussion of ancient weights and measures.

Industry

TEXTILES

Crowfoot 1931: description of methods of hand spinning in ancient Egypt; Roth 1951: a study of Egyptian and Greek looms.

WOODWORKING

Baker 1966: an account of furniture in the ancient world; Petrie 1917: a study of tools and weapons; Petrie 1937: a study of funerary furniture.

PLANT PRODUCTS

Manniche 1989: discussion of the uses of ancient Egyptian plants; Hepper 1990: a useful study of the botanical remains found in the tomb of Tutankhamun.

JEWELRY

Aldred 1971: comprehensive survey of the history and development of Egyptian jewelry.

MUMMIFICATION TECHNIQUES

Smith and Dawson 1991: classic account of mummification; Herodotus 1961: account of mummification; Diodorus Siculus 1954: account of mummification.

11

EVERYDAY
LIFE

Although evidence from ancient Egypt comes mainly from the tombs and funerary goods, the Egyptian ambition to re-create the conditions of their daily existence in the afterlife has resulted in the preservation both of tomb scenes, showing many facets of their lives, and of objects such as furniture, clothing, cosmetics, and jewelry.

HABITATION AND POPULATION

With regard to the population of ancient Egypt, the development of centers of habitation was largely directed by the geographical features of the country. The predynastic towns and villages remained the basis for this development; communities were strung out along the river, hedged in on one side by the desert and by the river on the other. Thus their direct contacts were with their neighbors who lived immediately to the north or south. Since the Nile was their only direct means of transport and communication, it was always difficult for people in the north to have contact with the far south. Gradually towns and villages came to form larger districts or provinces, each with its own deity, capital city, and traditions.

These provinces, or nomes, were used as government districts. Some of these in the Delta were quite large, whereas others in the south were much smaller; there were about twenty nomes in both Upper and Lower Egypt. Changes occurred over the centuries: At different times nomes appeared in some lists as independent units and in others as parts of other provinces, thus reflecting political or govern-

mental changes. Although their boundaries, areas, and status might change, however, the nomes remained the basic divisions of Egypt. There are no definite estimates of population figures during the historic period. Numbers supplied by the Egyptians in military campaigns, for example, are unreliable, and a "hundred thousand persons" probably simply meant "a very large number" rather than representing a specific figure. Nevertheless, it is known that the country was very fertile, and it probably supported a dense population within the narrow confines of the cultivation. Even with a high infant mortality and low average life expectancy, the Egyptians still found it necessary to limit the size of their families by using contraception. It can perhaps be estimated that, at its peak, the population reached between 5 and 7 million.

The racial mixture of the population is another uncertainty. According to the theory of a "Dynastic Race," the people who entered Egypt around 3400 BC may have come from the region of Mesopotamia, and it is argued that their fusion with the indigenous population may have provided the initial inspiration for the Nile Valley civilization. Many other groups entered Egypt in later times; there were prisoners of war taken captive in Egypt's Asiatic campaigns, and craftsmen, diplomats, technicians, and traders who came from neighboring lands. There were foreign rulers such as the Hyksos who ruled the country in Dynasties 15 and 16, and the New Kingdom saw the development of a cosmopolitan society with foreign queens and their entourages at court, traders bringing a variety of goods to Egypt, and immigrant craftsmen and servants working at building sites and in Egyptian households.

When the Egyptians were ruled by foreigners during the later dynasties, the Ethiopians, Assyrians, and Persians all had some influence, although it is generally accepted that their long-lasting impact was minimal. Under the Greeks and Romans major changes were introduced, and the arrival of a substantial minority of Greek settlers undoubtedly had an effect upon the overall population.

Despite these influxes, Egyptian civilization remained remarkably stable and homogeneous. Foreign influence was minimal in the formative years of the society, allowing the distinctive Egyptian traditions to become firmly established. The culture was so all-embracing and pervasive that, when it finally encountered foreign ideas and customs, these were either readily absorbed and Egyptianized or had little or no impact on the mainstream culture. Within Egyptian society, however, each community retained its physical separateness, although the inhabitants were generally crowded together in the Nile Valley. The population never truly combined to become one nation, and usually when the central government collapsed the country broke down again into its various geographical divisions.

The extent of the role of the foreigners within special communities, such as the pyramid workmen's town of Kahun, is particularly interesting. It is evident that there was a presence, perhaps significant in size, of foreign residents in the town. Legal papyri and temple lists show that "Asiatics" were employed at building works, in the temples, and in domestic service. It is also possible that a group of Minoan workmen may have been employed on the construction of the Lahun pyramid or engaged in producing goods for the royal funerary treasure. At this time Crete was experiencing stability and prosperity and quantities of Minoan pottery were being exported to Cyprus, Syria, and Egypt. Other workers may have come to Kahun from Cyprus and were perhaps partly responsible for the metalworking development seen in the tools and other items discovered at the town.

Thus, immigrants may have come to Kahun for a variety of reasons. Some were perhaps traders who decided to stay and settle; others were itinerant artisans whose skills were welcomed by their royal patrons; and there were also those who had probably been brought to Egypt as prisoners of war. The "foreigners" appear to have been readily accepted by the indigenous population; although they may have preserved some of their own religious and other customs, the newcomers clearly adapted themselves to their new home, and Kahun essentially remained an Egyptian town.

There is insufficient evidence from other sites to draw many general conclusions about the combination of native and immigrant features within Egyptian society. Foreigners seem to have been readily accepted, however, and in some cases were able to rise to important and responsible positions within the hierarchy. The Egyptians were generally tolerant of other people's customs and traditions. Since they posed no threat to their own lives, they allowed others to pursue their own beliefs.

THE FAMILY

The Egyptian family was a small, independent unit consisting of father, mother, and children, although it was sometimes extended to include unmarried or widowed female relatives. The financial position of women and children was protected by law, and even after marriage women retained ownership of their own property. If a woman's husband divorced her, she kept her own property and he had to pay her compensation. Bigamy and polygamy were rare among commoners, and consanguineous marriages outside the royal family were very infrequent before the Greco-Roman Period.

Marriage

Great consideration was given to women. The wisdom texts instructed husbands to love, feed, clothe, and seek to please their wives. Being a wife was regarded as a woman's main role in society, and a man was advised to marry as soon as he acquired property and when he had reached the age of twenty so that he could have children while he was still young. Outside the royal family it was not customary to have arranged marriages, although parents obviously hoped their children would make suitable alliances, and it was the duty of the older people to introduce young girls to reputable bachelors. At the betrothal there would have been an exchange of gifts, but there is no record of wedding rites or religious celebrations; probably, as in Islam, marriage was primarily a legal ceremony.

When he took a wife a man became head of his household, and his wife became "mistress of the house." They had equal legal rights and joint ownership of property within the marriage; after death, the wife could expect the same eternal life as her husband and an equal share in his tomb. When the couple died, their property was divided between their children in their will. There was no family name as such, but each individual had a personal name to which his or her father's name was added in any official documentation (*X* son of *Y*). In the funerary texts the name of one or both parents was given (*X* son of *Y*, born to the mistress of the house *Z*).

Household Arrangements

Legal documents provide insight into family units. At the pyramid town of Kahun archaeologists found some of the earliest known examples of particular types of documents. There are deeds that record the transfer of property from one person to another and include some types of will and marriage settlement. There seems to have been quite a degree of flexibility in these arrangements. For example, one man (an architect) left all his property and his Asiatic slaves to his brother, while the latter in turn transferred all this property to his wife, who could pass it on to any of their children.

Official lists of individual households also survive from Kahun, and these give the names of the family members, their serfs (servants), and slaves. It is interesting to observe that the names of female slaves and their children are included, but not male slaves, probably because they worked (and were listed) elsewhere—at the building sites or as soldiers or clerks. One list included the head of a household, his wife, a grandmother, and three of his father's sisters, while another indicates that households were combined when the male head of one household died, thus demonstrating how guardianship and accommodation of unmarried female relatives was achieved.

Children and Pregnancy

The Egyptians appear to have been devoted to their families and to have loved their children. Scarcity of cultivatable land, however, probably prompted them to consider contraceptive measures to limit the size of their families. Again, from Kahun, there is a famous medical papyrus containing gynecological prescriptions and various tests to ascertain sterility, pregnancy, and the sex of unborn children, as well as prescriptions concerned with fertility and contraception. Similar examples occur in other medical papyri.

Barrenness was considered a great personal tragedy for a couple, and if a wife could not bear children a female slave was sometimes brought to the household. If she then produced children they could be given full legal rights of inheritance when the father died. Pregnancy and childbirth were surrounded by great physical dangers, and many women died in childbirth or shortly afterward, while infants frequently did not survive the first few months of life.

Eldest Son

When a man died, his eldest son inherited the obligation to bury his father with the correct rites and also perhaps to place his statue in the local temple so that he could continue to receive benefit and spiritual sustenance from the rituals performed there. The family was also expected to continue to place food offerings at the tomb in perpetuity, although this duty was frequently delegated to a special priest (ka servant). In return for a continuing income from the deceased's estate, this man and his descendants were expected to perform the rites forevermore, although in reality this was often neglected.

Slaves

It is clear from extant legal documents that "slaves" were part of some households, but the definition of a slave in the Egyptian context differs from that of the modern world. No one in Egypt was completely devoid of legal rights, although some people were legally owned by others who could sell them, hand them over to a third party, or rent them out, as well as officially emancipate them. The king, the temples, and private individuals were in charge of substantial numbers of slaves who labored on building sites, in the workshops, and in the fields, as well as in private households. These included various categories such as Egyptian peasants,

convicted criminals, and, in later times, prisoners of war brought back from foreign campaigns. However, it would be wrong to conclude that these tied workers played a crucial role in the organization of the country. The pyramids of the Old Kingdom, for example, would have been constructed entirely by local serf labor.

In fact, there were no true slaves in ancient Egypt, since these individuals could own property and dispose of it as they wished. They could also own land and pass it to their children; the men could marry free women; and if they reached a certain level of prosperity they could employ their own servants. Nevertheless, although some achieved a good standard of living, their freedom of movement was always restricted.

THE HOME

Furnishings

Furniture has survived from the tombs—placed there to provide the owner with his comforts in the next life—and, much more rarely, from domestic contexts such as the town of Kahun. Individual pieces were functional and sometimes elegant; quality varied according to the status of the family. Pieces included beds, chests (for storing clothes, jewelry, and dishes), small tables, and stools. Rushes and palm leaves were used for the manufacture of mats, baskets, and parts of furniture (beds and chair seats), but wood was most often employed for furniture construction.

Chairs and couches were particularly fine. Those used by the upper classes were often made of ebony and ivory and incorporated feet carved to represent the paws of a lion. The earliest type of seat was a wooden stool, used with a cushion; this design remained popular down into the New Kingdom, although some changes were introduced in Dynasty 5. These seats had high sides and a back but they were obviously uncomfortable, and in the Middle Kingdom the back was altered and the sides were lowered. Other styles were introduced in the New Kingdom, and thick cushions were used with them in place of the leather seat found in earlier periods. Chairs were often used with footstools. Variations on the simple seat included folding stools (rather like camp stools) and low seats for older people. In some cases the furniture itself survives, but more frequently the evidence of the tomb murals provides the only detailed information.

The couch or bed apparently developed from the seat. Again, the lion's paws were used to decorate the feet. Sometimes cushions were piled onto these couches, and at least one example of an herb pillow (to assist sleep) has survived. Wooden headrests, however, frequently replaced pillows. The headrest was placed under the neck and allowed the owner to rest without removing his wig. There were no tables of the traditional type at which people sat on chairs to eat. Stands, often made of stone, were used, rather like our trays or "occasional" tables; each held a cup or jug and a flat basket as a plate. Instead of cupboards, their clothing, jewelry, cosmetics, and domestic items were stored in boxes and baskets. Some of the boxes incorporated devices allowing them to be sealed and secured.

In the kitchens and cellars there were clay ovens and large pottery jars for keeping wine, oil, and grain. Special jars were used to keep the precious water supply as cool as possible. Bathrooms and lavatories provided additional comfort in the wealthiest villas.

Rugs and hangings brought color to the decoration of a room. Woven, colored matting was suspended to cover the upper parts of the inner wall surfaces, and thick rugs covered the floors. The doors and windows (which were small and set high in the walls) were protected by mats hung over the openings; when not in use, these were raised on wooden rollers fixed at the top of each door or window. This afforded privacy and protection from the sun, but allowed cooling breezes to pass through the house.

Servants and Housekeeping

The upper classes lived in considerable style and employed many servants. The estates of the great nobles had their own slaughterhouses and bakeries, and these as well as the food stores had to be organized and managed. Within the house a butler attended to the master's drinks, and there were cooks, bakers, porters, gardeners, and other servants. At some periods many households seem to include foreign servants, some of whom held positions of considerable authority.

From the medical papyri we know something of their housekeeping methods. Plant recipes were used to get rid of vermin and insects; one prescription for flea infestation was to grind fleabane with charcoal and then dust the house with this mixture. Fumigation pellets were also used to improve or mask household smells, and scented oils were probably burned in the houses. To light their homes, candles made of plant fibers were dipped in sesame oil.

Flowers and Gardens

The Egyptians loved plants, flowers, and floral decorations, and these were widely used for the

A tomb scene (c.1400 BC) in which the owner and his wife are seated in a kiosk (left); stands loaded with food offerings and flowers are placed in front of them, and two servants (right) bring fruit, fowl, and flowers.

living and the dead because of their beauty and their religious and magical symbolism. Floristry was a well-organized industry, and the chief florist of the Temple of Amun at Karnak had the temple plant nurseries, which he supervised, depicted in a scene on his tomb wall. Ancient records indicate that Ramesses III presented nearly two million bouquets in this temple over a three-year period. Beyond their religious importance at festivals and their use as a presentation to the deceased on the day of burial, flowers and foliage were valued as a decoration for the home. Plants, garlands, and flowers decked the living rooms; outside, gardens were assiduously tended. Flowers were also made into elaborate table decorations for parties and banquets, and guests wore and carried lotus buds.

A wealth of plant remains from ancient Egypt, wall scenes in tombs and temples, and models of houses and villas all indicate that the Egyptians cultivated and even landscaped their gardens from as early as the Old Kingdom. The gardens were private retreats with shady trees, sweet-smelling flowers, and cool ponds and lakes.

Private domestic gardens are sometimes depicted on tomb walls, because the owner hoped to continue to enjoy his garden in the next life. The typical upper-class garden was walled to provide seclusion and privacy, and a porter's lodge was situated at the only entrance. In some examples, the whole area was subdivided into "rooms" containing different types of trees, shrubs, and flowers; some sections may have been devoted to rare trees, whereas others perhaps contained nursery plantations.

Gardens were formally arranged, with trees aligned in neat rows, and flowers planted in square beds or straight borders. There was often a pool with water plants and fish, and a seat, summerhouse, and line of shade trees where the owner could contemplate his garden. There were fruit trees and flowers chosen for their beauty and fragrance. Two species of blue and white lotuses grew in the ponds, and field flowers such as poppies and cornflowers were mixed in the borders with mandrake, iris, lilies, chrysanthemum, and delphinium. The Egyptians also imported exotic plants and trees such as the pomegranate and the fig. One poem recalls that a fig tree was brought from Syria as a love token, and gardens and flowers were generally associated with romantic love. Apart from these country gardens, even town houses were decorated with trees and shrubs planted in pots and containers and arranged along the facade of the house.

There are no tomb scenes that depict royal gardens, but they were undoubtedly splendid. The ivory panels on a casket found in Tutankhamun's tomb show scenes of the king and his wife passing time in their garden. The Great Papyrus Harris preserves the information that Ramesses III tried to create garden cities. He planted trees and papyrus plants in Thebes and had incense trees brought back from Punt to enhance the temple gardens. In a new city he founded in the Delta, great vineyards were created, and there were walks shaded by fruit trees. Some time earlier Queen Hatshepsut had also ordered incense trees to be transported from Punt and planted in the garden of her funerary temple at Deir el-Bahri, and in c.2000 BC King Mentuhotep Nebhepetre had planned a garden around his temple, which stands adjacent to Hatshepsut's own monument. Not only have the tree pits and tree cuttings been discovered there, but on a floor slab in the temple the garden plan sketched by the landscape artist in charge of the work can still be seen.

In the Temple of Karnak wall reliefs in one small chamber depict the plants which Tuthmosis III brought back from his military campaigns in Asia Minor and Syria. Generally, temple gardens were planted to delight the god and to provide the flowers and herbs for the daily offerings made to the god's statue. Sometimes, physic gardens were also established to provide produce for the priests to use in their medicines. The temple and domestic gardens closely resembled each other in design and purpose.

FOOD AND DRINK

Eating Habits

Food and drink were prepared to nourish both the living and the dead. In the Old Kingdom people squatted at low tables or stands to eat the food piled on the table, while their drinking bowls stood under the table or on another stand. In the New Kingdom these traditions continued for the poor, but wealthy people now sat on high chairs and were waited on by their servants. They ate with their fingers, and afterward water was poured over their hands from a ewer into a basin kept on a stand in the dining room.

Diet

The ritual menus shown on the walls of the tombs provide information about the diet of the wealthiest people, and occasionally repasts have been found in the tombs set out on individual dishes. It was customary for the relatives of the deceased to supply food offerings at the tomb to nourish his spirit. This duty was frequently delegated to a special priest, and to avoid starvation if this task were ever neglected, a menu inscribed in the tomb could be magically activated by the deceased. These funerary lists include ten sorts of meat, five kinds of fowl, sixteen kinds of bread and cake, six kinds of wine, four different beers, and eleven varieties of fruit.

There is sufficient evidence to show that fashions in dishes and food preparation changed over the centuries and that foreign recipes supplemented Egyptian cooking. In the New Kingdom delicacies were introduced from Syria and Asia Minor. The Egyptians enjoyed unusual breads and imported wine and beer, but sometimes foreigners resident in Egypt produced these new products locally.

The staple diet of the poor consisted of bread, beer, and onions. They lived and ate frugally, eking out their rations with any extra fruit and vegetables they could grow. Conversely, the nobles and landowners ate well from the produce of their estates, and the priests received payment for their temple duties in the form of the food and drink that reverted from the temple god's altar at the conclusion of the thrice-daily ritual.

The staple food of all classes was bread, and bread making was an important task of all households. Beer, produced from ground barley, was the Egyptians' favorite drink and was prepared in a "brewery" or special area of the kitchen devoted to this purpose. Wine was another favorite beverage, and even as early as the Old Kingdom there were six distinct types of wine grown in different parts of Egypt. From the New Kingdom onward various wines were mixed together in large vessels to provide a potent drink for the celebration of feasts and special occasions.

Meat and fowl appeared among the dishes enjoyed by the wealthy and included beef, goat, mutton, pork (although for some social and religious groups, this was forbidden), goose, and pigeon. Butchery is shown in tomb and temple scenes and was obviously well organized, but meat had to be consumed immediately after slaughter and was a food for feast days rather than part of the daily diet. Animal husbandry provided most of the meat and fowl since by the historic period, hunting had become a sport rather than a means of supplying food, except perhaps occasionally for the royal family or the temples. Fish were caught by many people and provided an important additional element to their diet.

Egypt produced a rich harvest of vegetables and fruit. These included figs, dates, pomegranates, grapes, onions, garlic, leeks, romaine lettuce, radishes, chicory, cucumbers, and melons. Others found in Egypt today (oranges, bananas, lemons, mangoes, peaches, almonds, tomatoes, and sugar cane) were only introduced in the Greco-Roman Period or later times. Popular herbs were coriander, dill, and mint. In harvesting their crops the ancient Egyptians sometimes employed the assistance of animals, such as the tame monkeys who are shown in the tomb scenes climbing the stout branches of the fig trees to help the gardeners gather figs. Milk was provided by farm animals, and in the absence of sugar, honey was used as a sweetener.

Food Preparation

Very little is known of how the food was prepared or cooked, as no Egyptian cookery book has yet been discovered. The contents of the tomb of Kha, a senior workman at Deir el-Medina, were found intact and are now housed in the Turin Museum, Italy. Food placed in his tomb included shredded vegetables, bunches of garlic and onions, bowls of dates, raisins, and persea fruits, and spices including juniper berries and cumin seeds.

Spit-roasting over live embers was the usual method of cooking a goose or fish. They also had stone hearths or metal braziers on which smaller pots were placed; larger pots were propped on two supports over the open fire, and in the late New Kingdom cooks used great metal cooking pots, presumably to prepare dishes where the vegetables, fish, herbs, spices, and occasionally fragments of meat and fowl were mixed together and braised slowly.

PERSONAL APPEARANCE

Hair

The Egyptians were very concerned with their personal appearance, and their hair proved no exception. Evidence of hair care and hairstyles is provided by wigs, inscriptions, tomb scenes, and statuary. As part of their routine to ensure cleanliness, many men and women used copper or bronze razors to shave their heads. The upper and middle classes wore wigs when they went outdoors to provide protection against the sun, and also when they attended social functions. Some were made entirely of real hair and others had hair mixed with vegetable fibers. Sometimes, they were worn even if the owner retained his own hair. According to the medical papyri, there were prescriptions to prevent baldness and to remedy grayness, but these were ineffectual. One ointment made of juniper berries and other berries was recommended as an antidote to

graying hair, and chopped lettuce, placed on a bald patch, was suggested as a cure for hair loss. To augment the natural hair on mummies, false plaits were woven into the real tresses. The dead were also equipped with wigs that were stored in boxes and kept in the tombs for use in the next world.

During the Old Kingdom men and women wore simple, short hairstyles, but there were many variations, and by the New Kingdom both sexes had longer hair, and flowers and ribbons were used as accessories. Priests, however, were required to remove all bodily hair in order to be ritually "pure" when they came into contact with the god's statue and his possessions. Children's heads were also shaved, although the "sidelock of youth" (one strand left at the side of the head) was worn until the age of puberty.

Cosmetics and Perfumes

Cosmetics were used by both sexes, initially to protect the skin against the harshness of Egypt's sunny, dry climate. Recipes have been found for removing spots and wrinkles and for improving the appearance of the skin. Toilet boxes and equipment have survived containing bronze or copper mirrors (highly effective when polished), combs, tweezers, ointment spoons (for pouring oils over the body), and pots and boxes for cosmetics.

Plant products were used for cosmetics and perfumes. The Egyptians were famous for their perfumes. One such perfume, The Egyptian, was made in the city of Mendes and exported to Rome. It had a long shelf life, and one perfumier in Greece kept a supply in his shop for eight years. It was also reputed to last well on the skin. To produce another famous perfumed ointment called Oil of Lilies, a thousand Madonna lilies were used for each batch; a constant supply was grown in special enclosed gardens.

People also wore wax cones, scented with herbs and spices, on their wigs when they attended parties; the cones would melt in the course of the evening and give forth a pleasant odor. Air fragrances were produced, including the famous "Kyphi," which was an oil free and fat free scent based on wine, raisins, and aromatic herbs. The recipe for this temple purifier was found engraved on the temple walls at Edfu and Philae and was repeated later in works of Classical writers. Fumigation pellets were also used to improve or at least mask household and clothing odors, as well as to freshen the breath,

following the daily example of the gods. Unfortunately, the smells of these perfumes and ointments have not survived in the residues found in the tombs because of chemical changes that have occurred in the fatty substances.

The Egyptians were greatly concerned with personal hygiene. Body and facial hair was removed with razors, tweezers, or depilatory creams. It was customary to apply a deodorant by rubbing ground carob into the skin. Facial cleansing creams were used such as the oil and lime mixture found in two jars among the tomb contents belonging to three queens of Tuthmosis III. A recommended antiwrinkle cream consisted of a mixture of frankincense, moringa

Small wooden boxes for storing cosmetics, jewelry, and trinkets. One held powdered hematite and juniper berries (center front) for coloring the face, and a bulbous-ended kohl stick (center front) for outlining the eyes. From Kahun, c.1890 BC.

oil, grass, and fermented fruit juice and was to be applied daily.

The Egyptians used two kinds of eye paint: Malachite (green ore of copper) and galena (dark gray ore of lead) were ground on palettes, mixed with ointment, and applied to the eyes. Eye makeup equipment was found in the earliest burials of the Predynastic Period and was obviously considered an essential accessory for the afterlife. Eye paint was probably originally regarded as a protection against the glare of the sun and the dust. Kohl was kept in small stone jars or in faience, stone, or wooden tubes and applied with a kohl stick (bulbous at one end) to outline the shape of the eye. Red ocher was used both as rouge and, mixed with oil or fat, as a lip gloss. Henna was applied to hair, feet, hands, and nails. From the evidence of the mummies, the feet and hands of the upper classes were carefully pedicured and manicured.

Clothing

The Egyptians generally used linen for their garments and mummy bandages. Wool was also worn but has been found less frequently because it was forbidden to include clothing made from animal products among the tomb goods. Linen was produced in several regions of the ancient world, but the finest quality was found in Egypt. Although it was traditional to wear white linen, dyes such as safflower, madder, and acacia were used to provide yellow, red, and blue cloth. Men are frequently shown with a short kilt that reached the knee; made from fine, stiffened linen, this was generally a luxury item worn only by the wealthiest classes. Women often wore a sheath dress of almost transparent linen, but occasionally model statues of servant girls show them wearing dresses of geometric patterned, multicolored textiles.

In the Old Kingdom the garments worn by men and women are simple, and there is no great variation between the classes, but in the New Kingdom the upper classes are represented in tomb paintings and statuary in elaborate, full-length costumes. These have fine pleating and often incorporate one almost transparent tunic over another garment. The most common footwear was a pair of sandals, made of rush or papyrus, but there were also leather shoes, and an example of a fur-lined boot was discovered at the pyramid workmen's town of Kahun.

Peasants wore simple linen clothes—men working in the fields are shown in loincloths while women were barely clad in simple linen dresses. Children went naked until puberty. Some professions and trades had official robes or distinctive garments associated with their work. By the Greco-Roman Period styles changed and were strongly influenced by Hellenistic and Roman fashion. At first these new styles were only worn by the foreign upper classes, but eventually some Egyptians also adopted them.

Jewelry

From earliest times the Egyptians adorned themselves with jewelry. The gods received clothing and jewelry every day when the priests performed the rituals for the divine statue in the temple sanctuary, and humans also felt the need to protect and decorate themselves with jewelry. It was worn by both the living and the dead and was believed to fulfill a number of functions. Magical charms (amulets) were used to protect the wearer (when alive or after death, on the mummy) against mysterious hostile forces such as wild animals, disease, accidents, and natural disasters. Sometimes, the charm was made in the shape of a limb so that if the owner had suffered an accident or injury to this part of the body, the substitute would attract good spirits who could cure this affliction. The forms of the amulets, representing sacred symbols such scarabs, the Eye of Horus, or the ankh (sign of life), were believed to provide magical protection, but also the materials from which the jewelry was made conveyed their own hidden powers. These materials included metals and gem stones and also shells, seeds, bone, and flowers.

Apart from the most important purpose of protecting the wearer, jewelry was also an indication of status and wealth or represented royal honors given to mark service or valor. Archaeological discoveries of royal jewelry, such as the treasure of the Middle Kingdom queens and princesses at Dahshur and Lahun, the contents of Tutankhamun's tomb at Thebes, and the wealth of objects found at Tanis, indicate the quality of the jeweler's craftmanship; in some instances, it cannot be equaled today. Wealthy Egyptians enjoyed a sophisticated lifestyle that was reflected in the care and effort they devoted to their personal appearance, and even the poorer classes wore simple jewelry to adorn and protect themselves.

ENTERTAINMENT

Children's Toys and Games

There is some difficulty in distinguishing true toys and games (intended to amuse and entertain their owners) from "dolls" or other figurines used for magical or religious purposes. Enough examples survive, however, to show that both children and adults played with and enjoyed a wide variety of toys and games. Young children played with dolls in cradles; animal toys, including crocodiles with movable jaws; puppets, including dancing dwarfs; rattles and tops; and miniature weapons.

Many toys were discovered at the town of Kahun. These ranged from simple clay figurines (human, hippopotamus, crocodile, ape) that the children probably modeled from Nile mud to sophisticated wooden dolls that were painted and had movable limbs. They were found in a room in one of the houses, together with a pile of hair pellets for insertion into holes in the dolls' heads. The excavator identified this as the workshop of a toy maker who was producing dolls on a small commercial scale.

Children also played ball games; tomb scenes show girls throwing balls. Boys fished with sticks, shot at targets, wrestled (a limestone figurine from Kahun shows two boys wrestling), ran, jumped, and performed tightrope walking. Another game depicted in the tombs is similar to leapfrog. At Kahun wooden and leather balls were found, as well as whiptops and tipcats (a game played by hitting the "cat"—usually a wooden peg—into the air with a bat or stick; before landing on the ground, it would be struck again, and the person who drove the cat farthest would be the winner). There was also a woven sling, found with three small stones that were probably thrown together as one shot, to kill birds and small animals.

Adult Sports and Games

Adults enjoyed playing a variety of sports and games. Kings and nobles engaged in target practice, and there are many scenes of hunting birds and animals in the marshes, harpooning fish, or striking duck with throwsticks. The Egyptians

Clay figurines, possibly modeled by children as toys. They include an ape (top left), a pig (top right), an unidentified animal (bottom left), a crocodile (center bottom), and a model boat (bottom right). From Kahun, c.1890 BC.

also hunted in the desert, where wild game and ostriches were favorite pursuits. King Amenhotep II in particular was proud of his sporting and athletic prowess and claimed that he was an excellent athlete, skilled charioteer, powerful archer, and expert horseman and trainer of horses. Many of the pharaohs were probably very physically fit in their early years, since they were expected to lead their troops into battle.

As well as participating in sports, the upper classes also enjoyed watching contests, and tomb scenes depict wrestling and javelin-throwing contests. (Wrestling, used to train army recruits, is shown in tomb scenes at Beni Hasan.)

Board games were popular too. These included serpent, dog-and-jackal, and senet. The latter is mentioned in chapter 17 of the Book of the Dead, where it is described as an occupation

A tomb scene (c.2000 BC) showing girls playing with balls. They display a range of skillful actions, juggling with the balls and performing acrobatic dances.

of the deceased in the next world. In the vignette accompanying this text, a man (often with his wife) is shown seated at a checkerboard, but no opponent is depicted. As early as the Old Kingdom tomb scenes show the owner playing this game, sometimes adjacent to scenes in which he listens to music or watches other kinds of entertainment.

Although senet boards have been discovered (they generally have three rows, each with ten squares of which five might be inscribed with hieroglyphs), the rules of the game are not clear. There were five or seven playing pieces (often conical) for each player, and each player probably tried to be first to reach the square at the angle of the L-shaped arrangement inscribed with the sign meaning "happiness, beauty." The moves were determined by throwing either knucklebones or four casting sticks. The game obviously appealed to all classes: Four boards were found in the tomb of King Tutankhamun, and two were uncovered at Kahun, one of which was painted in on the inside of a wooden box lid.

Dancing

Dancing was an important part of life in ancient Egypt. It had its origins in religious ritual and played a part in temple rites, festivals, and funer-

Children's toys, including wooden balls (top left), a leather ball (top center), wooden whiptops, and tipcats (bottom row). From Kahun, c.1890 BC.

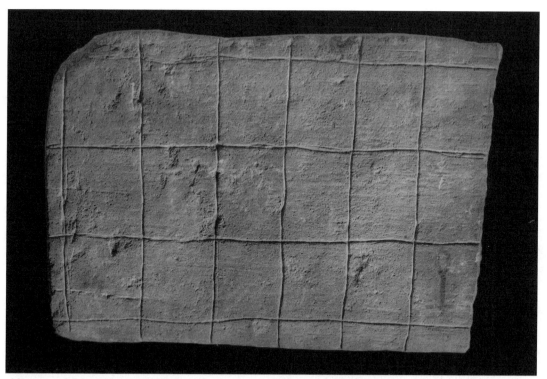

A limestone slab, roughly incised as a board for the game senet. It has three horizontal rows and, when the slab was complete, each row would have contained ten squares. In the top row, the hieroglyph nfr is marked in black, and immediately below it, in the middle row, there is a painted cross. From Kahun, c.1890 BC.

als. The dancers wore special costumes and masks to imitate the gods and followed a prescribed pattern of steps and rhythm. There were also special dances performed by local magicians: In a house at Kahun, ivory clappers, a canvas mask representing the god Bes, and a figurine of a magician/dancer wearing a mask and a false tail were discovered. The magician probably imitated Bes to utilize the god's great magical powers.

As well as the sacred dances there were also secular performances. These are depicted in tomb scenes and show the rhythmic and acrobatic actions of professional dancing girls who could be hired for entertaining guests at banquets and parties.

Music

Musical performances were given by professionals. In the temples priests played instruments to accompany the sacred hymns that were sung by the "chantresses." Musicians were employed to entertain nobles in their homes, and tomb scenes show the owner and his wife listening to performances by blind harpists or sharing a banquet where their guests are entertained by musicians and female dancers. At the burial ceremony, when the guests shared a meal at the tomb with the deceased, a harpist recited special songs that either urged the living to enjoy life to the fullest—because the afterlife was so uncertain—or emphasized the joys of eternal existence.

Musical instruments played by the Egyptians included various kinds of harp, the lute and lyre (both imported from Asia in the Hyksos Period, c.1550 BC), trumpet, flute, double clarinet, and double pipes. These wind instruments were made of wood. To mark the rhythm, drums, tambourines, ivory or wooden clappers, and hand clapping were used, and large bead collars and metal or faience sistra were shaken and rattled. Despite modern studies on methods of playing some of these instruments and on the scales of the flutes and pipes, we have no detailed knowledge of how Egyptian music was played or sounded.

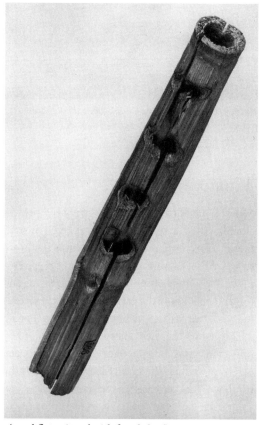

A reed flute pierced with four holes. It is quite rare for such fragile and well-used musical instruments to survive. From Gurob, c.1450 BC.

Songs and Sacred Drama

Songs were intended to honor the gods, entertain the living, and comfort mourners. There were liturgical hymns and chants, sung by choirs in the temples as part of the daily rites or festivals, and also in the sacred temple dramas performed to enact events in the gods' lives and bring their magical potency into effect. In the palaces and houses of the nobles, songs were performed by professionals to entertain the owners and their guests. The love songs of the New Kingdom were also apparently set to music and formed part of a formal entertainment. In the funerary processions and at the tomb, songs were an important part of the mourning process, and special songs were used in the treatment of the sick in the temples. In the fields and at major building sites, people sang their own refrains to ease the burden of their work and to provide a communal rhythm for their physical activities.

MEDICINE

Medical Concepts

Egyptian medicine was a mixture of magical and rational treatments. Both methods were considered equally valid; where the cause of the affliction was visible, objective and scientific treatments were used, and where the cause was hidden (and often attributed to the vengeance of the dead, punishment by the gods, and the ill wishes of enemies), magic was employed. The rational treatments were based on observation of patients and a good knowledge of anatomy (the result of mummification practices). Magic involved the use of spells or incantations accompanied by a ritual in which the practitioner performed acts or gestures over the patient. In the patient's absence, these were imitated on a figurine.)

The sick were always treated well, and no disease was considered untouchable; however, doctors did identify cases as curable, incurable, or of uncertain outcome. There were high standards of ethical behavior, and doctors were forbidden to divulge their patients' confidences or to look at the women in the households they visited. Patients were examined and questioned, and if possible the sickness was diagnosed and treatment was prescribed. If this were not immediately possible, the patient was confined to bed and reexamined later.

Probably because the internal organs were never examined during life but only postmortem as part of the process of mummification, the Egyptians had some erroneous ideas about body systems and functions. A concept that dominated their medicine was the belief that there was a system of conduits (the *metw*) that carried blood, tears, and all bodily fluids around the body. All vessels, ducts, and nerves were metw, and the center of this network was the heart, regarded as the seat of the intellect and emotions. Thus, according to this theory, sorrow felt in the heart would have the physical effect of sending tears to the tear ducts. Obstructions in the metw caused "floods" or "droughts," with their accompanying symptoms, in different parts of the body. The Egyptians' idea of physical functions within the body was probably directly based on their picture of Egypt as a country fed by canals.

Medical Sources

There are several sources for our knowledge of Egyptian medicine, although none provides a complete account: tomb scenes and s showing persons with diseases or aff. stelae (tomb stones) or physicians that pro their titles and give some indication of variou categories and career progression; and surgical instruments (although only from the Greco-Roman Period) and a wall scene in the Temple of Kom Ombo that may represent a panel of surgical instruments. The mummies themselves provide information about a variety of diseases; scientific techniques including radiology, histopathology, immunology, dental studies, and DNA and genetic identifications continue to provide researchers with new knowledge of disease and disease patterns.

One very important source is the ten major medical papyri that have been identified to date. Most date from c.1550 BC onward, but are probably copies of earlier works. They presumably represent only a very small proportion of the medical documents that once existed but are now either lost or awaiting discovery and identification. The papyri seem to include handbooks for surgeons' daily use, outlines for medical lectures, and lecture notes and clinical notebooks that doctors used when they were students and subsequently retained to help them practice their profession.

Each papyrus is not a book with any unity of composition and subject but contains information on a variety of subjects. In most papyri scientific or rational treatments are written alongside magical formulas, although the proportion of each varies from text to text. The inscriptions are usually written in hieratic (although some are in hieroglyphs) and present case studies with details of symptoms and recommended treatments. The papyri reveal the great complexity that existed in the structure of pharaonic medicine. The Edwin Smith Papyrus is famous as the world's first treatise on surgery, while the Kahun Papyrus supplies the earliest known record of gynecological treatments.

Doctors

The earliest medical practitioners were the chieftains of villages who extended their role as local leader to act as priest and magician (healer) for the community. As Egypt became a kingdom, the pharaoh (as supreme chieftain) also acquired power as the country's religious leader who possessed medical wisdom and healing ability. Indeed, the first pharaoh was credited by a later historian with the authorship of a treatise on anatomy and dissection. Medical practice and religion were therefore always closely associated, and the king's powers in both these areas were gradually delegated to the priest-doctors.

Doctors were specialized priests who had originally acted as religious mediators between the god and the patient, but over the centuries, they acquired detailed medical knowledge and experience. Even as early as the Old Kingdom, the medical profession appears to have been highly organized and incorporated rational as well as magical treatment of patients.

Little is known of the medical training and whether it was entirely practical or whether the students had to pass examinations. The temples appear to have played an important part both in medical training and the healing of patients. The "House of Life" was an area of the temple that, as a center of documentation where sacred papyri were written or copied, may also have been used as a teaching center for medical students.

At the highest level, doctors (who often specialized in particular areas of medicine) were called *wabau*, meaning that they were ritually pure and thus able to be in the god's presence. They were priests of the goddess Sekhmet and spent part of each year in the temple; for the rest of the time they practiced medicine in the community. There were also *swnw* who were general practitioners employed by the state and ap-pointed to the building sites, the army, burial grounds, or royal palaces. In addition, there were the *sau* who specialized in the use of magic and probably filled an important role in local communities. Nurses, masseurs, and bandagers assisted the doctors, and there were specialist midwives who were trained in the temple of Sais.

One doctor of paramount importance in Egypt was Imhotep, the vizier of King Djoser. The historian Manetho credits him with the invention of building in stone, and he was the architect of the Step Pyramid at Saqqara (the world's first monumental stone building). However, the Egyptians revered him as a great physician and the founder of medical science. In the Late Period he was worshiped as a god of healing and medicine, and the Greeks in Egypt later identified him with Asklepios, their own god of medicine. Buildings within various temples were dedicated to him, and there is a chapel built in his honor on the island of Philae.

Temples as Centers of Healing

Some temples had a special reputation for healing the sick. Cripples from all over Egypt visited Imhotep's chapel at Saqqara (the Asklepieion) in search of a cure, and the upper terrace of the Temple of Deir el-Bahri became a resort for invalids in the Greco-Roman Period. From the graffiti left there on the walls, it is evident that foreigners as well as Egyptians sought help.

Although such healing centers are best known from the Greek tradition, it is evident that temples in Egypt had been used for healing since much earlier times. Those at Sais and Heliopolis were famous in the Middle Kingdom (c.1900 BC), and a document relates that the Persian king Darius reorganized the medical school at Sais during the Persian occupation of Egypt. There was probably always a healing role and tradition associated with temples in Egypt.

One particularly interesting building has been discovered and excavated in the precincts of the Temple of Hathor at Denderah. This has been identified as a "sanatorium" or "hotel" where the mentally ill were accommodated and underwent preparation for the "Therapeutic Dream." The building was arranged around a corridor and central area; the corridor was lined with healing statues, and there were sanitary installations with a drainage system so that the sacred water that had passed over the statues was directed into a series of cubicles where the sick were bathed. Hathor (Isis) was the goddess attributed with the invention of most healing remedies.

At Denderah the sanatorium was of a late date, but there is evidence for the Therapeutic Dream (incubation) method in Egypt from at least the Middle Kingdom. Using isolation, silence, and lamps, the patient spent one or more nights at the center in a state of deep sleep when, it was believed, he could enter Nun, the dwelling of the dead. Here, the soul could act and travel and attempt to contact the gods, thus gaining knowledge of the future and of any dangers or evil spells that threatened him as well as achieving a cure for his ailments. During this sleep, Isis appeared to the patient, held him, and treated him for his illness. Because she herself had attained immortality, she could help humans and restore their health even when cure by rational means had failed.

Texts in papyri indicate that songs played an important part in the healing process, particularly in driving out mental illness. The earliest reference to the value of such songs occurs in the First Intermediate Period (c.2200 BC). Sometimes, the goddess gave direct healing to the patient through song, but in other instances this was achieved through the wise interpretation of the priests who prescribed treatment for the patient. The center for incubation was always close to the temple, either in a separate building or perhaps in a special chamber of the temple. It was essential to have a plain dark room in order to obtain this sleep, which was assisted by burning four pieces of sweet-smelling wood.

Gods of Healing

There was no one god of medicine or healing. Imhotep, the human founder of medical science, was deified and worshiped in the later periods. The lioness goddess Sekhmet, believed to be the destroyer and bringer of epidemics, was worshiped to placate her wrath, and the most senior doctors held priesthoods of Sekhmet. Her consort, Seth, was also regarded as a source of sickness and epidemics and received prayers. Thoth, patron god of scribes, was credited with the invention of the healing formulas, and Isis/Hathor was the patroness of magicians and regarded as the inventor of many healing treatments. Some deities played special roles: Horus and Amun were in charge of cures for eye diseases, and Tauert (the hippopotamus goddess) controlled all aspects of fecundity and childbirth.

Medical Treatment

The Egyptians used surgical and pharmaceutical procedures. Surgery was mainly employed for the superficial treatment of wounds, dislocations and fractures, and the excision of some tumors. There is also evidence, however, that they practiced trepanning and male circumcision. Anesthetics were available in the form of drugs derived from plants. One area of medicine that attracted particular attention was gynecology. In the medical papyri many entries are devoted to fertility and pregnancy tests, contraceptive measures, the treatment of women's ailments, and problems associated with childbirth.

As far as we are aware there were no specialized dentists, and there is no conclusive evidence of cosmetic dentistry. Although there are relatively few examples of caries (tooth decay) in the mummies of the Pharaonic Period, virtually everyone suffered from attrition (wear of the cusps) due to the gritty composition of the bread.

Pharmaceutical treatments included medicines to be taken orally or by fumigation and ointments to be applied externally. These incorporated substances from mineral, animal, and vegetable sources: Pulverized precious metals or stones and aromatic oils were included to attract good deities to the patient, thus improving his condition, whereas unpleasant or disagreeable ingredients (fat and blood of various animals, as well as their horns, hides, hooves, and bones, or excrement and urine) were thought to expel evil spirits from the sick person. Unpleasant medicines were taken in water, wine, milk, or beer or were disguised with honey. For the treatment of some ailments, including the common cold, magical spells were used.

Contribution to Medical History

The Egyptians made the first strides in developing medical science. They were the first to make observations in human and animal anatomy; conduct experiments in surgery and pharmacy; use splints, bandages, and compresses; and devise medical and anatomical terms. Because mummification familiarized them with the concept of autopsying the human body, there were no religious or popular objections to the process. In the later times Greeks came to Alexandria to practice systematic dissection, which was forbidden in their own country. Despite its many advances, however, Egyptian medicine retained the use of magical formulas alongside rational, scientific treatments, and some remedies were valueless.

Most concepts of medicine in Europe and the Near East owe their origin to ancient Egypt. This knowledge was passed down through medical practice and through literature from the Greek sources into medieval texts in Europe and through Arabic literature.

READING

The Family

David 1996: general account of the pyramid workmen's town of Kahun, with descriptions of legal practices; Bierbrier 1982: general account of the lives of the royal workmen at Deir el-Medina, including family law; Černý 1973: description of the lives and conditions of the workforce and their families at Deir el-Medina.

The Home

Tooley 1995: introductory book about tomb models, including houses; Winlock 1955: description of tomb models from the famous tomb of Meket-Re; Manniche 1989: the use of herbs and plants, with some reference to domestic applications.

Food and Drink

Manniche 1989: op. cit; Erman 1971: general description of civilization, including growing and production of food.

Personal Appearance

Manniche 1989: op. cit; Aldred 1971: description of uses and development of jewelry.

Entertainment

David 1996: description of toys and games found at Kahun; Erman 1971: includes description of forms of entertainment.

Medicine

Reeves 1992: introduction to Egyptian medicine; Brothwell and Chiarelli 1973: contributions by various authors to study of Egyptian population; David 1986: papers on aspects of disease found in mummies; Nunn 1996: general account of Egyptian medicine.

CHRONOLOGICAL TABLE

Predynastic Period (c.5000–3100 BC)

Unification of Egypt
(c.3100 BC)

Archaic Period

Dynasty 1 (c.3100–2890 BC)
Dynasty 2 (c.2890–2686)

Old Kingdom

Dynasty 3 (c.2686–2613 BC)
Dynasty 4 (c.2613–2494)
Dynasty 5 (c.2494–2345)
Dynasty 6 (c.2345– 2181)

First Intermediate Period

Dynasty 7 (c.2181–2173 BC)
Dynasty 8 (c.2173–2160)
Dynasty 9 (c.2160–2130)
Dynasty 10 (c.2130–2040)
Dynasty 11 (c.2133–1991)

Middle Kingdom

Dynasty 12 (1991–1786 BC)

Second Intermediate Period

Dynasty 13 (1786–1633 BC)
Dynasty 14 (1786–c.1603)
Dynasty 15 (1674–1567)
Dynasty 16 (c.1684–1567)
Dynasty 17 (c.1650–1567)

New Kingdom

Dynasty 18 (1567–1320 BC)
Dynasty 19 (1320–1200)
Dynasty 20 (1200–1085)

Third Intermediate Period

Dynasty 21 (c.1089–945 BC)
Dynasty 22 (945–730)
Dynasty 23 (c.818–793)
Dynasty 24 (c.727–715)
Dynasty 25 (c.780–656)
Dynasty 26 (664–525)

Late Period

Dynasty 27 (525–404 BC)
Dynasty 28 (404–399)
Dynasty 29 (399–380)
Dynasty 30 (380–343)

Dynasty 31 (343–332)

Conquest of Egypt by Alexander the Great (332 BC)

(Alexander ruled until his death in 323 BC)

Ptolemaic Period (323–30 BC)

Conquest of Egypt by Octavian (Augustus) (30 BC)

Roman Period (30 BC–c. AD 600)

Arab Conquest of Egypt (seventh century AD)

LIST OF MUSEUMS WITH EGYPTIAN COLLECTIONS

Australia

Melbourne: National Gallery of Victoria
Sydney: Australian Museum; Nicholson Museum of Antiquities

Austria

Vienna: Kunsthistorisches Museum

Belgium

Antwerp: Museum Vleeshuis
Brussels: Musées Royaux d'Art et d'Histoire
Liège: Musée Curtius
Mariemont: Musée de Mariemont

Brazil

Rio de Janeiro: Museu Nacional

Canada

Montreal: McGill University, Ethnological Museum; Museum of Fine Arts
Toronto: Royal Ontario Museum

Commonwealth of Independent States (formerly USSR)

Moscow: State Pushkin Museum of Fine Arts
St. Petersburg: The Hermitage Museum

Croatia

Zagreb: Archeoloski Muzej

Cuba

Havana: Museo Nacional

Czech Republic

Prague: Náprstkovo Museum

Denmark

Copenhagen: Nationalmuseet; Ny Carlsberg Museum; Thorwaldsen Museum

Egypt

Alexandria: Greco-Roman Museum
Aswan: Aswan Museum
Cairo: The Egyptian Museum

Luxor: The Luxor Museum of Ancient Egyptian Art
Mallawi: Mallawi Museum
Minya: Minya Museum

France

Avignon: Musée Calvet
Grenoble: Musée de Peinture et de Sculpture
Limoges: Musée Municipal
Lyons: Musée des Beaux-Arts; Musée Guimet
Marseilles: Musée d'Archéologie Méditerranéenne
Nantes: Musée des Arts Decoratifs
Orléans: Musée Historique et d'Archéologie de L'Orléanais
Paris: Bibliothèque Nationale; Louvre; Musée du Petit Palais; Musée Rodin
Strasbourg: Institut d'Égyptologie
Toulouse: Musée Georges Labit

Germany

Berlin: Staatliche Museen, Ägyptisches Museum; Staatliche Museen Preussischer Kulturbesitz, Ägyptisches Museum; Staatliche Museen, Papyrussammlung
Dresden: Albertinum
Essen: Folkwang Museum
Frankfurt-am-Main: Liebieghaus
Hamburg: Museum für Kunst und Gewerbe Museum für Völkerkunde
Hanover: Kestner-Museum
Heidelberg: Ägyptologisches Institut der Universität
Hildesheim: Roemer-Pelizaeus-Museum
Karlsruhe: Badisches Landesmuseum
Leipzig: Ägyptisches Museum
Munich: Staatliche Sammlung Ägyptischer Kunst
Tubingen: Ägyptologisches Institut der Universität

Würzburg: Martin von Wagner Museum der Universität

Greece
Athens: National Museum

Hungary
Budapest: Szépmüvészeti Múzeum

Ireland
Dublin: National Museum of Ireland

Israel
Jerusalem: The Israel Museum; Bible Lands Museum

Italy

Bologna: Museo Civico
Florence: Museo Egizio
Mantua: Museo del Palazzo Ducale
Milan: Museo Archeologico
Naples: Museo Nazionale
Parma: Museo Nazionale di Antichità
Palermo: Museo Nazionale
Rome: Museo Barracco; Museo Capitolino; Museo Nazionale Romano della Terme Diocleziane
Rovigo: Museo dell'Accademia dei Concordi
Trieste: Civico Museo di Storia ed Arte
Turin: Museo Egizio
Vatican City: Museo Gregoriano Egizio
Venice: Museo Archeologico del Palazzo Reale di Venezia

Japan
Kyoto: University Archaeological Museum

Mexico
Mexico City: Museo Nacional de Antropología

Netherlands

Amsterdam: Allard Pierson Museum
Leiden: Rijksmuseum van Oudheden
Otterlo: Rijksmuseum Kröller-Müller

Norway

Oslo: Universitetet i Oslo Etnografisk Museum

Poland

Krakow: Muzeum Narodowe; Muzeum Archeologiczne
Poznan: Muzeum Archeologiczne
Warsaw: Muzeum Narodowe; Parístwowe Muzeum Archeologiczne

Portugal

Lisbon: Fundaço Calouste Gulbenkian

Spain

Barcelona: Museu Arqueológic de Barcelona
Madrid: Museo Arqueológico Nacional

Sudan

Khartoum: National Museum

Sweden

Linköping: Östergöttlands Museum
Lund: Kulturhistoriska Museet
Stockholm: Medelhausmuseet
Uppsala: Victoriamuseum

Switzerland

Basel: Museum für Völkerkunde
Geneva: Musée d'Art et d'Histoire
Lausanne: Musée Cantonal d'Archéologie et d'Histoire; Musée Cantonal des Beaux-Arts
Neuchâtel: Musée d'Ethnographie
Riggisberg: Abegg-Stiftung

United Kingdom

Bristol: City Museum
Birmingham: City Museum and Art Gallery
Cambridge: Fitzwilliam Museum
Dundee: Museum and Art Gallery
Durham: Gulbenkian Museum of Oriental Art and Archaeology
Edinburgh: Royal Scottish Museum
Glasgow: Art Gallery and Museum; Burrell Collection; Hunterian Museum
Leicester: Museums and Art Gallery
Liverpool: National Museums and Galleries on Merseyside; School of Archaeology and Oriental Studies, University of Liverpool
London: British Museum; Horniman Museum; Petrie Museum, University College London; Victoria and Albert Museum
Manchester: University Museum
Norwich: Castle Museum
Oxford: Ashmolean Museum; Pitt Rivers Museum
Swansea: Wellcome Museum of Egyptian and Graeco-Roman Antiquities

United States

Baltimore (MD): Walters Art Gallery
Berkeley (CA): Robert H. Lowie Museum of Anthropology
Boston (MA): Museum of Fine Arts
Cambridge (MA): Fogg Art Museum, Harvard University; Semitic Museum, Harvard University
Chicago (IL): Field Museum of Natural History; Oriental Institute Museum
Cincinnati (OH): Art Museum
Cleveland (OH): Museum of Art
Denver (CO): Art Museum
Detroit (MI): Detroit Institute of Arts
Kansas City (MO): William Rockhill Nelson Gallery of Art
Los Angeles (CA): County Museum of Art

Minneapolis (MN): Institute of Arts Museum

New Haven (CT): Yale University Art Gallery

New York (NY): Brooklyn Museum; Metropolitan Museum of Art

Palo Alto (CA): Stanford University Museum

Philadelphia (PA): University of Pennsylvania Museum

Pittsburgh (PA): Museum of Art, Carnegie Institute

Princeton (NJ): University Art Museum

Providence (RI): Rhode Island School of Design

Richmond (VA): Virginia Museum of Fine Arts

St. Louis (MO): Art Museum

San Diego (CA): Museum of Man

San Francisco (CA): M. H. De Young Memorial Museum

San Jose (CA): Rosicrucian Museum

Seattle (WA): Art Museum

Toledo (OH): Museum of Art

Washington, DC: Smithsonian Institution

Worcester (MA): Art Museum

BIBLIOGRAPHY

Whenever possible, details of the latest revised edition are given.

Adams, B. *Ancient Hierakonpolis*. Warminster, England: Aris and Phillips, 1974.

Adams, W. Y. *Nubia: Corridor to Africa*. London: Allen Lane, 1977.

Africa, T. W. "Herodotus and Diodorus in Egypt." *Journal of Near Eastern Studies* 22 (1963): 254–58.

Aldred, C. *Akhenaten: King of Egypt*. London: Thames and Hudson, 1988.

———. *Art in Ancient Egypt: Old Kingdom*. London: Alec Tiranti Ltd., 1968.

———. *Jewels of the Pharaohs*. London: Thames and Hudson, 1971.

Allen, T. G. *The Egyptian Book of the Dead. Documents in the Oriental Institute Museum at the University of Chicago*. Chicago: Univ. of Chicago Press, 1935–61.

Andrews, C. *The Rosetta Stone*. London: British Museum Publications, 1981.

Austin, M. M. *The Hellenistic World from Alexander to the Roman Conquest*. Cambridge: Cambridge Univ. Press, 1981.

Badawy, A. "The Ideology of the Superstructure of the Mastaba Tomb in Egypt." *Journal of Near Eastern Studies* 15 (1956), 180–83.

———. "The Periodic System of Building a Pyramid." *Journal of Egyptian Archaeology* 63 (1977), 52–58.

Baines, J., and J. Málek. *Atlas of Ancient Egypt*. New York: Facts On File, 1980.

Bagnall, R. S. *Egypt in Late Antiquity*. Princeton, N.J.: Princeton Univ. Press, 1993.

Baker, H. S. *Furniture in the Ancient World*. New York: 1966.

Baumgartel, E. J. *The Cultures of Prehistoric Egypt*. Oxford: Oxford Univ. Press, 1955.

Bell, H. I. *Cults and Creeds in Graeco-Roman Egypt*. Liverpool: University Press, 1953.

———. *Egypt from Alexander the Great to the Arab Conquest*. Oxford: Oxford Univ. Press, 1956.

Bender, B. *Farming in Prehistory*. London: John Baker, 1975.

Bevan, E. *A History of Egypt under the Ptolemaic Dynasty*. London: Methuen, 1927.

Bierbrier, M. *The Tomb-Builders of the Pharaohs*. London: British Museum Press, 1982.

Blackman, A. M. "Libations to the Dead in Modern Nubia and Ancient Egypt." *Journal of Egyptian Archaeology* 3 (1916), 31–34.

———. *Middle Egyptian Stories*. Brussels: Bibliotheca Aegyptiaca, 1932.

———. "Myth and Ritual in Ancient Egypt." In *Myth and Ritual*, edited by S. H. Hooke. Oxford: Oxford Univ. Press, 1953.

———. "Oracles in Ancient Egypt." *Journal of Egyptian Archaeology* 11 (1925), 249–55, and 12 (1926), 176–85.

Bowersock, G. W. *Augustus and the Greek World*. Oxford: Oxford Univ. Press, 1965.

Bowman, A. K. *Egypt after the Pharaohs, 332 BC–AD 642*. London: British Museum Publications, 1986.

Breasted, J. H. *Ancient Records of Egypt*. 5 vols. Chicago: Univ. of Chicago Press, 1906–7.

———. *The Battle of Kadesh*. Chicago: Chicago Oriental Institute, 1903.

Brothwell, D., and B. A. Chiarelli, eds. *Population Biology of the Ancient Egyptians*. London: Academic Press, 1973.

Buck, A. de "The Judicial Papyrus of Turin." *Journal of Egyptian Archaeology* 23 (1937), 152–57.

Buck, A. de, and A. H. Gardiner, eds. *The Egyptian Coffin Texts*. 7 vols. Chicago: Univ. of Chicago Press, 1935–61.

Budge, E. A. *Osiris and the Egyptian Resurrection*. 2 vols. London: Medici Society, 1911.

Butzer, K. W. *Early Hydraulic Civilization in Egypt: A Study in Cultural Ecology*. Chicago: Univ. of Chicago Press, 1976.

Cambridge Ancient History. Cambridge: Cambridge Univ. Press, 1962–present.

Carter, H. *The Tomb of Tut-Ankh-Amen*. 3 vols. 1923–33. Reprint, London: Sphere Books Ltd., 1972.

Černý, J. *Ancient Egyptian Religion*. London: Routledge, 1952.

———. *A Community of Workmen at Thebes in the Ramesside Period*. Cairo: Institut Français d'Archéologie Orientale du Caire, 1973.

Clarke, S. "Ancient Egyptian Frontier Fortresses." *Journal of Egyptian Archaeology* 3 (1916), 155–79.

Clarke, S., and R. Engelbach. *Ancient Egyptian Masonry: The Building Craft*. London: Oxford Univ. Press, 1930.

Clayton, P. A. *The Rediscovery of Ancient Egypt: Artists and Travelers in the 19th Century*. London: Thames and Hudson, 1982.

Cockburn, A., and E. Cockburn, eds. *Mummies, Disease, and Ancient Cultures*. Cambridge: Cambridge Univ. Press, 1980.

Crowfoot, G. M. *Methods of Handspinning in Egypt and the Sudan*. Bankfield Museum, 2nd series, 12. Halifax, 1931.

David, A. R. *Discovering Ancient Egypt*. New York: Facts On File, 1994.

———. *A Guide to Religious Ritual at Abydos*. Warminster, England: Aris and Phillips, 1981.

———. *The Pyramid Builders of Ancient Egypt*. London: Routledge, 1997.

David, A. R., and E. Tapp. *The Mummy's Tale*. London: Michael O'Mara Books Ltd., 1992.

David, R. *Science in Egyptology*. Manchester, England: Manchester Univ. Press, 1986.

David, R., and A. E. David. *A Biographical Dictionary of Ancient Egypt*. London: Seaby, 1992.

Davies, N. de G. *The Mastaba of Ptah-hetep and Akhet-hetep at Saqqara*. 2 vols. London: Egypt Exploration Fund, 1900–1.

———. *The Rock Tombs of El Amarna*. 6 parts. Egypt Exploration Society, Archaeological Survey, 13–18. London, 1903–8.

Davies, Nina, and N. de G. Davies. *The Theban Tomb Series*. London: Egypt Exploration Society, 1915–33.

Derry, D. E. "The Dynastic Race in Egypt." *Journal of Egyptian Archaeology* 42 (1956), 80–85.

Diodorus Siculus. *Diodorus of Sicily*. 12 vols., bk. 1. Translated by Russel M. Geer. London: Loeb Classical Library, 1954.

Drescher, J. *Apa Mena. A Selection of Coptic Texts Relating to St. Menas*. Cairo: Soc. d'Archéologie Copte, 1946.

Drioton, E., and J. P. Lauer. *Sakkarah, The Monuments of Zoser*. Cairo: French Institute of Oriental Archaeology, 1939.

Dunham, D. *The Royal Cemeteries of Kush*. 2 vols. Boston: Museum of Fine Arts, 1950–55.

Edgerton, W. F. "The Government and the Governed in the Egyptian Empire." *Journal of Near Eastern Studies* 6 (1947), 152–57.

———. "The Strikes in Ramesses III's Twenty-ninth Year." *Journal of Near Eastern Studies* 10 (1951), 137–45.

———. *The Thutmosid Succession*. Chicago: Chicago Oriental Institute, 1933.

Edgerton, W., and J. A. Wilson. *Historical Records of Ramesses III*. Chicago: Chicago Oriental Institute, 1936.

Edwards, I. E. S. *The Pyramids of Egypt*. Harmondsworth, England: Penguin Books, 1985.

Emery, W. B. *Archaic Egypt*. Harmondsworth, England: Penguin Books, 1961.

———. *Egypt in Nubia*. London: Hutchinson, 1965.

———. *Great Tombs of the First Dynasty*. 2 vols. Cairo: Government Press, 1949. London: Egypt Exploration Society, 1954.

Engelbach, R. M. *The Hyksos Reconsidered*. Chicago: Univ. of Chicago Press, 1939.

The Epigraphic Survey, University of Chicago, Medinet Habu. 8 vols. Chicago: Univ. of Chicago Press, 1930–70.

The Epigraphic Survey, University of Chicago, Reliefs and Inscriptions at Karnak. 2 vols. Chicago: Univ. of Chicago Press, 1936.

Erman, A. *Life in Ancient Egypt*. Translated by H. M. Tirard, with introduction by J. Manchip White. New York: Dover Publications, 1971.

———. *The Literature of the Ancient Egyptians*. Translated by A. M. Blackman. 1927. Reprint, *The Ancient Egyptians: A Sourcebook of Their Writings*, with introduction by W. K. Simpson, New York: Harper Torchbooks, 1966.

Fagan, B. M. *The Rape of the Nile. Tomb Robbers, Tourists and Archaeologists in Egypt*. London: Macdonald and Jane's, 1975.

Fairman, H. W. "The Consecration of an Egyptian Temple According to the Use of Edfu." *Journal of Egyptian Archaeology* 32 (1945), 75–91.

———. "The Kingship Rituals of Egypt." In *Myth, Ritual and Kingship*, edited by S. H. Hooke. Oxford: Oxford Univ. Press, 1958.

———. "Town Planning in Pharaonic Egypt." *Town Planning Review* (Liverpool) 20 (April 1949), 33–51.

Faulkner, R. O. *The Ancient Egyptian Coffin Texts*. 3 vols. Warminster, England: Aris and Phillips, 1973–78.

———. *The Ancient Egyptian Pyramid Texts*. 2 vols. Oxford: Oxford Univ. Press, 1969.

———. *A Concise Dictionary of Middle Egyptian*. Oxford: Oxford Univ. Press, 1964.

———. "Egyptian Military Organisation." *Journal of Egyptian Archaeology* 39 (1953), 32–47.

———. "Egyptian Military Standards." *Journal of Egyptian Archaeology* 27 (1941), 12–18.

———. "Egyptian Seagoing Ships." *Journal of Egyptian Archaeology* 26 (1940), 3–9.

———. "The Wars of Sethos I." *Journal of Egyptian Archaeology* 33 (1947), 34–39.

Forbes, R. J. *Studies in Ancient Technology*. 6 vols. Leiden, Netherlands: Brill, 1956–66.

Frankfort, H. *Ancient Egyptian Religion*. New York: Columbia Univ. Press, 1961.

Fraser, P. M. *Ptolemaic Alexandria*. Oxford: Oxford Univ. Press, 1972.

Gardiner, A. H. "An Ancient List of the Fortresses of Nubia." *Journal of Egyptian Archaeology* 3 (1916), 184–92.

———. "The Baptism of Pharaoh." *Journal of Egyptian Archaeology* 36 (1950), 3–12.

———. *Egyptian Grammar*. 3rd ed. Oxford: Oxford Univ. Press, 1966.

———. "The Egyptian Origin of the Semitic Alphabet." *Journal of Egyptian Archaeology* 3 (1916), 1–16.

———. *Egypt of the Pharaohs*. Oxford: Oxford Univ. Press, 1961.

———. *Hieratic Papyri in the British Museum, 3rd Series: Chester Beatty Gift*. 2 vols. London: British Museum Publications, 1935.

———. *The Kadesh Inscriptions of Ramesses II*. Oxford: Griffith Institute, 1960.

———. *The Library of A. Chester Beatty: Description of Hieratic Papyrus with a Mythological Story, Love-songs and Other Miscellaneous Texts. The Chester Beatty Papyri, No. 1*. London: Emery Walker Ltd., 1931.

Glanville, S. R. K., ed. *Catalogue of Egyptian Antiquities in the British Museum, Volume 2: Wooden Boat Models*. London: British Museum Press, 1972.

Goedicke, H. "Was Magic Used in the Harem Conspiracy against Ramesses III?" *Journal of Egyptian Archaeology* 49 (1963), 71–92.

Griffiths, J. G. *The Origins of Osiris*. Berlin: Hessling, 1966.

———. *Plutarch, De Iside et Osiride*. Cardiff: Univ. of Wales Press, 1970.

Gunn, B. "Religion of the Poor in Ancient Egypt." *Journal of Egyptian Archaeology* 3 (1916), 81–94.

Hall, R. *Egyptian Textiles*. Princes Risborough, England: Shire Egyptology, 1990.

Harris, J. E., and E. F. Wente, eds. *An X-ray Atlas of the Royal Mummies*. Chicago: Univ. of Chicago Press, 1980.

Hayes, W. C. "Most Ancient Egypt." *Journal of Near Eastern Studies* 23 (1964), 74–273.

Hepper, F. N. *Pharaoh's Flowers. The Botanical Treasures of Tutankhamun*. London: HMSO, 1990.

Herodotus. *The Histories*. Bk. 2. Translated by Aubrey de Sélincourt. Harmondsworth, England: Penguin Books, 1961.

Hodges, H. *Technology in the Ancient World*. Harmondsworth, England: Pelican Books, 1970.

Hooker, J. T., ed. *Reading the Past: Ancient Writing from Cuneiform to the Alphabet*. London: British Museum Publications, 1990.

Hurry, J. B. *Imhotep*. Oxford: Oxford Univ. Press, 1926.

Ions, V. *Egyptian Mythology*. London: Hamlyn, 1968.

Iverson, E. *Canon and Proportions in Egyptian Art*. Warminster, England: Aris and Phillips, 1975.

Jacq, P. *Egyptian Magic*. Warminster, England: Aris and Phillips, 1985.

Jones, A. H. M. *The Later Roman Empire, 284–602*. Oxford: Oxford Univ. Press, 1964.

Jones, D. *Model Boats from the Tomb of Tutankhamun*. Griffith Institute, Tutankhamun's Tomb series, 9. Oxford, 1990.

Kantor, H. "The Early Relations of Egypt with Asia." *Journal of Near Eastern Studies* 1 (1942), 174–85.

———. "Further Evidence for Early Mesopotamian Relations with Egypt." *Journal of Near Eastern Studies* 11 (1952), 239–51.

Kees, H. *Ancient Egypt: A Cultural Topography*. Edited by T. G. H. James, translated by I. F.

D. Morrow. Chicago: Univ. of Chicago Press, 1961.

Kemp, B. J. "Abydos and the Royal Tombs of the First Dynasty." *Journal of Egyptian Archaeology* 52 (1966), 13–22.

———. "The Early Development of Towns in Egypt." *Antiquity* 51 (1977), 185–200.

———. "Preliminary Reports on the El-Amarna Survey, 1977 and 1979." *Journal of Egyptian Archaeology* 64 (1978), 22–34, and 66 (1980), 5–16.

———. "The 'Window of Appearance' at El-Amarna, and the Basic Structure of this City." *Journal of Egyptian Archaeology* 62 (1976), 81–99.

Khs-Burmester, O. H. E. *The Egyptian and Coptic Church. A Detailed Description of Her Liturgical Services.* Cairo: Soc. d'Archéologie Copte, 1967.

Kitchen, K. A. *Pharaoh Triumphant: The Life and Times of Ramesses II.* Warminster, England: Aris and Phillips, 1981.

———. *Ramesside Inscriptions: Historical and Biographical.* 8 vols. Oxford: Blackwell, 1975–90.

———. "Some New Light on the Asiatic Wars of Ramesses II." *Journal of Egyptian Archaeology* 50 (1964), 47–70.

———. *Suppiluliumas and the Amarna Pharaohs.* Liverpool: Univ. of Liverpool Press, 1962.

———. *The Third Intermediate Period in Egypt (1100–650 BC).* Warminster, England: Aris and Phillips, 1973.

Landström, B. *Ships of the Pharaohs, 4000 Years of Egyptian Ship-building.* London: Allen Lane, 1970.

Langdon, S., and A. H. Gardiner. "The Treaty of Alliance between Hattusili, King of the Hittites, and Pharaoh Ramesses II of Egypt." *Journal of Egyptian Archaeology* 6 (1920), 179–205.

Lange, K., and M. Hirmer. *Egypt: Architecture, Sculpture and Painting in 3,000 Years.* London: Phaidon, 1956.

Lauer, J.-P. *Saqqara. The Royal Cemetery of Memphis. Excavations and Discoveries since 1850.* London: Thames and Hudson, 1976.

Lichtheim, M. *Ancient Egyptian Literature.* 3 vols. Berkeley: Univ. of California Press, 1973, 1976, and 1980.

Littauer, M. A. and J. H. Crouwel. *Chariots and Related Equipment from the Tomb of Tutankhamun.* Oxford: Griffith Institute, 1985.

———. *Wheeled Vehicles and Ridden Animals in the Ancient Near East.* Leiden, Netherlands: Brill, 1979.

Lucas, A., and J. R. Harris. *Ancient Egyptian Materials and Industries.* London: Arnold, Ltd., 1962.

Manniche, L. *An Ancient Egyptian Herbal.* Austin: Univ. of Texas Press, 1989.

Martin, G. T. "Excavation Reports on the Tomb of Horemheb at Saqqara." *Journal of Egyptian Archaeology* 62 (1976), 5–13; 63 (1977), 13–19; 64 (1978), 5–9; 65 (1979), 13–18.

———. *The Royal Tomb at El-Amarna.* 2 vols. London: Egypt Exploration Society, 1974 and 1989.

Mendelssohn, K. "A Building Disaster at the Meidum Pyramid." *Journal of Egyptian Archaeology* 59 (1973), 60–71.

Mercer, S. A. B. *Horus, Royal God of Egypt.* Grafton, Mass.: Society of Oriental Research, 1962.

———. *The Pyramid Texts in Translation and Commentary.* New York, London, Toronto: Luzac, 1952; *Literary Criticism of the Pyramid Texts.* London: Luzac, 1956.

———. *The Tell el-Amarna Tablets.* 2 vols. Toronto: Luzac, 1939.

Millard, A. R. "The Infancy of the Alphabet." *World Archaeology* 17, no. 3 (1986), 390–98.

Montet, P. *Eternal Egypt*. London: Weidenfeld and Nicolson, 1965.

———. *La necropole royale de Tanis*. 3 vols. Paris: 1947–69.

Morenz, S. *Egyptian Religion*. Translated by A. Keep. London: Methuen, 1973.

Murray, M. A. "Nawruz or the Coptic New Year." *Ancient Egypt* 3 (1921), 79–81.

Nelson, H. H. *The Battle of Megiddo*. Chicago: Univ. of Chicago Press, 1913.

Neugebauer, O. "On the Orientation of Pyramids." *Centaurus* 24 (1980), 1–3.

Nour, M. Z., et al. *The Cheops Boat*. Vol. 1. Cairo: General Organisation for Government Press Offices, 1960.

Nunn, J. *Ancient Egyptian Medicine*. London: British Museum Press, 1996.

Otto, E. *Egyptian Art and the Cults of Amun and Osiris*. London: Thames and Hudson, 1966.

Pagels, E. *The Gnostic Gospels*. London: Weidenfeld and Nicolson, 1982.

Peet, T. E. "Fresh Light on the Tomb Robberies of the 20th Dynasty at Thebes." *Journal of Egyptian Archaeology* 11 (1925), 162–64.

———. "Mathematics in Ancient Egypt." *Bulletin of John Rylands Library, Manchester* 15 (1931), 409–41.

———. *The Rhind Mathematical Papyrus*. Liverpool: University Press, 1923.

Perry, W. J. "The Cult of the Sun and the Cult of the Dead." *Journal of Egyptian Archaeology* 11 (1925), 191–200.

Petrie, W. M. F. *Ancient Weights and Measures*. London: British School of Archaeology in Egypt Publications, 1926.

———. *Funeral Furniture and Stone Vessels*. Warminster, England: Aris and Phillips, 1977.

———. *Illahun, Kahun and Gurob*. London: D. Nutt, 1891.

———. *Kahun, Gurob and Hawara*. London: Kegan Paul, Trench, 1890.

———. *Objects of Daily Use*. London: British School of Archaeology in Egypt Publications, 1927.

———. *Royal Tombs of the Earliest Dynasties*. 2 vols. London: Egypt Exploration Fund, 1900–1.

———. *The Royal Tombs of the First Dynasty*. London: Egypt Exploration Fund, 1900.

———. *Tools and Weapons*. London: Egyptian Research Account, 1917.

Pinch, G. *Magic in Ancient Egypt*. London: British Museum Press, 1994.

Posener, G. *La première domination Perse en Egypte*. Cairo: Impr. de l'Institut Français d'Archéologie Orientale, 1936.

Pritchard, J. B., ed. *Ancient Near Eastern Texts Relating to the Old Testament*. Princeton, N.J.: Princeton Univ. Press, 1969.

Quibell, J. E., and F. W. Green. *Hierakonpolis*. 2 vols. London: Quaritch, 1900–2.

Ray, J. D. "The Emergence of Writing in Egypt." *World Archaeology* 17, no. 3 (1986), 307–16.

Redford, D. B. *Akhenaten. The Heretic King*. Princeton, N.J.: Princeton Univ. Press, 1984.

Reeves, C. N. *The Complete Tutankhamun*. London: Thames and Hudson, 1990.

———. *Egyptian Medicine*. Princes Risborough, England: Shire Egyptology, 1992.

———. *Valley of the Kings*. London: Kegan Paul, 1990.

Reisner, G. A. *The Development of the Egyptian Tomb Down to the Accession of Cheops*. Cambridge, Mass.: Harvard Univ. Press, 1936.

———. *A History of the Giza Necropolis*. 2 vols. Cambridge, Mass.: Harvard Univ. Press, 1942 and 1955.

Roth, H. Ling. *Ancient Egyptian and Greek Looms*. Halifax: Bankfield Museum, 1951.

Sandars, N. K. *The Sea Peoples*. London: Thames and Hudson, 1985.

Sandman, M. *Texts from the Time of Akhenaten.* Brussels: Bibliotheca Aegyptiaca, 1938.

Sauneron, S. *The Priests of Ancient Egypt.* New York: Grove Press, Inc., 1960.

Säve-Söderbergh, T. *The Navy of the Eighteenth Egyptian Dynasty.* Uppsala, Sweden: Uppsala Univ. Press, 1946.

Schäfer, H. *Principles of Egyptian Art.* Translated and edited by J. Baines, edited with epilogue by E. Brunner-Traut. Oxford: Oxford Univ. Press, 1974.

Schulman, A. R. *Military Rank, Title and Organisation in the Egyptian New Kingdom.* Berlin: Verlag Bruno Hessling, 1964.

Shaw, I. *Egyptian Warfare and Weapons.* Princes Risborough, England: Shire Egyptology, 1991.

Simpson, W. K., ed. *The Literature of Ancient Egypt: An Anthology of Stories, Instructions and Poetry.* New Haven, Conn.: Yale Univ. Press, 1973.

Singer, C., E. J. Holmyard, and A. R. Hall. *A History of Technology.* 2 vols. Oxford: Oxford Univ. Press, 1954 and 1956.

Smith, G. E. *The Royal Mummies.* Cairo: Impr. de l'Institut Français d'Archéologie Orientale, 1912.

Smith, G. E., and W. R. Dawson. *Egyptian Mummies.* London: Kegan Paul International, 1991.

Smith, R. W., and D. B. Redford. *The Initial Discoveries. Volume 1, The Akhenaten Temple Project.* Warminster, England: Aris and Phillips, 1977.

Smith, W. Stevenson. *The Art and Architecture of Ancient Egypt.* Harmondsworth, England: Penguin Books, 1958.

———. *A History of Egyptian Sculpture and Painting in the Old Kingdom.* London: Oxford Univ. Press, 1946.

Till, W. C. *Koptische Dialektgrammatik.* Munich: Beck, 1961.

Tooley, A. M. J. *Egyptian Models and Scenes.* Princes Risborough, England: Shire Egyptology, 1995.

Trigger, B. G. *Nubia under the Pharaohs.* London: Thames and Hudson, 1976.

Trigger, B. G., et al. *Ancient Egypt: A Social History.* Cambridge: Cambridge Univ. Press, 1983.

Ucko, P. J., and G. W. Dimbleby, eds. *The Domestication and Exploration of Plants and Animals.* Chicago: Aldine Pub. Co., 1969.

Ucko, P. J., R. Tringham, and G. W. Dimbleby, eds. *Man, Settlement and Urbanism.* London: Duckworth and Co., Ltd., 1972.

Van Seters, J. *The Hyksos: A New Investigation.* New Haven, Conn.: Yale Univ. Press, 1966.

Waddell, W. G., trans. *Manetho.* London: Loeb Classical Library, 1940.

Wainwright, G. A. "Pharaonic Survivals between Lake Chad and the West Coast." *Journal of Egyptian Archaeology* 35 (1949), 170–75.

———. "Some Sea-Peoples." *Journal of Egyptian Archaeology* 47 (1961), 71–90.

———. "Some Sea-Peoples and Others in the Hittite Archives." *Journal of Egyptian Archaeology* 25 (1939), 148–53.

Watterson, B. *Coptic Egypt.* Edinburgh: Scottish Academic Press Ltd., 1988.

———. *The Gods of Ancient Egypt.* London: B.T. Batsford, Ltd., 1984.

———. *Introducing Egyptian Hieroglyphs.* Edinburgh: Scottish Academic Press, 1993.

———. *More about Egyptian Hieroglyphs.* Edinburgh: Scottish Academic Press, 1986.

Weeks, K. R. "The Theban Mapping Project and Work in KV5," in *After Tutankhamun: Research and Excavation in the Royal Necropolis at Thebes,* C. N. Reeves, ed. London: Kegan Paul, 1992.

Wilcken, C. *Alexander the Great.* London: Chatto and Windus, 1932.

Williams, R. J. "Scribal Training in Ancient Egypt." *Journal of the American Oriental Society* 92 (1972), 214–21.

Wilson, H. *Egyptian Food and Drink*. Princes Risborough, England: Shire Egyptology, 1988.

Wilson, J. A. "The Artist of the Egyptian Old Kingdom." *Journal of Near Eastern Studies* 6 (1947), 231–48.

Winlock, H. E. *Models of Daily Life in Ancient Egypt from the Tomb of Meket-Re*. Cambridge, Mass.: Harvard Univ. Press, 1955.

———. *The Rise and Fall of the Middle Kingdom in Thebes*. New York: Macmillan, 1947.

Worrell, W. H. *A Short Account of the Copts*. Ann Arbor: Univ. of Michigan Press, 1945.

Yadin, Y. *The Art of Warfare in Biblical Lands in the Light of Archaeological Discovery*. London: Weidenfeld and Nicolson, 1963.

Zauzich, K-T. *Discovering Egyptian Hieroglyphs*. Translated and adapted by A. M. Roth. London: Thames and Hudson, 1992.

INDEX

Boldface page numbers indicate major treatment of a subject. Page numbers in *italics* with suffix *f* denote a figure.

cultus temples **105, 107**, 111, 112, 210, 218
cuneiform 19, 198, 251
currency 71, 272. *See also* coinage
cursive writing 194
customs posts 233–234, 266
cutters 313
Cynopolis 158
Cyprus 71, 249, 252, 304, 320
Cyrus II 41

D

Dahshur 8, 9, 23–24, 30, 49, **78**, 175, 330
Damietta 64
dancing *331f*, **332–333**
Daressy, G. 38
Darius I 13–14, 41–42, 336–337
Darius III 14
Day of Judgment 152, 157–158, 159, 199
dead/death. *See also* afterlife; burials; coffins; Day of Judgment; funerary beliefs/customs; graves; mummies/mummification; Osiris; pyramids; tombs
    deities for 148, 1**56–159**, **161**, 203
    festivals of 112
    needs of 139
    readings about **161**
death penalty 94
debts 96
Decius 15, 47, 132
decoration *133f*, *153f*, **185–186**, **187**, 199, 264
Dedun 127
Deir el-Bahri
    Amenhotep cult at 124
    in First Intermediate Period 28, 49
    gardens in 325
    as healing center 336
    monuments at 9, 238
    in New Kingdom 52
    and reburial of royal mummies 38
    temples at 10, 50, 80, 245–246, 265, 267–268, 270, 279, 314, 325
    and Third Intermediate Period 38
Deir el-Bersha (el-Bersha) 31, 76, **78**
Deir el-Gebrawi **78**
Deir el-Medina
    food preparation at 326–327
    foreign deities at 127
    houses in 183, 184–185
    library at 202

literature found in 210
Medjay in 232
religious worship at **117–119**
royal workforce at 49, 167, 168, 169, 180–181, 186
size of 181
slates found at 123
tombs at 326–327
wall art at 186
deities **102–105, 134, 156–159, 161.**
    See also Creation Myth; priests; religion; rituals; *specific diety;* temples
    animal characteristics of 101
    animals as 101
    appeals for help from 119
    assistant **104**
    birth house of 46
    cities associated with 24–25
    clothing for 127, 329
    cosmic **101–102**
    dancing and imitation of 333
    for death and resurrection 148, **156–159, 161**
    destruction of all 124
    and economic system 86
    of elements **103**
    of fertility 157, 158
    foreign 43, 118, **126–128**, 130, 158, 205, 227
    and funerary beliefs/customs 148, **156–159**
    in Greco-Roman Period 129
    of healing **337**
    household 101, **105, 117–119**, *120f*, 127, **134**, 185
    and industry 281
    jewelry for 329
    kings' relationship with 22–23, 26, 87, 88–89, 103, 104, 219
    and legitimacy of foreign rulers 211
    literature about 212–213
    local 24, 102, **104–105**, 107, 113, 117–118
    in Middle Kingdom **31**
    and military organization 228–229, 237
    mythologies about 112, **115–117**
    in New Kingdom 127–128
    in Nubia 51, **126–127**, 128, 242
    offerings to 109, 278, 325
    in Old Kingdom 24–25, 102, 127, 219
    painted 309
    pantheon of **102**, 126, 127, 261

possessions of **114–115**
powers of 102, 192
in predynastic Egypt 19–20
in Ptolemaic Egypt 43, 158
religion as compact between man and 112
restoration of traditional 89, 126
as rulers 6, 16, 19–20
state **102–104**
statues of 105, *113f*, 115, 121, 263
vegetation 157, 158
Delta
    agriculture in 65, 69, 200
    capital of 270
    cities and towns in 268
    and climate 61
    in Greco-Roman Period 271
    horse breeding in 261
    immigrants in 61, 251, 271
    impact on civilization of 59
    and inundation of Nile 64
    language and writing in 194
    and Libyan invasion of Egypt 250, 251
    literature about 215
    navy as protection for 249
    towns in 268
    and trade 268, 271
    transportation in 263, 265
demotic script **193, 194**, 196, 197, 198, 200, 211, **220**
Den 8
Denderah 43, 44, **78**, *106f*, 131, 265, 337
Denen 251
dentistry 338
Dep 19
desert 59, 60, 70, 71, **228**, 233. *See also* Sinai
deserters 94
diet **325–326**
Diocletian 15, 47, 132
Diodorus Siculus 7, 30, 41–42, 62, **214**, 289, 311, 313
Dioscorides 296
diplomacy 30, 50, 52, 93, 127, 225–226, 234, 278
divine possessions **114–115**
Divine Wife of Amun 89
divorce 95, 320
djed pillar *200f*
Djer 227, 240
Djoser 8, 25, **48**, 165, 166, 174, 287
doctors 313, 325, 335, **336**, 337
dolls and concubine figures 155

Theban conflict with 10, 32, **33–34**, 35, 74, 230
    weapons and equipment of 239
hymns 191, 198, 201, 205, 208, 210, 211–212

I

ideal man 124, 207–208. *See also* wisdom texts
ideograms **193**, 198
Ifaa 76
Imhotep 8, 48, 123, 165, 166–167, 174, 336, 337
immortality. *See* afterlife; resurrection
Imset 152, 159
incense **297**
    and foreign affairs 24
    and gardens 325
    and moving monuments 262–263
    and mummies/mummification 313–314
    in New Kingdom 50
    in Old Kingdom 24
    and plant products **297**
    for rituals *111f, 113f*, 119, 281
    trade for 24, 72, 74, *111f*, 240, 249, 257, 267–268, 269, 270, 281
India 272
industry **281–282, 314–315**. *See also specific industry*
Inha'pi 38
inheritance 85, 87, 95, 96, 139, 185, 229
inscriptions **199**, 247. *See also* hieroglyphs; *specific monument*; tomb art; wall art
Instructions in Wisdom. *See* wisdom texts
inundation. *See* Nile River, inundation of
Inyotef. *See* Antef
Ipuky 282
Ipy *68f*
iron 70, 165, 240, 268, 302, 303, **305**
irrigation system 18, 20, 61, 65, 68, *68f*, 271, 277, 281
Isesi 207
Ishtar 127, 226
Isis. *See also* Hathor
    and canopic jars 152
    as consort of Osiris 103, 157, 158
    cult of 129
    figures of *157f*
    and funerary beliefs/customs 158, 159

and Great Ennead 116
in Greco-Roman Period 129
in Greece 130
importance of 102
and Osiris myth 103, 157, 158, *200f*, 215
parents of 103
as state deity 102
as supreme mother goddess 103
Islam 3, 15, 47, 134
Island of Creation 103, 107, 111, 115–116, 121, 143
Israelites 128
Israel Stela 52, 250
Istnofret 52
It-towy 9, 29, 30, 49, 79
ivory **295–296**. *See also* bone
    and foreign affairs 24
    in furnishings 322
    in game instruments *295f*
    in graves 17
    and magicians 122
    in musical instruments 122, 333, 334
    in Neolithic Period 295
    in predynastic Egypt 17, 19, 295
    tablets 101
    in tombs 325
    trade in 24, 72, 228, 240, 267, 272, 295
    as tribute 268
    in weapons and equipment 249
Iwnw. *See* Heliopolis

J

Jeremiah 41
Jerusalem 38, 41, 132
jewelry/jewelers **307–309, 315, 329–330**. *See also* gemstones
    in Byblos 227
    for deities 329
    as divine possessions 114–115
    and economic system 95, 277
    functions of 114, 329–330
    and funerary beliefs/customs 5, *5f*, 24, 30, 37, 48, 147, 149, *150f*, *287f*, 307–308
    as gifts 308
    as hereditary craft 309
    and magic 121
    materials for making 71, *86f, 287f*, 305, 308–309, 330
    in Middle Kingdom 30, 307, 309, 330

in New Kingdom 308
Nubian 267
in Old Kingdom 24, 48, 309
for poor people 330
production process for **308–309**
in Ptolemaic Egypt *150f*
royal 37, 79, 307, 308, 309, 330
as source material 5
storage for 322, 323, *328f*
symbolization of 149, 308
in Third Intermediate Period 37
tools for 308
as tribute 267
workshops for 282, 308–309
Jews 40, 46, 132
Jonah of Tudela, Benjamin ben 216
Joppa 213
Joseph, biblical account of 313
Josephus, Flavius 6, 32, 33
Judah 13
Judaism 128
Judea 13
Judgment of the Dead 104
judiciary 21, **93–95**. *See also* legal system
Jupiter Amun 43
Justinian 47, 133

K

el-Kab 34, 79, 211, 230, 242, 243, 245
Kadesh 243, 268
    battle of 212, 225, 235, *236f*, **237**, 238, 240, 244–245, 249
Kagemni 79, 123, 207
Kahun **79**
    basketry and rush work from *298f*
    and brickmaking *284f*, 286
    building materials from 169
    deities in 126, 333
    footwear from 294–295, 329
    foreigners from 119, 320
    games and toys from 330, *331f*, 332, *332f, 333f*
    and household arrangements 321
    household articles from *17f*, 322
    houses in 183–184, 186
    library from 202
    magical objects from 122
    medical papyrus at 321, 335
    pottery from *28f, 292f*, 320
    and pyramid building 30
    religion in **119**
    royal workforce in 79, 167, 169, 179, 180–181
    and textiles 290

royal 26, 34, 36, 37–38, 43, 76, 87, 89, 127, 225–226, 245
of slaves 92
and stability 85
in Third Intermediate Period 37–38
marriage settlements 321
Mastabat Fara'un 8
mastaba tombs **144, 146, 172–173**
in Archaic Period 21, 22
architecture of 18, 139, 144, 146
brick 144
coffins in 149
functions of 144
as home for spirit 139, 144
as monuments 79
in Old Kingdom 144, 165
in predynastic Egypt 18
in pyramid complexes 175
revival of 8
scenes in 238
and social structure 144
Step Pyramid as 143
stone 70, 171
mathematics 206, **217–218**
mats/matting **299**
for burials 17, 101, 149, 172, 173
as furnishings 322, 323
plant products used in 69, 200, 296, 298–299
measurement 165, **217–218**, 266, **279–281**, 280f. *See also* weights
medical instruments 79
medical papyri 191, 203, 205, 323, 327, 335, 338
medicine **334–338, 339**. *See also* doctors; healing; pregnancy
and anatomical knowledge 334, 335, 338
contributions to history of **338**
deities associated with 336, **337**
in First Intermediate Period 337
in Greco-Roman Period 336
and healing centers **336–337**
Imhotep as god of 167
literature about 191, 213, 338
and magic 121, 201, 334–335, 336, 338
and medical treatments 201, **337–338**
in Middle Kingdom 336, 337
in Old Kingdom 336
plant products used in 68, 296–297
sources of information about **335**, 338

medieval literature 62, 191, 213, **215–216**
Medinet Habu
palaces at 182
temples at 12, 37, 52, 80, 212, 232, 235, 245, 249, 250–251, 285
Medjay 73, 92, 168, 231, 232
Megiddo, Battle at 237, 243
Meidum 8, 23–24, **79**, 175
Meir **79**
Memphis **79**. *See also* Saqqara
in Archaic Period 8, **21**, 86, 91
Assyrian attacks on 39
as capital 79, 91, 179
creation myth of 104, **116**
deities at **104**, 127, 158
as economic center 79
in Egyptian Empire 244
in First Intermediate Period 9, 27
founding of 79
as jewelry center 308, 309
in Late Period 41
and Libyan invasion 250
literature about 213
in Middle Kingdom 158
as naval port 246
in New Kingdom 35, 52
in Old Kingdom 21, 23–24, 25, 282, 309
palaces at 182
and Persian rule 41
as political center 79
Ptah as god at 25, 79
in Ptolemaic Egypt 43
pyramids at 30
quarries near 171
as religious center 25
and Rosetta Stone 197
Schoolboy Exercises found in 208
in Second Intermediate Period 32
in Third Intermediate Period 39
tombs at 282
workshops at 282, 308
Mendes 14, 327
Menes (Narmer) **48**
and King Lists 6
marriage of 21
Memphis founded by 79
military campaigns of 225
and unification of Egypt 6, 7, 8, 16, 18, 20, 21, 48, 65, 230
Menkheperre 38, 268
mental illness 337
Mentuhotep Nebhepetre 9, 27, 28–29, **48–49**, 238, 325

Mentuhotep Nebtowyre 9, 49
Mentuhotep S'ankhkare 9
mercenaries **231**
on expeditions 261–262
foreigners as 73, 225, 229, 239–240, 247, 257, 265
Greeks as 40, 41, 42, 231, 240, 247, 257, 264, 266
in Late Period **40**, 41
Libyans as 231, 247
Medjay as 232
in Middle Kingdom 231
in New Kingdom 127, 231
Nubians as 247
in Old Kingdom 231
Phoenicians as 247, 257, 264, 270
Sea Peoples as 231, 247, 252
Sherden as 249
Syro-Palestinians as 247, 265
merchants 42, 92–93, 266, 269, 272, 277. *See also* trade
in Middle Kingdom 29
in New Kingdom 319
Merenptah **52**, 182, 231, 249, 250, 251
Mereruka 79, 309
Meroë 39, 73, 128–129
Mertetseger 118
Meshwesh tribe 228, 231, 249, 250, 251
Mesopotamia
brickmaking in 286
deities in 126
and Dynastic Race origins 319
horses and chariots in 33, 239
influence in predynastic Egypt of 19
towns in 179
trade with 269, 270
weights and measurement in 280
writing in 198
metal
in chariots 260
in pharmaceuticals 338
in tomb goods 155
in tools *165f*, 172, *304f*
in weapons and equipment 238
metalworkers/metalworking 22, 34, 71, 166, 172, 239, 277, 281, **303–305**, 320. *See also specific metal*
middle class 29, 90, 123, 142, 149, 154, 206, 207, 281, 327
Middle Egyptian 209, 211
Middle Kingdom **9–10, 29–31, 49, 54**. *See also specific ruler or topic*
capitals during 9, 29, 49
dates of 9

O

obelisks 73, 143, 171–172, 196, 217, 261, 305, 307
obsidian 152
Octavian. *See* Augustus
Ogdoad, Hermopolitan 117, 205
Old Kingdom **8–9, 22–26, 48, 54.** *See also specific ruler or topic*
    capital in 23–24
    dates of 8
    decline/collapse of 9, 22, 25, **26,** 27
    democratization during 30–31
    kings' role in 22–23
    Manetho's determination of 3
Ombos 79
oracles 14, 94, 118, 121
Osireion cenotaph 76
Osiris **103**
    Abydos as center for 76, 247
    and afterlife 125, 142
    and Apis bulls 130, 158
    burial of 155
    and climatic impact on civilization 59
    consort of 102, 103, *200f*
    crown and insignia of *157f*
    cult of 31, 78, 103, 158
    and divine kingship 88
    festivals of 112
    in First Intermediate Period 26, 28, 31
    and foreign deities 158
    as foreign god 126
    and funerary beliefs/customs **156–159,** 157
    as god of dead and resurrection 148, **156–159,** *157f,* 203
    as god of vegetation and rebirth 64, 157, 158
    and Great Ennead 116
    in Greco-Roman Period 129
    and House of Life 203
    and Hyksos Period 33
    importance of 102
    and Judgment of the Dead 104
    kingdom of 142, 155
    at Memphis 158
    in Middle Kingdom 31, 103, 142
    as mummiform figure *157f*
    myth of **103,** 104, 112, 129, 148, 157, *200f,* 213, 215, 219
    origins and evolution of 142, 156–158

    parents of 103
    and Ptah 104
    in Ptolemaic Egypt 43
    replaces Re 88
    representation of *157f,* 158
    resurrection of 103, 112
    in Second Intermediate Period 33
    snake as symbol of 152
    as state god 102, **103**
    as supreme royal god 88
    temples for 79
Osorkon II 13
ostraca 194, 200, 206, 208
ownership 93–94. *See also* land ownership; property
Oxyrhynchus **79,** *292f*

P

Pachomius 195
paint, eye *23f, 28f, 328f,* 329
painters 166, 261–262
paints/pigments **309–310**
palaces 165, **181–183,** 186, **187,** 234
Paleolithic Period 59
Palermo Stone **7**
panel portraits *5f,* 78, **131–132,** 149, *150f, 312f*
pantheon of deities **102,** 126, 127, 261
panther skins 24, 72, 240, 267
paper making **300–301**
papyrus **200–202, 263–264, 300–301**
    as agricultural product 69
    and barter 278
    as coffin material 150
    footwear 329
    in Greco-Roman period 301
    manufacture of 200
    in Old Kingdom 301
    and paint/pigments 309
    in Pharaonic Period 301
    as plant product 297–298
    in predynastic Egypt 19
    processing of **200**
    in rope making *300f*
    in ships/boats 247, *247f,* **263–264,** *300f*
    as symbol 300
    trade in 86, 202, 272
    as writing material 194, 198, **200–202,** *201f,* 206, 208, 297, 300–301, *300f*
Papyrus Anastasi 208
Papyrus Chester Beatty I 213
Papyrus Chester Beatty IV 208

Papyrus Harris 500 213
Papyrus Lansing 208
Papyrus Leiden 27–28
Papyrus Leningrad 27
Papyrus Prisse 207
Papyrus Sallier 208
peasants
    afterlife for 142
    and agriculture 65, 67, 68
    and bureaucracy 92
    clothing of 329
    conscription of 91, 180, 226, 261
    in construction work 175
    and economic system 86
    on expeditions 70
    in Middle Kingdom 92
    in Old Kingdom 24, 92
    and police force 232
    as slaves 92, 322
    and social structure 91
    taxes of 91, 232. *See also* corvée system
Peleset tribe **251–252**
Pelusium 13, 41, 43, 235
Pepy I 9, 204
Pepy II 9, 26, 27, 72, 257
perfection, human 208
perfumes *28f, 33f,* 68, **327–329**
Peribsen 8
Per-medjeh 79
Persia/Persians **41–42**
    Alexander the Great conquers 14, 42
    coinage system of 96, 266, 272, 278, 279
    conquest of Egypt by 13–14, 41, 226
    empire of 75
    as enemies 225
    as foreign rulers 319–320
    influence on Egyptians of 42, 319–320
    in Late Period 13–14, **41–42**
    and medicine 336–337
    and religion 13–14
    and Saite rulers 266
    tombs of 79
    trade with 266, 271
personal appearance 110, *153f,* **327–330, 339.** *See also* clothing; cosmetics; jewelry
personality **140**
personal piety **122–124, 135**
Pe. *See* Buto
Pessimistic Literature 27, 192, 209

secular literature **221**
secular writing 198
Sedeinga 73
Sekhmer 225
Sekhmet 104, 336, 337
Sekmem 242
"self-sale" 96
Selim I 216
Selket 152, 158, 159
Semainian culture 16
Semitic people 33
Senusret I 9, 29, 30, 72, 79, 227, 241, 259, 306–307
Senusret II 9, 30, 79, 90, 180
Senusret III **49**
    and defensive/military architecture 234
    deification of 241
    expeditions of 227
    jewelry with name of *86f*
    major events during reign of 10, 29
    military campaigns of 72, 230, 241, 242
    pyramid for 30, 49, 78
Septimius Severus 15, 46–47, 132
Seqenenre Ta'o II 10, 34, 49, 230, 238, 242
sequence dating **16–17**
Serapeum 79–80, 104, 215
Serapis 43, 53, **130**, 158
serfs 277, 321
servants *68f*, **154–155**, 168, 169, 183, 260, *260f*, 319, **323**, *324f*, 329
Seshat 176, 178
Seth
    in Archaic Period 8
    consort of 103, 158
    as foreign deity 127
    forms of 104
    and gods of healing 337
    as god of warfare 225
    and Great Ennead 116
    as Hyksos' patron god 32–33
    Nagada as center for 79
    and Osiris myth 103, 157, 158, 215, 219
    parents of 103
    in Second Intermediate Period 32–33
    story about 213
Sethos I **51–52**
    and Egypt's empire 36
    and foreign affairs 76
    and King Lists 7

military campaigns of 226, 230, 244
    Nauri Decree of 246
    palace of 181–182
    temples for 76, 80, 176, 203, 232, 244
    well of 266
Setnakhte 52
"Setting out the Four Sides of the Enclosure" 176
Sextus Julius Africanus 6
Shabaka Stone 116
Shabako 13, 39, 242
Sham el-Nessim, Festival of 129
Sharuhen 231
Shebitku 39
Sheklesh tribe 250, **252**
Shepseskaf 8, 48
Sherden tribe 231, 239–240, 249, 250, **252–253**
ships/boats **155–156, 247–249, 254, 263–264**
    in afterlife 142
    building of 271
    decoration on 264
    design of 248
    in expeditions 228, 269–271
    and funerary beliefs/customs **155–156**, 247, 248
    in Middle Kingdom 264
    in military campaigns 75, **247–249**, 263
    in New Kingdom 247, 264
    as Nile transportation *247f*, **263–264**
    in Old Kingdom 248, 264
    papyrus 200, 247, *247f*, **263–264**, *300f*
    in Pharaonic Period 248
    plant products used in 296, 298, 299, 302
    in predynastic Egypt 263
    in religious ceremonies 101
    seagoing **264–265**
    Syrian 249
    as toys *331f*
    for trade 247, 249, 257, 269–271
    types of 247
    wood for 71, 171, **264**, 302
    and workshop system 282. *See also* Byblos boats/ships
Shipwrecked Sailor, Story of 259
Shoshenk I (Shishak) 12–13, 38
shrines 165, 199, 266
Shu 103, 116

Shuttarna 225
Sicard, Claude 62
silk 293
silver
    as coffin material 152
    in jewelry 308
    metalworking with 303
    in Middle Kingdom 305
    as standard of exchange 266, 278, 279
    as taxes 95
    trade in 71, 86, 268, 271–272, 278, 305
    as tribute 268
    value relative to gold 71, 305
    and weights and measurement 279
Sinai **227**
    expeditions to 24, 49, 50, **227**, 269
    and geography 62
    natural resources in 49, 71, 74, 269, *280f*, 304, 309
    in Old Kingdom 24
    trade with 257
sins 119, 156
Sinuhe, Story of 212, 259, 268, 271
Sitamun 124
Sit-Hathor-Iunut 30
Siwa 14, 43, 52
Slate Palette of Narmer **20–21**
slate palettes 17, 19, 101, 198
slaves
    definition of 322
    on expeditions 261–262
    in households 321, **322**
    lists of 321
    marriage of 92
    as military reward 231
    in Nubia 72, 73
    in Old Kingdom 24
    ownership by 92, 322
    peasants as 92, 322
    and royal workforce 168, 169
    and transportation of stones 261
    as tribute 73, 182, 241
    women as 168, 321
Smendes 12, 37, 271
Smenkhkare 50, 51
snakes 152
Sneferu 8, 27, 48, 78, 79, 175
Sobek 79, 104
Sobekneferu 10, 31
social structure **22–24**, **89–91**
    and administration 89
    and afterlife 142
    in Archaic Period 89